questions on the f...
① existentialist what
② Phenomena what it is

INTRODUCTION TO PHILOSOPHY

Scientist aspect of Phi.
" " "
linguistic " " "

Study

135 Philosopy of mind.
Know Merleau Ponty

INTRODUCTION TO PHILOSOPHY

H. GENE BLOCKER
Ohio University

WILLIAM HANNAFORD
University of Colorado

D. VAN NOSTRAND COMPANY
New York   Cincinnati   Toronto   London   Melbourne

D. Van Nostrand Company Regional Offices:
New York   Cincinnati   Millbrae

D. Van Nostrand Company International Offices:
London   Toronto   Melbourne

Copyright © 1974 by Litton Educational Publishing, Inc.

Library of Congress Catalog Card Number 73-14372
ISBN: 0-442-20827-8

All rights reserved. No part of this work covered by the copyright hereon may be reproduced or used in any form or by any means—graphic, electronic, or mechanical, including photocopying, recording, taping, or information storage and retrieval systems—without written permission of the publisher. Manufactured in the United States of America.

Published by D. Van Nostrand Company
450 West 33rd Street, New York, N. Y. 10001

Published simultaneously in Canada by
Van Nostrand Reinhold Ltd.

10 9 8 7 6 5 4 3 2

Acknowledgments

Page 179, 15 lines from the *Tao Te Ching* by Lao-Tzu, translated by Wing-tsit Chan (Bobbs-Merrill Company, Inc., 1963). Page 190, excerpts from poems by Shen-hsiu and Hui-neng, from *The Way of Zen*, by Alan W. Watts. Copyright © 1957 Pantheon Books, Inc. Reprinted by permission of Pantheon Books/A Division of Random House, Inc. Page 190, excerpts from poems by Wo-luan and Hui-neng; page 193, 4 lines from *Madhyamika Karikas*; page 195, 4 lines from the *Chung Lun*, from *A Source Book of Chinese Philosophy*, translated by Wing-tsit Chan, (Princeton University Press, 1963). Pages 197–198, 21 lines from *Haiku*, translated and edited by Harold Henderson (Doubleday & Company, Inc., 1958). Page 307, 12 lines from "Death" by William Butler Yeats. Reprinted with permission of Macmillan Publishing Co., Inc., from *Collected Poems* by William Butler Yeates. Copyright 1933 by Macmillan Publishing Co., Inc., renewed 1961 by Bertha Georgie Yeats. Page 307, 4 lines from "Stopping by Woods on a Snowy Evening" from *The Poetry of Robert Frost*, edited by Edward Connery Lathem (Holt, Rinehart, and Winston). Page 307, last two stanzas from "A Winter's Tale" from *The Poems of Dylan Thomas*. Copyright 1946 by New Directions Publishing Corporation. "A Winter's Tale" was first published in *Poetry*. Reprinted by permission of New Directions Publishing Corporation.

Preface

This book is devoted to the idea that philosophy is interesting, relevant, and comprehensible to the beginning student. Philosophy does not have to be *made* relevant because it *is* relevant, but it must nonetheless be *shown* to be so since its relevance is indirect. While it is true that the philosopher is probably no better equipped to settle the world's problems than the man on the street, he can show us how to go about solving them, especially where the solution depends on a clear understanding of the problem. Since, in the opinion of the authors, philosophy is defined more by its methodology than by its subject matter, it can in principle be used to examine any subject matter. The authors have tried to develop a broad notion of philosophy as a means of clarifying difficult problems, especially where the root of the problem lies in the way we are accustomed to thinking about it. This method of clarification is then directed toward various problems of continuing importance, grouped into chapters by subject matter—moral problems, aesthetic problems, and so on.

We believe that this approach provides the best way of teaching philosophy. Along with introducing the student to various fields of philosophy, we invite the student to think critically, and hence to philosophize, about subjects with which he is already concerned. From a prephilosophical interest in any one of a variety of ongoing concerns, the student is drawn into a greater conceptual awareness and sophistication of these problems. This process, we feel, serves to combine relevance with philosophical rigor. We begin where the student is. Are values relative? If God exists, how can there be so much evil in the world? Can one person ever really understand another? Does social conformity corrupt an inherently beautiful human nature? But we do not stop here. These problems are troubling precisely because of a lack of clarity in the terms in which they are expressed—assumptions, distinctions, arguments presupposed or taken for granted, the clarification of which is a distinctly philosophical enterprise.

This approach also provides the best justification for offering a beginning course in philosophy. Since most students do not intend to take many other courses in philosophy, much less plan a career in philosophy, the value of a single philosophy course cannot lie in its role in training professional philosophers. Its value for the student must lie in the development of his or her critical faculties through a growing awareness of personal assumptions and an increasing ability to tackle difficult problems in a sophisticated, critical manner.

The book is divided into chapters according to the type of problem in need of philosophical clarity: the philosophy of mind, the philosophy of society, the philosophy of art (aesthetics), the philosophy of knowledge (epistemology), the philosophy of morals (ethics), and the philosophy of reality (metaphysics). Two chapters, "Existentialism" and "Eastern Philosophy," fall somewhat outside this framework and reflect the great interest these types of philosophy continue to exhibit both in and outside of philosophical circles. Since it is expected that most introductory courses will cover no more than three or four of the nine areas in a single quarter or semester, the book offers considerable flexibility in the selection of chapters, accommodating itself to a wide range of interests on the part of professor and student. Those already familiar with philosophy will also find considerable flexibility in the balance among different schools, periods, and types of philosophy represented and in the relative degree of popular relevance and difficulty. The first chapter is unique in its attempt to provide an overview of the special nature of philosophical activity, and to that end contains a section on elementary techniques of reasoning (logic) and a section outlining the development of certain major themes in the history of philosophy, which provide the background and context the authors believe necessary to approach some of the problems discussed elsewhere in the book. Unlike the other chapters, this chapter would normally be considered a prerequisite to the others, pointing the student in a certain direction and giving him some idea of what to look for along the way.

Contents

1. PHILOSOPHICAL THINKING   1
    What Is Philosophy?
    The Use of Reason
    Historical Perspective
    Topics for Discussion
    Selected Bibliography

2. METAPHYSICS   44
    What Is Metaphysics?
    The Metaphysical Theory of Substance
    Aristotle's *Metaphysics*
    The Empiricist Critique of Metaphysics
    The Phenomenological Critique of Metaphysics
    Topics for Discussion
    Selected Bibliography

3. EPISTEMOLOGY: THEORIES OF KNOWLEDGE   85
    What Is Epistemology?
    The Sources of Knowledge
    Knowledge and Belief
    Practical Knowledge
    Conclusion
    Topics for Discussion
    Selected Bibliography

4. THE PHILOSOPHY OF MIND 132
What Is the Philosophy of Mind?
Dualism
Materialism
Behaviorism
Expression Theory
Criteriological View
Conclusion
Topics for Discussion
Selected Bibliography

5. EASTERN PHILOSOPHY 159
What Is Eastern Philosophy?
Why Eastern Philosophy?
A Brief History of Eastern Philosophy
The Finger and the Moon
Conclusion
Topics for Discussion
Selected Bibliography

6. ETHICS: THE PHILOSOPHY OF MORALITY 201
What is Ethics?
Normative Ethics
Metaethics
Moral Problems
Conclusion: Expediency versus Rightness
Topics for Discussion
Selected Bibliography

7. SOCIAL PHILOSOPHY 228
What Is Social Philosophy?
Freedom
Violence
Revolution
The Law and Civil Disobedience
Topics for Discussion
Selected Bibliography

8. EXISTENTIALISM: THE PHILOSOPHY OF THE ABSURD 242
What Is Existentialism?
Kierkegaard and Nietzsche: The Problem Stated

The Philosophy of Existence: Sartre and Heidegger
Meaning and Meaninglessness
The Tragic Sense of Meaninglessness
Conclusion
Topics for Discussion
Selected Bibliography

9. AESTHETICS: THE PHILOSOPHY OF ART 290
What Is Aesthetics?
The Concept of a Work of Art
Meaning in Art
Truth in Art
Topics for Discussion
Selected Bibliography

INDEX 327

INTRODUCTION TO PHILOSOPHY

CHAPTER 1

Philosophical Thinking

WHAT IS PHILOSOPHY?

It is extremely difficult to define "philosophy," and the attempt to do so forms an interesting and important part of philosophical investigation. Even though we should not expect a pat definition, we can try to get a clearer idea of what philosophers do. To those who have not studied the subject, the word "philosophy" might initially suggest two things: first, a kind of general theory or principle, as when we speak of a person's "philosophy of education" or the need for a "philosophy of leisure," and second, something abstract and mysterious—"profound" if you like such things, "worthless star-gazing" if you don't. This last characterization has been with philosophy for a very long time. There is a story told of the first Western philosopher, Thales, which illustrates this popular view of philosophy and philosophers.

People worried about Thales because he was always gazing at the stars. One day he became so absorbed in his astronomical pursuits, he actually fell into a well and had to be helped out. Everyone thought this typical of the absent-minded, impractical philosopher, but Thales had the last laugh! By careful observation of the stars he predicted that the following year would be a very good year for grapes. So he bought up all the wine presses around and, sure enough, made a killing the following year. The story is interesting, whether true or not, because it points up both the charge that philosophy is too abstract to be practical and the countercharge that the best practitioners are those with access to the most sophisticated theories, a view fully supported today by our technological application of the theoretical sciences. To most of us, then, philosophy conjures up the image of something general, theoretical, abstract, and somewhat mysterious. This popular conception of philosophy is neither entirely right nor completely mistaken. It sets us in the right direction, but it is too vague to be very helpful. After all, the sciences, too, are theoretical and abstract, and so are logic and mathematics, and religion is at least as mystifying as philosophy. How, then, does philosophy differ from these other pursuits?

Actually, the idea of philosophy has changed somewhat over the 2500 years of its existence. The word in Greek originally meant "love of wisdom," and at first "philosophy" meant any general theoretical concern, thus including what we now call the sciences but excluding religion (though not entirely). In the eighteenth century, for example, physics was still called "Natural Philosophy." Gradually, as each science became self-supporting, it broke away from the parent stock of philosophy and became an independent entity. This might seem to have shrunk the domain of philosophy, and some thought it had. But the main effect of this long series of breakaway movements was to sharpen the idea of philosophy and make it more precise. Especially in the nineteenth and twentieth centuries, as psychology, sociology, anthropology, political science, and other subjects made their escape from their philosophical mother, philosophers devoted a great deal of attention to clarifying precisely how their investigations differed from those of the scientist on the one hand and the social and moral critic on the other. The result of this clarification has actually been to broaden the scope of philosophy so that today almost any topic can become the subject of philosophical investigation. In 1971 the Council for Philosophical Studies published a book of essays by philosophers on *Violence* and in the following year a similar book on *Women's Lib*. A sampling of other philosophy books recently published reveals a broad range of subject matter: sex, drugs, revolution, Zen Buddhism, civil disobedience, pacifism, suicide, death, and communes, as well as the older, more traditional topics such as art, religion, science, politics, and morals. Obviously, philosophy cannot be the sum total of all these different disciplines and concerns. What then is common to the philosophical interest in all these different subjects?

Most philosophers today believe that philosophy is not a factual science describing important aspects of the world, but rather an analytic discipline for clarifying how we think about the world. According to this view, philosophy seeks to describe the concepts by which we conceive the world, not to describe the world itself. Philosophy is concerned less with the factual accuracy of statements than with their meaning. Ironically, this narrowing of function explains the recently broadened scope of philosophy. Since philosophy is not defined by its subject matter, it can in principle direct its attention to any subject matter. Unlike scientific inquiry, philosophical questions are not decided by examination of the facts (although the philosopher is interested in what we mean by the word "fact"). Philosophical debate turns on disagreements as how best to describe those facts.

The Philosophical Approach

So we can begin to think of philosophy primarily as the analysis of concepts. This does not mean that it is necessarily a trivial debate over words. Not all philosophical questions are of the quibbling, logic-chopping sort you may have heard about—how many angels can stand on the head of a pin, if a tree falls in the forest does it make a sound if no one is there to hear it, and so on. Many questions are both important and conceptual. Take the question of abortion. Some people claim that the abortionist is a murderer. Well, is he? How do we decide such a question? Certainly not by looking at the facts, because both the proabortionist and the antiabortionist agree on the facts—that the fetus develops progressively from a fertilized egg to a human infant, that it will die if removed from the mother's womb, that it will probably live if left there, and so on. Agreeing on all these facts, we are still left with the question of how to describe them—as "murder" or simply as "removing an unwanted growth"? To decide this question we must examine what we mean by "murder," and if we are going to succeed in communicating with others, our meaning must fall in line with that of others in our society. While there is a publicly accepted meaning for "murder," it must be admitted that it is not a very precise meaning. While the center of the concept is fixed, its boundaries are vaguely drawn and hence open to debate.

If we define murder as the deliberate killing of another

human being, what about the soldier who deliberately kills another soldier, or the hangman doing his job? Such cases are not generally held to be murder, except by some religious sects, because to be classed as murder the killing must be not only deliberate but illegal, though the question remains whether certain forms of killing should be legal. A soldier can legally kill another enemy combatant, though it would be murder for him to deliberately kill a civilian noncombatant. What then about the bombing of civilian centers of population such as Hiroshima, Dresden, London, and Hanoi? Is this murder? It's hard to say, isn't it? The decision involves two questions, both of which are conceptual in nature. Was the killing of these civilians deliberate, and were these people really noncombatants? Those who wish to defend such bombings usually argue that it was not murder because the pilots were deliberately bombing military installations and only accidentally killing civilians as a side effect, or that by working in munitions factories these people were not really noncombatants. How sound is the first defense, that the civilians were killed accidentally? There seems to be something fishy about it which has to do with our concept of what is accidental. In ordinary English I cannot call the consequence of my action accidental if I knew perfectly well beforehand that an unfortunate "side effect" would occur. Otherwise any gunman could claim that he never meant to kill anyone— he only pulled the trigger! What about the second defense, that the civilians are really combatants? This does stretch the usual meaning of the word "combatant" somewhat, but, on the other hand, the concept was not very precise to start with. In any case, the debate is decidedly conceptual.

It is along these fuzzy borders of ordinary concepts that philosophers battle, and if you have followed the discussion above, you have been doing philosophy! In the case of abortion, granting that it was recently declared legal, the debate centers on the moral question of whether the fetus is a human being. Again, it should be clear that this is not a factual question. A biologist is in no better position to say than a priest. All the disputants agree on the facts—what the fetus is like at three or four months, what it can and cannot do at that stage, that it will die if removed and probably live if allowed to remain. It is a fact that a fetus will probably become a human being, but it is a conceptual problem whether it *is* one. The main point of contention is at what precise stage of devlopment the fetus becomes a human being. We all know what the expression "human being" means—we can all pick out the people from the tables and chairs. But the ordinary meaning is not sufficiently sharp to settle such a borderline case. And so we must make a decision, but not an arbitrary one. Our decision must reflect at least some of the ordinary criteria by which human beings are differentiated from dogs, cats, and sunflowers. This type of decision and the grounds for it are the center of most philosophical debate.

Such debates are not mere squabbles over words. It would be monstrous to suggest that it doesn't matter how we define "human being" so long as we make it clear how we intend to use the word. Suppose we decided that "human being" would exclude anyone over the age of 50. This would amount to an open hunting season on uncles, aunts, and grandparents. This example seems farfetched because a member of *Homo sapiens* age 50 is very close to the center of our ordinary concept of a human being, and so, for those of us who know the language, there is no real debate here. But in the case of the fetus at four months or the invalid in an irreversible coma, there is.

Sometimes the natural course of events points up the limitations of our ordinary concepts and creates a need for philosophical clarification. No one wondered much about the criteria for calling someone dead until heart transplants became possible. Previously, if someone's heart stopped, breathing ceased, and body temperature lowered, he was declared dead, but today, of course, once the new heart is installed the patient revives. Do we want to say the person died and came back to life, or do we want to modify our criteria somewhat and say that heart stoppage is not a necessary condition for death? This is a conceptual decision and an important one, especially for the surgeon who wishes to avoid legal action on a possible murder charge.

Similarly, few of us turn to philosophy for help in distinguishing men from women. Nonetheless, an international scandal was created by certain questionable entrants in one of the women's events in the 1968 Olympic Games in Mexico City, which did raise the somewhat surprising question, "What exactly is a woman?" Ordinarily a woman is distinguished from her male companions by primary and secondary sex characteristics, as well as her "identity," that is, the fact that she thinks of herself as a woman and is so regarded by others. But some people, like the athletes in question, possess some of the characteristics of one sex but not all. A person may be female in terms of identity and secondary sex characteristics, but not in terms of primary sex characteristics. Is this person male or female? This depends on which of the ordinary criteria are considered the most important. Humanitarian considerations would stress the person's identity and so lean toward a female classification of the athletes, whereas medical grounds would probably insist on a male or at least non-female slot. Since our ordinary criteria are indecisive on this point, we might consider introducing some technical criteria to decide the matter, such as specific male and female genetic structure. But the Mexico City athletes straddled the fence on this point as well, fitting into neither category, and the question would still remain, in any case, why genetic structure should take precedence over other criteria. Perhaps the athletes were neither male nor female, but the Olympic officials only had these two categories of participants. Since the games had to go on, a difficult conceptual decision had to be made, and the participants were finally disqualified.

Sometimes the inadequacies of ordinary concepts are brought out into the open by the philosopher himself. In cases of this sort the philosopher takes some ordinary concept and derives from it by logically correct steps some puzzling and clearly unacceptable consequence. About 2500 years ago a Greek philosopher named Zeno argued on the basis of commonly accepted notions of space that it was impossible for a man to run across the equivalent of a football field! His argument went something like this. A football player takes the kickoff in his endzone and decides to run it out. Before he can reach the opposite goal line he must cross the 50 yard line, and before he can do that he must cross the 25, and before that the 12, the 6, and so on to infinity—according to the common Greek concept that space is infinitely divisible. So, no matter how hard he runs he will never make it, though he is very good and has a clear field ahead. The point of this argument is not to prove that a man *can't* run the length of a football field. This would be absurd. We all know that he can. The point is that an ordinary concept seemed to imply an absurd conclusion. There must, then, be something wrong with the ordinary concept, some unclarity which, until tested, was not known to exist. In this case, Zeno's argument showed that the Greek concepts were contradictory in holding that space is on the one hand infinitely divisible and on the other reducible to indivisible atomic units. Once we put it in this blatant way, it is obvious that it cannot be both, but it took Zeno's shock tactics to make this clear.

A philosopher is not always appreciated for performing this task. Socrates was put to death for his philosophical "gadflying," though he is now seen as a cultural hero from the safe distance of 2000 years.

A similar difficulty was discovered in the so-called problem of evil in reconciling the traditional idea of God with the existence of evil in the world. Both believers and atheists tend to define "God" as being good and all-powerful, but upon reflection this appears inconsistent with the existence of evil. If God is both good and all-powerful, how can there be any evil. If He is good, He would want to prevent evil, and if He is all-powerful, He would be able to. Therefore, if there is evil in the world, it is hard to see how God can be both good and all-powerful. God might be well-intentioned but unable to prevent evil, or He might be all-powerful and actually want there to be evil, but how can He be good *and* all-powerful? This no more proves that God is weak or malicious than Zeno's argument showed that a man can't run the length of a football field. What it shows is an apparent conceptual incompatibility between the properties attributed to God and the ways the world is described.

Philosophy is therefore probably best characterized as a rational examination or critique of the most basic elements of our everyday experience and beliefs. In this sense philosophy has been described recently as a "second-order" discipline. The biologist describes the biological aspect of the world, the physicist the physical aspect, and so on. The philosopher is interested in the concepts and arguments used by the biologist, the physicist, and others in talking about the world as they do. Among the various branches of contemporary philosophy we find philosophy of science, philosophy of history, philosophy of art, philosophy of mind, philosophy of morals, philosophy of law, philosophy of politics, and so on, some of which are included in this book. Philosophy is a concept-oriented discipline and as such its subject matter includes the fundamental principles of other disciplines.

Two consequences follow from this view of philosophy as "talk about talk": first, that philosophy cannot teach us anything totally new but can only clarify what we were already implicitly aware of, and second, that philosophy takes nothing for granted. Nothing escapes the light of philosophical criticism, not even the assumptions of the philosophers themselves. For this reason there are no absolute starting points in philosophy and in this sense philosophy is continually starting anew, constantly searching for a new point of departure. This is not, of course, a particularly happy thought for those who require definite answers and who want to "get somewhere" with philosophy in the way physicists have gotten somewhere with physics in the last several hundred years.

Philosophers typically examine the elementary assumptions of everyday life, such as freedom and justice. Although we think *with* these assumptions, we cannot think *about* these assumptions very easily in ordinary language. We cannot pull them out, so to speak, and examine them, because they are absolutely essential to our being able to examine anything at all. It would be like a man who can't see anything without his glasses trying to take them off to look at them. So the philosopher must develop new ways of speaking. At the same time, however, if he is to make any sense, he cannot abandon entirely ordinary language. No wonder philosophers are sometimes so hard to understand!

FREEDOM. One of the basic conceptual assumptions with which philosophers have traditionally been concerned is freedom. When we choose a certain course of action we assume we have selected one of several possible courses of action which were open to us. Indeed, this is part of the meaning of the word *choose*. If a man is tied to a post, it makes no sense for him to say, "I have chosen to stay here for a while." To choose logically implies alternatives. And this means there are other courses of action which the agent could have taken but decided against. It is on this basis that in everyday speech we distinguish a freely chosen act from one which we were forced to do. According to the everyday meaning of the words we use, a person is free to do something if and only if he could have done otherwise; he is not free if he could not have done otherwise. I am free to jump up on a chair if I choose to, but I am not free to jump over the moon because I am physically incapable of doing so.

Upon this foundation of the freely chosen act rests a great deal of our sense of moral responsibility, blame, and guilt. We only blame or punish a person for acts for which he is responsible, and we only hold him responsible for acts which he has freely chosen. You are not to blame for unavoidable and unintended accidents even though they may harm someone. It is not just a fact that we do this, it is part of our concept of "blame" and "responsibility" (see Chapter 6).

So far, so good. But notice, we also commonly assume that

there is an explanation for everything that happens, and this assumption, when clearly analyzed, appears to flatly contradict the first one! For if there is a reason which determines everything that happens, then there will be a reason determining your choice of a certain course of action. If an act was predetermined, then it wasn't freely chosen. Say I decide to take a course in elementary chemistry. But what caused me to make this decision? I wanted to get into medical school. Why? To become rich and respected. Why? Because I am the child of middle-class American parents. But I had no control over my heritage, and since this apparently has influenced what university courses I shall take, neither is my decision to take this chemistry course a completely free choice. This means that it has already been determined in advance how I am going to choose (even before I make up my mind), so that I am not really free to choose at all. Since there is no other alternative open to me I cannot really be said to have chosen it in the ordinary sense. And since the argument is completely general (applying to all choices), the conclusion seems to be that there is no such thing as a freely chosen act. We are just as bound to do everything we do as the man tied to the post. In an age in which concrete, workable proposals are being put forward for the kind of social conditioning and control which Alex received in *The Clockwork Orange*, this is obviously a conceptual question of enormous practical and moral consequences.

PERSONAL IDENTITY. We all take for granted that although we have changed over the years physically and mentally, we are nonetheless the same person we were ten yars ago. But if we reflect on these obvious facts, doubts begin to creep in. If I am taller and heavier than I was ten years ago, with different concerns and hopefully more knowledge of the world, am I really the same person I used to be? At one of his parole hearings Loeb, of the famous Leopold-Loeb murder and kidnapping trial of the 1920s, argued on similar grounds that he should be released because he was not the same person he was at the time of the murder, and so was not the same person as the murderer, and hence not the murderer. (He was not released!) Of course, it is true that we are more or less as we used to be. There are differences, but there are also similarities—some of the same memories which only I could have, and so on, but still, strictly speaking, it remains true that I am not the same as I was, and it seems to follow from this that I am not the same person. After all, what is a person or a self but a physical or mental consistency? Even the character in Kafka's *Metamorphosis* who awoke to find himsef turned into a cockroach was at least mentally consistent with his former self.

This is part of another, very old philosophical problem—the problem of identity through change. An object can change in certain ways and still remain the same object. Indeed, if the object became a different object each time something happened to it, think how hard it would be to talk or think or refer to things in everyday life. It would probably be impossible. If you try to criticize me for putting a dent in your new car, I will simply point out that this is not your car because *your* car didn't have any dents! Fortunately we allow that things can change and still remain the same. A tree can lose a limb and still remain a tree. But if the object changes in other ways it may no longer be the same object, and then we say that the original object has ceased to exist. If the tree is cut down, ground to sawdust and made into newsprint, the tree has ceased to exist and in its place paper has been created. Some changes transform an object into something else, while other changes do not, for the identity of an object depends on our concept of it. If the concept we are dealing with is "tree," then cutting it down into one-inch squares will destroy the object; if the concept is "wood," the cutting action will not destroy the object (since it remains "wood"), and if the concept is "piece of wood," cutting up a tree will produce a multitude of such objects. Thus, while the same act is performed on the same object, the object changes or remains the same according to our original concept of it.

So it is in the case of personal identity. It all depends on what our concept of a person is, though unfortunately we are not nearly so positive in this case as in the case of the tree and the wood. We are not so sure which changes will change the person and which changes will not. (If Mary's brain is transplanted in John's skull, is this a brain transplant for John or a body transplant for Mary? Who will emerge from the operation, John or Mary?) But notice, the problem does not end here. It's bad enough your being two people, but if you are different from what you were ten years ago, you are equally different from what you were five years ago, and if so, what is to stop this whittling away of your most precious possession, yourself? If you are not the same person you were a year ago, how about a day ago, or an hour ago, or a minute, or a second ago? Pretty soon we have not just many different persons all claiming to be you, but an infinite number.

And that means there is nothing left of you at all. As Zeno showed, divided infinitely, each "part" of a finite quantity is infinitely small and so nonexistent. You seem to have dissolved into empty space! Suddenly from the most commonplace assuption—the fact that in ordinary speech we call a person who grows and develops over the years the same person—we seem to have arrived, under pressure of a certain kind of rational inquiry, at the audacious and rather frightening conclusion that you don't really exist at all!

Nor is this a trivial playing about with words. Some Eastern philosophers (see Chapter 5) argue quite seriously on this basis that there is no such thing as the individual ego. And it makes a big difference whether there is or not. What happens when you die? As an individual ego you either live on in some afterlife or you simply cease to be. To many people this is frightening because we place tremendous value on this entity called self and we are not sure about immortality. But what if there is no such thing as the self or the ego? What if it is just a convenient way of speaking? The Buddhists directly challenge this assumption of an ego: "Why do you fear the annihilation of the ego, when there is no such thing to be annihilated in the first place?" The problem is conceptual. The Buddhist philosophers are not denying any of the empirical facts claimed by the Christian theologian. The difference lies in how they construe the same facts.

We tend to look at all the different things a person says and does as stemming from a single entity, his ego, because generally, in order to think or talk we tend to look at the world as a collection of stable things possessing fixed properties. This, too, is a conceptual matter, one of great interest to those philosophers known as metaphysicians (see Chapter 2).

Philosophical Analysis

Philosophy, then, is a kind of conceptual analysis, exposing the implications encased in the meanings of ordinary words, ideas, and beliefs. But is it only analysis? That is, don't philosophers also have ideas and opinions of their own, or do they, as we have perhaps suggested, simply look at all sides of a question equally? Philosophers themselves are not in complete agreement on this point. Philosophers do seem to come down more heavily on one side of an issue than another, and in this sense to put forward views which are not just analyses but true or false assertions. Some philosophers see themselves doing this more than others, and generally, it is fair to say that philosophers in the past saw themselves primarily as affirming positions and arguing for their truth, not just working out the logical implications of what others believed. For this reason some contemporary commentators draw a distinction between *philosophy proper*, which is concerned with establishing the truth of certain claims, and *metaphilosophy* which is pure analysis. However, while a distinction can be made between these two philosophical approaches, analysis is one of the basic tools of all philosophical investigation.

As we have already suggested, since the world as we are aware of it is at least partly conceptual in nature (a world which includes murder, abortion, violence, racism, and so on), the analysis of our concepts ("murder," "abortion," and so on) entails analysis of the world. We can just as easily frame our philosophical question in terms of things in the world as we can in terms of our concepts of the world. One of the earliest and best examples of philosophical writing is Plato's *The Republic*, parts of which are discussed in various sections of this book. The central question of *The Republic* is, What is justice? Plato does not initially ask simply for a definition of the word, but for an account of the true nature of justice per se. However, it is clear from *The Republic* that the kind of answer Plato wants is basically a definition of the word. Although Plato, along with many other philosophers for reasons we will discuss later, believed that everything which could be thought corresponded to something existing in the world (the word "justice" corresponding to a real justice), he also recognized that the only way to discover a real justice was to analyze our word for it. Even if you believe, with Plato, that in addition to our human concept of justice there is a real justice out there in the world, how can you discover the real nature of this justice except by analyzing what the word means?

One method of analysis might be to examine all the things called "justice" and figure out what they all have in common. This is what one of the antagonists, Thrasymachus, does in *The Republic*. He examines what goes by the name of justice and concludes that the one feature which all the cases have in common is their "being in the interest of the stronger." The ruler makes the laws to suit himself and then calls these justice. But is that what justice really is? Is it just for a ruler to pass laws which harm the mass of people but benefit the ruler? This, of course, is precisely an example of injustice. And this is exactly how Plato presses his attack on Thrasymachus. Even though we claim to be concerned with the object justice and not just the idea, we know that Thrasymachus is wrong in his account of justice simply because this is not what we *mean* by "justice." In other words, with things like justice, knowledge, good, art, and God, analyzing the concept and discovering the real nature of the object come down to much the same thing. What if someone "discovered" that God was really a small white pebble? Such a thing is not even possible because that's just not what me *mean* by "God."

Conceptual analysis can also masquerade as a description of our experience. The task of describing experience belongs to psychology. But since our experience of the world is colored by our view of it, the analysis of the structures of experience is really a philosophical analysis of meaning. Imagine two philosophers, Verbo and Psycho. Verbo insists that philosophy must analyze words, which Psycho rejects in favor of the philosophical analysis of experience. Independently they begin a philosophical analysis of a work of art. Verbo, the word analyzer, says, "What do we call a 'work of art,' what are the criteria for the correct application of this word? Would we call a tree a work of art, however beautiful? No. Why not? Because it has not been made by a human being to be viewed in a certain way. So one necessary feature of a work of art is that it be made by someone with the intention of being viewed in a certain way." Psycho analyzes our experience and comes up with this solution: "Imagine you are looking at outdoor sculpture. A wood carving stands next to a tree. Now examine your experience carefully. You experience both as lovely to look at, but your experience of the two is different. You experience the tree as a natural object; you approach the carving as a man-made object deliberately designed to 'speak to you' in some way. So one necessary feature of a work of art is that it be made by someone with the intention of being viewed in a certain way." Verbo and Psycho have taken different paths to the same conclusion. Because we interpret the world conceptually, both the world as we experience it and our experience of the world are concept-laden; and therefore concentration on either will yield conceptual analysis.

Finally, analysis may be a means of supporting belief. Suppose I believe that abortion is wrong. How can I show this? I need to show that the fetus is a human being. But it is only potentially a human being. So I need to show that what a thing is potentially it already *is* in some sense. And to do that I need to carefully analyze the relation of potentiality to actuality. Or I may begin my analysis with a more open mind, with a view to arriving at a decision on the basis of my analysis. I'm not sure about abortion, so I hold off making any judgment until I have examined carefully all the conceptual (and factual) issues involved. Then on the basis of my analysis I come to a decision—that abortion is wrong, or right, or the lesser of two evils, or a toss-up.

Or, suppose I am really upset by the "problem of evil" mentioned above and want to solve it. Since the problem is conceptual in nature, it can be settled only by logically resolving the apparent contradiction in the meanings of the three statements involved:

1. God is good.
2. God is all-powerful.
3. Evil exists.

One way to solve the problem would simply be to deny one of the three statements which make up the problem; any two of the three are compatible so long as we reject the third. God is good but unable to prevent evil (1 and 3, rejecting 2). God could prevent evil but doesn't want to (2 and 3, rejecting 1). Because God is good and all-powerful, there *is* no evil (1 and 2, rejecting 3). But the first two alternatives do not coincide with what we ordinarily mean by "God," and the third seems to fly in the face of the facts. We want to hold on to all three statements, since the denial of any one of them appears to contradict common sense and ordinary speech. As in the problem of "Freedom and Determinism," the problem is how to have one's cake and eat it too.

Perhaps the three statements above are not really as incompatible as they at first appear, and maybe we can dissolve the conflict through analysis. Perhaps the world is evil only in a human sense while God is good in a divine sense. We could then rewrite our three statements in a way which removes any suggestion of contradiction:

1. God is good in a divine sense.
2. God is all-powerful.
3. The world contains evil in a human sense.

(But then, what does the first statement mean? What is divine goodness? We are only familiar with human goodness, and not much of that.) Another possibility would be to deny that God's goodness and omnipotence are incompatible with evil. Perhaps God prefers that there be no evil at all and could prevent it (that is, He is good and all-powerful). But He also wants people to be free, so He allows them to choose evil, which they frequently do; therefore evil exists. Our analysis has shown that there is no real incompatibility. Of course, it is also true that some of the evil that exists is not man-made, such as floods, hurricanes, and so on. But perhaps these things are not actually evil in the broad scope of things known only to God. In each case we are using analysis to support our belief that God is good and all-powerful even though evil does exist.

What we have been doing is philosophical analysis, leading up to or at least supporting a conclusion. As a matter of fact, the bulk of philosophical writing is concerned with the conceptual foundations for a theory or position. Consider, for example, one of the basic arguments for the existence of God, the "Ontological Argument," first formulated by St. Anselm (1033–1109). His argument is that since "God" is defined as a necessarily existing being, He must necessarily exist. The point of the argument is to establish something about God Himself and not just the word "God," but the argument nonetheless turns on the definition of God as a necessary being. Subsequent philosophical debate over Anselm's argument has focused on the definition of God, as well as the more general problem of the relation of a word to the object it refers to. David Hume (1711–1776) suggested, for example, that "necessary existence" was a contradiction in terms, and so made no sense. Immanuel Kant (1724–1804) argued that although the idea of a necessary being made sense, it did not follow that there was an object out there in the world corresponding to it (just as nothing corresponds in the real world to the concept we have of a unicorn).

So, while we may distinguish between those philosophers (largely contemporary) who are consciously analyzing words and concepts and those philosophers (largely traditional) who supposed they were investigating real objects or aspects of the real world, or between philosophy which has an "ax to grind" and philosophy which has little or no "ax to grind," or between the conclusions philosophers reach and the conceptual analyses leading up to or at least supporting those conclusions, there is probably no great difference between philosophers past and present on the score of analysis. In the sense in which we have defined it and in so far as it can be defined at all, all philosophy is basically conceptual analysis.

THE USE OF REASON

If the philosopher is not directly concerned with objects in the world, but primarily with the concepts we use to describe the world, how do we know if his analysis is correct? When he presents an analysis, what sort of evidence is he appealing to which will enable us to choose between competing philosophical accounts of the same thing? If you and I are arguing whether a mutual friend has blue or brown eyes, we settle the dispute simply by looking. But this obviously won't settle a dispute over whether he is a just administrator or not. Such conceptual disputes can be settled only by recourse to reason. One constant thread running through the entire history of philosophy is its appeal to reason, argumentation, and logic.

We all use arguments in everyday life to support our opinions and to attempt to refute other people's views with which we disagree. Basically, an argument is simply the reasons (called the *premises*) which are offered for or against a position (called the *conclusion*). Logic is the systematic study of the rules for the correct use of these supporting reasons, rules we can use to distinguish good arguments from bad ones.

Deductive Arguments

Consider the following argument. "Murder is the deliberate taking of human life by another human being; abortion is the deliberate destruction of a human fetus; the human fetus is human life; therefore, abortion is murder." This argument is valid in that the conclusion (abortion is murder) must be true if we accept the other statements as true. These premises may not be true, but if they are, then the conclusion must be true as well because the conclusion follows simply from an analysis of the premises. If the meaning of "fetus" implies the concept of "human life," then the destruction of the human fetus is by definition the taking of human life; and if this is what we mean by "murder," then simply by the meanings of these words, it follows that abortion is murder. This kind of argument is known as a *deductive argument*. A deductive argument is simply an extended analysis of the meaning of words. The conclusion is supported by the premises in that the conclusion simply restates what the premises themselves stated or implied.

Take a still simpler case. "If John is a bachelor, then he is unmarried." We know this is so simply by knowing what the words mean. A bachelor is by definition an unmarried man, and obviously unmarried men cannot be married. Looking at it another way, what prevents us from asserting that a bachelor could be married? Simply the desire not to contradict ourselves. To say that a bachelor is married is to assert that an unmarried man is married. This, of course, makes no sense; by saying one thing (he's married) and denying it in the same breath (he's not married), we effectively cancel out anything we may have wanted to say and so have succeeded in saying nothing. As Aristotle said, if you want to say anything, you must be consistent.

The same principle holds true in the above argument on abortion: to accept the premises and deny the conclusion would mean contradicting ourselves and therefore asserting nothing. Suppose we accepted all the premises but nonetheless insisted that abortion is not murder. This could only be done by denying at least one of the premises. If abortion is not murder, then by the definition of "murder," it does not involve one human being deliberately taking the life of another human being. But an abortion is by definition the deliberate human destruction of the fetus. Now the doctor is certainly a human being and he is surely acting deliberately. So if it is not murder, it could only be because the fetus is not human. But this directly contradicts one of the premises of the argument, that "the fetus is human." So, if we accept the truth of the premises and deny the conclusion, we are in effect saying that the fetus is and is not human. But what does that mean? Nothing. Therefore we can't say it; that is, the strength of the argument is that we can't reject it and still mean something. The argument turns exclusively on meaning.

Logic

Argumentation is an indispensable tool of the philosopher, and thus the arguments must be sound and reasonable. The job of devising tests to determine which arguments are valid and which are not belongs to that branch of philosophy known as *logic*. Suppose we take a survey of arguments we know intuitively to be valid and then try to discover what it is about these arguments which makes them valid. We can then apply this test to new arguments, ones too complex to certify intuitively. We would then be constructing a "logic."

VALID ARGUMENTS. For example, consider our argument above: if abortion is the destruction of the human fetus and if the destruction of the fetus is the deliberate taking of human life, and if the deliberate taking of human life is murder, then abortion is murder. This seems valid, but why, what makes it so? Consider another argument of a similar form. "If whales are mammals and mammals have hair, then whales must have hair"; or, "If this is an essay for Prof. Brown and Prof. Brown requires that essays be typed, then this essay must be typed." These three arguments are valid for the same reason: each asserts that if the objects belonging in one class or category (A) also being to a second category (B), and all those in the second category belong to a third category (C), then all those in the first category must belong to the third. This gives us a way of constructing a test for the validity of arguments of this kind. If an argument has this form:

If all A is B, and
All B is C,
Then all A is C,

then it is valid. This is what Aristotle called a *syllogism*: an argument made up of three statements, two of which are premises and the other conclusion, with three and only three terms (A, B, and C) each of which names a distinct class of objects. It is a logic of class inclusion which presupposes our intuitive idea of classes and the meanings of words like "all," "and," and "is" (which here means "is included in"). If everything included in class A is included in class B and all those things are included in class C, then all those in A will have to be included in C. Now we have a way of testing new arguments; if they fit this pattern, or can be arranged to fit this pattern, they are valid. Arguments expressed in terms of such a pattern are known as *formal arguments*. The same argument expressed in ordinary English is an *informal argument*. Our abortion argument is an extension of this syllogistic principle since it includes three premises and four terms.

> If all *A* is *B*, and
> All *B* is *C*, and
> All *C* is *D*,
> Then all *A* is *D*.

INVALID ARGUMENTS. We can also discover patterns of invalidity as well. A common form of argument goes like this: "The leaders of peace movements are political activists. But this is precisely what Communists are. So these leaders must be Communists." Is this valid? From our previous analysis of validity, is it possible for the premises to be true and the conclusion to be false? There are many kinds of political activists—some Communist, some right-wing, some anarchist, and some unaffiliated with any political movement; thus it is possible that even though the peace leaders are activists they are not Communist activists. So the argument is invalid. The same goes for any argument which has this form, and if we can isolate the form we will have a test for invalidity. What the argument states is that if all the members of one class (*A*) belong to a second class (*B*) and if all the members of a third class (*C*) also belong to this second class, then the members of the first class belong to the third class. That is,

> If all *A* is *B*, and
> All *C* is *B*,
> Then all *A* is *C*.

Having shown that one instance of this argument-form is invalid, we know that it is always possible for the premises to be true and the conclusion false, and therefore that all arguments of this form are invalid.

However, the conclusion of an invalid argument is not always false. In our argument above, it is possible that the particular peace leaders in question are Communists, even though that conclusion is not established by the premises. Nor is the conclusion of a valid argument always true. Because of the nature of validity, there are two basic strategies open to anyone who finds the conclusion to an apparently valid argument unacceptable. He can either show that the argument is not really valid after all, or he can show that while it is valid the conclusion need not be true because one of the premises is false. If it turns out, for example, that Prof. Brown does not always insist on typed essays, then it is possible that I don't have to type this essay. But the argument is still valid since it only claims that the conclusion is true if the premises are true. What if I accept the validity of an argument and the truth of the premises, but still reject the conclusion? Then I am being unreasonable, and we will discuss in a moment what is wrong with that.

Hypothetical Reasoning

The logic of class-inclusion can also be expressed in terms of sentence-implication. Instead of using terms (A and B) representing classes joined together by connectives like "all," "and," and "is," modern logicians often use a logic of sentences (p and q) joined together with "if," "and," and "then." In our earlier argument on abortion, for example, let p represent "it is an abortion"; and q: "it is the destruction of a human fetus"; and r: "it is the deliberate taking of human life"; and s: "it is murder." The argument in the sentence-logic, called the *sentential calculus*, looks like this:

If p, then q; and
If q, then r; and
If r, then s.
Therefore, if p, then s.

This is an extended version of what is called the *hypothetical syllogism:* if p implies q and q implies r and r implies s, then p implies s.

The advantage of the sentential calculus is that it exposes the essential nature of argumentation. An argument in its most basic form states that *if* the premises are true, *then* the conclusion is true. All argumentation is therefore of a hypothetical nature, speculating on what would happen if such and such were true, which is aptly summarized in the "if–then" relation. This basic form of reasoning can be found not only in philosophical analysis, but in science and everyday life as well.

DIALECTICAL REASONING. In Plato's *Phaedo*, the character representing Socrates describes his hypothetical method of doing philosophy by criticizing other people's views.

> This was the method I adopted; I first assumed some principle which I judged to be the strongest, and then I affirmed as true whatever seemed to agree with this, . . . and that which disagreed I regarded as untrue. [Plato, *Phaedo*]

This is the Socratic Method of the early Platonic dialogues in which Socrates examines some common belief by "knowledgeable" people to see what its logical implications are. Usually these consequences reveal some inconsistency and thus the unacceptability of the original belief. Thus the form of the procedure is hypothetical. "Suppose p is true; if so, then q, but if q, then r; but r is clearly unacceptable; so we can't accept p, after all." This is called an *Argumentum ad Absurdum*—assuming the truth of a premise in order to show, by its absurd consequences, its falseness.

In *The Republic* Socrates asks, What is justice? To this Cephalus, a respected and honorable merchant, replies that justice is speaking the truth and paying your debts. Socrates' response is to see where such a view leads, that is, to determine whether its consequences are acceptable or not.

> Suppose that a friend when in his right mind has deposited arms with me and he asks for them when he is not in his right mind, ought I to give them back to him? No one would say that . . . I should be right in doing so, any more than they would say that I ought always to speak the truth to one who is in his condition. [Plato, *The Republic*]

So, Cephalus' definition is unacceptable and another definition is proposed which also founders on inconsistencies, and so on through much of the first part of the dialogue. This negative form of argument, called *denying the consequent*, can be summarized:

> If p, then q;
> But not q:
> Therefore, not p.

This is a common form of argumentation in everyday life: "If the Senator were a wise legislator, then our state would have benefited during his twelve years in office; but in all important respects the fortunes of our state have declined these past twelve years; therefore, I conclude that the Senator has not been a wise legislator."

The hypothetical method need not be negative. In *Meno*, another Platonic dialogue, Socrates and Meno try to determine whether virtue can be taught, as claimed by the professional teachers of the day, the Sophists. This question can only be answered, Socrates says, relative to an hypothesis, or supposition. All we are able to determine about such nonempirical concepts is whether they imply or are implied by other concepts. We cannot determine their truth absolutely, in isolation. If virtue is knowledge, Socrates hypothesizes, then virtue can be taught. But this does not prove that virtue can be taught, it only shows that it can be taught if it is knowledge. But is it knowledge? This can only be answered relative to another hypothesis. If virtue is profitable, then virtue is knowledge (and if it is knowledge, remember, then it can be taught). The form of the argument is that of the hypothetical syllogism considered earlier.

If p, then q; and
If q, then r:
Therefore, if p, then r,

where

p: virtue is profitable,
q: virtue is knowledge,
r: virtue can be taught.

Notice that in the first case (Cephalus' definition of justice) we started out with a premise (p) and worked "down" to the consequence (q) which turned out to be unacceptable, whereas in the second case (defining virtue in *Meno*) we did just the reverse, starting out with the conclusion (r) and working back "up" to those premises which logically support it (p and q). This is an important form of reasoning which Plato called *Dialectic* and Kant called *Transcendental*. Plato argued that all the sciences, including mathematics, are hypothetical in nature. They all begin with certain assumptions from which they derive other consequences.

The mathematician Euclid used this type of reasoning in developing his *Elements of Geometry* in the third century B.C. Euclid began with certain unproved, "self-evident" axioms from which he logically derived all the other theorems in his geometrical system. The truth of the consequences (the theorems) depends upon the truth of the initial starting points (the axioms), just as

Socrates' conclusion that virtue can be taught is contingent upon the supposition that virtue is profitable and that it is knowledge. The axioms upon which Euclid built his system of geometry cannot be proved within that system, and if Euclid's axioms are wrong, then the entire system is wrong.

In order to test or prove the axioms, Euclid must move to a "higher-order" discipline, like philosophy, in order to find the principles from which the axioms follow as consequences. These could then be derived from still higher principles and so on. For Plato the highest type of knowledge was knowledge of the Good, which we will discuss in Chapter 6.

> You are aware that students of geometry, arithmetic, and the kindred sciences assume the odd and the even and the figures and three kinds of angles and the like in their several branches of science; these are their hypotheses, which they and everybody are supposed to know, and therefore they do not deign to give any account of them either to themselves or to others, but they begin with them, and go on until they arrive at last, and in a consistent manner, at their conclusion. . . . [But philosophical wisdom], which reason herself attains by the power of dialectic, uses these hypotheses not as first principles, but only as hypotheses, in order that she may soar beyond them to the first principle of the whole; and clinging to this and then to that which depends on this, by successive steps she descends again without the aid of any sensible object, from ideas, through ideas, and in ideas she ends. [Plato, *The Republic*]

Kant employs a similar form of argument, called *Transcendental* (not to be confused with "transcendent" which refers to a reality beyond this one). He begins with some commonly accepted fact and asks, What assumptions are we required to make in order for this to be possible, and what assumptions are required to make these assumptions plausible, and so on? In the *Critique of Pure Reason*, for example, Kant argues that since scientific laws presuppose causal connections which in turn presuppose the existence of a principle of causality operating throughout nature, such a causal principle must exist. This is a powerful form of argument which we will encounter frequently in the course of this book.

24   Philosophical Thinking

SCIENTIFIC REASONING.   The same double use of hypothetical reasoning (from premise to conclusion and from conclusion to premise) is also the cornerstone of modern science. At some point in school most of us were told that scientific theories are generated by a process of *inductive* generalization from particular instances. "This swan is white, that one is white, and so on; therefore, all swans are white." This was a very popular view of science until a closer examination of scientific methods revealed that this simply was not what scientists did. With a little reflection it is easy to see why such a program, were it actually carried out, would prove ineffectual. Without some specific problem to be solved or question to be answered, inductive generalizations would be aimless and quite useless. There are many observable similarities among objects in the world which could stimulate generalizations, but most of them are not of great importance. Stones, for example, generally lie on the ground, while peaches are found higher up in trees, with insects somewhere in between, but so what? Only some special concern would make such generalizations worth noting. Theorizing must be directed, and it is the question or problem which provides this direction.

Inductive generalization alone, assuming we used it, would be hopelessly weak as a form of reasoning. Suppose I notice that all the animals on my farm are white (a white dog, a white horse, several white sheep, and so on). Would I be justified in concluding that all animals were white? Of course not. Even the generalization that all swans are white has been disproved by the discovery of a group of black swans in Australia. The weakness of this form of reasoning is that it always argues from the fact that some A is B to the conclusion that all A is B, which is obviously invalid (that is, it is always possible for the premises to be true and the conclusion false). The induction method is useful only when it is supplemented by a great deal more implied information. If we already know, for example, that the color of birds' eggs is specific to a particular bird, then from the fact that these Mallard eggs are blue, we can infer that all Mallard eggs are blue. Because we already know the general theory for birds' eggs, we do not need more blue Mallard eggs to support our argument.

The appeal to empirical facts is important in the formualtion of scientific theories, of course. The question is, How is it important? Empirical facts are not collected like birds' eggs, as the Empiricists often argue (see Chapter 3); they are used to test hypotheses which have been formulated to solve a particular question, and this process involves the dual role of hypothetical reasoning discussed above. Suppose we notice that two widely separated groups of people, A and C, speak a similar language. This is puzzling; we would expect that the more remote the groups are in space and time, the greater the language differences between them. How can we explain this problematic phenomenon? We begin with a problem—some fact which needs explaining. We must then formulate one or more possible solutions, or hypotheses. Since there is always more than one possible explanation for anything, this requires a certain amount of imagination. We certainly cannot hope to answer our question by just staring at all the facts; investigations, whether scientific or not, require a creative effort. Perhaps A and C were originally one people driven apart in some remote period of history by an invasion of an alien group, B, which now separates them. In formulating this hypothesis we are reasoning *transcendentally*; that is, we treat our problematic fact as the *conclusion* of an argument for which we construct a *hypothetical premise*. We are asking what is essentially a *dialectical* question: "What must have happened to account for the facts as we know them; what supposition can we come up with which would logically imply that A and C speak a similar language?"

Sometimes the scientist constructs higher-order hypotheses to account, not for specific events, as in our present example, but for other hypotheses. Here the scientist's approach resembles even more closely the philosophical task of dialectic outlined by Plato in *The Republic*. The value of these higher-order hypotheses and the test of their credibility lie in their ability to account for (that is, to logically imply) other hypotheses, bringing many separate hypotheses under one large umbrella. Part of Newton's success was his ability to infer from his general laws almost all the important hypotheses of his predecessors, Kepler and Galileo, and the acceptance of Einstein's General Theory of Relativity was due in large part to Einstein's success in deriving from it not only the work of Newton, which it then replaced as a higher-order theory, but the most significant work of his contemporaries, until then widely divergent theories of electromagnetism, radiation, and subatomic particles.

Generally, the hypothesis is formulated to account for (or imply) some more specific event which needs to be explained, a supposition, for example, which if true would explain the fact that A and C speak similar languages. Our hypothetical reasoning, then, is

> If A and C were driven apart by B,
> Then A and C would speak a similar language today (which they do).

But we don't know that B drove them apart; this is merely assumed as a possible solution. How can we determine if this is indeed the correct answer? What right have we to assume that this provides a better answer than some other possibility? It is at this point that empirical testing becomes important. We must now try to infer from our hypothesis some new, empirically observable phenomenon which we can then proceed to test. We stake the truth of our hypothesis, in other words, on a prediction which can be empirically decided one way or the other. In the earlier stages of our reasoning, in formulating our hypothesis, we argued dialectically "upward" from conclusion to premise (from the fact that A and C are apart to the hypothetical cause, B). To test our hypothesis, we reason "downward" from premise to conclusion, that is, from our hypothesis to some new empirically observable event. We reason, for example, that if A and C had been separated by the warlike activities of B (that is, if our hypothesis is true), then A and C would still be telling similar stories about the cruel B people, and B would still be telling a different story about the brave exploits of their ancestors scattering their enemies when B first came to the land. Having staked our claim to observable facts, we can proceed to test our hypothesis. We record the stories of A, B, and C and if they are not as predicted, we have falsified our hypothesis and have to start all over again. But if things turn out as we predicted, we have confirmed and supported our hypothesis—though we have not yet proved it. Our test procedure is based on the reasoning that

> If p, then q; and
> q.
> Therefore, p.

Setting up our argument in this form, we have:

> If A and C were originally one people, then they will have similar mythologies.

They do have similar mythologies.
Therefore, they were originally one people.

However, upon close scrutiny, we find that this is not a valid form of argument. It is possible that the premises are true and the conclusion false. Consider another argument of this form:

If John is sick, he won't make it to class today.
He didn't make it to class.
Therefore, he must be sick.

However, suppose we know for a fact that John is at that very moment sitting in a bar having a beer. But since any argument which takes this form is invalid, then, in our argument about peoples A, B, and C, it is entirely possible that the conclusion is false. Thus, anticipating something we will discuss in Chapter 3, we find it is easier to falsify a theory than to prove it.

A valid argument can, however, be formulated to prove the falsity of a theory.

If p, then q; and
Not q.
Therefore, not p.

This is the kind of argument we identified earlier as *denying the consequent*. The first premise asserts that the truth of p is dependent on q; this means that if q is false then p is also false. According to the second premise, q is false, so p must be false as well. If the premises are true, the conclusion must be true, and so the argument is valid.

INFORMAL REASONING. There is nothing mysterious about this form of reasoning—it is precisely what we do every day in solving problems which crop up in the normal course of events. Suppose that toward the end of the semester you decide to pay a visit to a college friend and find that he is not in. Where could he be? You hypothesize: perhaps his exams are over and he has gone home for the semester break. But how can you be sure? Well, if he has gone home his car will be gone, which you can check. If the car is not in the garage, you can be reasonably sure he has gone away for the week. If you find the car in the garage, however, you must begin thinking of alternative hypotheses. Maybe

28 Philosophical Thinking

he is at Mary's, which you can test by going there to see for yourself.

Your form of reasoning is precisely that of the scientist. You began with a puzzling fact (John is not in). You constructed an hypothesis (he has gone home for the break) which if true would account for the unexplained fact. From this hypothesis you inferred a new testable consequence (that his garage would be empty), which you went on to check. From all this you concluded that he has probably gone home for the break.

Inductive Arguments

Of course, not all forms of reasoning are valid. Some arguments, such as the one above, do not prove the truth of their conclusions beyond all doubt but only confirm or support them up to a point. Correctly predicting something previously unknown is very persuasive, though it is not a complete proof. Instead of looking at induction in the old way as "going from the particular to the general," it is probably better to think of induction as all those forms of argument whose premises support but do not necessarily prove the conclusions. By contrast, premises in deductive arguments do necessitate the conclusions. Some people think that since inductive arguments are not valid, they are mistaken or *fallacious*. In many instances, however, they lend support or weight to a conclusion and are a legitimate source of evidence. The only mistake would be in pretending that inductive arguments are deductive!

Does it follow, for example, that because most drivers under 25 are insurance risks, that you are an insurance risk simply because you are under 25? The conclusion does not logically or necessarily follow from the premises, but the insurance company is correct in supposing that their statistical information about drivers lends some weight to the claim that, other things being equal, you are probably not as safe a driver as your mother. If you dispute this claim, you can only do so by another argument of the same form. You may say, "But look, I have never had an accident, have no police record, and do not take drugs or alcohol in excess." This might carry some weight. You are assuming that since most people who have had no accidents, who do not have a police record, and so on, are less accident prone, that you are a safe driver. But this no more follows from the premises than the original argument by your would-be insurance company. (Don't worry, your argument is better since it includes a more complete profile of yourself.)

Another kind of inductive argument (as we are using the term) frequently used by philosophers is the *argument from analogy*. This argument, as the name implies, is based on an analogy drawn between the relation of A and B to that of C and X, where A, B and C are known quantities and X is unknown. This type of reasoning rests on the claim that if two things resemble each other in one respect, they are likely to resemble each other in some other respect which the argument seeks to establish. One argument for the existence of God, for example, goes like this. The world is as well-organized as a clock; since a clock could only have been made by a skilled craftsman, the world must have been created by a Divine Craftsman. The argument exploits the analogy that the world is to the Supreme Craftsman what the clock is to the clockmaker. We are using our knowledge of three of the terms (clocks, clockmakers, and the natural world) to infer something about the fourth (God), which is in question. The argument rests on the similarity of the "products" (the clock and the world) and is only as strong as the degree of similarity between the clock and the world. Is the world like a clock? How similar are they? Not very, according to some philosophers. In *Dialogues Concerning Natural Religion*, the eighteenth-century Scottish philosopher David Hume argued that the world was as much like a plant (which is not "manufactured") as a clock, from which he concluded that the grounds for supposing that the world was created by an intelligent agent were no greater than the grounds for supposing it just grew like a weed!

In Chapter 4, we will consider in some detail the analogical argument for the existence of "other minds" (minds other than one's own), but for now let us consider a similar argument. Why do we suppose that animals suffer pain as we do? We can't see or feel their pain, but we can see that they behave as we do when we are in pain. Our reasoning, then, is analogical. Our feeling is to our behavior as their feeling is to their behavior. From an observable similarity in behavior, an unobservable similarity in feeling is inferred. Since animals behave as we do when we know we are in pain, we conclude that they must also experience pain when they behave in a similar way. Again, the question is, how similar is the behavior of people and animals? This argument seems somewhat stronger than the clock/world one because it presupposes a great deal more information, not stated in the argument, about the similarity of people and animals (a similar nervous system and a common evolutionary history, for example).

The Critique of Reason

As you can see from this brief sketch, and as you will see from the chapters which lie ahead, analytical reasoning is an indispensable tool not only of the philosopher but of the scientist and the man on the street. However, reason, intellect, logic, and analysis have all come under heavy fire in recent years. The revolt against reason can be traced to the nineteenth-century Romantic poets (Coleridge, Wordsworth, Keats, and Shelley) and their twentieth-century cousins, the existentialists, whom we shall discuss in Chapter 8. John Keats included a critique of philosophy at the end of the poem *Lamia:*

> Do not all charms fly
> At the mere touch of cold philosophy?
> There was an awful rainbow once in heaven;
> We know her woof, her texture; she is given
> In the dull catalogue of common things.
> Philosophy will clip an angel's wings,
> Conquer all mysteries by rule and line,
> Empty the haunted air, and gnomed mine—
> Unweave a rainbow, as it erewhile made
> The tender-person'd Lamia melt into a shade.

The poet Samuel Taylor Coleridge remarked that reason only "kills to dissect." The Romantics viewed reason as cold, inhuman, dull, aloof, abstract, cut off from the whole man of dreams and passions. Why do we need all this argumentation, this endless analysis? Why can't we just "let it be"?

Admittedly, there is a certain persuasiveness in this charge, but it is not directed against reason itself but against the objectification of reason. The Zen Buddhists have a marvelous expression: when you point to the moon, "don't mistake the finger for the moon"—that is, don't confuse your idea of a thing for that thing itself. Reasoning as a human activity for solving problems and resolving conflicts is an indispensable feature of human existence. But it does not follow, as many philosophers have supposed, that the universe must be rational through and through just because our explanations are rational. Much of Western philosophy has been dominated by this tempting fallacy of objectifying reason which the recent critique of reason quite rightly rejects. Reason is a feature not of the world but of our dealings with the world. The world is what we reason about, and reason is an activity we direct at the world.

When we offer a reasonable explanation or an analysis of something, it is tempting to suppose that our explanation and our analysis have somehow exposed the real, underlying rational character of the world. Parmenides, one of the first philosophers, stated that, "Whatever can be rationally thought must exist and what cannot be rationally thought cannot exist"; the German philosopher Hegel said some 2000 years later, "What is real is rational and what is rational is real," as though the world were a mirror simply reflecting human reason-giving. This is a mistake. A rational explanation does not discover a new reality which is rational but simply clarifies the old one. The point of explanation and analysis is not to find a substitute for our everyday experience of the world but to make it clearer in our own minds. There is only one world, but there are many different human ways of relating to it.

Take love for example. Love is something which happens to people. They can feel it and they can also describe it, analyze it, explain it, and even computorize it, but the love relation itself does not change from the feeling of it to the analysis of it. All that changes is the level of human interest in it. People like to make love and they like to talk about it. All our talk, whether everyday, philosophic, or scientific, is directed at the ordinary world we all live in and is no better than the light it sheds on this reality. A poem, a philosophical analysis, a psychological study, a neurophysiological dissertation, or a sociological explanation of love are all different attempts to articulate the same basic phenomenon—love. Far from killing or replacing the feeling of love, all these articulations presuppose it and would make no sense without it, and in the final analysis they must all be judged by how well they relate to the phenomenon being described. Analysis can only make explicit what is already known implicitly.

Reason is neither the underlying reality of the world nor an autonomous human enterprise, but a human way of interpreting and ordering the world as we experience it to make it more intelligible to ourselves. It is we who use reason in certain situations who are reasonable, not the universe. What are the situations in which we feel the need to use reason and intellect? What is the role (and thereby the value) of reason-giving in human experience? As the philosopher David Hume pointed out, we do not usually need logic or analysis to direct our affairs. Most of the time we do quite well with what is variously called feeling, instinct, or intuition. We absent-mindedly go about our daily concerns directed mostly by habit and familiarity. But occasionally situations arise where feeling alone is useless, and these are generally situations in which problems or disputes arise. Then we turn to reason. Imagine that on your way to an important appointment you come upon what looks like an accident—a man lying in the middle of the road surrounded by a small group of onlookers. Should you stop and help? If you do, you will probably miss your appointment. Which is more important? You're not sure. Perhaps you could simply call the police without waiting for help to arrive. On the other hand, the man may simply be drunk and just need a hand across the street. Maybe one of the onlookers has already called for help, but you can't be sure. Perhaps you should ask, but then you may become "involved." Intuition won't help you solve this problem because the problem is simply the conflict you are experiencing among your own intuitions and contradictory feelings toward the situation. It is feeling which is pulling you apart, and the solution calls for a calm ordering of these emotions. You are not abnegating your feelings; they are the center of your problem. What you are trying to do is sort them out, and especially to resolve their conflicts. Far from rejecting feelings, you are trying to pull them together.

Another sort of situation which calls for the use of reason is in resolving disputes between people. The conflict here is not among your own feelings, but between your feelings and those of a friend. Ordinarily, we need not resort to formal logic and careful analysis to communicate with those we feel closest to. Hopefully, love is all you need. But suppose a disagreement arises. Your friend's intuitions strongly affirm what yours vehemently deny; your two feelings are equally sincere and intense, though contradictory. Obviously, you can't resolve the dispute on the level of intuition; more feeling will only exaggerate the conflict. Suppose you say, "You feel what you feel and I'll feel what I feel." But that settles nothing; the dispute still hangs in the air, and the effect of your remark is not to heal the cleavage between you but to emphasize it. What is required is a spirit of reasonableness: "I feel very hostile to your view, but if you will try to explain why you feel this way, I will make an effort to see it from your point of view, though this is alien to my most basic instincts." This is what we mean by being reasonable—to be willing to offer reasons for our views and to listen to the reasons of others. Why be reasonable? Ironically, to keep lines of communication open. Love is *not* all you need.

Similarly in a heated political situation. Suppose you and I march to the courthouse and ask to present our grievances to the mayor who refuses to see us. We respond in anger and frustration. The stage is being set for a potentially violent confrontation because reasonable lines of communication have been rejected. So long as we feel we have a chance of explaining our side of the story and the possibility, at least, of effecting change if we can make a good case for it, we will usually go through established procedures for settling complaints however we may disagree with those in authority. But where there is no way for a reasonable person to present his case concerning legitimate grievances and where reasonable complaints are rejected through the force of the power-structure, he may resort to violence. Violence can be seen, then, as a poor substitute for reason, when all lines of communication have failed.

So, in our enthusiasm to criticize reason, we must not throw out the baby with the water. Reason as the supposed inner reality of the world corresponding to man's supposed true inner nature we are happy to reject; but reason-giving as a human enterprise for solving problems, settling disputes, and establishing lines of communication we desperately need, today probably more than ever.

HISTORICAL PERSPECTIVE

There are basically two ways to approach the study of philosophy—either from the standpoint of its history or from the standpoint of the major problems which philosophers try to answer. The latter is probably the best avenue for the general student who does not intend to go on in philosophy, but who does wish to gain a general understanding of what philosophy is and how it might be relevant. It is more important to develop techniques and habits of critical thinking than it is to know that it was Berkeley, rather than Leibniz, who said, "to be is to be perceived." Accordingly, the problematic approach has been adopted in this book. Nonetheless, a brief overview of the major devolopments in the history of philosophy might be helpful at this point, for in the following chapters we will move about rather freely among different theories from different historical periods and geographical areas. How and when did philosophy first appear? What have been the major trends, and what are the major periods and personalities which make up its history? In the remainder of this chapter we will try to answer these questions with the hope of drawing a kind of map which can be used as a guide to help you through the rest of the book.

Western philosophy appeared in Greece in the sixth century B.C. as the first attempt to provide a thoroughly secular and rational explanation of the natural world. People have always tried to explain the world, of course, but they had previously framed their theories in religious, mythological and magical terms, leaning mainly on mystical and magical grounds for support. The first group of philosophers, known as the pre-Socratic Milesians, limited their explanation of the world to natural elements, such as air, water, heat, and condensation, and their mode of justification to analytical reason and logic.

The question which dominated this early period was, What is the basic reality underlying the world, the changeless stuff of which all things are made? This question arises from a pessimistic view of change: Everything is transient, nothing seems permanent. The early philosophers felt there must be some "ageless, deathless" reality underlying the world as we know it—something eternal and unchanging from which everything else is derived. Thales (624–550 B.C.) said it was water, perhaps from his unfortunate experience in the well. Anaximander (611–547 B.C.) objected that if everything had to come from one basic stuff, this primary substance would have to be "boundless" or indeterminate in character. Anaximenes (588–524 B.C.) responded that everything could be produced from one definite element, which he thought was air, if it could be differentiated into various forms by opposing principles, which he designated as the rarification and condensation of air. Already two important themes of Western philosophy had been struck: the concern with reality as an underlying substratum and the problem of the "one and the many"—how to account for the many different objects in the world of ordinary experience on the basis of one unchanging substance.

The implications of this quest gradually became clear. The

basic reality had to be eternal, unchanging, and undifferentiated. This definition of reality has dominated philosophy ever since, and early in its history led to two quite different schools of thought, remnants of which continue up to the present day: the Eleatics (Parmenides (c. 495 B.C.) and Zeno (c. 490–430 B.C.)) and the Atomists (Democritus (460–370 B.C.) and Leucippus (c. 440 B.C)).

The Eleatics (so named after Parmenides' native town, Elea) argued that the one unchanging, eternal reality could not be identified with any of the elements known to ordinary experience, but had to be defined simply as the proper object of logical thought (whatever that turned out to be). That is, the only thing that really answers the criterion for reality is, ironically, what we think. Everyday things like tables and trees are not unchanging and so are not real. What is real is a special kind of object defined in terms of rational thought. When you think logically, you must be thinking about something, and that something is real, though it is not the kind of thing you can see, touch, or locate in space and time.

What was gradually emerging, though it did not become clear until much later, was that area of philosophy known as Idealism (nothing exists but what is thought; "to be is to be perceived"), or as Rationalism ("whatever is real is rational and whatever is rational is real"). In analyzing the Milesian requirements for the primary substance, Parmenides found that its main element was noncontradiction (that it must not contradict itself). Since noncontradiction is a logical requirement of thought, reality was thus defined as whatever can be consistently thought. If this is not something in the physical world, then there must be some other kind of object specially suited to reason which we think about when we think logically. This is an instance of the misuse of reason we referred to earlier as the objectification of reasoning as a principle of reality.

Supporting this early trend toward idealism and rationalism were the Pythagoreans (Pythagoras, 572–497 B.C.) who maintained that the basic substance of the world consisted of mathematical entities—numbers, relations, geometrical figures, and so on. This sounds odd, but it is not hard to understand in terms of the objectification of reason. Many of our explanations of things are framed in terms of mathematics. This was especially true of the Pythagoreans, who were the first to develop mathematics as we understand it today as a set of propositions derived logically from

36 Philosophical Thinking

primitive axioms in a hypothetical, deductive system. The Pythagoreans also saw that although mathematics dealt with pure abstract entities (numbers, triangles, and so on), it could be used to explain the ordinary world of sense experience. This suggested to them that the underlying reality of the world was mathematical and ideal, a view still popular among scientists and philosophers of science.

The Pythagoreans, for example, discovered that the musical triad (tonic chord) was based on the relation 3:4:6. This applied to all such musical sounds and therefore seemed to be the one underlying principle behind them all. Whether you fill bottles with water or cut bamboo gongs, as long as the ratio is 3 to 4 to 6, the sound produced will be that of the triadic chord. The underlying reality of the chord seems to be the mathematical relation. If the explanation is relational, then the reality must be relational as well. We make a similar assumption today when we speak of the scientist discovering the "laws" of nature, as though there were a rational system of relationships in the world corresponding to the mathematical formula which the scientist uses in his explanation. Thus, one major development arising out of the Milesian investigation into the one underlying substance of the world was the view that the underlying reality consisted of abstract, ideal objects of thought. From the very beginning the philosopher's concern with the world was rational and conceptual.

The Atomists, on the other hand, argued that there were many unchanging, eternal, self-consistent entities of a physical nature which they called "atoms." There is nothing in reality, they said, but these atoms and empty space; everything else is to be explained as different arrangements of atoms. By emphasizing the material elements over their arrangement, the Atomists established themselves as the forerunners of modern Materialism. Pythagoras, of course, would argue that the immaterial arrangement of the atoms was more important for explaining why things are as they are, and this was the beginning of a long debate between the Idealists and the Materialists.

The next major philosophical development was that of Plato (427–347 B.C.) and his prize student, Aristotle (384–322 B.C.), who together established a powerful synthesis of pre-Socratic thought, setting it forth in a clear and compelling way which survived almost unchanged for 2000 years. Plato was inspired by the life and doctrines of Socrates (469–399 B.C.), one of the most interesting figures in Western civilization. Socrates never wrote anything, but spent most of his time dialectically annoying the smug, self-satisfied establishment, for which he was tried and sentenced to death. Socrates was interested primarily in moral problems of justice, piety, and so on, and this made a powerful impression on Plato. Plato combined the Pythagorean and Eleatic conception of reality with the Socratic concern with morality, and explained the multiplicity of the ordinary physical world on the basis of eternal, unchanging, ideal entities. Justice, Plato argued, is an ideal entity, along with the mathematical entities of the Pythagoreans, and these ideal entities are the only genuinely real things in the world. Like the Eleatics and Pythagoreans, Plato noted the discrepancy between our ideas and those things in the world to which those ideas refer. We talk about justice, equality, goodness, and beauty, for example, but it is hard to find anything in the world exactly corresponding to these ideas. No single instance of beauty, for example, can be identified with beauty itself because it is only one of many beautiful things and because it is not perfectly beautiful. Therefore, Plato reasoned, when we talk about beauty, we must be talking about something else, some ideal Beauty of which ordinary instances of beauty in the day to day world of sense experience are but dim reflections. Since Plato found the latter involved in the same sort of contradictions charged by the Eleatics, Plato made the bold claim that the ideal entities (the Forms) were more real than their ordinary counterparts which we actually encounter in daily life (see Chapter 2).

But unlike the Pythagoreans or Eleatics, Plato went on to try to explain the ordinary world of sense particulars on the basis of the universal Forms. The Eleatics held that only the One was real. But what about all the other things in the ordinary physical world? The Eleatics never seriously tried to explain these; they just said that if you apply your logical principle of reality (that a thing cannot both be and not be at the same time), you will see that these things are not real. But this is very unsatisfying. If they are not real, then what are they? Plato said we must somehow account for these appearances.

Plato's solution was to blend Eleaticism with Materialism. There is a basic material "stuff." It is not completely real, but it is not exactly nothing either. By shaping this stuff, like a potter, into different forms resembling the ideal Forms which make up reality, God creates the ordinary physical world of tables, chairs, trees, animals, and people. These things "participate" or share in reality and more or less resemble it, but they are not identical with it. This is Plato's way of expressing the point made earlier that the world and our experience of it is concept-laden, except that Plato is also objectifying the concepts into ideal objects, called the Forms. When we inquire into justice, we are not asking about a particular law, state, or person; we are trying to define the essential characteristic of the real Form, Justice, which all the other things we call "just" more or less resemble. Plato, then, represents a compromise which favors the idealist aspects of pre-Socratic thought.

Aristotle, who is sometimes called the philosopher of common sense, objected to some of Plato's reasoning. He argued that while it is true that reality is conceptual, ideal, one, unchanging, and so on, it is not true that these ideal entities can exist by themselves. The Forms can only exist in particular physical things, and these ordinary objects composed of matter and form are what make up the real world. Still, Aristotle did admit that what is most real about these particular things is their form and that the more form a thing had the more real it was, so his position did not really differ too much from Plato's.

The primary philosophical task of the Middle Ages was to wed philosophy to the requirements of the expanding Christian religion. The theological synthesis was achieved by defining God as the most real being (i.e., pure Form) in the Platonic-Aristotelian sense and by treating the Greek Forms as ideas in the mind of God. Otherwise Greek philosophy survived the transition intact, and the debate over the reality of the Forms continued. Realists such as Thomas Aquinas (1225–1274) and Duns Scotus (1270–1308) argued with Aristotle that Forms were real but only in particular things; Nominalists such as William of Occam (1300–1350) argued with the early Atomists that Forms are only names to which no abstract entity corresponds in reality. The basic realities, Occam argued, are particular things, but in order to talk about specific things, we must introduce general terms and relations into our language. But just because there is a word for something (e.g., "justice"), it does not follow that there is a real object corresponding to it (Justice).

With the rise of the New Science toward the end of the Renaissance (late sixteenth and early seventeenth centuries), philosophy took a new turn and the period known as Modern Philosophy began (the seventeenth through the twentieth centuries). If the previous (Classical) philosophy is characterized by an overriding concern with the nature of reality (see Chapter 2), Modern

Philosophy is dominated by a concern with knowledge (see Chapter 3). This was an exciting period in which Europeans felt themselves on the verge of a dramatic new breakthrough in accurate scientific understanding of the world, and they wanted to get off to a good start. The primary goal, therefore, was to discover the most secure foundation possible for our knowledge of the external world.

René Descartes (1596–1650) is the first major figure of this period. Knowledge must be erected on a solid foundation of certainty, he argued; nothing less than complete certainty will do. But although the purpose was to secure our scientific knowledge of the physical world, the logical implications of this initial starting point was, ironically, toward subjective idealism! It was held that what we are most sure of is our own thought (just as it had been held much earlier that what answered the criterion of reality was what can be thought). I may not know how things really stand, but at least I know what I think about them. The gaze outward toward the physical world therefore turned inward toward the self, and Descartes' "I think, therefore I am" became the foundation for all subsequent developments in Modern Philosophy until the early part of this century.

This idealist trend took two forms: the Continental Rationalists (Descartes, Spinoza (1632–1677), and Leibniz (1646–1716)) who stressed the importance of reason in the acquisition of knowledge, and the British Empiricists (Hobbes (1588–1679), Locke (1632–1704), Berkeley (1685–1753), and Hume (1711–1776)) who stressed the role of sensation and observation. The Rationalists looked primarily to Plato as their source of inspiration, while the Empiricists called upon the authority of Aristotle and the Atomists. Both groups were in essential agreement that our knowledge of the external world had to be constructed out of subjective certainties, regardless of whether they were derived from our reasoning faculty or our faculty of sensation. The Empiricists began, with Hobbes and Locke, on the materialist note that our sensations are caused by the interaction of our bodies with the physical world. But as it gradually became clear, to Berkeley and Hume, that this was only a supposition of which we could by no means be certain, Empiricism moved progressively toward a kind of idealism known as Phenomenalism.

Much of the debate between the Rationalists and the Empiricists centered on the possibility of *a priori* knowledge. Did all knowledge come from sensation, as the Empiricists claimed, or did all or some of it come innately from within by pure reason, as the Rationalists insisted? In Chapter 3 we will reconstruct part of this controversy as an imaginary debate between Locke and Plato. The Rationalists naturally stressed logical and mathematical knowledge as the basis of knowledge, emphasizing the uncertainties of opinions about the physical world, while the Empiricists stressed perceptual knowledge, explaining logical and mathematical certainty nominalistically, as being true simply by definition.

Just as Plato worked out a lasting compromise between competing views of his predecessors, so the eighteenth-century German philosopher Immanuel Kant (1724–1804), came up with an ingenious resolution of Rationalism and Empiricism which held together for several centuries and is still important today. Borrowing Plato's distinction of matter and form, Kant held that the materials of our knowledge come from sensation (conceding to the Empiricists), while the form of our knowledge comes from reason and the other cognitive faculties (which he interpreted the Rationalists to mean). Kant was one of the first to see how concept-laden our everyday experience of the world is. We cannot perceive, much less think, raw sense impressions; we can only assimilate information which has been "programmed" through our own forms of perception and reason. Just as Aristotle had said that neither matter nor form could exist alone but that things could only exist as a mixture of form in matter, so Kant argued that the objects of our experience can never be pure sensation (matter) nor pure thought (form), but must always be a combination of the two.

But the roots of the old controversy went too deep, and during the nineteenth century the old battle lines were gradually redrawn along the English Channel, emerging in a somewhat different form today as the split between contemporary Anglo-American "analytic" philosophers and European "phenomenologists" (not to be confused with the phenomenalists).

The twentieth century is characterized by revolution against the past. The dominant mood among philosophers of this century has been to denounce all previous philosophy as a colossal mistake, and to begin reexamining the nature of philosophy and the reconstruction of its foundations. The more positive character of this revolution can be described as a break with the metaphysical dream of discovering the real nature of the world and a new conception (though not really so new, as we saw) of the role of philosophy as the analysis of meaning. For the analysts (Wittgenstein, Ryle, Austin, Strawson), this meant the analysis and meaning of words and concepts; for the phenomenologists (Husserl, Heidegger, Sartre, Merleau-Ponty), it was the analysis and meaning of the most general structures of our experience.

Probably as time goes on, the differences between these contemporary schools will seem less radical. In our discussion of Verbo and Psycho (which you can now appreciate as caricatures of the analyst and the phenomenologist) we suggested that the two approaches might be reconciled. Much of the difference between these two important philosophical movements results from differences in historical background and style rather than in substance. Analytic philosophers pride themselves on their tough-minded rigor; they thrive on logic and avoid discussions of such things as sex, death, and anxiety. The phenomenologists tend to revel in more tender, emotional, relevant issues which they deal with in a more literary style. The phenomenologists tell the analysts they are too mechanical, aloof, trivial, and irrelevant. The analysts respond that the phenomenologists are vague, wishy-washy, and too poetical. In the following chapters major contributions by both groups will be discussed.

What about the future? If we may venture a cautious prediction, philosophy in the near future will probably be a reconciliation between philosophy past and present, British and Continental. Indeed, as our world shrinks before our eyes, philosophers are beginning to absorb currents of thought outside their own Western tradition—from Africa, the Middle East, and especially the Far East (see Chapter 5). What precise direction this will take depends on the work of philosophers from your own generation.

This book will give you a taste of what philosophy is like and hopefully will whet your appetite for more. What follows is a more detailed sampling of some of the major areas of lasting philosophical concern. The philosopher, we have been saying, begins with common-sense assumptions, so he is criticizing *your* view of the world as well as his own. As we go along you will doubtlessly raise considerations of your own, and it will be up to you to test your positions rationally against the philosophers. Remember that philosophers love nothing better than logically hassling one another. In the end, as Socrates said, everyone must be his own philosopher. In refining your views, you will at the same time be strengthening your own reflective, analytic habits of mind.

TOPICS FOR DISCUSSION

1. What effect might the discovery of new factual information have on the abortion question? How, in general, is empirical data relevant to settling philosophical questions?
2. Can you think of other conceptual boundary disputes which might be of interest to philosophers? How would you go about trying to solve them?
3. What are the criteria for personal identity? If you woke up one morning to find you had turned into a cockroach, how would you know it was you? How could you convince your family that it was you?
4. See what further patterns of validity and invalidity you can come up with on your own. After checking these against any good logic text, such as Copi's, use your newly devised rules to test the validity of a random sample of arguments from friends, radio, television, and newspaper.

SELECTED BIBLIOGRAPHY

Primary Source

Cohen, Morris and Ernest Nagel. *An Introduction to Logic and Scientific Method.* New York: Harcourt, Brace and Co., 1934.
Copi, Irving. *Introduction to Logic.* New York: Macmillan, 1968.
Hume, David. *Dialogues Concerning Natural Religion.* 1748. New York: Hafner, 1948.
Plato. *Meno.* Translated by Benjamin Jowett. New York: Liberal Arts Press, 1957.
———. *Phaedo.* Translated by E. F. Church. New York: Liberal Arts Press, 1951.
———. *The Republic.* Translated by Benjamin Jowett. New York: Random House, 1957.

Secondary Source

Avery, Albert. *Handbook in the History of Philosophy.* New York: Barnes and Noble, 1954.
Copleston, Frederick. *A History of Philosophy.* New York: Doubleday, 1966.

Danto, Arthur. *What Philosophy Is.* New York: Harper and Row, 1968.
Organ, Troy. *The Art of Critical Thinking.* Boston: Houghton Mifflin, 1965.
Rachels, James, ed. *Moral Problems.* New York: Harper and Row, 1968.
Shaffer, Jerome, ed. *Violence.* New York: David McKay, 1971.
Thouless, Robert. *How to Think Straight.* New York: Hart Publishing, 1939.

CHAPTER 2

Metaphysics

WHAT IS METAPHYSICS?

Until the eighteenth century, philosophy was largely identified with metaphysics. Philosophers were concerned with what is real, what really exists in this world. Beginning in the seventeenth and eighteenth centuries, philosophers shifted their attention to what we can be sure we really *know*, and this question tended to cast doubt on the possibility of knowing anything of a metaphysical or extrasensory nature. This doubt gained ground until a group of science-oriented philosophers in the 1930s, the Logical Positivists, tried to eliminate metaphysics altogether as meaningless nonsense. More recently, attempts have been made to redefine the legitimate scope of metaphysical inquiry.

What is this controversy all about? What, after all, is metaphysics? In an age of science and technology, the traditional view of metaphysics as a science of extrasensory reality appears highly suspect. According to a more recent interpretation, however, metaphysics is part of the broader philosophical enterprise of analysis, concentrating on the most fundamental aspects of our experience of the world. This approach might seem a more creditable enterprise, but whether this is what metaphysicians through the years have really been up to it is still hard to say.

Most metaphysical theories do attempt to determine the real nature of things; they try to say what there really is in the world. A metaphysician will argue, for example, that the basic reality of everything is mental, or that it is material, or that it consists solely of atoms and empty space. But how does the philosopher know this and what sort of evidence does he appeal to? Behind this type of inquiry seems to lie the deep-seated belief that things as they appear to us in everyday life are a distortion, or misrepresentation, or even contradiction of the real nature of things. But how can the metaphysician know that things are different from the way we normally experience them? Certainly not empirically, from experience. Metaphysicians hold that there is a certain idea, prior to all experience, of what it means for something to be real, and they feel that this idea is contradicted by most of the things we experience in everyday life. Things in the world, in other words, do not seem to live up to our concept of reality.

Because metaphysical thinking is based not on our direct experience but on the idea we have prior to experience of what reality should or must be, metaphysics is rejected by many contemporary philosophers, such as A. J. Ayer and the Logical Positivists, who believe that knowledge can only come from direct sense experience, as in science. The disagreement between these philosophers and the metaphysicians parallels that between the Rationalists and Empiricists discussed earlier (see Chapter 3). The Rationalists hold that at least some knowledge is gained independently of sense experience. This is called *a priori* knowledge because it is logically prior to experience. The Empiricists, on the other hand, hold that all knowledge is gained through experience. This is called *a posteriori* knowledge since it comes after experience. As you might expect, the Rationalists have been sympathetic and the Empiricists hostile to metaphysics.

In our everyday experience, objects appear to have genuine spatial and temporal properties, as well as qualities of color and shape. Many philosophers, including Parmenides, Plato, and the twentieth-century British metaphysician F. H. Bradley, have argued that our experience of these properties is so contradictory that they cannot be the real features of things, but only an appearance or semblance of reality. If, for example, a grapefruit is first green and then yellow, then it is both green and not green. This is a contradiction; therefore, they say, the color of the grapefruit must be an illusion which does not really exist in the grapefruit. The argument applies to all perceived qualities of an object.

But notice, the metaphysician does not banish what he calls appearance entirely. He admits that it is there in a sense, but he denies that it exists in the fullest or best sense. As Plato put it, appearance rolls about between being and nonbeing, neither fully one nor the other. This is what the metaphysician means when he says "It *seems* to exist but doesn't *really.*" Metaphysicians appear to upgrade one sort of key concept, such as matter or mind, as "reality," and downgrade another sort of concept as "appearance." The materialist would designate matter as reality and the mind as appearance; the idealist would do the opposite.

Appearance is usually said to *depend on* the category called reality. The materialist does not want to flatly deny that there are minds in the world. He admits that there is something which we call "mental," but he insists that this is dependent on or a product of something more basic—namely, the human body, including that part of the body we call the brain. Nor does the idealist mean to deny the existence of things like sticks and stones. When Dr. Samuel Johnson, the famous eighteenth-century English critic, first read the idealist philosopher Bishop Berkeley, he reportedly went out and kicked a stone to prove that physical objects did exist. But he only succeeded in hurting his toe. He was not refuting the good Bishop, since Berkeley admitted there were things we call stones and that they were hard and heavy. What Berkeley objected to was the interpretation of these things as matter. As far as the stone was concerned, far from denying its existence, Berkeley tried to account for it as a visual or tactile idea in the mind of the person looking at or touching the stone—the idea of hardness as it vividly existed in Dr. Johnson's mind when he kicked the stone.

Now, this puts a different light on the harsh antiempiricist charge laid against metaphysics. Far from denying our experience of the world, metaphysics is an attempt to account for it. This is what Plato called "saving the appearances," which he pointed out was fundamental to any rational investigation. After all, we can no more see electrons or field forces than we can the metaphysician's mind or matter, yet the physicist finds the former useful in explaining what we can and do see. Plato's own theory of the Forms may be seen as just such an attempt to "save the appearances." Plato reasoned that since properties like the ordinary green and yellow of a grapefruit were too changeable and contradictory to be real, there must be another sort of greenness and yellowness which are the real green and the real yellow we are referring to when we say a grapefruit is first green and then yellow. "Real greenness" and "real yellowness," in Plato's sense, could never change into their opposites and thus contradict themselves, but will always remain one and the same—a yellow that could never be anything but yellow and a green that could never be anything but green. Thus, like electrons and field forces, these are not colors one can see with one's eyes but ideal colors which we know must exist by reason alone.

This argument is used to account for or "save" our ordinary experience of the changing colors of objects. Plato argued that what we call the grapefruit's changing from green to yellow is really the reflection in the fruit of the Ideal Green followed by the reflection of the Ideal Yellow, neither of which has itself undergone any change whatsoever. Plato "saves the appearance" in the sense that what had first appeared self-contradictory and therefore utterly impossible has now been accounted for in a perfectly rational and consistent, if unusual, manner. Plato thus retains his idea of what reality must be like while he finds a place for things as we normally experience them. But, of course, in order to resolve the apparent contradiction involved, Plato has had to postulate the existence of some rather strange entities, an ideal Greenness and Yellowness which one can never actually see or locate in the ordinary world of space and time.

But then so does the scientist. It was discovered by eighteenth-century scientists that two parts of one substance chemically combined with one part of another formed two, not three, equal parts of a third substance—somehow, they ended up with less than they started with! Scientists then began speculating on what might be going on "behind the scenes" to account for this strange phenomenon. They assumed as a rational criterion, contrary to their direct experience, that the overall quantity of matter could not be lost but must be preserved. Their job was to work out a theory which would save the appearances, that is, one which would reconcile their observations with the principle of the Conservation of Matter. They accomplished this by postulating the existence of atoms and molecules. They could not see the atoms or molecules but they introduced them to explain what they had observed. By supposing that the same atoms could group and regroup to form different molecules which were all of approximately the same size, they were able to have their cake and eat it too. The total quantity of atoms remained the same, thus preserving the Conservation of Matter principle, while their different groupings into molecules accounted for the apparent loss of matter in the final mixture. Imagine three car loads of people arriving for a dance with two people in each car; only two car loads leave the dance, this time with three people in each. There is one less car, but the same number of people.

48 Metaphysics

So it is not quite fair to say that metaphysicians simply turn their backs on the world of everyday experience in order to build castles of air. While metaphysicians may sometimes be deeply offended by what they see as the transient, illogical nature of everyday appearances, they nonetheless try to account for every item of experience in much the same way that the scientist does. In the short run the atomists might appear to be denying our everyday experience of the world, but in the long run the atomic theory provides a more coherent and unified picture of the world as we experience it.

THE METAPHYSICAL THEORY OF SUBSTANCE

The single most important question in the entire history of metaphysics has been the question of "substance" or the reality of objects. This question has attracted the attention of philosophers from Aristotle in the fourth century B.C. to the twentieth-century Oxford philosopher P. F. Strawson. "Substance" is an anglicized form of the Latinized Greek word *ousia*, a form of the verb "to be." The question as Aristotle first saw it was, What is it for something to exist, that is, what are the criteria necessary for something to be—not to be a specific thing, for this is answered by the particular sciences of biology, physics, geology, and so on, but just *to be* in the first place?

Objects and Their Properties

Since philosophy, as we have been saying, is an articulation of common-sense assumptions, let us approach this question, as Aristotle does, in the nontechnical language of common sense and ordinary speech. Notice first of all that in everyday speech we distinguish an object from the properties which we say the object has. We distinguish, in other words, what we say about a thing from that thing itself. An object is one in number, though it can have many different properties. There are many parts and properties of a table, for example, all of which we nonetheless treat as belonging to one thing, the table. This distinction is supported by the grammar of our language. We speak of "a book," "a table," and "the pen," but not of "a circular," "the shady," or "the blue." If we do occasionally speak of "blue" as the subject of a sentence (e.g., "This blue is very nice"), we do so only in the relative sense that the blue of this cloth or this book is nice, not the blue itself. The subject of a sentence is usually an object like a pen, a tree, or a book, while the predicate of the sentence is normally some property which we wish to attribute to the object, e.g., "is blue," "is fast," "is shady," and so on. And even though "blue" may sometimes be the predicate and sometimes the subject of a sentence, things like tables, pens, and trees can only be the subject of a sentence and never the predicate.

But wait! Can't we say "This is a table" or "The elm is a tree" where "a table" and "a tree" appear as parts of the predicate? In these cases we don't mean by "a tree" a particular tree, but the whole class of trees, or the general property of being a tree. We mean that an elm belongs to the class of trees or has the property of being a tree. The only time the term for a particular thing is treated as a predicate of a sentence is in identity statements, e.g., "The girl over there is the one you met last night." Here we are not predicating one thing of something else; we are saying that the objects denoted by these two expressions are one and the same. We will return to this complication in a moment.

First, let's go back to the distinction between objects and their properties. What sort of things make up the world according to common sense? We do not ordinarily think of properties, for example, as existing in their own right in addition to objects. The existence of properties is normally thought to be dependent on the existence of physical objects. If you take away all the objects in the world, you have thereby removed all the blueness, redness, and squareness in the world. So, it begins to look as though *to be* is *to be an object*. And this is the assumption on which all Western metaphysics has proceded from Aristotle to the present. However, this raises the question, What is an object?

INDEPENDENCE. In common sense we tend to think of the tree as being more real than its shadiness, which we consider to be dependent on the tree for existence. Thus, objects, like a tree and a pen and things of this sort, are relatively self-subsistent and exist relatively independently of other things. They also exist independently of you and me and the question of whether we perceive them or not. Compare this with the case of a rainbow. Is it a real, self-existing object? It is at best a border-line case. We cannot touch a rainbow and give it a definite spatial location, and we know the rainbow exists only as a reflection of drops of water visible to people from a certain vantage point and under certain conditions. It does not seem to have any existence in and of itself. If we try to locate the pot of gold at the end of the rainbow we find the rainbow "moving" as we approach it, which suggests that it exists only within the mind of the beholder.

An object is also independent of its properties in the sense that the object does not change just because some of its properties change. If I paint my brown table red, it is still a table. What if I pick a leaf off a tree, isn't it still a tree, and the same tree it was? Yes, according to common sense; the number of leaves has changed, but the tree itself has not ceased to be a tree nor has it ceased to be this particular tree. It remains that tree throughout a prolonged period, in spite of minor changes, day by day, month by month. Compare this with a wave breaking along the beach. As soon as I am able to spot it, to pick it out from among the others, it is gone. If it were a real object, in the usual sense of the word, I could separate it from the other waves and take it home with me, or at least I could give it a name and come back to see it again tomorrow. But, of course, we can not do this with the wave. And this is what inclines us to say that the wave is simply a *manifestation* of the sea. The sea is real; the wave is just a momentary feature *of* the sea. If a child were to ask, "Where has the wave gone?" we would be puzzled as to how to answer him because this is the kind of question we can only meaningfully ask about an object. The child who asks this question is still developing his concept of an object.

All we have said so far is simply an articulation of what is implied in our common-sense concept of an object and the sense in which it exists as a real thing. When we say that a thing exists we mean that it is an object of some kind, meaning that it is relatively stable and permanent, that it exists relatively independently of other things, and that it is the subject of discourse rather than what we predicate of the subject.

EFFECTS OF CHANGE. We said that an object is relatively unchanging. Let's examine this more closely. Take a tree, for instance. A tree is constantly changing in one way or another; here it gains a leaf, there it loses a leaf, today it is a little greener, tomorrow a little less green, each day a little taller, and so on. Yet these changes do not alter its being a tree. But if I remove all the leaves, cut off all the branches, and saw it off at the base, we would say it is no longer a tree. These changes make it cease to be a tree while the other changes did not because after such alterations it can no longer function as a tree—it no longer possesses enough of the essential criteria for being a tree to be included in the class of trees.

This brings us back to an ambiguity we noted earlier. When we said that a tree was always the subject of a sentence and never the predicate, it was objected that in "An elm is a tree," "a tree" functions as the predicate. We pointed out that in this case "is a tree" means "belongs to the class of trees" or "has the property of being a tree," which is very different from "a tree" in the sense of a particular tree. In one sense "a tree" is general and applicable to many trees; in another it is particular and applicable only to one individual tree. It now becomes apparent that the two are not altogether unrelated. The existence of this *particular* tree as an object is directly related to the *general* concept we have of a tree. How would you know when a tree ceases to be a tree unless you have an understanding of the general concept of what it means to be a tree? As soon as this particular thing ceases to match up to the idea you have of a tree, you say it has ceased to *exist*. Notice that as a mere thing the tree has not ceased to exist when it is transformed into a log. It simply ceased to exist as a tree. Consider the tree as simply a hunk of wood. The properties which make it cease to exist as wood are different from what they were when we considered the object as a tree. If we cut it down it is still a hunk of wood; if we cut it in half, either half is still a hunk of wood. Indeed, far from eliminating objects from the world, we have multiplied them! But if we grind it up into sawdust, or burn it to ashes, or make paper out of it, *then* it ceases to exist as a hunk of wood.

Kinds of Objects

To be an object, then, is always to be an object of a certain *kind*, and the kind of thing it is determines what changes are irrelevant to its existence and which are relevant.

Of course, our idea of treehood does not affect the tree itself, but it does affect how we understand the existence of that thing. As we noted in the first chapter, the world as we experience it is concept-laden. We are able to identify a tree because we have learned to call and recognize it as such. It *could* mean something different; imagine a group of people who do not distinguish in their language between trees and logs—they would not understand what it means to destroy a tree by cutting it down. It makes sense to us because of our concepts of a tree and of a log. The existence of a particular object is related to the idea we have of a class of objects to which the particular thing belongs.

An understanding of this concept is crucial for an understanding of Aristotle's view in Book Z of *Metaphysics* that in one sense the *substance* of a thing is also its *essence*. All objects are objects of a certain kind. Ironically, the existence of objects is tied to the way we classify things into kinds. Suppose you had never seen a city and had no idea of what a city was, and suppose that to show you I simply took you into the middle of Manhattan and announced, "This is a city." Would you understand what I meant? "Where is the city?" you would wonder. "Here is a house, there is a car, there is a tree, here are people walking about—is this a city or part of one?" You wouldn't know. You don't know what a thing is until you have an idea of the kind of thing it is, and until you know this, you can not know what makes an individual member of that group exist as a self-subsistent, permanent entity in its own right. Does an object cease to exist when I cut it in half? Well, it depends on what kind of thing it is. There is no answer to such a question in general. Break a piece of chalk in half and either half is still a piece of chalk; but cut a car in two, and neither half is a car. So, an object must be not only relatively permanent and self-subsistent; it must also be classifiable into a definite group or kind of thing.

Philosophy arises out of common sense, but it often travels far afield in the course of developing an initial idea. So, for example, the original common-sense notion of an existing object as relatively permanent has undergone significant changes in the hands of successive philosophers. Any object we can actually find in the world is only relatively permanent. Trees cease to exist, men die, and so on. If permanence is an essential characteristic of a real object we might wonder whether any of these relatively permanent things is a real object. Would not an absolutely permanent entity, if there were such, be more real than a tree or a pen? Take the idea of a perfect triangle, for example; it never changes, it is always precisely three straight lines enclosing 180°. If our criterion of reality is permanence, then isn't the triangle more real than a tree? This is the sort of consideration which led Plato to hold that abstract, ideal entities were more real than ordinary physical objects. Or consider the independent character of an object. If shadiness is less real than the tree because shadiness depends on it for its existence, then isn't the tree less real than the material elements it depends on to live and remain a tree? This type of reflection leads naturally to materialism, the view that only material elements are real. If we believe in God, then isn't everything in the world dependent, in some sense, on God, and if so, then isn't God the only real object in the world? This was the position developed in the seventeenth century by the exiled Jewish philosopher Spinoza. This example illustrates the way in which philosophers can begin with ordinary common-sense notions, but by trying to make them more rigorous or exact, can arrive at conceptions very far removed from common sense.

ARISTOTLE'S *METAPHYSICS*

One of the earliest, probably the best, and certainly the most influential work in metaphysics is Aristotle's book which gave the subject its name, *Metaphysics*. (As a matter of fact the book is probably a collection of his students' lecture notes.) When we look at Aristotle in *Metaphysics*, we see him torn between the common-sense notion of a real thing and a philosophically exaggerated extension of that common-sense idea. Officially, Aristotle seems to hold that metaphysics deals only with absolutely permanent, independent, supersensible entities, such as God, the "intelligences" which he thought moved the planets, and abstract forms or essences, as Plato also believed. In practice, most of Aristotle's concern in *Metaphysics* is with the nature and reality of individual, concrete existing things in the perceptible world of space and time, things like trees and houses, which Aristotle calls *ousia*, or as it is translated into English via the Latin, "substance." Aristotle wants to know what general characteristics any individual thing must have in order to be and to be known. Just as biology asks, "What is it to be a living thing?" and physics, "What is it to be a physical thing?", so metaphysics, according to Aristotle, asks the more general question, in a sense preliminary to the others, "What is it to *be*," meaning "What are the conditions or criteria necessary for a concrete individual object to exist?"

Aristotle deals with this question in two different but closely related ways, and any understanding of Aristotle's theory of substance must take into account the relationship between these two approaches. The first is a linguistic, logical account of what it is to be the subject matter of any discourse, what it is to be a thing which one can talk about. The second approach is the biologically, scientifically-oriented question of what is it to be something which exists in its own right but which also comes into the world as a result of change. What is it, in other words, to be the kind of thing that *becomes* what it is, such as a tree from a seed, a person from his parents, or a house from wood and the builder's craft? We'll begin with the first, the linguistic or logical approach to substance as the ultimate subject matter of all thought and conversation.

The Linguistic Approach to Substance

For Aristotle, to be is to be something, that is, some concrete, determinate object which answers the question, "What is it?" Aristotle acknowledges both in *Categories* and in *Metaphysics* that we use the expression "to be" in different senses, that we speak of colors or plans or relationships existing in a different sense than we speak of a grasshopper existing. Aristotle argues that only that which answers the question "What is it?" exists in the primary sense of the word. When we ask this question we expect answers like "a man" or "a grasshopper." Anything else, whether properties or relations or whatever, exists only derivatively as properties or relations of a substance. They do not exist in their own right. As Aristotle puts it, "That which is primarily is substance."

Historically, from that point on the study of being was limited to the study of the being of substances, which had tremendous consequences for the history of Western thought. Things other than substances—like hopes, fears, plans, properties, and relations—are regarded or defined either as attributes of substances or as unusual kinds of substances. Only concrete, determinate objects (a table or whatever) are substances, and for Aristotle these are the ultimately real things in the world. But Aristotle also wants to know what it is about these things which differentiates them from properties and relations. He wants to know what it is about such objects which makes them answerable to the question "What is it?" However, there is a deep ambiguity in Aristotle's way of putting the question which permeates his whole discussion and indeed the entire history of metaphysics. In our earlier discussion of the expression "a tree," we noted an ambiguity: the term could refer to a particular tree or to the general class of trees. A similar ambiguity results when we speak of "a substance"; we may mean this particular substance, this book or this tree, or we may mean the idea of substantiality in general, what makes a substance a substance. Since Aristotle is interested in a science of substance, he is primarily interested in substance in the second sense. He does not want a mere list of substances: trees, tables, grasshoppers, pens, and so on; he wants a definition or explanation of substance in general. But because of the ambiguity involved, we are apt to confuse the idea of a particular substance with the idea of substantiality in general. A tree is a tree, that is, a particular tree falls under the general class of trees. But a particular tree is not the same thing as a general class or property—a tree grows in the ground, a class or property does not. Sometimes Aristotle keeps this distinction straight and sometimes he does not, which often makes him hard to understand.

The Scientific Approach to Substance

In his study of substantiality, Aristotle found several common-sense candidates for substance which had already been suggested by previous philosophers. The materialists argued that substance is material since the house we plan to build does not exist until it has actually materialized. Others, such as Plato, held that substance is the abstract Idea or Form which makes a thing real. Whatever limited reality a particular bed may have, Plato said, is due entirely to its resemblance to the abstract idea of a bed. Another possible approach was that substance is whatever is essential to that thing being the particular thing it is, that without which it would be something else. And finally there was the suggestion that substance is a concrete, sensible entity consisting of both matter and form—the house-plans actually carried out in wood, concrete, and metal.

All of these different interpretations of substance (substantiality) are supported at least partially by common sense. It is typical of philosophical analysis to uncover not one but several roots of any given common-sense concept. The philosopher frequently discovers that a concept which appeared to have only one meaning in common usage has several quite distinct and even contradictory meanings when analyzed carefully. And frequently subsequent philosophers follow up on one aspect of the concept, ignoring the others, and end up with a definition or theory having little resemblance to common sense. Aristotle recognized in Book Z of *Metaphysics* that in one sense substance is matter, while in another sense it is the abstract idea of a thing, while in still another sense it is a combination of matter and form. Following Aristotle and continuing right up to the present, philosophers have seized upon some one of these possibilities to the exclusion of the others. Since isolating any one of these involves denying part of the common-sense notion of substance, all these philosophical refinements of Aristotle's original analysis appear strange to common sense. Each of these distinct interpretations of substance are ambiguously contained in our ordinary concept of a real entity.

SUBSTANCE AS MATTER. We have already suggested that the independent existence of a thing is a relative notion and that just as the properties of a table are dependent on the individual table, so the table is dependent on the wood from which it is made. The same applies to the permanence of a thing. A table is more permanent than a spot of light reflected on it, but the wood from which the table is made is more permanent still. If we cut up the table it ceases to be a table, but it remains wood. But even the wood is not absolutely permanent, for it can be destroyed by burning. But even so, the basic chemical elements which make up the wood have not changed. The wood is composed of carbon, nitrogen, oxygen, and so on, but so are the ashes and smoke which result from burning it. These chemical elements have remained exactly the same from the time it was wood until it was reduced to smoke and ashes, so the elements seem to be the most permanent of all. If our everyday criterion for something's being real is that it be independent and permanent, then shouldn't we say that the ultimate material elements out of which the wood and the table are composed are more real than either the table or the wood? If being real means being permanent and independent then the material ingredients are the most real, but this makes it sound as though the table is somehow less than real, contrary to common sense.

This philosophical analysis led Aristotle to state that in one sense substance is matter. The early Western philosophers, including Thales, Anaximander, and Anaximenes, thought of substance in this manner, as the basic stuff out of which all the particular things in the universe were made. This is also the central position of philosophical and scientific materialism to this day. Many people still feel that the particles of nitrogen, hydrogen, oxygen, and so on are more real than an actual table, which is viewed simply as a particular arrangement of the real particles of matter. When the atom was split and found to be composed of still more elementary matter, the tendency was to say that these subatomic particles were even more real than the atoms. This trend toward materialism is the philosophical heir of Aristotle's analysis of substance as matter, which, in turn, is a reflection on common sense.

Aristotle acknowledges, then, that matter is one of the reasons why a thing is what it is. For Aristotle there are four basic causes, or ways of explaining what a thing is, and one of these is the material cause. One reason a bell has the properties which make it a bell is that it is made of brass. But Aristotle saw that this could not be the only thing that made a bell a bell. Brass alone would fail to differentiate a brass bell from, say, a brass monkey. For Aristotle, substance is what a thing is and that which tells us what it is and makes it what it is—and matter, although it is one meaning of substance, cannot be the whole explanation.

SUBSTANCE AS IDEA. Substance, as well as being permanent and independent, should also determine what an individual thing is. What makes a table identifiable to us as a table—what tells us that it is a table—is the *idea* we have of a table. An idea is independent of every other idea, since it is the idea of that thing and nothing else. It is also permanent. You can destroy the table, but you cannot destroy the idea of a table. This is the line of reasoning Plato and the later Realists developed, that Ideas of tablehood, treehood, and so on could exist on their own and were the ultimately real things in the universe. A number of philosophers, like Whitehead and Santayana, have tried to reinstate this position in twentieth-century thought. But just as Materialism contradicts the common-sense belief in the reality of individual physical things, so too does Realism. We can see, feel, touch, taste, and smell objects in this world, and for most of us, they are much more real than the idea of treehood, tablehood, or yellowness. But in both cases the philosophical idea has grown out of common sense, and thus Aristotle concludes that one possible interpretation of substance is that it is Idea in the Platonic sense.

While this is one legitimate sense of "substance," it cannot be the only one since it does not give a complete account of why a particular thing is the kind of thing it is. One reason this tree is the kind of thing it is, namely a tree, is the Idea of treehood. This leads Aristotle to acknowledge the importance of what he calls the Formal Cause. What makes that thing a bell?—both the fact that it is made of brass (the *Material Cause*) and also the fact that this brass was shaped into the form of a bell (the *Formal Cause*). But Aristotle sees that the Form is not sufficient to explain how this thing got to be a bell. His main objection to Plato's theory of Ideas, or Forms, is that it does not really explain anything. If the Ideas are completely independent, self-contained, and unchanging, then why should anything but these Ideas exist? If they are so stable and permanent, then why should the particular tables, trees, and other objects have ever come into existence? Dreaming of a million dollars does not make me a wealthy man!

Aristotle's final verdict on all these proposals is that no one alone can completely explain what makes an individual thing the particular thing it is. All along Aristotle is judging the various interpretations of substance against the common-sense view that substance is a particular thing of a certain kind—a tree, a table, and so on. The two definitions of substance Aristotle seems to favor most are that substance is essence and that substance is a combination of matter and form.

SUBSTANCE AS MATTER AND FORM. The definition of substance as a combination of matter and form is probably the closest to the common-sense idea of a particular thing. A bell is the brass material molded into the shape of a bell. Aristotle uses another set of terms to distinguish matter and form: *potentiality* and *actuality*. The lump of brass is actually a lump of brass, but potentially it is a bell; the brass bell is actually a bell but potentially an ornament for a bracelet, and so on. This is simply another way of expressing the fact that brass is the material for the bell, while the bell is the material for the bracelet. Both the matter-form and the potentiality-actuality distinctions are thus relative distinctions. Brass is the *form* of the material elements of tin and copper, but it is the *material* out of which the bell is made.

How well does this explain why a certain thing is the particular thing it is? The matter-form theory can explain why this thing is a bell, but can it explain why it is this *particular* bell?

It explains the *kind* of thing I am (a human being), but does it explain why I am me and not you? Can it account for the difference between us? My matter (flesh and bones) is the same kind of matter as your matter, and my form (human nature) is the same as yours, but surely we are different people. This is a problem for Aristotle, and it springs directly out of the ambiguity we discussed earlier between substance as a particular entity and substance as that which makes an entity what it is. Aristotle tries to answer this problem by saying that what differentiates two people is not the matter out of which they are directly composed, but a more indirect or ultimate matter. By this he means that while all human beings are made out of flesh and bones, flesh and bones are themselves made out of (hence the "form" of) still more primitive matter, and so on. While the kind of flesh and bone out of which we are made is the same, the ultimate, most primitive matter is different, and this is what differentiates us from one another, according to Aristotle. However, since the only thing we can understand about an object is the kind of thing it is, that is, its form, this ultimate, *pure* matter cannot be known or understood. So, it is gratuitous and useless for explaining anything! How can I tell the difference between this person and that person if what differentiates them is something ultimately unknowable?

+ This is part of a very general philosophical problem known as the *essence-existence problem*. If all we ever know of an object is conceptual and general, then it is difficult to explain how we know and differentiate individual things and distinguish them from imaginary ones. What do you know about a particular piece of chalk? That it is white, cylindrical, and so on. But these are general terms applicable to other pieces of chalk, including imaginary ones, as well as to cigarettes and other look-alikes. The problem is not *whether* we know particular things or not, which we surely do, but *how* we know them, that is, how well we can account for our knowledge of them. Most traditional philosophical answers rely on the notion of intuition, or knowledge by acquaintance, but even by intuition or acquaintance I can only know something as a certain *kind* of thing. I may be acquainted with you, but only as a man or a woman or a student or a friend. It appears we can only know things as a member of an identifiable class or group, that is, in general and not in particular. This problem is a major preoccupation of the existentialists which we will discuss in Chapter 8.

The essence-existence problem led to the first suspicion that metaphysics was an unknowable and therefore worthless subject. John Locke (1632–1704) first noted that since we can only know various generalized attributes of an object, we could never know that concrete object itself. We can know various properties of X but never the substance X itself. George Berkeley (1685–1753) and David Hume (1711–1776) immediately objected that, if this were so, then the whole notion of properties being dependent on substance was worthless. This naturally enough led either to scepticism (that we cannot know the real object) or to idealism (that an object is nothing more nor less than the sum of ideas we have about it). The German philosopher Leibniz (1646–1716) had an interesting suggestion. He proposed to salvage the idea of substance by simply identifying an object with all its properties. This had the paradoxical consequence, however, that no two objects could have the same properties. If an object is nothing but its properties, different objects will have to have different properties. All of these proposals and counterproposals are ramifications of Aristotle's initial discussion.

The essence-existence problem is another indication of the strong intellectualist bias running through Western philosophy. What we know intellectually, philosophers tend to identify with what is real. Though Aristotle denies the independent existence of the Forms, he agrees with Plato in identifying reality with form. Form and actuality are always more real for Aristotle than matter and potentiality because he regards matter as a mere potentiality for *becoming* something real. The thing is most real when it has finally arrived at what it truly is, when the seed becomes a tree, and so on. Aristotle does say that form must be combined with matter; the form of a tree cannot exist by itself but must be made actual in this bit of wood. But he also recognizes that even though the form cannot exist by itself, it is always the degree of form which determines the degree of reality a thing has. The reality of a thing is therefore fixed by its form. The bell as matter for the ornament is less ultimately matter than the brass as matter for the bell, and so on until we come to pure, ultimate matter which has no form at all but is pure potentiality for becoming. And on the other end of the scale, form becomes progressively purified of matter until we arrive at pure form without any mixture of matter, and this is God, the most real being. This view was systematized by Thomas Aquinas in the thirteenth century to form the core of Scholastic metaphysics. As Jean-Paul

Sartre, the contemporary French existentialist, says, the traditional view has always been that essence precedes existence.

SUBSTANCE AS ESSENCE. Aristotle's final definition of substance, and the one he seems to favor, is that substance is essence. We have already suggested that Aristotle has some very good reasons for supposing that what makes a thing the particular thing it is is the *kind* of thing that it is. But what exactly does Aristotle mean by "essence"? Is the essence of something the same as our concept of that thing? Not quite, for Aristotle objectifies some of our concepts just as Plato does. For Aristotle, there is a very important distinction between ideas like treehood and ideas like hunk of wood. Aristotle holds that the idea of treehood actually belongs to the object, that it is really a part of the objective, external world, whereas "hunk of wood" is just a conventional, human way of speaking. As later philosophers put it, "hunk of wood" is a nominal essence, while "treehood" is a real essence. What exactly is the difference between the two? I think we can see what Aristotle is driving at, though we may not agree with him, if we consider examples from Aristotle's pet subject, biology. Consider the animals in Africa. How can we classify them? We can divide the animals up any way we choose, and having done so proceed to make true assertions about the animals which fall into this or that group. For example, we can divide animals into those that live in Sierra Leone, those that live in Ivory Coast, those that live in Guinea, and so on. If I classify them this way, then it will be false to say lions are Sierra Leone animals and true to say that monkeys are Sierra Leone animals. Similarly, we could divide animals into different categories according to height—group A up to one foot, group B from one to two feet, and so on. But we all feel that these are arbitrary categories which we have imposed on the world, not categories we discover in the world. On the other hand, when we classify animals as lions, monkeys, snakes, lizards, and so on, we all feel that we are classifying the animals into their real, or natural, groupings. There seems to be something fixed and stable about this system of classification which is absent from the others. Leaving aside the question of evolution for the moment, animals have always fallen into these groups and no animal can be a member of more than one such group, whereas a Sierra Leone animal might well wander off into adjoining Guinea and suddenly become a Guinean animal, or after a good grazing season a young antelope might suddenly grow from a group A animal into a group B animal. The most important factor, however, is that horses only have horses as offspring and never anything else, and no other animal ever has a horse as an offspring, whereas every B and C animal has young A animals for offspring.

Let's pursue this idea further. Aristotle's question about substance is always, What makes this particular thing the particular thing it is? If we ask of a snake egg what makes it grow into a snake rather than a bird, a lizard, or a frog, we are inclined to answer that there is something in the egg which already contains the determining grounds for becoming a snake. Today we understand this in terms of genetic structure. Aristotle said it was the essence of snakehood potentially present in the egg that determines what it will become. What determines what a seed, for example, will grow into? The kind of seed it is. We call a pumpkin seed a *pumpkin* seed, not because it is a pumpkin, but because we know it will become one. Essences differ from other concepts in that an essence is said to really belong to a thing, making it the particular thing it is. In Chapter 8 we will return to this notion of the real essence or nature of a thing when we discuss the modern problem of meaninglessness. Notice that if we deny the objective reality of essences, we are led either into idealism (that what makes a thing exist as an entity is simply our idea of it) or meaninglessness (that things do not mean anything in and of themselves).

There is an important point of difference between *essence* in Aristotle's sense and *Idea* in Plato's sense. If the essence really belongs to a particular thing, then the essence is a part of the particular thing and does not exist independently of it as the Platonic Idea does. But is this really so different from Plato? Aristotle says the essence is always *in* the particular thing, but if the essence of this tree is the same for all trees of this species, then the essence must be general while the tree is particular. What sense does it make to say that the general idea of treehood resides in this particular tree? This essence is not destroyed when the tree burns down, for example. What Aristotle probably has in mind is just that the general essence is *in* the particular thing in the sense that the idea of treehood is what makes this the particular thing it is. But this is precisely what Plato held: the Idea of bed is what makes this particular thing a bed. If all of us have the same human essence or nature, then doesn't that human nature transcend each one of us? When a man dies, does a little part of human nature die? No, human nature is independent of the existence of any particular person. And how much more than this did Plato say? The difference between Plato and Aristotle on this point is probably one more of emphasis than principle.

The point is that concepts have a life of their own. They have logical implications and contain the seeds of philosophical ideas. When a philosopher begins analyzing a concept from common sense, he may well find it leading him to say things he does not wish to say. So it was in this case. What Aristotle wished to say was that substance was always concrete, individual, physical, and sensible. But what the logic of the concept led him to say, among other things, was that substance is formal essence. Once you take the wrong turn down a country lane, it is often difficult to get off of it!

THE EMPIRICIST CRITIQUE OF METAPHYSICS

The puzzling consequences of Aristotle's original analysis of substance began to surface prominently in the work of subsequent thinkers. The whole discussion of substance sank into deeper and deeper difficulties as more of its logical implications were worked out and wilder and wilder claims were made *vis-à-vis* common sense. In the seventeenth and eighteenth centuries metaphysics fell into disrepute, and in the twentieth century it was totally rejected by the Logical Positivists, whose most prominent spokesman was A. J. Ayer.

The Two Classes of Meaningful Propositions

Ayer objected to metaphysics in general and to the metaphysics of substance in particular because he felt that *all* metaphysical statements were devoid of literal meaning: while these statements purport to be genuine propositions about the world, they are neither true nor false. Ayer followed the argument of the eighteenth-century Scottish philosopher David Hume that there are only two classes of meaningful propositions which can be said to be true or false: (1) those which are analytic and a priori—statements such as "All bachelors are unmarried," which are true and which we know to be necessarily true simply from the meanings of the words used; and (2) those which are synthetic and a posteriori, those factual statements about the empirical world whose truth can only be learned, either directly or indirectly, from sense experience. What Hume and Ayer are saying is that the only statements whose truth can be determined independently of sense experience (that is, a priori) are those which are true simply by definition (that is, analytic) and therefore uninformative (for example, "Either it will rain or it won't). On the other hand, the only informative (that is, synthetic) statements possible which actually assert something about the world (for example, "It is raining") are those which we learn from sense experience (that is, a posteriori). You can have factually uninformative statements of logic and mathematics, or you can have factually significant statements like those of science and ordinary common sense, which are grounded on sense experience. But you cannot have metaphysical statements which supply information about an extrasensory reality inaccessible to sense experience. The claim of philosophers like Hume and Ayer, then, is that metaphysical statements belong to neither class of meaningful propositions.

ANALYTIC A PRIORI. The first category of meaningful propositions are verbal tautologies, such as "Either it will rain or it will not rain," which are true by definition. It is clear that metaphysical statements are not statements of this kind. The test of whether a statement is a logical tautology or an analytic statement is whether the denial of that statement results in a self-contradiction. For example, if we want to check to see if the statement "All bachelors are unmarried" is a tautology, we deny the proposition and get "Some bachelors are married." But since "bachelor" simply means an unmarried man, this proposition clearly contradicts itself, for it asserts that "Some unmarried men are married"! Since the denial of the proposition is self-contradictory, we can safely conclude that the proposition itself is a tautology. But what happens when we apply this test to metaphysical statements? Take Spinoza's claim that there is only one substance. Is its denial, "There is more than one substance," self-contradictory? No. Therefore, it is not a tautology. So metaphysical statements do not fall into the first class of meaningful propositions, those which are analytic a priori. The question is, Do they fall within the second class of statements?

SYNTHETIC A POSTERIORI. The second type of statement are factual assertions. Their denial does not yield a self-

The Empiricist Critique of Metaphysics 65

contradiction, and the only way you can tell whether they are true or false is to look and see. These statements describe the actual course of events in the world and in order to be meaningful must therefore be empirically verifiable—that is, it must be possible to determine by our sense experience whether the statement is true or false. For example, the truth of the statement "The Empire State building is a mile high" can be determined and the statement verified either by measuring its height or reading reports of the building's specifications. A. J. Ayer points out that in order to be meaningful, it is not necessary that a factual statement be completely or conclusively verifiable or falsifiable, but he does insist that there be some empirical evidence which would count for or against the claim, even if it does not establish its truth or falsity completely, once and for all. For Ayer it is not necessary to have the means, here and now, of verifying a statement before it can be said to be meaningful; but it must be *possible in principle* to verify the statement. Twenty years ago it was impossible to verify physically that the far side of the moon resembled the near side. But the statement was nonetheless verifiable because it was conceivable that one could verify the statement by going to the far side of the moon or, as actually happened, by flying around it with cameras. This is what is called the *Verifiability Criterion:* what we experience of the world in sensation must have some bearing or impact on our factual beliefs. If a statement truly describes the world, then it must be possible for the future course of events in the world to confirm or disconfirm the truth of that statement. A person who holds beliefs which no sense experience would confirm or disconfirm is simply constructing castles of air.

The question is, Do empirical facts make any difference to the truth or falsity of metaphysical statements? Is there any empirically noticeable difference, for example, between Spinoza's position that there is only one substance and Descartes' view that there are three substances, God, mind, and matter? Can you imagine anything which you can observe which could possibly confirm or disconfirm either view? If not, then, according to Ayer, these two views come down to much the same thing. There is no real dispute between Spinoza and Descartes. Theirs is a bogus, or phony controversy. There is no more empirical difference between Descartes' and Spinoza's positions than there is between the man who believes in goblins which become invisible the instant you look at them and the man who denies that such goblins exist.

66 Metaphysics

Whether they do or do not exist, the world would be exactly the same as far as we could tell. And so, for all metaphysical disputes, according to Ayer, "we must conclude that neither assertion is significant."

It appears, then, that metaphysical statements are neither tautologies nor factual statements, and since these are the only kinds of meaningful propositions allowed, it follows that metaphysical statements have no literal meaning. They may express some emotional or religious attitude, but they are neither true nor false. Since metaphysical statements can not be proved or disproved, for Ayer and the Positivists, discussing such statements is a waste of time. This is precisely what Hume said over 200 years ago at the very end of his *Enquiry Concerning Human Understanding*:

> When we run over libraries, persuaded of these principles, what havoc must we make? If we take in our hand any volume of divinity or school metaphysics, for instance—let us ask, *Does it contain any abstract reasoning concerning quantity or number?* No. *Does it contain any experimental reasoning concerning matters of fact and existence?* No. Commit it then to the flames, for it can contain nothing but sophistry and illusion.

Ayer's Logical Analysis of Meaning

How does the metaphysician come to commit these terrible blunders, imagining that he is making sense, but is really talking a lot of nonsense? Ayer argues that the source of the philosopher's error is his general failure to stick to his own job. Instead of doing what philosophers ought to have been doing, traditional metaphysicians were off meddling in other people's work, trying to do the job of the scientist, for example, and therefore failing both as a scientist and as a philosopher. The real job of the philosopher, according to Ayer, is giving a proper logical analysis of the meaning of statements, not constructing substantive theories about some supersensible reality outside space and time. Because the metaphysicians were not paying attention to what they should have been doing, i.e., logical analysis, they made bad mistakes in the analyses they did give, which led to subsequent errors.

For example, metaphysicians noticed that in most Indo-

The Empiricist Critique of Metaphysics 67

European languages we describe an object by specifying a subject term, which we are describing, and a predicate term, which is our description of that object. From this accidental grammatical feature of language, philosophers jumped to the conclusion that there must exist two quite different sorts of entities in the world, objects and properties, or, more technically, substances and their attributes. According to Ayer, this conclusion results from a faulty analysis of language and a confusion of grammatical distinctions with real distinctions. The analysis is based on the mistaken notion that every word gets its meaning by referring to an existing object, or in other words, that the meaning of a word *is* that object to which it refers. The philosopher assumes that because the word "John" in "John is dropping out of school" refers to an existing entity, *all* words must refer to existing entities. Thus the philosopher reasons that in the statement "The apple is red" there are two things being referred to, the apple and the redness, and the statement is asserting some relation between these two entities, just as the statement "John loves Mary" asserts a relation between two existing entities, John and Mary. As Ayer put it, the metaphysician is "deceived by grammar," or as Hume said a few centuries earlier, "[metaphysical questions] can never be decided, and are to be regarded rather as grammatical than as philosophical difficulties." Thus metaphysicians would not have made mistakes if they had paid more attention to the correct logical analysis of language and meaning.

Since the grammar of a language is not always an adequate reflection of real distinctions, it is the task of the philosopher to discover by analysis the real meaning of statements. According to Ayer, philosophical analysis will always eliminate metaphysical statements simply because metaphysical statements are based on incorrect analyses. When the analysis is corrected and the meaning of statements is analyzed correctly, the metaphysical problems and questions disappear. The proper analysis of "The apple is red," for example, will reveal not that there are two things being referred to, the apple and its redness, but only one thing which we first *identify* as an apple and then go on to *describe* as red. The distinction is not between two kinds of entities but between two kinds of linguistic functions: identification and description.

Even if we agree with Ayer that philosophy is the analysis of meaning, it is not clear that logical analysis excludes metaphysics. It all depends on what we mean by logical analysis. To illustrate this unclarity let's consider for a moment a difficulty in Ayer's own criterion of meaning, the "Verifiability Criterion." Shortly after the publication of Ayer's most popular book, *Language, Truth and Logic* (1936), a philosopher-priest named Copleston raised an interesting objection. What would happen, he asked, if we applied the Verifiability Criterion to the Verifiability Criterion itself? Ayer asserts that *all* meaningful propositions are either tautologies or empirically verifiable; Copleston questions whether this statement is meaningful or not. Copleston concludes that Ayer's statement is not a tautology, since it is not self-contradictory to deny that there are only these two types of meaningful statement. Nor is it a factual statement since there are no empirically observable facts which either confirm or disconfirm Ayer's assertion. Indeed, people do consider many other types of statements to be meaningful. Ayer makes a value judgment, contending that there are only two types of statement which ought to be considered meaningful, but there is no empirical evidence to support this. So, the Verifiability Criterion of meaning must be meaningless on its own grounds! Ayer seemed to be damned out of his own mouth, and, though he was genuinely embarrassed by this objection, he never succeeded in providing a completely satisfactory answer to it. Ayer's own theory seems to result from a kind of philosophical analysis which does not fit the simple model of "logical analysis" which he proposes for all philosophical investigation.

There appear to be at least two types of philosophical analysis: one very narrow and particular, the other more broad and general. The one examines the meaning of individual statements piecemeal, the other looks to the conditions of meaningfulness in general. The one asks, "Is this statement meaningful or meaningless?" and the other asks, "What conditions must be present before *any* statement can have meaning?" When Ayer explains his Verifiability Criterion he does the latter—inquires into the general conditions which must be met before any statement can be meaningful—and this, ironically, begins to look very much like metaphysics! Ayer's formulation of the Verifiability Principle is neither a tautology nor a factual statement; it is in fact a metaphysical assertion analyzing the most general empirical requirements of factual meaning. Ayer could have avoided Copleston's objection by admitting that while some metaphyical assertions are conceptually barren, others provide logical analyses of the general conditions of meaningful experience and discourse which are part of the broad, legitimate scope of philosophical inquiry.

Transcendental Analysis

Metaphysical statements which examine the general conditions of meaningfulness, although they are neither tautologies nor factual statements, are an important part of philosophical analysis. The contemporary British philosopher P. F. Strawson realized the value of such statements and analyzed Aristotle's theory of substance accordingly. Rather than trying to refute and dismiss metaphysics as others had done, Strawson reinterpreted it. In Strawson's view, the metaphysical theory of substance is an analysis of the general conditions which must exist in order for us to be able to identify, name, or refer to individually existing things, and this ability to identify is itself a necessary condition for our being able to think or speak or perceive at all. This type of analysis, known as *transcendental analysis*, is widely used in traditional metaphysics and was employed by Ayer in the Verifiability Principle.

IMMANUEL KANT The reknowned German philosopher Immanuel Kant (1724–1804) used transcendental analysis to prove the strictly metaphysical thesis that there must be genuine cause/effect relations in the empirical world, and that perceptual qualities *must* belong to substances. Kant maintained that without these basic assumptions we could not have the meaningful, coherent experience we do in fact have. Kant argued that since the world as we actually experience it is composed of reasonably stable objects, then there must be a cause/effect relationship existing between objects and events in the world. In order for objects to be reasonably stable, they must be disposed to act in fairly constant ways (the leaves of the tree change color each fall, for example, and then drop off). If there were no consistent cause/effect relationship, then any object could do anything, any time, and in such a world one would lose the ability to pick out objects and reidentify them. If that happened, there would not *be* any objects for us. And in that event, would we have a world at all? For what is it to "have a world" but to experience stable objects behaving in predictable ways in constant relations with one another? And if we did not experience a world of objects, can we really be said even to have experience? Can you have an experience without experiencing something?

Returning to Kant's defense of substance underlying properties, try to identify an object without presupposing that its properties all belong to some one thing. Take a piece of chalk. Now it is in the tray (property-1), now it is in my hand (property-2). But is this thing which was in the tray the same thing as the one in my hand? We can no longer tell; all we have left, since we have given up the idea of an underlying substance, are various properties, and these properties—being in the tray and being in my hand—are contrary to one another. Therefore, it looks as though they do *not* belong to the same object. In fact, what can we now mean by the word "object"? Just a class of properties, presumably. If so, then every time the chalk gets worn down a little by being used to write on the blackboard or changes its spatial position, the class of its properties changes, and since the object is now defined as the class of its properties, we must now say that we have as many different objects as we have changes. But the changes are infinite in number. Do we want to say we have an infinity of objects in this little piece of chalk? This comes pretty close to saying there is no object at all!

The conclusion is that we cannot meaningfully speak of an "object" or identify it unless we assume that various properties commonly belong to it—in short, to something very much like the philosophers' substance. And if there were no objects, it would not be possible to talk or even think. You couldn't say anything about anything, because there would be no more things to talk about. Suppose I wanted to tell you about the chalk's being shorter than it was a week ago, but this presupposes what we have just given up, that this piece of chalk and that one a week ago are one and the same. But we can and do talk and think about things, and since this requires objects, then we must suppose that there are such objects. This is a transcendental defense of the traditional notion of substance.

Transcendental analysis falls into neither of Ayer's categories of meaningful assertions, though it smacks a little of both. Statements of this kind are neither tautologies nor empirically verifiable; they are an attempt to account for sense experience. Since they are concerned with the most general *preconditions* of all meaningful experience, they can hardly be themselves empirically verifiable. If p is a precondition for your being able to see or hear anything at all, you could not empirically verify p without presupposing p, thus arguing in a circle like a dog chasing its tail. If you wear rose-colored glasses, things will, of course, look rose-colored, but you cannot use this to prove that things are rose-colored. Sense experience must conform to any supposed preconditions for experience, but it cannot establish an independent criterion which would prove or disprove their existence.

ARISTOTLE. Transcendental metaphysics, or *descriptive metaphysics*, as Strawson calls it, involves the legitimate philosophical task of conceptual analysis. This is what Strawson and Kant were discussing, and what Aristotle discusses in parts of *Metaphysics*. Books 12 and 13, where Aristotle talks about God and other immaterial substances, include the kind of metaphysics which Ayer criticized and rejected as meaningless. But the rest of the work and especially Book Z can easily be read as a piece of descriptive or transcendental metaphysics.

In saying that substance is essence and also that substance is particular, Aristotle in effect means that in order to be able to see, or refer to, or speak about a particular thing one must first classify and regard this thing as a thing of a certain kind. A necessary condition of our being able to identify individual entities as we do is that we be able to state what kind of thing it is, that is, into what class of things it falls. Or, to put the same point differently, if we did not first treat things as belonging to classes, it would be impossible for us to determine when one individual ceased to exist and another different individual took its place and when it had merely changed without ceasing to exist. Particular things are constantly changing in different respects—size, shape, color, position, and so on—and, as we saw before, it is the *kind* of thing which the object is that determines what changes make it cease to exist and what changes are consistent with its remaining that thing. In order for us to be able to understand and speak about individual objects, we must treat *particular* things as belonging to *kinds*, and, if we follow Strawson's example, this is how we will understand Aristotle's assertion that substance is both a particular and also essence. Looking at it in this way, I think we must conclude that this metaphysical assertion, at least, is a meaningful and important piece of philosophical analysis which is neither tautological nor empirically verifiable.

KANT'S EMPIRICAL CRITERION OF MEANING. Metaphysical statements of this sort are not empirically verifiable, but they are related to facts. In the first place, they are necessary in order for us to be able to perceive and discuss the empirical world. Secondly, they are *interpretations of* empirical matters and hence consistent with them. If a metaphysical statement is true, we will expect the world to look a certain way. But the fact that the world looks this way does not prove that the statement is true, since there may be other, and possibly better, ways of interpreting the same facts. As we noted in the first chapter, we cannot prove the truth of hypotheses empirically, even in science. The fact that the sun "rises and sets" every day means either that the sun travels around the earth from east to west or that the earth spins on its axis eastwardly. Since both are equally consistent with the facts, these facts alone cannot prove or disprove either hypothesis. And so it is in the case of metaphysical hypotheses. Can we, for example, *see* Aristotelian substances? In the sense in which the word "substance" stands for particular, tangible objects like tables and trees, we certainly can and do see them. But we can not see substances in the sense that we can not determine by sense experience alone whether tables and trees *ought* to be interpreted and understood as substances, whether they ought to be *called* substances. Metaphysical concepts like substance and causality are categories which enable us to interpret sense experiences. In this sense metaphysical statements about substance or causality are more closely related to empirical facts and experience than, say, statements about how many angels can balance on the head of a pin, which are not interpretations or classifications of sense experience and which are therefore totally unrelated to empirical facts. This is what Kant meant when he said that any legitimate concept, metaphysical or otherwise, must be capable of being *exemplified* in sense experience.

Like Hume and Ayer, Kant believed that sense experience defined the boundary or limits of meaning. If a concept or a statement based on a concept went beyond sense experience, Kant held that it was theoretically meaningless. But he gave a broader interpretation to this empirical criterion of meaning. He contended that any statement or any concept for which we could find examples or illustrations in sense experience was empirically meaningful. This would include many statements and concepts which are not empirically verifiable. I can show you an *example* of a substance and its property simply by exhibiting a red apple, but I cannot empirically verify that there is an underlying substance to which this property belongs. The concept of substance and statements about substances, at least of the sort which Aristotle typically made, are interpretations of sense experience for which we can always find examples, but which we can not empirically verify.

An interpretation must be more or less correct, and the correctness or accuracy of the interpretation depends on its correspondence with the empirical facts. This defines a further relationship between metaphysical statements and empirical facts. For even though you can never verify or falsify a metaphysical statement, it is nonetheless true that certain empirical facts are more compatible with some theories than others, and that some metaphysical hypotheses are more in line with the facts than others. What if you woke up one morning and found that everything was continually changing in unpredictable ways. Instead of fixed objects you found only a mass of fleeting sense impressions, a chaotic, swirling whirlpool of colors, shapes, and sounds in which nothing could be related to anything else? Would this new empirical information have any bearing on the Aristotelian theory of substance? Yes, it would. This sort of sense experience would tend to disconfirm or falsify Aristotle's theory. But of course that is not the world we actually live in, and it is difficult to either confirm or disconfirm Aristotle's theory within the empirical world in which we actually find ourselves. Or, consider the theory of Leibniz, the seventeenth-century German philosopher, that no two objects can have the same properties. Wouldn't two indistinguishable leaves tend to challenge Leibniz' theory? It would not absolutely refute the theory since Leibniz could always maintain that there were differences too small to be seen. But wouldn't this at least prove an embarrassment for Leibniz? And wouldn't he feel easier if, as microscopes improved, differences in the two leaves could be detected? Certainly, Leibniz would not turn his back on these findings or be completely indifferent to them. The very fact that he would feel the need to patch up the theory indicates that he felt the "pinch" from sense experience. Because sense experience has this disconfirming impact on the theory, he would feel the need to alter the theory to account for the discrepancy.

P. F. STRAWSON. Not all metaphysical theories can be analyzed or described as transcendental philosophy. P. F. Strawson recognized two types of metaphysics: *descriptive metaphysics*, which he says is "content to describe the actual structure of our thought about the world," and *revisionist metaphysics* which attempts "to produce a better structure." The latter cannot be saved from the Positivists' critique and so must be thrown to the Humian flames.

Strawson's own contributions to contemporary descriptive

metaphysics is remarkably similar to many of the things we now want to interpret Aristotle as saying about substance. Like Aristotle, Strawson's concern is to analyze the most general conditions which must exist in order for us to be able to refer to, identify, name, and talk about particular things. He begins with the common-sense view of the world—our everyday conceptual scheme of an external world composed of semipermanent, three-dimensional physical objects, spread out in space and time and existing as they do independently of what we think about them. Strawson accepts this as given and then goes on to ask what are the necessary conditions for our having this conceptual scheme for viewing the world in this way, and without which we could not have the common-sense view we do have. It is, in short, a transcendental analysis arguing from the way we do experience and think about the world to what must be the case in order for this to be possible.

Strawson's argument in a nutshell is that in order to have the common-sense view of the world we do have, we must be able to identify particular things in the world. In order to identify particular things in the world, we must be able to *uniquely* identify them. The ability to uniquely identify particulars presupposes the existence of a single, all-inclusive system which applies to all particulars and in which each particular has its place—this can only be satisfied by our unified system of space and time. Finally, if we are to be able to locate every particular in this single spatiotemporal system, we must be able to reidentify particulars where our perception of them has been broken by gaps of time. This is the kind of transcendental analysis which is both a conceptual analysis and a kind of metaphysics. In analyzing the concepts through which we view the world, the philosopher is analyzing such concepts as *object, property, space, time, causality* and their interrelationships. The analysis of these concepts is, of course, metaphysics. But, according to the view of Kant and Strawson, the metaphysician is not studying extrasensory objects; he is simply analyzing the concepts which we use in our ordinary sense experience of the world. We perceive the world in terms of objects and properties, and the metaphysician asks what it is to be an object or a property. As we indicated in the first chapter, conceptual analysis does not mean turning one's back on the world in order to pursue a world of concepts. Since the shared world as we experience it is formed by certain basic concepts, the analysis of those concepts is at the same time an analysis of the world. We live in a world of objects with properties in space and time, involved in causal relations. To analyze the concepts of object, property, space, time, and causality is therefore to analyze the world metaphysically.

Strawson's analysis is remarkably similar to Aristotle's analysis. Like Aristotle, Strawson affirms the priority of the substance-property distinction, which Ayer attacked as a mistake of language. Like Aristotle, Strawson asserts that relatively stable, re-identifiable individual objects are the basic entities in the world, and he relates this to the subject-predicate form of ordinary language. The main difference between Strawson and Aristotle is that for Aristotle matter is the individuating factor which differentiates one individual from another of the same kind and a real individual from an imaginary one of the same kind, whereas for Strawson the individuating factor is the system of space and time. In other words, Aristotle and Strawson have different solutions to the essence-existence problem, but both are engaged in a similar metaphysical investigation. Strawson has thus successfully defended Aristotle and others against the charges of Ayer, the Logical Positivists, and others that all metaphysics was meaningless nonsense. He has established that metaphysics involves the legitimate philosophical task of conceptual analysis which seeks to describe the actual structure of the world as we experience it.

THE PHENOMENOLOGICAL CRITIQUE OF METAPHYSICS

In its long history, there have been other serious objections to traditional metaphysics. Certain contemporary philosophers have charged that the particular metaphysics inherited from Aristotle is an inadequate metaphysics primarily because of its treatment of being as the being of objects. This method of analyzing being has proved especially troubling in theological accounts of God as a kind of super-object and in the well-known "mind-body problem."

The Mind-Body Problem

The mind-body problem arises out of a philosophical way of distinguishing mind and body, which in turn arises out of a related distinction in common sense. In everyday speech we distinguish a person's mind from his body. We may say that someone has a beautiful body but a rather shallow mind. Sometimes we doubt whether our bodily activities, such as speech and writing, really convey the thoughts which lie deep within the privacy of our own minds. If we get sleepy during a lecture but feel that we ought to stay awake, we express this to ourselves by saying with St. Paul that the mind is willing but the body is weak, and so on. All of these examples suggest a distinction between mind and body. Similarly, even if we do not believe in the immortality or the transmigration of the soul, we are still able to contemplate the separation of the soul from the body and the entry of the soul into a different body. And to be able even to contemplate this presupposes a distinction between mind and body.

So, we do draw some distinction in common sense between mind and body, but we do not draw this distinction in such a way as to present special problems or difficulties. But the philosopher, in reflecting critically on this common-sense distinction, comes to the conclusion that it is problematic and contradictory. He claims that if we are to hold the distinction between mind and body, we must, in logical consistency, give up another important common-sense view, that minds and bodies nonetheless interact in important ways. Common sense presupposes that mind and body interact, for example, in the way we express our feelings in bodily movement, gestures, sounds, and the like, in our interpretation of other people's behavior as representing their thoughts and feelings, and especially in our ability to move and to feel our own bodies. The philosopher asks, How can a physical object have any effect on a mind or vice versa, since these are distinct sorts of things? The philosopher tries to show that it is logically contradictory to assert *both* that mind and body are distinct and that mind and body nevertheless interact with one another. If the first is true, then the second is false; if the second it true, then the first is false.

Sources of the Problem

The history of philosophy is filled with ingenious attempts to solve this problem, which we will discuss in considerable detail in Chapter 4. Recently an interesting attempt has been made to show how the problem itself rests on a mistaken emphasis on the being of objects in traditional metaphysics. What makes the problem so apparently insoluble is the philosophical interpretation of the common-sense distinction of mind and body as two completely independent *substances*. Although Gilbert Ryle and Martin Heidegger are generally thought to represent two diametrically opposed schools of contemporary philosophical thought, British Analysis and German Phenomenology, their views on the philosophy of mind are remarkably similar, especially in their opposition to the traditional assumption that mind must be treated as a kind of substance.

GILBERT RYLE. Ryle calls this a "category mistake," the mistake of trying to put into one category of things something which belongs to a quite different category. As an example, Ryle mentions the foreigner who, after he had been shown all the buildings, the playing field, and the halls of residence of some university, asked to see the university. The man obviously made a mistake in thinking that a university is one more thing of the same kind which he had been viewing all afternoon. He thinks that he can add to the list of buildings, dining halls, playing fields, etc., the university itself. But the university belongs to a different list or category altogether.

When one puts something into a certain logical category, there are certain questions one can legitimately and meaningfully ask of anything in that category. If the foreigner in Ryle's example says, "Now show me the halls of residence," his statement makes sense, and if he asks, "And where is the playing field?" his question makes sense, because these are the sort of questions one can legitimately ask and the sort of statements one can reasonably make about the various things which together make up what we call a university. When the foreigner supposes that he can include in this category the university itself, he is naturally led to believe that he can ask similar questions and make similar statements and requests. So he says, "Now show me the university," or he asks, "This is all very nice, but where exactly is the university?" But these questions make no sense; they are illegitimate—that is, they are not allowed by the unspoken rules of the English language.

Of course, in this example the category mistake is so obvious that it becomes something of a joke; it is simply a funny story. But when the philosopher makes a category mistake, it is not so obvious, and the result is not a sense of the ridiculous, but a sense of bewilderment and mystery. When we think of substances, we most naturally think of things like trees, animals, houses, tables, and so on—three-dimensional, semipermanent, heavy, spatially extended, physical objects located in space and time and causally related to one another. Therefore, there is a certain type of question and a certain type of statement which it is legitimate to ask or assert about substances. We can ask where they are, how large they are, how heavy they are, whether they are hard or soft, how long they last, whether they can be moved or crushed or cut in half or lifted, and so on. All these questions and the statements which make up their answers are allowed by the rules of English grammar because all these objects, however different they may be otherwise, belong to the same category of substances.

Now, when we consider that minds are also substances, we begin to think of them in the same way we think of the other substances—after all, they belong to the same category, they are all substances. And so we naturally suppose that the same sorts of questions and statements will be legitimate and meaningful in regard to mental substances which are legitimate and meaningful in regard to material substances. Thus we are led to ask, "Where is the mind?" "Is it very small or is it large?" "Is it light like air or water or is it solid like a stone?" "Is it made up of parts so that it could be taken apart, or is it simple like an atom?" "Can minds move or split physical objects?" "Can physical objects damage or hurt the mind?" But these questions cannot be answered one way or the other; they make no sense. They all assume that the mind is a kind of object, though not a physical object.

Minds are substances but they are not like material substances, they *are* im*material. Minds, we say, have a *non*material existence, a *non*spatial reality, an *im*material causality—in other words, we seem unable to describe mental substance except by negations of physical substance. Thus we are still thinking of mental substance along the same lines as we think of material substances. It is just the opposite side of the same coin. If a material substance has weight, then we say a mental substance is weightless; if a material substance is spatially extended, we say a mental substance is unextended; if a material substance has a physical causal power, we say that mental substance has a mental causal power. The idea we have of mental substance is strictly parallel to and dependent on our idea of physical substance.

But what do we really understand by these negative properties of mental substance? Try to think of a thing which has no spatial location at all, has no spatial extension, which could not be seen, felt, or heard—now, what sort of idea is this? Are you really entertaining *any* clear idea? Or don't you find that the attempt to think of such a thing simply creates a sense of confusion in your mind, an uneasy feeling of bewildered amazement or mystery? If you do succeed in thinking of such a thing, aren't you really cheating? That is, if you succeed in imagining such a thing, are you really thinking of it as being completely immaterial or are you thinking of it as you think of air, or something very small? This is how Descartes tried to think of mind when he spoke of it as being a subtle, volatile ether or gas located in the tiny pineal gland inside the head. But this is cheating. You are supposed to be thinking of an immaterial substance, whereas air and vapor and the like are material substances no less than sticks and stones. In short, this whole way of thinking about mind is very confusing, and every attempt to make it clearer only succeeds in making it more confusing.

The main problem with this way of construing minds concerns their causal relations. If we regard the mind as a distinct substance, then how are we going to explain the inter-working of mind and body in the case of human behavior? In everyday speech we assume that there is some interaction between mind and body; we say that a person decided to drive down the hill, and this clearly implies that the physical act of driving the car was induced by the thought of driving into town. But how can a mind cause a body to move? What kind of causality is this? Clearly, it cannot be a material or mechanical sort of causality, because that kind of causality can occur only between two material bodies.

We all know that we can raise our arms if and when we have a mind to do so. First we have the desire to raise our arms, and then we do it. Thus it looks as though the mind is raising a physical object, our arm. But consider this a moment. The arm is held down by a certain gravitational force, and in order to raise the arm that gravitational force must be overcome. But how can one sort of physical force be overcome except by another physical force? What is going to push or pull the arm up? Whatever it is, it will at least have to get into contact with the arm, or into contact with some other object which is in contact with the arm. But how can the mind get into contact with any physical object? Only a physical object can touch another physical object. Thoughts cannot by definition occupy space. How then can an immaterial thing get hold of my arm to pull it up? How can something which has no weight, solidity, density, or volume push

80 Metaphysics

my arm up? How else can it be raised? It is not only difficult to conceive of this, it seems quite impossible.

The same sort of problem confronts us when we consider the fact that physical objects can produce effects within our minds. A sharp object causes pain in the mind, a cool object causes a feeling of pleasure in the mind, a rough object causes a sense of irritation in the mind, and so on. In each case, a physical object is presumably producing an effect on a mind. But how is such a thing possible? A sharp object can only puncture another physical object, how can it stab a mind? A cool object can only cool another material object. Again, we have no way of making sense of this supposition.

But this whole way of looking at the problem is wrong, and the mistake, according to Ryle, is trying to treat mind as though it were a substance. Heidegger would agree, though his principal concern is to explain *why* philosophers have thought it necessary to treat mind as a special kind of substance, and the reason he comes up with is that philosophers felt that substance was the only kind of real thing there could be. Thus if they thought mind was real, which it surely is in some sense, then they felt compelled to say that mind was a kind of substance, though a very different kind from material substance.

MARTIN HEIDEGGER. For Heidegger, the ultimate source of this problem is an oversimplified and therefore inadequate account of being, starting with Aristotle and continuing right up to the present day. Aristotle's original question, you will remember, was, What is it *to be* in the broadest possible sense? But in the end, as we saw, Aristotle fixes on one important, though limited, sphere of being—the being of real, substantial objects. This obscured the basic question of being by playing down the being of dreams, feelings, emotions, imaginary objects, and fictional entities, as well as properties, shadows, relations, and so on. There *is* the property of redness, there *is* a number 3, there *is* the relation bigger, there *is* a character named Tom Sawyer, and there *is* the possibility that you will get an A in this course. In what sense *are* such things? By fastening onto the being of real objects we lose the ability to answer this question. In fact all we seem able to say is that there *are not* really such things, that they just *seem* to be. But this simply postpones the question; what is it to *seem* to be, what kind of being is that?

Heidegger became interested in Aristotle's idea of the "analogy of being" presented in *Categories*. According to Heidegger, Aristotle almost discovered a theory of being which would have been far more adequate and which would have made the entire history of philosophy turn out much better from Heidegger's point of view. In *Categories*, Aristotle notes that being can be predicated of things in each of the main grammatical categories, and not just in the category of substance. Aristotle's point is that we can say that things *are* in each of these categories—substance, property, relation, quantity—though in a different sense in each case. In one sense we can say that there is a horse; this is the sense in which we speak of the being of substances. In a different sense, we can say that there is a color darker than red; and in another sense, that there is a relation "larger than"; and in still another sense, that there is a number between 2 and 4. Heidegger regards this as a most important suggestion, for had Aristotle stuck with it and developed it, he would not have said, as he did say, that substance was the only proper sense of "being"; instead he would have said that substances were real in one sense, while properties were equally real though in a different sense, and relations were real in still a further sense. Had Aristotle developed this line of thought, there would have been no tendency, as there in fact has been, to say that if a thing is real it must be or be part of a substance, from which it follows, as we have seen, that if mind is real it must be or be a part of a substance. Instead, philosophers would have argued that mind was real but that it was not a substance; they would have said that it was real but that it was not real in the same way in which substances are real.

However, Aristotle did not develop this line of thought. What he goes on to say in *Categories* and more explicitly in *Metaphysics* is that although being can be predicated of categories other than substance, only substance has reality in the primary sense, while the other categories have reality only in so far as they are properties *of*, or relations *of*, or quantities *of* substances. But it is inconsistent to say that there are two different senses and that one is dependent on the other. To say that is just to say that there is only one sense which is sometimes used more strictly than at other times. What Aristotle says (at least in the "analogy") is that properties exist in a different sense from the way in which substances exist, but what he seems to mean is that properties exist in exactly the same sense as substances, although properties exist in this sense relatively while substances exist in this sense absolutely.

Heidegger's suggestion, then, is that we regard the being of the mind in ways other than the being of substance. However, even if we take Heidegger's suggestion seriously, how else can we conceive the existence of mind except as an object? We might try, as Strawson does in *Individuals*, treating both mind and body as different functioning aspects of the same entity: a person. In the Strawsonian scheme, mental and physical are not essential attributes of two substances, but only two different ways of apprehending, describing, and referring to a person. Strawson does not say that mental attributes are attributes of a material substance or that material attributes are attributes of a mental substance. He simply says that in common sense we can talk about a person in one of two more or less distinct ways—either physically or mentally. In ordinary speech a person is not a material substance or a mental substance, or a combination of the two. The ordinary concept of a person is prior to, or more primitive than, the concept of either a physical substance or a mental substance. Before we have done any philosophy we all have a common notion of a person. But we can *conceive* of a person in different ways. A person can be described and comprehended in one of two parallel though largely distinct ways. If we are fitting clothes on a person, or lifting a sleeping person, or loading people into a small compact car, we naturally think of a person in purely material terms: how large, how heavy, what shape, and so on. But if we are talking to the person or evaluating his work, we tend to think of him in terms of intelligence, diligence, charm, and so on, in other words, in mental concepts. There are many problems with Strawson's proposal, but it may well be a start in the right direction.

The solution to old problems like the mind-body problem may well lie in a *metaphysical* reordering. Doing good work in philosophy may require doing *better* metaphysics, not *less*. In fact the attempt to abandon metaphysics is often, as we saw in Ayer's case, simply doing metaphysics badly and blindly, unaware that we are doing so. It is an inescapable feature of human beings to interpret the world according to their own concepts. Therefore, the world as we know it is "concept-laden." Our experience of the world consequently has an inevitable metaphysical dimension, and to give a thorough account of the world of everyday experience will eventually result in a metaphysical analysis. This is in no way antiscientific since the scientist himself employs a metaphysical view of the world. He assumes, for example, that there exists a material universe, distinct from God and human decision-making, spread throughout time and space, which uniformly obeys mathematically precise laws. In the end it looks as though metaphysics, in one form or another, is a necessary feature of all theoretical inquiry.

TOPICS FOR DISCUSSION

1. Both science and metaphysics attempt to account for the world as we experience it. How do they differ?
2. We don't have to conceptualize the world as we do. But, on the other hand, is it merely an accident that we break up the world as we do into trees, people, and grapefruit?
3. What problems can you see which might arise from the metaphysical treatment of God as a substance? What do the "new theologians," like Karl Barth, say about this?
4. Is it really impossible, as Kant thought, to think or talk except in terms of objects and properties, or is this just one way of thinking and talking? Can you find consistent alternatives?

SELECTED BIBLIOGRAPHY

Primary Source

Aristotle. *Metaphysics.* Translated by David Ross. In *The Basic Works of Aristotle*, edited by Richard McKeon. New York: Random House, 1941.
Ayer, A. J. *Language, Truth and Logic.* London: Victor Gollancz, 1936.
Berkeley, George. *Three Dialogues between Hylas and Philonous.* 1713. New York: Liberal Arts Press, 1954.
Descartes, René. *Meditations on First Philosophy,* 1641, and *Principles of Philosophy,* 1644. In *Descartes Selections,* edited by Ralph Eaton. New York: Scribner's, 1927.
Hume, David. *An Inquiry Concerning Human Understanding.* 1748. New York: Liberal Arts Press, 1955.
Kant, Immanuel. *Prolegomena to Any Future Metaphysics.* 1783. Translated by Paul Carus. New York: Liberal Arts Press, 1951.
Plato. *Phaedo.* Translated by F. J. Church. New York: Liberal Arts Press, 1951.

―――. *The Republic.* Translated by Benjamin Jowett. New York: Random House, 1957.
―――. *Timaeus.* Translated by Benjamin Jowett. New York: Liberal Arts Press, 1959.
Strawson, P. F. *Individuals.* Garden City, New York: Doubleday, 1959.
Whitehead, A. N. *Process and Reality.* New York: Macmillan, 1929.

Secondary Source

Barth, Karl. *The Humanity of God.* Richmond: John Knox Press, 1960.
Canfield, John, ed. *Purpose in Nature.* Englewood Cliffs, New Jersey: Prentice-Hall, 1966.
Hook, Sidney, ed. *Determinism and Freedom.* New York: Collier, 1961.
Kiefer, Howard E., and Milton K. Munits, eds. *Language, Belief and Metaphysics.* Albany, New York: State University of New York Press, 1970.
Loux, Michael, ed. *Universals and Particulars.* Garden City, New York: Doubleday, 1970.
Plantinga, Alvin, ed. *The Ontological Argument.* Garden City, New York: Doubleday, 1965.
Smart, J. J. C., ed. *Problems of Space and Time.* New York: Macmillan, 1964.
Van Iten, Richard, ed. *The Problem of Universals.* New York: Appleton-Century-Crofts, 1970.

CHAPTER 3

Epistemology
Theory of Knowledge

WHAT IS EPISTEMOLOGY?

Philosophers have long questioned the possibility and extent of human knowledge. In everyday life we think of knowledge in many different ways: we speak of intuitive knowledge, religious knowledge, practical knowledge (or know-how), encyclopedic knowledge, and so on. The philosopher's interest in knowledge is much narrower. In general, *epistemology* is that branch of philosophy which studies the nature, sources, and validity of knowledge. Its main concern, however, is with knowledge as a kind of insurance policy against error. The goal of epistemology (the theory of knowledge) is to find a criterion for certainty. Just as the logician analyzes arguments which he knows are sound in order to find the source of their validity (see Chapter 1), so the epistemologist analyzes what we already know about knowledge in order to discover the grounds for its trustworthiness.

We all believe many things, and sometimes our beliefs are proved wrong, often with disastrous consequences. When we examine the range of our beliefs, we find that some seem to be generally more trustworthy than others. If we can find a pattern among these beliefs, we can use this to formulate a test for reliability. Any candidate for knowledge which meets this test could then be certified and given a kind of guarantee. Since in ordinary speech the word "knowledge" is used, among other things, as a term of honor to mark off those beliefs of proven reliability, the criterion we are looking for is precisely a criterion of knowledge. Which beliefs deserve this commendatory title and why?

Epistemology—Theory of Knowledge

Suppose we found, for example, that as a general rule secondhand information was less reliable and more liable to error than firsthand information. This suggests that one general criterion for knowledge is directness. This rule could serve as a general test of trustworthiness which we can express as a definition or theory of knowledge: "Real knowledge is based directly on sense perception; anything else is mere hearsay."

Philosophers have always been interested in problems of knowledge. At times they have proposed some strange theories and radical points of view, and it has always been clear that the credibility of such assertions would be greatly increased by a general defense of the means used to arrive at those conclusions. As a result, most philosophical theories of morals, politics, religion, and so on are supported by a defense of their *epistemological* foundations. But epistemology became an obsession in the Modern Period (seventeenth to the twentieth centuries), temporarily obscuring other philosophical areas, because of the need to provide a firm foundation for the new physical sciences.

Historically there have been two major contenders for the certification of knowledge: sense experience (championed by the Empiricists) and reason (championed by the Rationalists). In this chapter we will examine the two main centers of this debate: (1) the sources of knowledge and (2) the distinction between *knowledge* and *belief*. We will also take a brief look at the important distinction between theoretical and practical knowledge.

THE SOURCES OF KNOWLEDGE

For centuries philosophers have tried to answer the question, Where do we get all our ideas? What is the ultimate source of our knowledge? At first we may be inclined to say that our ideas come from a variety of sources; some ideas we learn from our parents, some from our teachers, some from our own experience, others from books, pictures, movies, and other media. When we reflect on this further, it seems that these sources ultimately rest on experience—we hear what our parents say, we see what the books say, and so on. Also, of course, what books and people tell us rests on their experiences or the firsthand experiences of other people. Your teacher tells you that Jefferson was the third president of the United States; she learned this from her teacher who learned it from books which were based on documents reporting the firsthand experience of eyewitnesses. At first glance, then, it seems fairly obvious that all our ideas come from sense experience.

The Empiricist Position

The seventeenth-century English philosopher John Locke (1632–1704) is one of the chief spokesman of Empiricism, the view that all knowledge comes from sense experience:

> Let us then suppose the mind to be, as we say, white paper void of all characters, without any ideas. How comes it to be furnished? Whence comes it by that vast store which the busy and boundless fancy of man has painted on it with an almost endless variety? To this I answer, in one word, from EXPERIENCE. In that all our knowledge is founded; and from that it ultimately derives itself. Our observation, employed either about external sensible, or about the internal operations of our minds..., is that which supplies our understandings with all the materials of thinking. These two are the fountains of knowledge, from whence all the ideas we have ... do spring. [Locke, *An Essay Concerning Human Understanding*]

Perhaps because of the influence of men like Locke, this seems to be an entirely reasonable hypothesis, one perhaps too obvious to be of much interest. When children are born they do not appear to have many ideas, and it is only when they begin looking out upon the world that they begin to learn about things and formulate opinions about them. As Locke says in *An Essay Concerning Human Understanding* (1690):

> He that attentively considers the state of a child, at his first coming into the world will have little reason to think him stored with plenty of ideas, that are to be the matter of his future knowledge. It is by *degrees* he comes to be furnished with them. And though the ideas of obvious and familiar qualities imprint themselves before the memory begins to keep a register of time or order, yet it is often so late before some unusual qualities come in the way, that there are few men that cannot recollect the beginnings of their acquaintance with them. And if it were worth while, no doubt a child might be so ordered as to have but very few,

even of the ordinary ideas, till he were grown up to a man. It will be granted easily, that if a child were kept in a place where he never saw any other but black and white till he were a man, he would have no more ideas of scarlet or green, than he that from his childhood never tasted an oyster, or a pineapple, has of those particular relishes.

The Rationalist Position

Other philosophers, especially the Rationalists, disagree with the Empiricist view that all knowledge is based on experience. Plato (427–347 B.C.), a charter member of the Rationalist school, concedes that what we call *opinion* comes from sense experience, but he denies that any of our *knowledge* comes from that source. Instead Plato believes that ideas come from a purely intellectual grasp of abstract, immaterial entities at a time before we are born, and that all learning is merely a process of recollecting what we previously knew but have since forgotten!

> The soul, then, as being immortal, and having been born again many times, and having seen all things that exist, whether in this world or in the world below, has knowledge of them all; and it is no wonder that she should be able to call to remembrance all that she ever knew about virtue and about everything; for as all nature is akin, and the soul has learned all things, there is no difficulty in her eliciting, or as men say "learning" out of a single recollection, all the rest, if a man is strenuous and does not faint; for all inquiry and all learning is but recollection. [Plato, *Meno*]

Plato often expressed his theory of the preexistence of the soul in a mythological form, and we do not know how literally Plato meant to be interpreted. Perhaps he only wished to illustrate a more mundane point in a colorful and picturesque way. In other dialogues such as *Phaedrus* and *Symposium*, Plato presents this mythical story in some detail. The objects of knowledge, the Ideas or Forms, do not exist in the world of space and time and cannot be perceived by means of ordinary sense perception. We can know such things (and there is nothing else we can know) only when the soul is separated from the body and bodily sensations. Before a person is born his soul is free to travel about among these ideal Forms and get to know all those things which

Plato believes constitute ultimate reality. So, when a person is born he already knows all there is to know, but unfortunately, being born, he is back inside a body, looking out through deceptive sense organs upon a world which is not completely real. In this fallen state the person begins to forget all he had known. But just as a person can sometimes remember something he has forgotten, so we can sometimes recollect this forgotten knowledge—this is what we call learning.

Plato's theory implies an interesting view of education. Many people today consider learning a matter of stuffing information into someone's head. For Plato, all a teacher can do is act as a midwife, helping the student to give birth to ideas which come entirely from within himself. Plato does not say that a person's experience of the world is entirely irrelevant to learning by recollection. He insists that certain experiences in the sense world *remind* us of Ideas we experienced in the ideal world before we were born. Thus certain sense experiences, although they cannot teach us anything new, can be instrumental in helping to recollect previous knowledge which had been forgotten. In *Phaedo* Plato compares this process with what modern psychologists call the "association of ideas."

> The knowledge of a lyre is not the same as the knowledge of a man. . . . And yet what is the feeling of lovers when they recognize a lyre, or a garment, or anything else which the beloved has been in the habit of using: Do not they, from knowing the lyre, form in the mind's eye an image of the youth to whom the lyre belongs? And this is recollection. In like manner any one who sees Simmias may remember [his brother] Cebes; and there are endless examples of the same thing. [Plato, *Phaedo*]

Plato does not deny that sense experience is instrumental in learning, he simply denies that it can do any more than remind a person of something which he already knows. Plato's interpretation of the role of sense experience nonetheless is very different from that of Empiricists like Locke. Plato contends that seeing a beautiful object simply reminds one of the Idea of absolute Beauty which cannot be experienced through any of the five senses.

To prove that all knowledge is recollection, Plato's teacher Socrates tried to show (in *Meno*) how an uneducated servant can give the correct answer to a complicated geometrical problem without being told the answer and without ever having studied geometry. (It is interesting for reasons we shall discuss shortly that Plato selects an example of logical or deductive knowledge.) He does not ask the servant a factual question such as in what year Pericles delivered his famous funeral oration. He asks him something which can only be known by logical inference from certain initial premises. Socrates never actually tells him the answer, though he helps him along by asking questions which lead by stages to the right answer. At one point the servant replies to a question that doubling the sides of a square doubles the area. Socrates does not tell him this is wrong, but he asks him what the area would be if only one of the sides were doubled. The servant immediately sees that this would double the area and that the square whose sides were all doubled would be four times as big. Plato argues that since the servant gave the answer at last out of his own head without being told, he must have already had the answer in the back of his mind.

If you momentarily forget a friend's name, but know that you will eventually remember it, would you say that you know his name or not? In a sense you do and in a sense you do not. In the sense that you are not conscious of it and able to say it right away, you do not know it. In the sense that you know you will be able to remember it without being told, you do know it. Plato claims that this is precisely the state of mind of the servant before Socrates begins questioning him. He is not aware of the answer, but he is capable of giving the right answer without being told. Plato argues that this means he must have known the answer previously. Otherwise, how could he recollect it? If you had never learned the name of your friend, it would be impossible for you to think of it later. The servant was never told the answer and had never studied geometry or even considered this problem before. Therefore, Plato argues, he must have learned it in some previous existence before he was born.

With all due respect, I think we must conclude that this is a little farfetched. Why does Plato defend such a view? Plato was not interested simply in expounding an occult theory of reincarnation. Epistemologically, the theory serves to elucidate certain features of our knowledge which he believed the Empiricists did not account for. Plato argues "transcendentally" for the pre-existence and preknowledge of the soul based upon the nature of the knowledge we actually possess. He looks at the various kinds of knowledge we have, especially logic and mathematics, and finds that sense experience by itself could never produce such knowledge. He concludes that there must be a source of knowledge other than sense experience.

MATHEMATICAL KNOWLEDGE. To illustrate Plato's point, let us consider how one would determine the sum of the interior angles of a triangle. First, will sense experience give us the correct answer, and second, will it give us the same kind of necessary, certain knowledge provided by mathematics? Let's say we started out to determine the sum of the angles of a triangle by empirical means. We called in the best draftsmen in the country and had them draw a number of triangles. We then purchased the most precise instruments for measuring angles and set to work, measuring one angle, writing it down, measuring and recording the other angles, and then adding up the total for each triangle. What sort of answer would we actually get? Scientists tell us that any physical measurement must be given with a certain margin of error or deviation. No matter how precise the measurement, the scientist will always give his measurement in terms of the deviation, for example, "22.0003 plus or minus 0.0001." So, the sum of the angles we measured would read something like this: "179.99 plus or minus 0.02, 180.0001 plus or minus 0.0004, 181.002 plus or minus 0.003," and so on. Averaging these sums, we would come up with an answer, say, of 179.999 plus or minus 0.002. But is this the right answer? Is the sum of the angles of a triangle anything more or less than 180°? No, the sum of the angles is *exactly* 180°. But how do we know this? Not from experience, as our example shows. Any empirical evidence, no matter how precise, would always of necessity be either slightly more or slightly less than 180°, for a number of reasons.

One reason is that no physical triangle is really perfectly triangular. A triangle must be composed of absolutely straight lines, but no physical instrument will ever produce a perfectly straight line. The better the instrument the straighter the line, but it will always be possible to produce a straighter one. This is not due to any temporary shortage of precise instruments but to logical necessity. It is the nature of physical measurement that it always be possible to produce a straighter line, a more perfect circle or triangle, and so on. There is also the possibility of human error in carrying out the measurement and in adding the totals. The instrument may register 89.9 but I read it to be 88.9, and while the total of three angles may be 179.9, I may add it up to be 178.9. For these reasons empirical means could never give us an exact answer of 180° plus or minus nothing.

Even if we accept the answer that a triangle has angles totaling somewhere between 179.9° and 180.1°, how would we know that this holds true of all triangles? We have measured some 400, let us say, but there are many more triangles than this. How do we know that all other triangles will have no more than 180.1° and no less than 179.9°? What about triangles which will be drawn tomorrow and the next day—how many degrees will their interior angles have? All we can say on *empirical* grounds is that they will *probably* remain more or less the same, and that all over the world triangles are likely to be more or less alike, so far as we know. This kind of knowledge is only probable, whereas mathematical knowledge is known with complete certainty. We not only know that the angles do add up to 180°, we know that they *must* add up to 180°. We know there could not be a triangle with 181°, and if we "found" such a thing we would simply throw it out, along with the empirical evidence supporting it, rather than change the general rule about triangles. We would say there must have been some mistake, even if we didn't know what mistake, since triangles *must* contain exactly 180°. Similarly, once we know what the interior angles are, additional empirical evidence adds no weight whatever to our mathematical knowledge. Mathematics is simply not known empirically.

The same is true of any piece of logical or analytical knowledge, such as "2 plus 2 is 4," "All bachelors are unmarried," "It cannot be both raining and not raining at the same time in the same place," and so on. In all these examples, sense experience is insufficient to explain how we come to have the kind of knowledge we actually possess. It is preposterous to suppose we know such things empirically. Empirical means do not give us and cannot give us the kind of knowledge we actually have in logic. Sense experience will explain how we come to have an idea of what a bachelor is, how we know what the word "two" means, and what rain is, but it cannot explain how we come to know that bachelors must be unmarried, that two plus two is four, and so on. Hence, Plato argues that sense experience cannot be our sole source of knowledge.

EVALUATIVE KNOWLEDGE. Sense experience, according to the Rationalists, cannot explain how people know or think that what they experience in the world is somehow imperfect. There is hardly anyone who has not thought at some time or other that the actual world of his experience is imperfect in some respect —he finds either that people are too stupid, or too dishonest, or too cruel, or that life is too harsh, too short, too long, or too painful. Plato asks, in effect, how such judgments are possible. It is unlikely that they are based on experience. How could experience fall short of standards gained exclusively from experience? Imagine someone who was born in a concentration camp and lived there all his life, never seeing or hearing anything of the outside world. According to Locke's theory that all ideas come from experience, whatever idea of justice this person has comes exclusively from his experience in the concentration camp. His idea of justice and injustice will be defined entirely by how he is treated within the camp.

If he is usually fed one bowl of soup a day, then he will think it just that he should be given his bowl of soup each day and unjust if he is fed only once every two days. If he is beaten once a week, he will think it just that he should be beaten once a week and unjust if he is beaten more than that. This is what we would expect, the Platonist might argue, if Locke were correct. However, it is more likely that the person would judge the whole concentration camp by standards completely alien to that way of life. From Nazi Germany to South Africa it has proved impossible thus far to psychologically condition people to accept servitude and deprivation as a natural, normal, much less just, way of life. The person in our example would probably begin to think that it is unjust that he should be forced to live in such a place at all and that he should ever go hungry or suffer pain. This idea, the Platonist would argue, could not have come from his experience but must have been something he was born with; if he experienced it at all, he could only have experienced it in some kind of ideal realm before he was born. This debate has been recently revived in the psychological controversy over the "nature-nurture" input into human development, with the "nature" supporters (heirs of Rationalism) enjoying at least a momentary comeback in the last ten years.

A less extreme case can be made for any critic of his own society or any of its institutions. If Locke is right, all of our ideas and standards have come from our experience in a particular society, in which case how could these ideas ever come into conflict with our experience of that society? The criticism of the society in which one acquires all his experience must be based on criteria which did not come from sense experience. The idea of perfect justice might conceivably be got by arranging unjust acts from more to less and then projecting the ascending order of increasing justice beyond experience to the idea of perfect justice, in somewhat the same way scientists are able to conceive without experiencing "absolute zero." But Plato insists that the idea of perfect equality or perfect justice is not taken from experience, or imprinted by experience, since no single instance of such a thing can possibly be found in experience. It is only suggested by experience to someone with the proper mental equipment and frame of mind. Newton's theory of gravitation may have been suggested by a falling apple, but the theory did not *come from* that experience, or we would have had the theory of gravity much sooner. Sense experience may be necessary, but it is certainly not sufficient.

In order to arrange cases of justice from more to less we must first know what justice is. Arranging anything on a scale presupposes we already have a sense of what the cases before us have in common. In all of the preceding examples, it is sense experience which must conform to our ideas, not the other way round. A "bachelor" who claims to be married we refuse to call a bachelor. When we discover a "triangle" with 178° we declare that it cannot be a triangle, or a very good one, for a triangle must have 180°, whatever sense experience may reveal.

Reconciliation

Plato adequately illustrated that sense experience alone, at least in the sense of merely accumulating more and more sense impressions, is insufficient to explain certain kinds of knowledge and certain kinds of ideas and that it cannot be the only source of knowledge. But this does not establish that the other source of ideas is direct, prenatal acquaintance with abstract ideas, the position opposed so vigorously by Empiricists like Locke. Just as the doctrine of innate ideas is not established by the fact that sense experience cannot be the only source of knowledge, so Locke's argument that there are no innate ideas does not show that all our knowledge is the mere accumulation of sense experience. To prove your opponent wrong does not necessarily prove you right, unless your position and his are mutually exclusive contradictories (e.g., either John is in bed asleep or he is not). If they are merely contraries (e.g., John is either in bed asleep or in class), then it is possible that both positions are false (e.g., it turns out that John is out somewhere having a beer). It is possible, then, that both the Rationalist theory of innate ideas and the Empiricist position that all knowledge comes from sense experience are false.

It is not completely clear that the positions held by Locke and Plato are contrary to one another since both are couched in extremely ambiguous language. What does it mean, for example, to say that knowledge "comes from" sense experience? Does this mean that sense experience simply provides the initial materials or starting points for thought (which Plato does not really oppose), or that sensation alone is sufficient to explain all our knowledge (an extreme position Locke himself never endorses without qualification)? A similar ambiguity persists in the contemporary debate between those, such as Skinner and Pettigrew, who say that all human activity is a learned response based on social *nurture* and those, such as Chomsky and Jensen, who insist that much of this is based on an innate human *nature*. This debate has become especially important today because of its social and political implications. Much of the drive toward equality of education in this country over the past thirty years has been based on the assumption that differences in intelligence and school performance were due more to environmental factors than to hereditary factors. Now evidence is coming in which emphasizes the innate genetic factor. Of course, both factors are important, but, as in the earlier Rationalist–Empiricist debate, the question is, Which is more important and how much more so?

THE ROLE OF SENSE EXPERIENCE. The Empiricist often talks as though we acquired knowledge simply by adding more and more sense impressions to our existing store of ideas, but it is difficult to see how this could ever lead to knowledge, whether common-sense knowledge or mathematical and scientific knowledge. It is too easy to imagine a man looking at things and accumulating more and more ideas without ever coming up with any knowledge—either because he did not sufficiently "process" the raw data or because he processed it incorrectly. The Empiricist seems unable to account for either the processing or the correct processing, both of which are essential for knowledge. If knowledge comes from sense experience, so does error! Put together correctly, sense ideas give us knowledge; put together incorrectly, they produce mistakes. How can we tell which is which? Locke does not say. If the point of a philosophical theory of knowledge is to demonstrate the *justifiability* in our knowledge claims, then Locke's Empiricist account will not do.

Locke was also engaged in a psychological investigation. Locke is often considered the father of modern psychology, an empirical science which at the time he was writing in the seventeenth century had not yet distinguished itself from philosophy. The empirical psychologist asks how we come to have the ideas we do have; the epistemologist asks how we can determine which of these ideas are truthful. Locke confused the psychological question of the history of our ideas with the philosophical question of their epistemological warrant. As a result, all the early Empiricists—Locke, George Berkeley (1685–1753), and David Hume (1711–1776)—had trouble explaining the difference between veridical experience and shere fantasy. As Descartes asked earlier, what is the difference between waking experience and dreams? Since both "come from" experience, how can they be psychologically differentiated? Hume said veridical experience was always more vivid, but it is not clear that this is always the case. Nightmares, for example, can be very vivid! It is hard to see how any *psychological* criterion can do what is essentially an *epistemological* job of certification. Sensation simply cannot certify itself.

Locke, along with the other Empiricists, spoke of the activity of the mind organizing and processing ideas, and this, as we will see in a moment, might explain how we get from sense experience to knowledge. Being an Empiricist, however, Locke generally played down the role of the mind in organizing sense materials and limited its function to the mere collecting, adding, or separating of simple ideas of sensation. For example, he says we get the idea of milk by combining the simple ideas of white, liquid, and its taste, and the idea of chalk by combining white with hard and cylindrical. According to Locke, we get the abstract idea of white by separating out what the complex ideas of milk and chalk have in common. But even this elementary combining-separating of ideas might prove difficult to explain within an Empiricist framework. In playing down the activity of the mind, Empiricists tend to assume that ideas will group themselves automatically on the basis of similarity and difference. But *how* are any two ideas similar or different—in what respect? In color, shape, size, length, cost, or what? There is no absolute similarity, and the respect in which things are judged alike is a conceptual affair, prior to experience, depending on the sorts of distinctions we as human beings are interested in. Think of all the erroneous and silly ideas which could be got by grouping sense impressions on the basis of arbitrary similarity. Peaches, for example, resemble house tops in their elevation off the ground, but so what? This is irrelevant. What makes a comparison relevant is some human concern, and this is a conceptual matter and not a question of sensation alone. Again, the Empiricists are hard put to supply epistemological criteria, whether of relevance or of correctness.

It is especially difficult to see how combining or separating simple ideas would ever yield mathematics or natural science. If you watched the stars every night for ten years and did nothing else, merely adding more and more ideas together, would you ever discover that some of these stars (the planets) traveled in separate orbits around a fixed point independently of the other stars? Scientific investigations, like all investigations, begin with a conceptual problem. The ancient Greeks had noticed that all the stars retained their same relative position with respect to one another, month after month, in a yearly rotation around the earth in a single orbit—all but five rebellious wanderers (called in Greek, "planets") which seemed to shift position randomly. Some hypothesis had to be constructed to account for these misfits. But for Plato and his followers there was a special problem involved. These were heavenly bodies; it was scandalous to suppose them zipping around randomly like flies! As celestial objects they must move in regular, orderly, rational paths. But they appeared to zigzag. How to save this appearance? This was Plato's famous question to his students. Construct a hypothetical model for these planets assuming they move in perfect circles around the earth. His students were allowed any leeway they needed in the number, size, or direction of the orbits necessary to account for the apparent random motion. The result was the orbital theory of our solar system which we still accept today. Copernicus changed the focal point in the fifteenth century from the earth to the sun, and more planets were discovered with the invention of the telescope, but the basic model has remained. The point is that the Greeks could not *see* the circular orbits, nor the planets moving in an apparently circular fashion. This idea did not "come from" sense experience, but was merely assumed hypothetically to account for the zigzag movement they could see.

Sense experience is important in this kind of investigation.

In order to interpret our experience, any theory has to be logically consistent with it. Assuming that the Greek theory is true, would a person standing on the earth see on a given night what we do in fact see? Secondly, though this only came later, the theory implies new experiences of the apparent positions of the planets at various times of the year from observation points other than the surface of the earth—a prediction which could only be tested and confirmed in the twentieth century with the advent of space travel. Sense experience is important in certifying a theory, but not by the psychological device of simply adding more and more sensations. While Locke appears to be right about innate ideas, he seems to be wrong in thinking that all our knowledge can be explained on the basis of sense experience.

WHAT DOES "INNATE" MEAN? But this does not mean that ideas are innate. What exactly is meant by the claim that something is "innate"? Does it mean that everyone can recite all there is to know at birth, which Plato never held, or that everyone will assent to such information under the appropriate conditions, which is not so different from Locke's view that people are simply able to learn them? Does it mean that people are born with ideas, or simply with the mental ability to "process" sense ideas? This is why we must be very clear about a philosophical question before we can hope to answer it meaningfully.

Take the question of universal assent. Locke takes this to mean that everyone knows and believes all sorts of mathematical and logical truths from the moment they are born, which he quite rightly rejects as totally false. But Plato does not mean this at all; he means that everyone would assent to these propositions if they were given the chance, as Meno's servant is by Socrates' questioning. Locke's reply is that this amounts to nothing more than the claim that everyone will assent to whatever he has been taught. Locke's argument is that, taken in this way, the doctrine of innate ideas would prove too much, reducing the claim to the absurdity that a child has innate ideas of important historical dates simply because he readily assents to them as soon as his teacher tells him what they are! Locke certainly has a point; he has shown in a rather devastating way the factually unverifiable, and therefore psychologically worthless, character of innate ideas.

But epistemologically Locke seems to have missed the point. Even though students will generally accept whatever they are taught, there is a very important difference, which Plato's theory at least takes into account, between empirical and logical *grounds* of belief. One may challenge a factual claim in a way one does not question mathematical or logical claims. We accept many factual matters largely on trust, trusting our teacher or our history book, whereas in the case of mathematical or logical knowledge, if it is presented correctly, we see for ourselves what the answer is. Even if we take the time to examine the empirical evidence for some scientific claim, we can at best see for ourselves what the answer is likely to be in all probability, whereas in logical and mathematical proofs we see what the answer *must* be.

Epistemologically, the warrant for these beliefs is very different. This is the point about the servant's answers in *Meno*. Socrates has not pumped the boy with information which he can repeat on demand; Socrates has helped him to see for himself what the answer must be. Whether the theory of the preexistence of the soul is literally true or not, it at least succeeds in calling our attenion to this important justification for our analytical knowledge, which Locke's theory does not.

What, then, is really in dispute between the Rationalists and the Empiricists? In one way, a great deal; in another way, not very much. It is precisely this sort of dispute which has led contemporary philosophers, like Ayer, to condemn most philosophical disputes as meaningless because they are unverifiable (see Chapter 2). Plato's theory of innate ideas does not greatly differ from Locke's in terms we can all verify. Both admit that the child at birth is unable to answer complex questions correctly; both agree that a child can only give the correct answers after he has mastered the language; both admit that he can only understand the language after he has had sufficient experience of the world; both agree that a person can figure certain things out without being told explicitly; and both agree that there is an important difference between empirical knowledge and analytic knowledge. They differ in that Plato says all ideas are innate, while Locke says all our knowledge comes from experience. What this difference amounts to, however, is far from clear. Whatever verifiable explanation Plato could give of "innate" Locke would probably accept, and whatever verifiable explanation Locke could give about knowledge "coming from" experience Plato would probably accept. As in most philosophical disputes, they differ on how best to *interpret* the agreed-upon facts. On a factual level, the difference between them may seem negligible and the dispute, imaginary. Epistemologically, however, as a means of certification, there are important differences.

THE NEED FOR CLARIFICATION. In a sense Locke and Plato are arguing at cross-purposes. Locke is concerned with the source of our idea in the psychological sense of the genesis of the materials on which the mind operates, and he thinks that this, along with simple additive-subtractive functions of mind, will account for all types of knowledge. Plato is more interested in the epistemological question of how we come to have the assurance and clarity of ideas and proofs in mathematics and logic, and he assumes that this can be explained by the peculiar (prenatal) genesis of our ideas. Locke is thus mainly interested in the psychological history of those experiences we call "having an idea"; Plato, in the epistemological source of their justification. Both confuse the two questions which are surely different! It is one thing to entertain the idea that I am the president of the United States; it is quite another to have a reasonable assurance that this idea is true. Wherever I got this idea, before or after birth, it is simply wrong. Both Plato and Locke are mistaken in supposing that a good account of its origins will provide a good account of its credibility, that the origin of an idea will certify its truthfulness.

Part of the difficulty, as we have seen, springs from ambiguities in words like "idea" and "source." Locke defines an idea as whatever we think about when we think (that is, the objects of thought). This is confusing since we do not normally think *about* ideas; we usually *have* ideas *about* objects. In ordinary speech there are two main senses of "idea." On the one hand, we can speak of an idea in the sense of that which occurs within us when we think of things like a tree or the number 2. Despite his definition, this is the kind of image-idea Locke is really interested in—psychological entities, like feelings, which we *have*. Plato would probably agree that at least most of our ideas, in this sense, are gotten by way of sense experience. Ironically, it is Plato who is interested in ideas in the sense in which Locke defines them! When Plato speaks of the idea of Justice or Equality, he does not mean the psychological process or image which occurs inside of us; he means that thing which we are talking *about*, namely, Justice or Equality. But, on the other hand, we also speak of ideas in the sense of our idea *that* 2 plus 2 must be 4. This is an idea in the sense of propositional knowledge and belief. We not only have ideas in this sense, but we also believe, question, doubt, prove, or refute them. The crucial question here is whether the idea is true or not, but the truth of an idea cannot be certified simply by *having* that idea, since we can have false ideas as well as true ones.

The Empiricists try to explain propositional belief and knowledge by the mere addition of ideas in the first sense. But this clearly won't do, for once I *have* the idea of a dragon as the combination of "lizard," "winged," and "fire-breathing," I must go on to doubt or affirm that idea, and once I affirm or deny it I must go on to justify its truth or falsity. The justification of a proposition presupposes asserting it which in turn presupposes entertaining that idea, but these are nonetheless three distinct epistemological functions. Falsity is not just another idea added on to "winged, fire-breathing lizard," but a decision rejecting the certification of the propositional idea that such things exist. Locke is primarily interested in the "source" of those things which go on in us when we think; Plato is primarily interested in the "source" of our assurance that some of these ideas are true. Unfortunately both these meanings are ambiguously contained in the expression, "the source of our ideas," and both Plato and Locke confuse the two by supposing that genetic-source will provide justification-source and that a kind of entity-idea will support a kind of propositional-idea. We can now begin to see why contemporary philosophers are so concerned with the analysis and clarification of meaning. Just as philosophers in the early modern period recognized that all their metaphysical investigations could be thrown into jeopardy by inadequate epistemological foundations, so twentieth-century philosophers have come to see that the answers to epistemological questions are worthless if the questions themselves are unclear!

CONCLUSION. We can conclude from this discussion that Plato is right when he says that the mere accumulation of sense experience is insufficient to explain all the kinds of knowledge we have, but he is not justified when he says, assuming he means this literally, that we know things before we were born. Locke is right when he says that there are no innate ideas, but he is wrong when he says, or implies, that the mere accumulation of sense experience, along with the mind combining and separating simple ideas, is sufficient for explaining our knowledge. But, as we saw before, Plato's and Locke's views are not contradictories; they are contraries and are not mutually exclusive. What we want to ask now is how we can preserve Plato's insight that the mere accumulation of sense experience is insufficient to explain all our knowledge without accepting Plato's theory of innate ideas.

Locke tried to reduce the "objects of thought" to psychological entities, like mental images; Plato tried to reduce them to real entities. Locke's mistake is in confusing the Empire State building I am thinking about with the image which occurs to me when I think of it. The image is in my mind and belongs to me, but not the Empire State building! Plato's mistake is assuming that if we know something there must exist something in the world which corresponds to that knowledge. Indeed this seems to be reflected in the very grammar of our language. To know is to know something. If I know something, there must be something which I know! Plato assumes that if we know mathematics there must exist triangles, equality, etc. which are the objects of our knowledge, and since these objects cannot be known through sense experience they must have been experienced in some other world when the soul was separate from the body and bodily sensations. However, Plato's argument does not prove that for every piece of knowledge there is something existing in the world corresponding to it. For example, I know that the Pilgrim Fathers did not watch television, but what is it that I actually know? Simply "the fact" that the Pilgrim Fathers did not watch television. But this "fact" is not some real object existing in the world, along side of ships, trees, and chairs, but is simply a grammatical object, the object of the verb "to know." Plato introduces the Forms in part to account for analytic knowledge, but there are better ways of explaining this, and we should consider two such alternatives briefly—those of Aristotle and Kant.

Alternative Theories

ARISTOTLE. Aristotle (384–322 B.C.) appears as a kind of compromise between Plato and Locke. He agrees with the Empiricists that there is no knowledge without sense experience, but he also agrees with Plato that knowledge is more than the accumulation of sense experience. Knowledge, according to Aristotle, begins with sense experience. More and more sense experience leads to the formation of general concepts and general laws of nature. Having acquired a certain amount of experience, for example, we know that water is wet, that fire is hot, that water will put fire out, and so on. Aristotle contends that the mind can proceed to acquire additional knowledge on the basis of these general laws and concepts without the addition of any further experience. Moreover, further experience is not required to confirm or support such knowledge. For example, if we know that fire requires air, we can deduce that nothing will burn inside a vacuum. If we know from experience what pairs of things are and have had some experience with counting, then we can go on without any further experience to deduce the new knowledge that 200 plus 200 is 400 and to work out the whole of mathematics entirely in our heads. Similarly, if we know from experience what "all" and "is" mean, then we can deduce, from this alone, that if all S is P and all P is R, then all S must be R, without any new experience. Aristotle gives a plausible account of a kind of knowledge which depends partly but not entirely on sense experience and not at all on innate ideas.

KANT. Another possibility is provided by Immanuel Kant (1724–1804) who argued that there is no form of knowledge, however elementary, which is the result of sense experience alone. From the very beginning, raw sense data must be processed; all sensation must be conceptualized in order to be experienced at all. To see a table one has to know that his sense experience falls within the general concept of a table; even to see that *as* a table is not a matter for sensation alone but a conceptual question of what counts as a table. To know as you walk around a table that the different sensations you receive are not different objects but different views of only one object is an intellectual, conceptual interpretation and not just sensation. If all we had to go on was sensation, we would have to suppose that there were as many objects as we had views or sensations of them. According to sensation, the tree I see in the fall is different from the tree I saw last spring. Everyday perception, as well as scientific, mathematical, or logical knowledge, depends on something besides sensation —namely the activities of the intellect: sorting, selecting, arranging, categorizing, and so on.

On the other hand, Kant disagrees with Plato that intellect has access to a new source of ideas or a new source of reality. For Kant, intellect is concerned only with the form of our thought. Reason can teach us that it is either raining or it is not, but this does not give us any new information! It is not getting a glimpse of a new realm of reality; it is simply seeing the pattern which all our thinking must take. The reason we know that a thing cannot both be and not be at the same time is that without this rule all thinking would be impossible. If we abandon this rule, we could not say anything, for as soon as we said that a ball was round it would be equally true to assert that it was not round, but then we would not have said anything! The result would be the end of all thought as well as speech.

Logical knowledge discovers general laws of thought which the mind must use if it is to be able to think at all. Here, again, we have an explanation of a kind of knowledge which is not entirely dependent on sense experience and which is not dependent on innate ideas. How do you know, for example, that every event has a cause, to take one of Kant's favorite examples? You don't know it by experience because you haven't experienced every event. What if your knowledge were based only on a generalization from sense experience—for example, we knew from past experience that most events had causes and so assumed as a general rule that all events would have causes. Suppose that you were trying to discover the cause of cancer and worked for years without discovering the cause. If your knowledge were really based on sense experience, you would have to conclude that you had discovered one event which apparently did not have a cause, and that it was therefore false that all events have causes. But this is not what we do at all. We go right on looking for a cause despite experience. As we saw before, it is often experience which must conform to our ideas, not the other way around.

Where does this idea that all events have a cause come from? Kant says that it is something which we must think if we are to have an intelligible experience and if we are to have science. Even if this assumption were false, we would still have to think and act as though it were true in order to have an intelligible world of everyday experience. Our world is intelligible because we can explain things in it, and we can explain things only by giving causes. Thus we must think of events having causes in order to have a meaningful, intelligible world (see Chapter 2).

Most of the materials of our knowledge, then, come from sense experience, but sense experience is not sufficient to explain our knowledge of the world. This does not mean that we have innate ideas, for we can find other, more adequate ways of explaining how we come to have the knowledge we possess. First there is the activity of the mind—sorting, combining, questioning, drawing conclusions, framing and testing hypotheses, categorizing, and so on. Second there is the purely intellectual deduction from general ideas already obtained from sense experience without the need of any additional experience, as when I deduce from the concepts of "bachelor" and "married" that all bachelors must be unmarried. Finally there is knowledge of the general laws of thought, those general rules of thinking which must be followed if thinking is to be possible. None of these kinds of knowledge gives us new information or puts us in contact with a new reality; they analyze, clarify, and draw inferences from ideas which we already have. Plato's mistake was in thinking that any knowledge must be about something, that all knowledge must have as its object something existing somewhere. So he reasoned that mathematical knowledge must be about mathematical entities, and since these entities could not exist in this world they had to exist in some other world. The view of most contemporary philosophers is that analytic knowledge is not about anything. It simply traces out the consequences of our thought.

KNOWLEDGE AND BELIEF

Philosophers have long pondered another fundamental question about knowledge: What is the difference between *knowledge* and *belief*? Is belief simply a low-grade kind of knowledge, or is knowledge a high-grade belief? Or are they two entirely different things? Can belief be converted into knowledge, and if so how? Is it true, as the Relativists maintain, that there is no difference, that knowing something is simply believing it?

Traditionally, philosophers were interested in belief only as an aid or hinderance to knowledge; they saw it almost exclusively as either leading to knowledge or taking the place of it. As such, belief has always been considered a poor substitute or shoddy masquerade for genuine knowledge. In their enthusiasm to acquire reliable knowledge, most philosophers from Plato to the present have felt compelled to distinguish true knowledge from mere belief as sharply as possible.

Plato's View

Plato distinguishes knowledge from belief in the sharpest possible way. For Plato, the difference between knowledge and belief consists in the absolute difference in the *objects* of knowledge and belief. In other words, for Plato, the things which one can know are an entirely different sort of thing from those which one can believe. The sort of thing one can know is real, and hence eternal and unchanging; the sort of thing one can believe is only an appearance, and thus contingent, temporal, and changing. This is the position Plato develops in *The Republic*. His argument is that to know something there must be something which you know, and this must be something real and unchanging.

Plato argues that if you know something, what you know *must* be true, and therefore cannot be otherwise than it is. It is impossible for me to know that Boston is larger than New York because this is not true, and we cannot know what is false. What we know must exist just as we conceive it to be. This sounds fairly plausible, but notice what appears to follow from it. Let's say I entertain two thoughts: one that the road to Alaska is unpaved, and the other that 2 plus 2 is 4. Both of these thoughts are true, but which of them do I know and which do I merely believe? If I *know* that the road is unpaved then it *must* be unpaved. But the road need not be unpaved; it might be paved, and someday, hopefully, it will be. We certainly cannot say that it *must* be unpaved. Plato would argue that therefore this is not something which I know, but only something which I believe. On the other hand, 2 plus 2 *must* be 4 and cannot be otherwise, and therefore, Plato argues, I can be said to know rather than believe it.

This point is further complicated by the temporal claim that the only things that *must* be true are those that do not change. By joining these two points, Plato is led to the conclusion that nothing can be known about the changing empirical world, and that the things we can know, the real things, are incapable of change and exist outside the framework of the space-time material universe—an idea which has dominated Western thought ever since. If I know that X is Y, then X *must* be Y and therefore cannot change from Y to Z. If I know that 2 plus 2 is 4, then 2 plus 2 can only be 4; it cannot be 4 today, 5 tomorrow, and 3½ the day after. In the case of the road to Alaska we have to admit (and indeed welcome) the possibility of its being unpaved this year and paved next year. First it is unpaved and then it is paved—can you be said to *know* things of this sort, Plato asks? Certainly not.

But this is a confusion of the logical point that we cannot

know something which is both paved and not paved with the temporal point that we cannot know something which is unpaved today and paved tomorrow. In Plato's analysis, change always involves a contradiction, and for this reason he holds that things which change can be neither real nor known (see Chapter 2). He analyzes the fact that a grapefruit is green today and yellow a week later as the proposition that the grapefruit is both green and yellow and thus that it is both green and not green. He reduces a fact of change to a contradiction in terms, something which cannot be consistently thought, much less real or known. What sort of thing is never changing in this sense, what is it which is always one thing and never anything else? The only conceivable answer, tailor-made for the question, is the Forms or Ideas. The Idea of Green is always green; it is never yellow. A person may be thin today and fat tomorrow, but Thinness itself can never be anything but thin! Everything that changes is only an "appearance" about which we can have opinions but no knowledge. This will include everything which occurs in time. But this includes the entire everyday, empirical, factual world of sense experience. It includes all history, common sense, geography, biology, and so on, none of which can be the object of knowledge but can only be believed.

Knowledge and Certainty

If we separate the temporal and the logical problems, which Plato confuses, and concentrate on the latter, we see that Plato is concerned primarily with the difference in the degree of certainty attached to belief and knowledge. What Plato seems to have in mind when he says that the objects of belief are constantly changing is that what we only believe to be true but do not know *could* be false. He confuses the two questions because he feels that in the process of change the object of belief contradicts itself. The object of knowledge, then, is defined most precisely in terms of the degree of certainty with which it is known—when we know something it is such that it could not be otherwise. This leads to the position that knowledge must always be expressed in the form of a statement which never contradicts itself, for example, beauty is beauty, knowledge is knowledge, and so on. This view reduces knowledge to the kind of certainty one finds in logic and mathematics, and this is the view one finds throughout Western philosophy from Aristotle to Descartes. In the *Nicomachean Ethics*, Aristotle says that "what we know is not even capable of being otherwise; of things capable of being otherwise we do not know." "Therefore," he says, "the object of scientific knowledge is of necessity. Therefore it is eternal: for things that are of necessity . . . are all eternal."

Like Plato, Aristotle confuses the logical point about *necessity* and the temporal point about *eternity*. It is not possible for the statement "All bachelors are unmarried" to be false, but this does not mean that the statement has always been true, or that it has been true for a long time and will continue to be true for months to come. Time has nothing to do with the truth or falsity of the statement. The truth of a contingent, factual statement lasts just as long as the truth of a necessary statement. If it is true that George Washington was the first U. S. President, then it will always be true, but it did not *have* to be true. The question of how long a proposition remains true has no bearing on whether its truth is necessary or only contingent.

The Problem

Plato's view has provided the framework for most discussions of knowledge ever since. For example, Aristotle says in the *Posterior Analytics*:

> Scientific knowledge and its object differ from opinion and the object of opinion in that scientific knowledge is commensurately universal and proceeds by necessary connexions, and that which is necessary cannot be otherwise . . . Opinion . . . is concerned with that which may be true or false, and can be otherwise.
> Demonstrative knowledge must rest on necessary truths, for the object of scientific knowledge cannot be other than it is.

Most philosophers have agreed with Plato and Aristotle that all knowledge is logical, deductive knowledge—the sort of knowledge one finds in syllogisms and mathematical proofs. But immediately a serious problem arises. Aristotle calls this "scientific knowledge," but is scientific knowledge deductive and incapable of being other than it is? Can we discover the truths of the natural sciences, such as biology, physics, and geology, simply by logical analysis? Are we absolutely certain of these scientific claims; are they incapable of being false? This introduces the head-splitting problem philosophers face in trying to define knowledge in terms of certainty: can scientific, factual information properly be called knowledge; how we can say on such a theory that we *know* the conclusions of the natural sciences? How indeed can we be said to know anything!

Descartes (1596–1650) also distinguishes knowledge from belief in this way. Descartes defines knowledge as absolute certainty; in *Meditations* (1641), Descartes vowed to reject anything which could in any way be doubted. This view is reflected to a certain extent in common sense and everyday speech when we say, "I think so, but I'm not sure," or "I know he will be here; I'm certain of it." The philosopher's treatment of this theme is an exaggeration of the common-sense view which never insists on complete certainty and so never gets into hot water. Complete certainty means that it is not possible for the statement to be false. If we insist that knowledge is absolute certainty, then what exactly can we know? Very little at best! Can we prove beyond the shadow of a doubt any of the statements of biology, physics, and the other natural sciences? Even if they are true, *must* they be true? Can we demonstrate with complete confidence that there even exists an external world? Is it absolutely impossible, for example, that our everyday experience is nothing but a dream? If not, then we cannot be said to *know* such things—*if* we insist on defining knowledge in terms of the complete certainty of mathematics and logic. If we set our standards too high, then we seem unable to find anything which will live up to those standards.

Having written the first three parts of *An Essay Concerning Human Understanding*, a book specifically designed to determine the limits of our knowledge, Locke found himself in the embarrassing position of having to admit that there is practically nothing we can know if we define knowledge as absolute certainty. Locke says we have only three kinds of knowledge: 1) knowledge by intuition of the immediate agreement between ideas, which includes immediate deductive inferences of the form "If all cats are mammals, then this cat is a mammal," as well as analytic statements like "All bachelors are unmarried" and "Either it will rain or it will not rain," in which the inference proceeds in a single step; 2) knowledge by reason of logical or mathematical proofs involving more than one step, such as a syllogism or any extended deductive argument; and 3) what Locke calls *sensitive knowledge*

—knowledge of only the bare *existence* of objects in the outside world. According to Locke, strictly speaking we do not know anything about the external world; we only know that it exists, and even this crumb both Locke and Descartes admit only very hesitantly. Descartes is willing to accept the existence of an external world only on what he understands to be the authority of God Himself; Locke cautiously admits that our belief in an outside world, though falling short of absolute logical certitude, is nonetheless more like deductive knowledge than mere opinion.

Descartes and Locke are hesitant to accept such belief as genuine knowledge because it falls short of the ideal of certainty by which they define knowledge. On the other hand, they are reluctant to deny that we do know something about the external world for fear of seeming ridiculous. Having painted himself into a corner, Locke tries desperately to extricate himself.

> These two, viz. intuition and demonstration, are the degrees of our *knowledge*; whatever comes short of one of these, with what assurance soever embraced, is but *faith* or *opinion*, but not knowledge, at least in all general truths. There is, indeed, another perception of the mind, employed about *the particular existence of finite beings without us*, which, going beyond bare probability, and yet not reaching perfectly to either of the foregoing degrees of certainty, passes under the name of knowledge. [Locke, *An Essay Concerning Human Understanding*]

By hedging a bit, Locke is able to admit with great difficulty and less consistency that we know there exists an external world. But what this world is like—whether there are trees, people in it, whether water is wet and ice is cold—Locke is obliged to admit with some embarrassment we don't know at all! It begins to look like the certainty criterion of knowledge can only lead to skepticism.

The Solutions

THE EMPIRICIST SOLUTION. It is interesting to see how philosophers have tried to solve this dilemma. Most attempts take the form of raising belief up to the level of knowledge. Empiricist philosophers contend that beliefs such as "The tomato is red" can be translated into statements about sensations—"I am now experiencing a red patch of color"—about which one could be absolutely certain and from which one could logically derive all knowledge of the external world. However, the certainty of the sensation-statements depends upon personal feeling; they are primarily about the *speaker* from which no objective truth about the *world* can be derived. Their certainty rests on the technicality that by saying "This is how things *seem* to me," I discount all the ordinary ways statements about things are falsified (by not being in fact what they seemed to be). A statement is false if it fails to correspond to the outside world. By constructing sensation-statements which are not about the outside world, we can construct statements which are not false. But then we are no longer talking about the external world. If I say "It seems cold to me," nothing can prove me wrong, not even a thermometer registering 110°, but I am certainly not talking about the 110° weather. Similarly, even if I am dreaming, the sensation-statement about the "red patch" is true, though it is hard to see how to get from there to objective knowledge of the physical world. Despite some verbal similarities between the object-statement and the sensation-statement (the red tomato and the red patch), the transition from the one to the other can never be bridged because the word "red," which in the object-statement refers to an object, refers only to my sensation in the sensation-statement. Historically, all attempts to bridge this gap have failed, but the program of extracting factual, empirical knowledge out of absolutely certain foundations has been persistent even in the twentieth century.

THE RATIONALIST SOLUTION. Others have sought to redefine knowledge of the physical world as knowledge of the eternal pattern which the external world imitates or reflects in some inferior way. The Platonic or Rationalist view, very popular today among scientists and philosophers of science, holds that the natural sciences are a form of knowledge in the sense that they express the eternal pattern which underlies the empirical world and which the empirical world more or less approximates. What the modern scientist seeks, according to these theorists, is an abstract mathematical pattern or schema which matches the behavior of empirical phenomena sufficiently to serve as an explanatory model for such phenomena. This pattern itself can be known in the purely deductive, logical way by which knowledge is defined, while at the same time it can provide a looser kind of knowledge of the factual, contingent world by reflecting certain of its patterns of behavior. This appears to be what Plato meant to say about the empirical world, that strictly speaking it cannot be known since what we know is another world altogether (the Forms), while in a looser sense, one *can* know the empirical world in so far as and to the extent that the shape of that world is determined by or reflected in the Forms. To that extent, knowledge of the Forms becomes knowledge of the empirical world, or at least of what is most real and important about the empirical world.

Despite its counter-intuitive flavor, this position has gained a certain currency in recent discussions of science. Boyle's laws of gases and Galileo's law of falling bodies do not describe real gases and real bodies. The scientist claims that they *would* if the container were not itself composed of atoms which interact with the gas molecules, and if air friction were completely eliminated, and so on. In other words, these laws hold not of real gases and bodies but of ideal systems which the real gases and bodies resemble fairly closely. These ideal systems do not exist; there are no ideal containers or complete vaccums. However, the theories can be applied to and will hold more or less for real gases and bodies because they are very much like their ideal counterparts; our theory for the one will do very well for the other.

Descartes, for example, maintains that geometry defines the underlying reality of the empirical world. He holds that the essence of the material world is spatial extension because this aspect of the material world is most amenable to mathematical, deductive treatment. In other words, whatever holds for mathematical triangles in pure mathematical space according to the science of geometry will also hold more or less for any triangular piece of land, pie, or stone. The findings of geometry will never apply to the material world exactly, because, as said before, there are no perfect triangles or straight lines in the material world. But there are approximations, and to the extent that they approach abstract geometrical figures, the science of geometry will be more or less applicable to the material world. Descartes thus felt that the absolute science of geometry could also, in a looser sense, become a science of the physical world. And since this aspect of the world is most amenable to mathematical knowledge, there is a tendency to assume that this is the most real aspect of the world.

However, Descartes' approach is really no more successful than the Empiricist attempt to deduce physical reality from sense-data; no matter how Plato and Descartes try to hide it, the fact remains that in this view of natural science we still don't really know the physical world at all. What we do know is an abstract world of ideal mathematical formulae. We believe the empirical world approximates to this, but we cannot be sure, and even so, it is not an exact fit. That the physical world approximates this ideal system can only yield approximate information which, according to the Platonic and Cartesian definitions, can never be more than belief.

PROBABILITY. One of the most successful attempts to solve this problem is the theory of probability. This relatively modern theory treats knowledge as 100 percent probability and belief as all degrees of probability ranging from 51 to 99 percent. If I flip a coin there is a 50 percent chance that it will turn up heads, and there is a 100 percent chance that it will land either heads or tails (unless it lands on its edge or is picked out of the air by a passing thief—perhaps probability theory also describes an ideal system). We *know* that it will be either heads or tails, but we only *believe* that it will be heads. But the point is, there are degrees of reliability to our beliefs which the probability calculus measures. As the probability of our belief gets higher and higher, it becomes more and more like knowledge, and there finally comes a point, no one can say exactly where, when the belief will be so much more like knowledge than belief that it will be less misleading to call it knowledge than belief. Thus, for example, the belief that the first ball picked up at random from a bag containing 999 red balls and one white one will be red can be called "knowledge" for all practical purposes. And so with my belief that the sun will rise tomorrow or that an object thrown into the air will fall to the ground again. These are not absolutely certain, but the probability is so high that no one will object if we boast a little and say that we *know* such things.

The problem with this type of solution is that the classical theory of knowledge in terms of which it is framed draws an *absolute* distinction between 100 percent probability and anything less. According to the traditional theory there is no difference in principle between 99 percent and 51 percent probability. Like putting on the golf green, a miss is a miss, however close you get to the hole. Knowledge is absolute certainty and anything less is simply not knowledge. In other words, when all is said and done, the probability theory has done nothing to correct the view that 99 percent probability is almost but not quite knowledge. Strictly speaking, it still remains true that only 100 percent probability counts as knowledge and this excludes all scientific and commonsense beliefs about the external world.

Since none of these solutions appears to work, must we conclude from this that we can't know anything about the external world? On the contrary, the fact that all these solutions are so inadequate has raised doubts about the traditional conception of knowledge as absolute certainty. Rather than trying to *solve* the problem, modern critics have challenged that conception of knowledge without which the problem simply doesn't arise. Instead of attempting an answer, they attack the question!

THE ANALYTIC/SYNTHETIC DISTINCTION. The first such view is developed from the analytic/synthetic distinction. Locke hints at such a distinction, though Hume was the first to state it clearly and to understand its importance philosophically. As pointed out earlier (see Chapter 2), the analytic/synthetic distinction concerns the factual content of statements, while the *a priori/a posteriori* distinction concerns the kind of evidence supporting the statement. A "synthetic" statement has factual content in the sense that it asserts something true or false of the actual world (for example, "The cat is on the mat"), while an "analytic" statement is true simply by definition of the words used and makes no claim or assertion about the real world (for example, "A bachelor is an unmarried man," "A unicorn is a horned animal"). As the words suggest, *a priori* means prior to or before experience and *a posteriori* means after experience, although in this context we are referring to a logical or evidential priority and posteriority. A proposition is a priori if it is known independently of experience, and an a posteriori proposition is one whose truth can only be determined empirically through experience. Generally it was felt that since no empirical data could falsify a priori statements, they could be known with complete certainty. Obviously, empirical statements are both a posteriori and synthetic, while mathematical and logical statements are both a priori and analytic. The only interesting question, therefore, is whether there are or can be statements which are synthetic and a priori, that is, significant information known independently of experience and with complete certainty. The mainstream of Western epistemology certainly thought so, since this was the goal of the continued quest for certainty—nontrivial, infallible knowledge.

Hume thought otherwise. Hume's position was that all necessary or a priori knowledge was merely "analytic" (true by definition), and that all truly informative, or "synthetic," knowledge was merely contingent. He contends that all necessary statements concern only the relations between ideas which we already have and hence yield no new information about anything in the world, and that all significant, informative, factual statements about the world can only be contingent. If we desire certainty, we will have to be content with trivial, uninformative statements like "Either it is raining or it is not," "A circle is a circle," and so on; if more informative, factual statements which tell us something about the world are desired, then we will have to settle for statements which are possibly true but also are possibly false. Hume's view collapses the traditional theory of knowledge by removing the ideal of an informative knowledge of reality which is completely certain. If Hume is right, then the traditional goal of having one's cake and eating it too is based on an impossible ideal. It is not that knowledge of matters of fact is an inferior grade of knowledge because it fails to attain complete certainty; it is rather a completely different kind of knowledge which can tell us something about the world. It is not an accident of sloppy, reckless thinking, but the very nature of this kind of knowledge that it cannot be, even as an ideal, absolutely certain.

To speak figuratively, the price we pay for the priviledge of referring to an actual world and saying something true about it is the possibility of the empirical world proving us wrong. To say something about the actual world, you have to stick your neck out. This is the whole point of scientific experimentation and the kind of thing we find in everyday life. If I say that it is raining at Pebble Beach, I have committed myself to that part of the empirical world we call Pebble Beach being in the state we call rain, and thus, having ascribed this rainy state to the beach, it remains an open possibility that the weather at Pebble Beach will prove me wrong. If I refuse to stick my neck out and am overly cautious, then I must restrict myself to the rather uninteresting and uninformative, though absolutely certain, statement that it is either raining at the beach or it is not. As we noted earlier, it is the failure to correspond with reality which makes a statement false. Because analytic statements are not *about* the world they cannot fail to correspond with it, and in this sense they are technically beyond doubt. Like sensation-statements, they are incapable of being false because they are incapable of being true of the real world!

KNOWLEDGE AS REASONABLE, TRUE BELIEF. Ironically, probably the best "modern" solution is found in a later work of Plato, *Theaetetus*, a book which marks an important change in the direction of Plato's thought away from the sharp distinction he drew in *The Republic* between the objects of knowledge and belief. In *Theaetetus*, Plato begins to see that knowledge is not simply the perception of a special kind of object, the Forms, but that it has more to do with the way we justify our assertions about the world. The modern account derived from *Theaetetus* is that knowledge can be defined in terms of three necessary and jointly sufficient conditions. Interestingly, one of the conditions is belief, thus softening Plato's earlier dichotomy between belief and knowledge.

After considering many different definitions and theories of knowledge, all of which he finds lacking in some way or other, Plato finally identifies knowledge as true opinion accompanied by rational justification, or good reasons.

Plato first posits that a person must believe something before he can be said to know it. To test this premise we can ask ourselves what we would say in certain situations to see if the proposed definition is in line with accepted linguistic usage. Imagine a child who is told by his teacher that the earth is round. He doesn't believe this for a moment, but he knows that he will fail his examination if he does not *say* that the earth is round, which he does in the exam. In this case, the person says p but does not believe p. So, this is a test case for our definition of knowledge. What do you say? Does he know that the earth is round or not? I think we will all agree that he does not know it, because, as Plato suggests, belief in p is a necessary condition for knowing p.

This is just common sense. As we have said before, philosophy does not teach us anything new, it simply clarifies our thought by making explicit what has previously been merely presupposed. Now let us ask if belief in p is a sufficient condition for knowing p. And again we try to invent a kind of imaginative test case. We can all think of cases in which someone believes something fervently but does not know it simply because what he believes is not the case. This brings us to the second necessary condition, the *truth* of p. I can believe that Guadalajara is the capital of Mexico, but I cannot be said to know it because it is a false belief—Guadalajara is not the capital of Mexico. A person can, of course, *claim* to know something which he believes but which is in fact false. Frequently, something we believe and claim to know is true turns out to be false, and we have to retract our claim to know it. In such cases, we usually say, "Well, I didn't know it after all, but I certainly thought so." A person cannot say, "I *know* it and it is false," but he can say, "It is false though I *believed* it to be true." It appears, then, that there is a link between knowledge and truth and between belief and falsity. We will say we know something only so long as we think it is true; as soon as we discover it is false we will retract and say we only believed it.

This introduces the disparity between first-person knowledge claims, in which I examine my own knowledge, and third-person knowledge claims, in which I examine someone else's claim to know. It is much more difficult, in examining one's own beliefs, to distinguish what is true from what one only thinks is true. If you were asked to write down a list of all the things which are true and another list of all the things which you believe to be true, the two lists would probably be identical. What you will claim to be true, if you are speaking candidly, is what you believe to be true. However, if we were to examine the beliefs of a third person, we could more easily distinguish what is true from what he only believes to be true. To a certain extent the two lists will overlap, but each will contain some items not found in the other —the person may believe something which is not true and there may be something true which he does not believe, either because he thinks it is false or simply because he has never considered it. Although we may not always be able to tell the difference between what is true and what we think is true, there is a meaningful distinction between *subjective* beliefs and *true* beliefs. Failure to keep such a distinction clearly in mind leads to epistemological relativism.

Relativism is a currently popular view that knowledge and truth depend entirely upon the point of view of each person, and that there is no absolute or objective truth. The relativist sees no difference between the statements "I believe *p*" and "I know *p*," except that the latter is a more conceited or intolerant claim. If a person says that he believes something or knows something, then, according to the relativist, this is true simply because truth is an entirely subjective matter. The great weakness of the relativist's position is that it contradicts our common-sense notion that some beliefs are false.

Despite the difficulty of distinguishing in our own case which of our beliefs we know to be true, there is a meaningful distinction between knowledge and belief, especially as this is expressed in third-person knowledge claims. "He believes p" does not mean the same as "He knows p." And this is a useful distinction in expressing our dissatisfaction either with other people's beliefs ("He thinks so, but it's not"), or with our own previous beliefs ("I used to accept a lot of things which weren't true").

This is also an important distinction in overcoming the weakness in the first-person approach to knowledge. Descartes, for example, places the criterion for knowledge on our feeling of certainty. But this is an internal, subjective criterion which cannot guarantee the objectivity of knowledge. Descartes reasons that since you cannot know something you are uncertain about, you will automatically know anything which you are certain of. But this clearly is not so. No amount of certainty will guarantee that what we believe is true. The truth or falsity of what we believe is an objective factor which has to do with the relationship of what we think to the actual facts; it is a relation of thought to reality, and no subjective determination of thought, such as feeling sure, can determine the correspondence of that thought with reality. Of course, what Descartes is really worried about is how to tell which of our beliefs correspond to reality, and this, as we will see in Chapter 8, is part of the human predicament never to be able to do absolutely! One of the great advantages of Plato's formulation in *Theatetus* is that it indicates both the subjective factor in knowledge, that a person must believe p, as well as the objective factor, that p must be true.

Now we can see Plato's earlier mistake in supposing we can only know what must be true. When I say, in ordinary speech, that to know p, p must be true, I only mean that it is a necessary condition of someone's knowing p that p be true, not that p be necessarily true. I don't mean that in order to know p, p must be analytically true, but only that it must be true. In *The Republic*, Plato confuses these two and, as a result, compounds these two types of necessity. He maintains not only that it is a necessary condition of knowledge that p be true, but that p be necessarily true. To be on the safe side, let us express this second condition by saying that a necessary condition for knowing p is simply that p be true.

It is not enough that p be true, as we saw in the example of the school boy who said what was true but did not believe it. Nor is it enough merely to believe something in order for it to be true. But if neither of these two necessary conditions is sufficient by itself, is the conjunction of the two sufficient for knowledge? Can a person believe something which is true and yet not know it? If so, what is the difference between true belief and knowledge? This brings us to the most important shift in Plato's thinking from *The Republic* to *Theaetetus*. In *The Republic*, Plato separates belief and knowledge completely, but in *Theaetetus* he admits that knowledge is a kind of belief. All knowledge is belief, but all belief is not knowledge. As we have seen, a false belief does not constitute knowledge. So, we can narrow the field and say that all knowledge is *true belief*, but does it follow that all true belief is knowledge? Plato's answer is no—all true belief is not knowledge; in order to qualify as knowledge, a true belief must always be accompanied by a rational explanation. Plato thus sets down three conditions for knowledge, and many philosophers today maintain that these three conditions together are sufficient for knowledge. Not only is it true that all knowledge is true opinion with rational explanation, but all true opinion with rational explanation is knowledge.

Now let's put Plato's third condition to the test. It is easy to imagine a case in which a person believed something which was true but did not know it. We have all probably made at some time a lucky guess—a case of true opinion which we would not classify as knowledge. We might get a hot tip from an old aunt that the winner of the Kentucky Derby will be Johnny Luck, and despite the fact that the horse is a 20 to 1 underdog, he wins. When asked how she knew such a thing, she replies that it is all very simple: Johnny Luck's jockey was Jim Lance; the winner of last year's race was Jerry Lane whose jockey was Justice Lagg—and since all these have the same initials, J. L., and Johnny Luck was the only horse in this year's race to have such initials, he had to win. Could we truly say she *knew* who was going to win? Most probably we would be inclined to say she didn't know because her reasons were ridiculous. (Of course, if she guesses everything correctly on such a basis we might change our mind, but only because we would begin to suspect that there is some sound basis to her reasoning which we can't explain—it is still the case that she *knows* only if her reasons are *good* ones.)

A person might also accept an opinion as true simply on the basis of authority, as in the case of a student who believes that the sum of the interior angles of a triangle is 180° just because his teacher says so. His belief is correct, but is it knowledge? Here there are good, though not conclusive reasons for excluding such true opinion from knowledge. Our indecisiveness rests on the question whether the boy believes it simply because someone of authority says so (which is a bad reason) or whether he believes it partly because he thinks there is a good chance that his teacher, with her training and degree, knows what she is talking about (which is a fair reason). Most actual cases are probably a mixture of the two, and the more the case tends to the former the less we are inclined to call it knowledge, while the more it tends to the latter, the more confident we are that it is knowledge.

This has important practical bearings on education. The student who merely repeats definitions and answers from memory has little solid understanding of the subject—he can merely recite without knowing. Conversely, students expect a professor not only to tell them that an argument or a line of poetry is bad, but why it is bad. As Aristotle said, we do not normally think a person has really learned something until he can explain it to someone else. Indeed, the best way to learn something is often to try to explain it to another person. As you explain it, you may begin to realize how weak some of your reasons are, and hence how thin your knowledge is. Plato pointed out that true opinion which is accompanied by good reasons is also more stable than true opinion accepted without reasons. You have probably noticed this in regard to religious belief. If a person seriously questions any religious belief and inquires into the reasons why it is true, one of two things will generally happen. Either he will lose his belief, which supports Plato's contention that belief without explanation is unstable, or else his belief will become much stronger than it was before, which also supports Plato's point. And although we cannot always distinguish, as Descartes hoped, between what is true and what is false, we can be reasonable and act on the basis of the best evidence available at the time.

Plato's three conditions do accord remarkably well with the ordinary criteria of knowledge, and his theory has been widely accepted. However, it still leaves many questions unanswered, for there are many different kinds of reasons which can be given for something's being true, and different degrees of weight which a reason can contribute to a theory. Plato's theory does not tell us what kind of reasons are to count toward knowledge and how good these reasons have to be. If someone says it will rain tomorrow because he has just been reading about the tropical rains of Central Africa, we would surely not count this reason as sufficient for knowledge. But if I say that it will rain tomorrow because the weatherman said it would, it is unclear whether this reason is strong enough. And if it is not, how strong do the reasons have to be? If we demand that the reasons be so strong as to exclude the logical possibility of p's being false, we are right back where we started, defining knowledge as complete certainty. In ordinary speech the idea seems to be "enough is enough," that is, enough in a given situation or context. But there are no clear guidelines laid down in ordinary speech, and it is questionable whether this is good enough for a philosophical account.

PRACTICAL KNOWLEDGE

So far we have been talking exclusively about theoretical knowledge. But a wise man is not always the man who possesses the most theoretical information. What about wisdom, or practical knowledge? This is a question of great interest to philosophers as well as one of immense practical importance to everyone. Indeed, a proper understanding of the role of practical knowledge and how it differs from theoretical knowledge could revolutionize university and secondary school education.

Practical knowledge is knowing what to do and how to do it. The traditional philosophical view construes knowing what to do and how to do it as a piece of theoretical knowledge. However, recently this position has come under fierce attack by contemporary philosophers such as Gilbert Ryle (*Concept of Mind*, 1949). If I am a university student, it is a practical question what university courses I ought to take, and on the traditional account my knowledge would take the following form. I know that I want to become a successful, respected, and wealthy member of the community, and I know that one way of achieving this is to become a lawyer or a doctor; however, I know that there are already many lawyers and doctors and that more trained engineers will be needed in the future; thus I know that the chances of success in engineering are greater than in law or medicine. I know that if I want to become an engineer I must take certain courses in the engineering and mathematics departments. On this basis I decide what university courses to take. The bulk of this argument is based on *theoretical* knowledge. The reasoning begins with the desired objective to be rich and respected, and ends with a choice and a decision to take certain courses, both of which are practical matters. But the intervening steps in the reasoning process are based on nonpractical, theoretical considerations—the theory that more engineers will be needed in the future, that they will be better paid, that engineers must have a university degree, and so on. These theories are either true or false. But my desire to be rich and famous and the choice of courses are neither true nor false, but wise or foolish, realistic or unrealistic, shortsighted or farsighted, and so on. The desires and choices are not theories to be proved or disproved, but matters of practical importance. According to the traditional view, if the desires and choices display practical wisdom, then they must be accompanied by a theoretical underpinning. Thus, the traditional view construes practical knowledge as composed of two distinct phases, cited by Ryle as "a bit of theory and then . . . a bit of practice."

Ryle and other philosophers oppose the idea that practical knowledge is always accompanied by theorizing. It suggests that before a person can perform any intelligent action he must first theorize and analyze and conduct a rational argument in his mind. Ryle argues that in fact this does not always or necessarily occur in intelligent action and that, moreover, it suggests a false picture of the relation between thought and action. It suggests a sharp dichotomy between action, which is physical and thus public and external, and the thought preceding it, which is mental, private, and internal. This implies that in any intelligent action there are two distinct things going on, the thought and the bodily behavior, and secondly, that credit for the intelligence of the action goes to the hidden thought processes. According to the traditional view, then, labeling a person's action as intelligent is simply describing what goes on in the mind, reducing behavior to a mere symptom or indication of the internal process. Ryle finds this ridiculous and sides with what he regards as the common-sense view that there is only one activity going on, the person's overt behavior, and that this is what we are describing when we say an action is intelligent, and not some anterior, ghostly mental process.

But is this the common-sense view? Don't we say in everyday language that intelligent people are those who think before they act? Don't we often think, in a common-sense way, of intelligent action as that which follows and is guided by a careful consideration of all the pros and cons? In short, isn't our common-sense view more like the traditional view, and isn't Ryle denying part of this common-sense view? Is he denying that we do sometimes think about what we are going to do before doing it? Is he denying the existence of mental phenomena when he attributes intelligence to bodily behavior? Before we try to answer these questions, let's consider in more detail what exactly Ryle is saying. According to Ryle, the difference between an intelligent action and an unintelligent one is not the fact that the one is accompanied by rational thought and the other is not, but a difference in the quality of the two acts, a quality which can be detected by most experienced observers. He resents the traditional philosopher's bias in thinking of intelligence as possession of theoretical knowledge, and he opposes the Greek view of the intelligent man as one in whom reason is in control of wild and chaotic passions and appetites.

Ryle reacts to the intellectualist bias which is still present today. Many people think of learning and education as the accumulation of information, rather than as the application and use of information. Ryle contends that theorizing itself is an activity which can be done either intelligently or unintelligently. If we think of intelligent activity as presupposing the mental act of theorizing, and we agree that theorizing is itself an activity, then we find ourselves in an infinite regress, for in order to act intelligently we must theorize and theorizing is itself an activity which can be done intelligently or unintelligently; if it is done intelligently, then according to the traditional view, it must be preceded by a second bit of theorizing, but this too must be done intelligently, which presupposes another bit of theorizing, and so on to infinity. Reasoning, thinking, and theorizing are not the causes of intelligent activity but are themselves human activities which can be done either intelligently or unintelligently.

Ryle further points out that intelligent practice need not be preceded by theorizing. There are times when in a good, animated discussion we may talk well, put forth sound arguments, and make valid objections to another's view, seemingly off the top of our heads and without first analyzing what we say. Secondly, Ryle shows that theorizing, where it is involved, will not always result in intelligent activity because the theorizing could very well be done stupidly. Thirdly, he argues that to patch up this last difficulty by postulating that in intelligent action the theorizing must be performed well, only leads to the infinite regress mentioned above.

In Ryle's positive account, intelligent action entails applying criteria or rules in a self-critical, self-correcting way which constantly improves on its own mistakes. There are two ways of following a rule which Ryle says are *not* intelligent. The first is explicitly, consciously thinking of the rule and then applying it mechanically. This is what we do when we are first learning how to cook or play tennis, but no one would describe these awkward beginnings as the intelligent application of the rules. The rules for playing tennis don't cover every situation; they don't tell you what to do in every emergency, and the person who simply memorizes the rules and applies them verbatim will be at a loss when some novel situation turns up for which no rule or interpretation has been given. The second sort of unintelligent observance of rules comes later when the person has played tennis or whatever so much that the rules have become second nature to him. When a person starts driving a car, at first he may memorize certain rules, but after he has driven a great deal, all these rules become habitual. When he sees a car approaching an intersection ahead he does not say to himself, "The rule says always yield to the car to reach the intersection first, this car will get there before me, therefore I will yield to him," before he begins to slow down. He sees the car out of the corner of his eye and without any deliberation or thought, he slows down. This makes for competent, average driving, but it does not produce a really skilled driver because habitual driving tends to be careless. Such a driver is driving automatically, scarcely thinking about what he is doing; he is talking, listening to the radio, and applying little attention to his driving. He can drive competently without devoting much of his attention to it because his observance of the rules has become "second nature." If some unusual situation comes up—if an animal were suddenly to run in front of his car—he is more likely to hit the animal than is the driver who is paying attention to what he is doing. Skilled or intelligent action is not merely habitual behavior; it is self-correcting, critical behavior which practice has made largely habitual but not entirely so. In such behavior there is room for imaginative deviation when the occasion demands and for constant revision and correction of the habitual pattern itself.

Ryle's attitude toward intelligence resembles that of the twentieth-century American philosopher John Dewey (1859–1952), writing some twenty or thirty years earlier. Dewey also held that intelligent action was self-correcting habit, which he analyzed as the product of two opposed but complementary ingredients: "habit" and "impulse." When habit is at work, the rules of action have become so much a part of one's whole person that there is no need for conscious, explicit thinking or theorizing. Conscious thought is awakened as soon as some problem or hitch arises, and this is where "impulse" comes in. If you are walking down a country lane, you are not thinking along the way, "Right, now first I lift the left foot and then swing forward on the right leg; now put the left foot down; so far so good; now I lift the right foot," and so on. No, the action is purely mechanical and habitual; there simply is no thinking or theorizing whatever about the walking itself. If you are thinking at all, you may be thinking about an essay you have to write the following Monday or about the party Saturday night. If we do become self-conscious of our walking, as we might when walking across the stage during graduation to receive our degree, the action generally becomes awkward and inept. As an anonymous poet put it,

> A centipede was happy quite,
> Until a frog in fun
> Said, "Pray, which leg comes after which?"
> This raised her mind to such a pitch,
> She lay distracted in a ditch
> Considering how to run!

But now, to add some drama to our story, suppose that there is a poisonous snake right in the middle of the road ahead. If your walking is too mechanical and absent-minded, you may not live to tell the tale. But if you are acting intelligently and paying attention to what you are doing, you will see the snake, realize the danger, and very rapidly bring to an end the absent-minded revery about the party or whatever. You are fully awakened to the situation—the problem of getting past the snake without getting bitten. This is precisely where conscious thought and theorizing come to play. You could wait for the snake to slither off the road, or attack it with stones, or walk around it. Having weighed the various alternatives, you might try the one you consider best, keeping constantly in mind your desire to get past the snake maintaining your own safety in doing so. Once you are safely past the snake and have proceeded some distance, your walking slips back into its mechanical mode. Of course, if you're walking along a rough mountain path, or mountain climbing, you are jogged out of the habitual, thoughtless routine more frequently —here is an overhanging branch, there a large stone, here the path branches in two directions, and so on.

Basically, then, intelligent action is habit which is self-correcting, following rules in an imaginative rather than blind, mechanical manner. Ryle points out that in many cases we do not start off by memorizing the rules; in some cases we simply learn by doing, and this kind of action can be just as intelligent as that in which the person begins by memorizing and repeating the rules. In learning to fish or cook, for example, you might prefer to watch an experienced person in the field rather than read a book on it. After watching and practicing, the principles become "second nature" without your having consciously learned and memorized the rules. If someone asks you for a list of rules for catching fish or for cooking a particular dish, you may find yourself quite unable to put into words the principles you are obviously quite skilled in applying. This is the kind of situation in which we may feel like saying, "Look, let me just show you." A good example would be learning how to tie knots, a notoriously difficult thing to explain.

In other cases we are able to reduce our skill to rules, but this comes after we are already skilled in the art of cooking or fishing or whatever. The point is, we do not need these thought-out rules for the skillful, intelligent performance of the activity. You would need them if you were asked to write a book on cooking or to appear on radio and explain how to cook your speciality. An occasion such as this requires the ability to put practical knowledge into words, but you don't need this in order to cook. The art of putting things into words is itself a practical matter. Some people are just no good at putting things into words, and yet they may be highly intelligent and spend a great deal of time thinking and theorizing about things. A person may think a great deal about physics, for example, and be utterly lacking in the art of getting the subject across to beginning university students. Again, that this is primarily a practical affair is shown by the fact that it can be improved by practice. Experienced teachers are often better than inexperienced ones not because they engage in more theorizing, but because they have had more practice and self-correcting experience in trying to communicate ideas to students. It is possible for someone to be good at getting ideas across to students in a live classroom situation and yet be an utter bore doing the same thing on television (or vice versa), because good television performance is a different sort of skill or knack than teaching, a different kind of practical knowledge.

Ryle does not deny that we sometimes plan a course of action before we engage in it; but he denies that this always happens and contends that even when it does occur the planning is a practical activity which can be done either intelligently or unintelligently. Neither does Ryle deny that we do sometimes think silently to ourselves; what he denies is that this is required for intelligent action and will automatically produce it. Ryle's main objection is to the intellectualist's legend which makes intelligence exclusively the product of mental events and never, except indirectly, of bodily behavior. Ryle does not identify intelligent action with mere behavior. Human action is behavior which is understood in terms of motives and trained dispositions to respond in regular controlled ways. This is what enables us to distinguish between lucky accidents and skilled activity. The same move in a game of chess, for example, can be the result of a brilliant play or a lucky guess. The intellectualist legend which Ryle opposes assumes that the intelligent action was preceded by a bit of theorizing while the guess was not. Ryle answers that we judge the one to be intelligent behavior because we know it was the product of intelligent application of rules, the result of a long-standing, self-correcting habit or disposition to play chess well. If we know that Jones has played intelligent chess for years, then we say the move was intelligent since it proceeded from Jones's long-standing disposition to play good chess. If the same move was made by a child of three and a half who had never seen a chess board before and who immediately thereafter proceeded to eat the rook he had just moved, we would say that was *not* an intelligent piece of chess-playing (nor indeed a piece of chess-playing at all), but simply a coincidence. It is not the mere behavior which is said to be intelligent, but only that behavior which is understood to result from the intelligent application of rules, that is, the expression of a stable disposition to play chess well.

If the intellectualist legend, that is, the traditional account of practical knowledge, is mistaken, why have so many otherwise intelligent people believed it? Ryle suggests that the traditional view is based on a misunderstanding of the fact that people can talk and read silently to themselves, which has exaggerated the place and value of such activity in guiding or directing other sorts of activities, like cooking, fishing, driving and so on. Dewey offers a much fuller account of what some of these reasons might be. He emphasizes the Greek bias in favor of intellectual pursuits and activities. Both Plato and Aristotle thought that sitting quietly and contemplating silently within oneself was the noblest and best sort of human activity possible. The Greeks had slaves to do most of their heavy manual work, so they developed a scorn for all menial physical labor. When they came to think about practical activity, they felt that if this was to be intelligent, it could only be intelligent because it shared in the contemplative, intellectual life of theorizing, and so they developed the notion of practical knowledge as a bit of theory and then a bit of practice. The irony of this, according to Dewey, is that this contemplative life was only possible because of the high level of Greek technology! Thus Dewey, like Ryle, thinks the Greeks, or at least the Greek philosophers, put the cart before the horse.

A shift in our concept of practical knowledge would have a marked effect on our educational practices. We would move away from the idea of knowledge as the retention of information (after all, this is what encyclopedias are for) and begin to develop the notion of knowledge as the ability to deal with problems in a skillful and intelligent way. We would encourage students to *do* some history, to *perform* some literary criticism, to *construct* arguments, to *become* critical and analytical.

CONCLUSION

Admittedly, the history of epistemology has been a rough road of frequent detours and occasional false starts. Yet on balance some valuable contributions have been made toward clarifying the troubling relationships among knowledge, belief, evidence, sense experience, and certainty. Although debate on these matters continues, and is in fact one of the liveliest sources of philosophical thought today, there is considerable agreement on the main contributions from the past: that the originating source of an idea cannot guarantee its validity; that the importance of empirical evidence is not so much as a fountain of ideas but as a means of testing and confirming ideas; that information-gathering, to be fruitful, must be guided by leading questions, or hypotheses; that the goal of an absolutely certain science (synthetic a priori) is an impossible ideal—and a rather worthless one at that; that the difference between knowledge and belief turns on evidence rather than certainty; and that the theory/practice distinction must be redrawn to allow the importance of practice in theoretical activity.

TOPICS FOR DISCUSSION

1. Can you know something you are not completely sure of?
2. Many experiments of the kind suggested by Locke on "sensory deprivation" have actually been performed in recent years (see Hunt and Solomon in "Selected Bibliography"). What conclusions can be drawn from these experiments and what is their philosophical significance, if any?
3. How does the certainty criterion of knowledge lead to scepticism?
4. Examine the literary influence of Plato's theory of reincarnation on writers such as Wordsworth ("Lines above Tintern Abbey" and "Immortality Ode") and Thomas Mann (see "Selected Bibliography").
5. What is the philosophical import, if any, of the contemporary "nature-nurture" debate in psychology (see Piaget, Chomsky, and Jensen vs. Skinner and Pettigrew in "Selected Bibliography")?
6. How can we tell the difference between waking and dreaming?
7. Compare Freud and Plato on the need to control the passions. To what do you attribute this pervasive uptightness?

SELECTED BIBLIOGRAPHY

Primary Source

Aristotle. *Posterior Analytics.* Translated by G. R. Mure. In *The Basic Works of Aristotle,* edited by Richard McKeon. New York: Random House, 1941.

Austin, J. L. "Other Minds." 1946. In *Philosophical Papers.* Oxford: Clarendon Press, 1961.

Chomsky, Noam. *For Reasons of State.* New York: Pantheon, 1973.

Descartes, René. *Meditations on First Philosophy.* 1641. In *Descartes Selections,* edited by Ralph Eaton. New York: Scribner's, 1927.

Dewey, John. *Human Nature and Conduct*. New York: Random House, 1922.
Freud, Sigmund. *Civilization and Its Discontents*. 1930. Translated by James Strachey. New York: Norton, 1962.
Hume, David. *An Inquiry Concerning Human Understanding*. 1748. New York: Liberal Arts Press, 1955.
Jensen, Arthur. *Genetics and Education*. London: Methuen, 1972.
Kant, Immanuel. *Critique of Pure Reason*. 1781. Translated by Norman Kemp Smith. London: Macmillan, 1958.
Locke, John. *An Essay Concerning Human Understanding*. 1690. New York: Dutton, 1948.
Mann, Thomas. *Death in Venice*. 1924. Translated by Kenneth Burke. New York: Alfred A. Knopf, 1965.
Piaget, Jean. *Genetic Epistemology*. Translated by Eleanor Duckworth. New York: Columbia University Press, 1970.
———. *The Origins of Intelligence in Children*. Translated by Margaret Cook. New York: International Universities Press, 1969.
Plato. *Meno*. Translated by Benjamin Jowett. New York: Liberal Arts Press, 1949.
———. *Phaedo*. Translated by F. J. Church. New York: Liberal Arts Press, 1951.
———. *Phaedrus*. Translated by W. C. Helmbold and W. G. Rabinowitz. New York: Liberal Arts Press, 1956.
———. *Symposium*. Translated by Benjamin Jowett. New York: Liberal Arts Press, 1956.
Ryle, Gilbert. *The Concept of Mind*. New York: Barnes and Noble, 1949.
Skinner, B. F. *Beyond Freedom and Dignity*. New York: Alfred A. Knopf, 1971.
———. *Walden Two*. New York: Macmillan, 1962.

Secondary Source

Armstrong, D. M. *Belief, Truth and Knowledge*. Cambridge: Cambridge University Press, 1973.
Aune, Bruce. *Knowledge, Mind and Nature*. New York: Random House, 1967.
Chisolm, Roderick, and Robert Swartz, eds. *Empirical Knowledge*. Englewood Cliffs, New Jersey: Prentice-Hall, 1973.
Danto, Arthur. *Analytical Philosophy of Knowledge*. Cambridge: Cambridge University Press, 1968.

Selected Bibliography

Griffiths, A. Phillips, ed. *Knowledge and Belief.* Oxford: Oxford University Press, 1967.

Hamlyn, D. W. *The Theory of Knowledge.* Garden City, New York: Doubleday, 1970.

Hunt, J. M. *Intelligence and Experience.* New York: Ronald Press, 1961.

Koffka, K. *The Growth of the Mind.* New York: Russell and Russell, 1962.

Pears, David. *What is Knowledge?* New York: Harper and Row, 1971.

Popper, Karl. *Objective Knowledge.* Oxford: Clarendon Press, 1972.

Solomon, Philip, et al. *Sensory Deprivation: A Symposium Held at Harvard Medical School.* Cambridge, Mass.: Harvard University Press, 1961.

Stroll, Avrum, ed. *Epistemology.* New York: Harper and Row, 1967.

CHAPTER 4

The Philosophy of Mind

WHAT IS THE PHILOSOPHY OF MIND?

The philosophy of mind dates back to the very beginnings of philosophy. Both Plato (427–347 B.C.), in *Phaedo* and *The Republic*, and Aristotle (384–322 B.C.), in the *De Anima*, were greatly concerned with the issues and problems found in the philosophy of mind, and most philosophers since have had something to say on the topic. Modern philosophy of mind began in the seventeenth century with the philosopher René Descartes (1596–1650). In the twentieth century, no other area of philosophy has enjoyed more attention; hundreds of books, anthologies, and journal articles concentrate, at least in part, on the philosophy of mind.

The philosophy of mind or philosophical psychology, so-called because it deals philosophically with psychological issues and concepts, is that branch of philosophy which is concerned almost exclusively with certain theories of mind. Most people have wondered, at one time or another in their lives, whether or not there are souls or minds, and if there are souls or minds, what they look like, where they are located, and so forth. There are, of course, basically two views about souls or minds: (1) that they exist and (2) that they do not exist. The first view is usually coupled with the view that bodies also exist and is called *dualism* because it claims that two kinds of things exist, minds and bodies. The second view is called *monism*, for it maintains that only one kind of thing exists, namely bodies. When a person claims that souls go to heaven after the body dies or that thinking goes on in the mind, he is taking a dualistic position. Doctors, dentists, and physiological psychologists, on the other hand, often take monistic positions when they argue that pain goes on in the brain or is a brain process. These are the kinds of issues brought out by the debate over whether or not there are souls or minds, and this debate is the central concern in the philosophy of mind.

The two main problems of the philosophy of mind are (1) the mind-body problem and (2) the problem of other minds. Most of the other problems which concern philosophers of mind spring directly from these. The mind-body problem is the problem of just how minds and bodies can interact. If they are two different entities, one mental and one physical, how can there be causal interaction between them? The problem of other minds is the problem of how we can come to know other minds or indeed whether other minds exist at all. From the dualist's argument that minds are different from bodies and empirically unobservable, the problem arises as to how we can know what is going on in the mind of another person, or whether another person has a mind at all. More specifically, how can we know that another person is in pain or is thinking? This problem gives rise to a view called *solipsism*: "I know only of my own experiences, i.e., my own pains and thoughts, and I can never know the experiences of another." Thus, in this view, other persons might not have minds at all, or if they do I cannot know that they do. The dualist seems to have greater difficulty solving these problems than does the monist, for when he argues that minds exist, he must then show how minds are related to bodies and how the minds of others can be known. The monist, on the other hand, might simply argue that these problems are not really problems for there are no minds, just bodies.

An understanding of the philosophy of mind involves an understanding of certain key psychological concepts, such as "thinking," "understanding," and "sensation." The explanation of these concepts given by a dualist will differ greatly from that given by a monist. The dualist might argue that "thinking" is an event which goes on in the mind. The monist, on the other hand, cannot argue this and be consistent with his view. The monist must argue that thinking is a brain process, or a bit of behavior.

Theories of mind can be looked at from the point of view of how they approach and attempt to solve the mind-body problem and the problem of other minds. Dualism, especially Descartes' dualism, seems to have given rise to the problems. The various monistic theories such as materialism and behaviorism, and even the expression theory and the criteriological view which are not monistic, have been expounded in order to solve the problems or at least to get rid of them. Theories in the philosophy of mind stand or fall according to how well they handle the two central problems discussed above. In what follows we will spend more time discussing materialism than any of the other theories because materialism seems to have emerged as the most important alternative to dualism.

DUALISM

There are many different kinds of dualism. They all have in common the fact that they posit a universe in which there exist at least two different kinds of entities or substances: mental and physical. All dualists claim that there are both minds and bodies, mental entities and events and physical entities and events, in the universe. The problem is in showing just how these two sets of entities and events are related. To explain this relationship some special kind of law must be invoked, a psychophysical law.

There are at least three kinds of dualism which have been widely discussed in both philosophy and psychology: (1) interactionism, (2) parallelism, and (3) epiphenomenalism. Each of these theories can be characterized in terms of how it handles the problem of mind-body interaction. By far the most important of these theories is interactionism; it is the most widely discussed in the philosophy of mind, and it is the theory against which many other theories of mind have been written.

Parallelism is the theory that there are two corresponding sets of entities, mental and physical, but that there is no causal interaction between the mental and the physical. This theory in a limited way does solve the mind-body problem, but it does not solve the problem or in any way account for the existence of other minds. *Epiphenomenalism* is the theory that minds and bodies are causally related but the causality is only one-way: bodies can causally affect minds but minds cannot affect bodies. But this theory does not solve the mind-body problem, for it claims that minds are merely epi-phenomena, fleeting offshoots of the body. The question of how we can come to know the minds of others is also not answered by this theory. *Interactionism*, the form of dualism espoused by Descartes, is the theory that minds and bodies are causally related and that the causal relation is two-way—minds can affect bodies and bodies can affect minds. It is the most widely expounded form of dualism and the form of dualism most often linked with the mind-body problem and the problem of other minds.

Descartes' Proofs

Descartes claims that minds and bodies are two very different kinds of entities or substances. Minds are indivisible, unextended or thinking, and incorporeal substances. Bodies are divisible, extended or unthinking, and corporeal substances. Thus, the properties which can be predicated of minds cannot be predicated of bodies, and conversely, those which can be predicated of bodies cannot be predicated of minds.

Descartes gives at least three arguments which purport to prove that mind and body are distinct and that the mind is the essence of human beings.

> Argument from ignorance
>> I know that thinking belongs to my essence.
>> I know of nothing else that does.
>> Therefore, only thinking belongs to my essence.
>
> Argument from doubt
>> I can doubt that I have a body.
>> I cannot doubt that I have a mind.
>> Therefore, I am not a body.
>
> Argument from the indivisibility of mind
>> My mind is indivisible.
>> My body is divisible.
>> Therefore, my mind and body are distinct and separate.

All of the arguments above claim to show that properties are not held in common by both minds and bodies. Bodies are the kind of entity whose existence can be doubted, minds are not; bodies are divisible, minds are not; and bodies are not thinking substances, minds are. But, as we shall see, each of these arguments is deceptive and misleading. By substituting different premises and setting up the arguments in the same manner, we can see that Descartes' reasoning is faulty.

> Argument from ignorance
>> I know that "appears in the morning" belongs to the essence of the Morning Star.
>> I know of nothing else that does.
>> Therefore, only "appears in the morning" belongs to the essence of the Morning Star.

Argument from doubt
 I can doubt that Shakespeare is the author of *Hamlet*.
 I cannot doubt that Shakespeare existed.
 Therefore, Shakespeare is not the author of *Hamlet*.
Argument from the indivisibility of mind
 The Morning Star appears in the morning.
 The Evening Star appears in the evening.
 Therefore, the Morning Star and the Evening Star are distinct and separate.

That each of these arguments is fallacious is obvious. In the argument from ignorance, it is obvious that it does not follow from the fact that "appears in the morning" belongs to the essence of the Morning Star and we do not know of anything else that does this, that nothing else does. The same holds true for Descartes argument; it does not follow from the fact that a certain person *knows* only of one property belonging to his essense that only one property does. It may be the case that this person is ignorant: the Morning Star might very well also appear in the evening, as in fact it does. The next two arguments are fallacious for much the same reasons. In the argument from doubt, it does not follow from the fact that I can *doubt* that Shakespeare is the author of *Hamlet* that Shakespeare is not the author of *Hamlet*. In the argument from the indivisibility of mind, it does not follow from the fact that the Morning Star appears in the morning and the Evening Star appears in the evening that the Morning Star and the Evening Star are distinct and separate. They are, indeed, identical. In all these proofs, the arguments are faulty because the conclusions do not logically follow from the premises. Descartes' arguments are invalid; while the conclusions might be true, his analysis of them does not *prove* them to be so. Thus, Descartes does not seem to argue well that minds and bodies are distinct and that thinking is the essence of human beings.

Cogito, Ergo Sum

In his *Discourse on Method* (1637), Descartes sets forth another argument which is summed up in the Latin phrase *Cogito, ergo sum*, "I think, therefore I am." Does he argue well for this position? At first glance, Descartes seems to be giving a straightforward inferential argument: he passes from one statement, considered as true, to another whose truth is believed to follow from that of the former. For Descartes, it follows from the fact that "I think" that "I am." This interpretation is strengthened by the *ergo* ("therefore") in *Cogito, ergo sum*. But there are several difficulties with this interpretation. First of all, if the argument is inferential, it does not *prove* the truth of the statement "I am" and it is just an argument that existence is a necessary condition for thinking. If this is the case, then the formula *Ambulo, ergo sum* ("I walk, therefore I am") also works, for existence is also a necessary condition for walking. In other words, if the argument is inferential, then "cogito" does not seem to have any special status. Further, it might be argued that thinking does not necessarily imply existence. If this were true, we might argue that Hamlet thinks even though he does not exist.

It is better to look at Descartes' *Cogito, ergo sum* as a performance (the act of uttering or thinking) and not as an inference. This view seems to be the most widely held interpretation at present. Descartes says in the *Meditations* that "I am, I exist, is necessarily true every time that I pronounce it or conceive it in my mind."[1] The role of the "cogito," the pronouncing or conceiving, is to show that "I exist" is a self-verifying statement; each time it is pronounced or conceived or thought by the individual referred to by "I," the individual is confirming his existence. "I do not exist," on the other hand, would be self-defeating if it were uttered or thought by the individual referred to by "I." The "cogito" in *Cogito, ergo sum* indicates that the act of pronouncing or thinking "I exist" verifies that I do, indeed, exist. This interpretation avoids the pitfalls of the inferential argument. "Cogito" holds a very special position that cannot be filled with "ambulo" or anything like it.

Even though Descartes' proofs for the distinction between mind and body and the claim that thinking is the essence of human beings (summed up in his formula *Sum res cogitans*) do not hold up under scrutiny, his formula *Cogito, ergo sum* does if it is given a certain interpretation, namely the performative one. Both *Sum res cogitans* and *Cogito, ergo sum* are entirely independent of dualism and are consistent with monistic positions such as materialism and behaviorism as long as thinking is not

---

1. René Descartes, *Discourse on Method and Meditations,* trans. Laurence J. Lafleur (New York: Bobbs-Merrill, 1960), p. 82.

interpreted as a mental activity. Only the distinction between mind and body does indeed imply dualism.

In the development and proof of the dualistic theory that minds and bodies are distinct and separate, the mind-body problem and the problem of other minds naturally arise. If minds and bodies are, as Descartes maintained, two very different kinds of substances, the problem then is to explain just how they can interact with one another—how mental and physical events can causally affect one another. Descartes' explanation of this causal interaction is that the mind is closely linked with the brain and, in fact, receives its impressions from the brain through the pineal gland. This will not do because the pineal gland itself is just another part of the body, namely the brain. This ploy just begs the question. Descartes seems to be left with no adequate way to explain the relationship between minds and bodies.

The Argument from Analogy

The distinction between minds and bodies also gives rise to the problem of other minds. Only bodies, behavior, and so on can be observed, minds cannot. And if minds cannot be observed, how can we know what goes on in other minds? In answer to this question dualists generally maintain that we can know what goes on in another person's mind by inference. The argument that is given by the dualists has come to be called the *argument from analogy*. An analogy is made between one's own mental experiences and behavior and the mental experiences and behavior of another person. It goes something like this. I can know what goes on in my mind when I behave in a certain way, i.e., I have direct access to my own mental experiences. But I do not have such access to another's mental goings-on; my access is, at best, indirect. Therefore, I can only *infer* that what is going on in the mind of another is *like* what goes on in my mind when that person is behaving in ways similar to my behavior. The great fault with this argument is that the inference is made on the grounds of only one case, my own, and this is not enough to justify the conclusion that what is going on in another person's mind is similar to what is going on in my mind. This inference would work only if the relation between another person's behavior and mental experiences were similar to the relation between my behavior and mental experiences, but this is just what needs to be determined. If this is the case, then Descartes and possibly any dualist seem to be left with a solipsistic position that a person can know only what goes on in his own mind.

MATERIALISM

Materialism has been expounded as a way to solve or get rid of the mind-body problem and the problem of other minds. In direct opposition to dualism, it claims that nothing exists in the universe except physical entities. Materialism actually is just one part of a larger theory of mind, the identity theory, which holds that conscious experiences, such as sensations and after-images, are brain processes.

Smart and the Identity Theory

One of the leading exponents of the identity theory is the contemporary philosopher J. J. C. Smart. His version of the identity theory, which can be called the translation form, attempts to translate statements about conscious experience into neutral statements (whereas another version, the so-called disappearance form, attempts to show that such statements might better be allowed to disappear from ordinary language). Smart's version of the identity theory makes at least the following three claims: (1) "conscious experience" is a report of certain inner goings-on; (2) "conscious experience" does not have the same meaning as "brain process"; and (3) conscious experiences are nothing over and above brain processes.[2] The first claim requires us to accept reports of conscious experiences—after-images or pains—as genuine reports, but there has been some controversy over this claim. Smart disputes the view that statements such as "I am having an after-image" or "I am having a pain" are not reports. He calls such expressions *open reports*. When a person reports such an experience, he is reporting that something is going on in him but he leaves it open as to just what it is that is going on. The report

---

2. J. J. C. Smart, "Sensations and Brain Processes," in *The Philosophy of Mind*, ed. V. C. Chappell (Englewood Cliffs, N.J.: Prentice-Hall, 1962), pp. 162–172.

that I am having an after-image or pain, in and of itself, does not commit me to any specific kind of goings-on. What is going on in me may be either physical or mental.

Further, Smart claims, "When a person says, 'I see a yellowish-orange after-image,' he is saying something like this: 'There is something going on in me which is like what is going on in me when I have my eyes open, am awake, and there is an orange illuminated in good light in front of me, that is, when I really see an orange.' "[3] The same would also hold for pain. When a person says, "I am in pain," he is saying something like the following: "There is something going on in me which is like what goes on in me when a pin is stuck in me." The point of this analysis is that reports of conscious experiences are *topic-neutral* —they report likenesses of what is going on in me, they do not report exactly what is going on in me. If they did, they would not be topic-neutral or open.

Thus, reports of conscious experience, according to Smart, even though they are genuine reports of inner goings-on, report only likenesses, or lack of likenesses, between these inner goings-on. It is just this report of likeness, the "What is going on in me is like what goes on in me when . . . ," which is, in effect, the translation of a report of conscious experience. The report is open or topic-neutral because it is only a report of likeness and because it does not indicate what it is that is being reported, that is, either a mental or physical something.

The second claim that "conscious experience" does not have the same meaning as or is not synonymous with "brain process" is closely related to two other claims: (1) conscious-experience statements cannot be translated into brain-process statements, and (2) the logic of conscious-experience statements is not the same as that of brain-process statements. For Smart, these three claims amount to the same thing: a statement such as "I am in pain" cannot be translated into and does not have the same logic as "My C-fibers are firing."

Now what does saying that "conscious experience" and "brain process" are not synonymous come to for Smart? For one thing it means that one can report pain, for example, without knowing that what one is reporting is really a brain process. A man may be acquainted with Sir Walter Scott and know him as the author of *Ivanhoe*, but not know him as the author of

---

3. Ibid.

Waverley. Yet it is the case that the author of *Waverley* and the author of *Ivanhoe* are identical. It is possible, then, for one to report pain without knowing that what one is reporting is a brain process in the same way that one can know Scott as the author of *Ivanhoe* without knowing him as the author of *Waverley*. All that this comes to is one thing: "There can be contingent statements of the form 'A is identical with B,' and a person may know that something is an A without knowing it is a B."[4]

Secondly, saying that "pain" does not mean the same as "brain process" for Smart means that pain may be characterized as having different properties or may be described differently than brain processes. For example, the Morning Star may be characterized by "appears in the morning," while the Evening Star may be characterized by "appears in the evening." Similarly, we do not characterize conscious experience as being swift or slow, yet brain processes may be swift or slow. But, according to Smart, this does not block the identity of the Morning Star and the Evening Star or conscious experiences and brain processes.

The whole point of making this second claim, for Smart, is to show that even though two words have different meanings, they may very well refer to the same thing or process. Thus, conscious experiences may be brain processes, not because "pain" is synonymous with "brain process," but because "pain" and "brain process" may refer to the same event. "Pain" and "brain process" may have the same referent even though they have a different sense.

The third claim that sensations are nothing over and above brain processes is Smart's form of materialism. He says that "by 'materialism,' I mean the theory that there is nothing in the world over and above those entities which are postulated by physics (or, of course, those entities which will be postulated by future and more adequate physical theories)."[5] In other words, materialism is the theory that the ultimate entities of physics make up the universe. Materialism is concerned only with these entities and the laws which govern them.

This third claim seems to allow no explanation of psychological concepts other than the brain-process theory, that is, the identity theory. Not only are the conscious experiences men-

---

4. Ibid.
5. J. J. C. Smart, "Materialism," *Journal of Philosophy* 60, no. 22 (October 1963): 659.

tioned earlier brain states, but by this explanation so are all psychological concepts such as thinking and understanding. Smart claims that all sensations are nothing over and above brain processes. His purpose in making this claim is "to deny that in the world, there are nonphysical entities ... In particular I wish to deny the doctrine of psychophysical dualism."[6] Smart, then, wishes to deny the existence of those entities whose existence dualists like Descartes wish to affirm. In other words, Smart wishes to deny the existence of mental entities. Along with this, he also denies the existence of mental properties and psychophysical laws. For Smart, after-images, pains, and the like do not, in effect, exist. What does exist is the conscious experience of having after-images, pains, and the like. If this is the case, then there are no mental properties, that is, there are no properties of after-images, pains, and so on, and no psychophysical laws needed to explain nonphysical entities and properties.

Smart denies the existence of nonphysical entities and properties because these are what have come to be called *nomological danglers*, nonphysical leftovers which do not fit within a scientific framework. In short, Smart denies the existence of those "spooks" and "ghosts" which have plagued philosophers for so long. If he is successful, then he has done philosophy a great service, for no discipline wants to be left with concepts or entities which are difficult or impossible to explain.

Why does Smart prefer materialism, which denies the existence of nonphysical entities, properties, and laws, over dualism, which affirms them? Materialism has two main advantages over dualism: (1) materialism tells us how things really are and (2) it does so in a concise and systematic manner.

Materialism tells us that the world is made up entirely of the ultimate entities of physics and does not contain any unexplainable "spooks" and "ghosts." Smart suggests that "it may be the true nature of our inner experiences, as revealed by science, to be brain processes, just as to be a motion of electric charges is the true nature of lightning, what lightning really is."[7] Science can reveal the true nature of anything and everything included in the materialists' world because everything in that world is a physical entity of one sort or another. Since materialism says that only

---

6. Ibid., p. 652.
7. J. J. C. Smart, *Philosophy and Scientific Realism* (London: Routledge & Kegan Paul, 1963), p. 93.

physical entities exist and since science can explain all these, Smart argued that materialism is superior to dualism. Materialism is the key to clarity in explaining how the world is. Dualism takes second place at best because it claims that some entites and properties are not physical. Thus, if dualism were to hold, science could not explain some of the things existing in the world.

Materialism is also preferable because it is more concise and systematic than dualism. Materialism has a world view which is vastly simpler than that of dualism; materialism does not have to contend with "nomological danglers" or with the psychophysical laws needed to explain them. Materialism has only one kind of entity and law to contend with, dualism has two.

The three claims which we have been discussing are those which according to Smart make up the identity theory. Smart's identity theory can be summarized as follows. Conscious experiences are brain processes, even though "conscious experience" and "brain process" are not synonymous, because a report of a conscious experience is a report of certain inner goings-on, or at least of likenesses to them. These inner goings-on could be either mental or physical because reports of conscious experiences are themselves neutral between the two possibilities. But there is good reason to argue that what is reported is really physical (that is, a brain process): a world with only physical entities can be explained by science in a more concise way than a world with physical entities and laws plus mental entities and psychophysical laws. Conscious experiences are really nothing over and above brain processes.

In effect, what Smart has argued for in his identity theory is a metaphysical world view which attempts to bring all intellectual disciplines into a harmonious relationship with the sciences. Science, its objects and its language, are the models for all other intellectual disciplines. With this materialistic world view everything can, at least theoretically, be accounted for; those things for which there is no scientific explanation are dismissed.

Objections to Smart's Theory

Many objections have been raised against Smart's identity theory, and much can be learned about the identity theory by looking at some of the criticisms of it. The objections to this theory may be categorized in several ways. When the criterion for classification is the kind of reply that Smart gives to the objection, there are three main categories: (1) those objections to which Smart replies that "conscious experience" and "brain process" are not synonymous; (2) those to which he replies that reports of conscious experiences are topic-neutral; and (3) the objection to which he replies that it is the experience of an after-image, for example, which is the brain process, not the after-image itself. These objections might also be categorized as (1) the objections which play on the difference in meaning of "conscious experience" and "brain process"; (2) the objections which insist that conscious experiences and brain processes have different properties; and (3) the objection which insists that after-images are not brain processes.

Smart himself raises one of the first-category objections: "Aristotle, or for that matter an illiterate peasant, can report his images and aches and pains, and yet nevertheless may not know that the brain has anything to do with thinking . . . therefore what Aristotle or the peasant reports cannot be a brain process . . ."[8] According to this objection, since an illiterate peasant may report that he is in pain and yet know nothing of the brain or brain physiology, pain cannot be a brain process. The same holds for Aristotle who thought that the function of the brain was to cool the blood. If this argument is true, then conscious experiences cannot be brain processes.

In defense Smart argues that Aristotle or the peasant may know about pains and not brain processes precisely because "pain" and "brain process" do not have the same meaning. The same is true of the Morning Star and the Evening Star: they, too, do not have the same meaning. This does not prove, though, that pains are not brain processes or that the Morning Star and the Evening Star are not identical.

The second category of objections is that to which Smart replies that reports of conscious experience are topic-neutral. This category has by far the most objections in it and has been the most important.

The contemporary philosopher J. T. Stevenson begins his objection by trying to arrive at what Smart could mean by "strict identity." If two things are identical, then they must have the same properties. Thus, if sensations are identical to brain pro-

---

8. Ibid., p. 92.

cesses, then both must have the same properties. Stevenson argues that they do not have the same properties.

If Smart claims that (1) "sensation" is not synonymous with "brain process" and that (2) sensations are strictly identical with brain processes, and it seems clear that he does, then he has "not got rid of the danglers" according to Stevenson "for sensations were nomological danglers in virtue of certain properties which they had, and we have in no way eliminated these properties."[9] The properties of sensations, which Stevenson calls P-properties, dangle precisely because they cannot be defined or redefined in terms of materialistic properties, which Stevenson calls M-properties. That is, "sensation" is not synonymous with "brain process," #1 above.

Further, and this is a nice twist on Stevenson's part, not only are sensations still danglers, but brain processes must dangle too because sensations are strictly identical with brain processes, #2 above. Thus, the properties which make sensations dangle also make brain processes dangle.

There is another objection in this second category of objections which centers on the controversy of whether conscious experiences are public or private. It is argued that conscious experiences are private while brain processes are public and thus that the two cannot be identical. Kurt Baier argues this point in the following way. When, for example, I say that "I have a pain," I am reporting something private in the sense that my report is about something which is necessarily owned in that it is had by someone; necessarily exclusive or unsharable in that it is my pain, not yours, though you may have one like it; necessarily imperceptible by the senses in that it cannot be seen, heard, tasted, and so on by anyone else; and necessarily asymmetrical in that it makes sense to say "I could see (or hear) that he had a pain," but not "I could see (or hear) that I had a pain."

Further, according to Baier, when I report that I have a pain, what I am reporting is private in that I have the final epistemological authority over what I am reporting for it does not make sense to say "I have a pain unless I am mistaken." Having a pain is not the kind of thing about which I can normally be mistaken, though Baier admits that perhaps it is misleading to speak of first-

9. J. T. Stevenson, "Sensations and Brain Processes: a Reply to J. J. C. Smart," *Philosophical Review* 69 (1960): 506.

person sensation reports as incorrigible, for mistakes regarding sensations may be made. An individual has the final epistemological authority over those matters where he is "the person necessarily in the best position to discover his mistake or to confirm his belief . . ."[10] For example, other people can come to know that I have barbed wire in my foot in the same manner that I do, namely by looking at my foot; in this case, I do not have the final epistemological authority because others might be in just as good a position as I am to know and prove to me that I have barbed wire in my foot. But no one can prove to me that I am in pain. Here I have the final epistemological authority. Asymmetry occurs only where there is final epistemological authority, where the individual has a way of coming to know not open to others.

When someone says "I am in pain," that person is reporting something private in the above sense of private, according to Baier. This person has the final epistemological authority for it would make no sense to say to this person "But surely you are mistaken"; this person is necessarily in the best position to confirm or disconfirm his own report. Further, no amount of physiological evidence could convince this person that he is not really in pain. For example, if a person who is reporting pain is hooked up to an electroencephalograph and then told that he cannot be in pain because the machine does not register the proper brain process, he will not, of course, be convinced that he is not in pain. It does not matter what physiological responses the machine registers, for none of these responses can convince us either that we are or are not in pain.

From the foregoing, Baier claims, it is quite evident that brain processes are different from conscious experiences. Reports of brain processes are not reports of something necessarily owned, imperceptible to the senses, or asymmetrical. Neither do I have the final epistemological authority over what I am reporting when I say "I have a brain process of sort X." Brain processes need not be owned by anyone; they are perceptible by the senses; it makes as much sense to say "I could see that I was having a brain process of sort X" as it does to say "I could see that he was having a brain process of sort X"; and finally, I am not necessarily in a better position to know what is going on in my brain than you are.

10. Kurt Baier, "Smart on Sensations," *Australasian Journal of Philosophy* 40 (1962): 59.

Introspective reports, then, reports of conscious experiences, are reports of something private whereas reports of brain processes are not, in the above sense of private. If this is the case, then according to Baier, conscious experiences cannot be brain processes.

Smart replies to the objections in this category by arguing to topic-neutrality. He replies to Stevenson's objection by denying that there are any P-properties. He does this on the grounds that sensation reports are open. That is, if reports of conscious experiences are neutral, then we need not admit that the properties of conscious experiences are P-properties. They might just as well be M-properties. It is hard to pin properties on what is reported until we know just what it is that is reported. If reports of conscious experiences are open, then the features or properties of what is reported are elusive.

Smart's reply to Baier's objection is that the situation envisaged by Baier, the electroencephalograph example, is a logical possibility. That is, it is logically possible that a person report pain and be correct when the machine does not register the proper brain process. Smart answers, "I do not think that any such situation would in fact occur. It should be recalled that I put forward the brain process thesis as a factual identification, not as a logically necessary one."[11] If such a situation did arise, Smart admits that he would have to give up his identity theory though, of course, he would not be logically compelled to.

In any event, Smart does not think that the incorrigibility of sensation reports as compared to the findings of physiology is a stumbling block to the identity theory, for the theory is that the identity of conscious experiences and brain processes is contingent, not logical. Further, Smart contends, it is precisely the neutrality of ordinary language reports of sensation which enables him to "explain the relative incorrigibility of sensation reports as compared with the findings of physiology."[12] Sensation reports are neutral between dualism and materialism, and so these reports are compatible with the physiological findings. Thus, Smart argues that he can admit that sensation reports are incorrigible and yet still hold that this is compatible with the findings of physiology

---

11. J. J. C. Smart, "Brain Processes and Incorrigibility: a Reply to Professor Baier," *Australasian Journal of Philosophy* 40 (1962): 68.
12. Ibid.

which are not, of course, incorrigible, just because sensation reports are neutral.

In other words, even though it might be argued, as Baier has argued, that reports of conscious experiences are, in some cases, incorrigible, the reports themselves, because they are neutral, are compatible with either incorrigibility or corrigibility. That is, the reports might be either incorrigible or corrigible. The reports are neutral between the two possibilities.

Moreover, since the reports of conscious experiences are neutral between dualism and materialism, they are also neutral in regards to the public-private controversy. The reports themselves do not commit us to viewing what is reported as public or private. They are open to either possibility.

According to Smart, the third and final category of objections results from a confusion between, for example, after-images and experiences of after-images. The objection is this: "The after-image is not in physical space. The brain process is. So the after-image is not a brain process."[13] In other words, after-images cannot be brain processes because after-images and brain processes have different properties.

Smart's reply to this objection is very simple: "I am not arguing that the after-image is a brain process, but that the experience of having an after-image is a brain process. It is the experience which is reported in the introspective report."[14] Thus, to say that an after-image cannot be a brain process, because the former is not in physical space while the latter is, is not an objection to the identity theory, according to Smart, for the identity theory does not claim that after-images are brain processes.

Whether or not Smart's replies to his critics are adequate is an interesting and difficult question to answer. This debate is still being waged among philosophers in papers, journal articles, and books; the debate is, as most philosophical debates, not an easy one to decide. I leave it to the reader to ponder his answer. In any event, materialism is one way of solving the traditional problems in the philosophy of mind. The mind-body problem is solved, in effect, by denying the existence of one of the poles involved in the problem, namely minds. Minds are danglers and are done away with by the materialist. The problem of other minds is also solved again by denying the existence of minds. One can know what is

---

13. Smart, "Sensations and Brain Processes," p. 168.
14. Ibid.

going on in another's "mind" because "minds" just are brains, and one can know what is going on in another's brain just as easily as one can know what is going on in one's own brain. Thus, both problems are solved by denying the existence of minds, and this existence is denied by arguing that minds are brains, that mental events are really physical events.

BEHAVIORISM

In his well-known book, *The Concept of Mind*, Gilbert Ryle presents his philosophy of mind in opposition to Descartes' dualism, which Ryle calls the official doctrine. Ryle has been called a behaviorist, and most likely is, though he would probably not admit to being one. Behaviorism, in its simplest form, is the theory that mental phenomena, conscious experiences, are just bits of behavior. For example, the simple behaviorist would claim that pain is just pain-behavior. This differs greatly from both dualism and materialism for the former would hold that pain is a mental event going on in the mind while the latter would hold that pain is a physical event going on in the brain. In any event, Ryle certainly is not a simple behaviorist who holds that mental phenomena are pieces and bits of behavior. Ryle's version of behaviorism is more sophisticated and includes not only behavior but also dispositions to behave. Before we discuss Ryle's theory of mind, let us look at what he has to say about Descartes' doctrine.

Descartes' doctrine is the doctrine that every human being has both a mind and a body. The body and the mind are connected and interact upon one another. After death, the mind continues to exist and function. Bodies are physical: they exist in space and are subject to the laws of physics. Minds, on the other hand, are not physical: they do not exist in space, and they are not subject to the laws of physics. Bodies are public and are observable by all; minds are private and are observable only by the persons to whom they belong. Ryle contends that this doctrine alone has given rise to both the mind-body problem and the problem of other minds.

Ryle calls Descartes' doctrine the dogma of the ghost in the machine, and according to him it is all one big category-mistake. Ryle defines a category as "the set of ways in which it is logically legitimate to operate with" a concept.[15] For example, the concept of mind belongs in a certain category, and this category defines the ways in which this concept can be used. A category-mistake is made when a concept is put into the wrong category. For example, we would be committing a category-mistake if we were to say that the number 2 is red; the number 2 does not belong in the category of things which can be colored. In the same way, Ryle claims, it is a mistake to put mind into the category of thing and to represent minds as different sorts of things than bodies. Let us see if this notion of category-mistake can be articulated in a more careful way, and let us do it with the proposition "The number 2 is red."

"The number 2 is red" represents the number 2 as being in the category of things which can be red. We, of course, want to argue that the number 2 cannot be red. But if we say this, then we are left open to the possibility that the number 2 is blue. "The number 2 is not red" and "The number 2 is blue" are perfectly consistent. What we need to do is to deny that the number 2 can be colored at all. In order to do this, we need to reject both the proposition "The number 2 is red" and the proposition "The number 2 is not red." Both propositions make sense only within a context where the number 2 can be colored, and this is just what we must deny. We can articulate the notion of category-mistake in the following way: an individual (here, the number 2) and a property (here, the color red) are mismatched when we can neither affirm nor deny the predication of the property to the individual.

This same analysis works for the concept of mind. It is a mistake to say that the mind is a mental thing, but if we deny this, then it is possible that the mind is a physical thing. Ryle argues that minds are not to be placed in the category of thing at all. To talk of minds is not to talk of things, places, storehouses, and so on; "it is to talk of . . . abilities, liabilities and inclinations to do and undergo certain sorts of things, and of the doing and undergoing of these things in the ordinary world."[16]

Thus, Ryle argues, it is a mistake to place both mind and body in the same category. It is a mistake to argue that minds are things, but different sorts of things from bodies, that minds are

---

15. Gilbert Ryle, *The Concept of Mind* (New York: Barnes & Noble, 1962), p. 8.
16. Ibid., p. 199.

machines like bodies, but spectral machines, that minds are the center of causal processes as are bodies, but mental rather than physical.

Ryle's theory of mind differs from dualism by holding that psychological concepts do not refer to or describe the occult episodes of the dualist, but rather they refer to or describe overt acts and utterances or dispositions. Ryle considers a large number of psychological concepts, the most important of which is the family of concepts named "intelligence," for it is intelligence, in the dualist's sense, which is thought to separate man from all other creatures.

When a person is described as being intelligent, we may say of that person that he is careful, observant, logical, sensible, and so on. With regard to intelligent performances, it might be said that the person doing them is thinking what he is doing while he is performing. In other words, intelligent behavior can be characterized as thinking what one is doing while one is doing it. An example of intelligent behavior is playing chess: before one makes a move he must concentrate and deliberate if he intends to win.

According to the dualist, thinking what one is doing while doing it involves two operations: (1) doing whatever one is doing and (2) thinking about what one is doing. Ryle calls this the intellectualist legend, one of the dualists' legends. This legend claims that thinking always preceeds and guides intelligent behavior. First one theorizes, and then one acts. Theorizing is a mental activity going on in a mind; acting is a physical activity going on in the physical world. Thus, when a person plays chess, mental activity preceeds and causes physical activity. Both mind and body are involved in all intelligent activity. It is just this kind of analysis which Ryle wishes to refute.

Many intelligent activities, practices of taste and good manners for example, involve standards and criteria which are unformulated. In these cases there is no theorizing, no considering certain appropriate propositions, which enjoin one to do something. Being intelligent, knowing how to do something, or having a certain ability does not amount to knowing certain truths or general principles. Further, if every intelligent performance involved prior theorizing, and if this theorizing is itself an intelligent activity, then an infinite regress is generated. Ryle concludes that intelligent activity does not involve doing two things. "Intelligent" cannot be defined in terms of certain mental activity, namely intellectual theorizing.

To behave intelligently is, according to Ryle, to do only one thing but to do it well. Intelligent activity has certain procedures and criteria, not antecedents. What is done must be done correctly, efficiently, and successfully; that is, the intelligent performance has to meet or satisfy certain standards or criteria. Further, these criteria must not be merely satisfied but also applied. This means that the agent performing must be responsible for the performance; he must be able to correct, repeat, compensate, and so on, what he does.

Ryle contends that judging someone's performance or activity as intelligent does not require occult episodes going on in a mind. It does not require our knowing anything about the intellectual theorizing which the dualist views as preceeding and causing the intelligent activity or behavior.

Ryle is not just a simple behaviorist, though. For Ryle, judging someone's performance as intelligent amounts in some cases to more than just looking at the behavior itself. Looking beyond the behavior does not mean looking for hidden mental causes but for capacities, skills, bents, and so on. Ryle's form of behaviorism involves dispositions. To have a disposition to behave is to be bound or liable to behave in a certain way when a certain set of circumstances occurs. In some cases, to be in pain involves more than pain-behavior; it involves the disposition to pain behave. A psychological concept is applied to a person according to how that person behaves or according to how the person is disposed to behave. A person is said to be intelligent if he behaves in a certain way or if he can be counted on to behave in a certain way given certain conditions.

In his analysis, Ryle attempts to rid psychological concepts of their dualistic denotations; he argues that these concepts do not refer to or denote any internal goings-on, any mental events. For Ryle psychological concepts refer to or denote behavioral and dispositional characteristics. If he is successful, then Ryle has solved both of the main problems encountered by any theory of mind. If there are no minds or inner places, then there can be no mind-body problem. The problem of other minds is solved because one can know what is going on in another's mind by looking at the other person's behavior or by knowing how that person is disposed to behave.

There are some, A. J. Ayer for example, who say that Ryle seems to be espousing a very strong form of behaviorism, logical behaviorism, and that he fails in doing so. Logical behaviorism is the attempt to eliminate any reference to inner, mental goings-on by showing that language about mental life can be reformulated into language about behavior. For Ryle, this amounts to rephrasing mental talk in terms of dispositional statements about people's behavior.

Does Ryle eliminate all reference to inner processes, to ghosts in the machine? The answer seems to be no. Ryle does seem to be left with certain mental residues—itches, pangs, daydreams, and the like do seem to require an inner-process story, as do the processes of which the modes of perception are the achievement. Ryle admits, for example, that looking and seeing are episodic verbs; the former is the task, the latter is the achievement. If Ryle is left with inner processes, why then is he not plagued with the ghost which he attempts to avoid?

Instead of logical behaviorism, Ryle seems to be left with a weaker form of behaviorism: there may be certain inner processes which accompany or precede performances, but there need not be. The inner process is not necessary to any analysis of psychological concepts. This claim is weaker than logical behaviorism because it at least admits the possibility of inner processes; logical behaviorism does not.

Ryle, like Smart, attempts to rid the universe of ghosts, but he does so in a different manner. Both Ryle and Smart are monists and both deny the existence of minds; one analyzes psychological concepts in terms of behavior while the other analyzes them in terms of brain processes. The end result, the denial of minds, is similar; however, the means to the end are different and constitute two separate theories of mind.

EXPRESSION THEORY

The expression theory and the criteriological view go hand in hand in that the latter will not work unless the former does. Both theories had their beginnings with one of the most famous and important philosophers of the twentieth century, Ludwig Wittgenstein; these two theories have been further developed by one of Wittgenstein's students, Norman Malcolm. Though neither theory is really monistic (neither equates pain and pain-behavior or pain and brain possesses, for example), taken together they offer a solution to both the mind-body problem and the problem of other minds. The expression theory concerns first-person sensation statements and the mind-body problem; the criteriological view involves third-person sensation statements and the problem of other minds.

In his *Philosophical Investigations* Wittgenstein asked: "How do words refer to sensations?—There doesn't seem to be any problem here; don't we talk about sensations every day, and give them names? But how is the connexion between the name and the thing named set up? This question is the same as: how does a human being learn the meaning of the names of sensations?—of the word "pain" for example."[17]

The dualist's answer is that the word "pain" refers to a private sensation going on in one's own mind. I name the sensation by fixing my attention on it and calling it "pain." "Pain" refers to or describes what is going on in me. Thus, only I can know when or that I am in pain, for only I can know the connection between the word "pain" and pain in my own case. This analysis generates both the mind-body problem—what is the relation between my mind and my body?—and the problem of other minds —if I can know only what is in my own mind, can I ever know the mind of another?

Wittgenstein argues that "I am in pain" is not a report of an inner going-on. "Pain" does not refer to or describe a private sensation. Wittgenstein answers the question "How do words refer to sensations?" in the following way: "Words are connected with the primitive, the natural, expressions of the sensation and used in their place. A child has hurt himself and he cries; and then adults talk to him and teach him exclamations and, later, sentences. They teach the child new pain-behavior."[18] The word "pain" is an expression of pain; it does not refer to or describe pain. In Wittgenstein's analysis, sensation statements are tied up or connected with natural expressions of sensation, "ooow," for example, and replace them; sensation statements are expressions, not reports or descriptions. When a person is young, he expresses his pain by uttering natural pain expressions, such as "ooow"; when he is older, he replaces the natural expression with a learned one, such as "It hurts." Now this is not to deny that "It hurts" or "I am in pain" are never reports or descriptions, but in these cases they are not. Further, sensation statements are incorrigible

---

17. Ludwig Wittgenstein, *Philosophical Investigations*, trans. G. E. M. Anscombe (New York: Macmillan, 1953), p. 89e.
18. Ibid.

on this account. A person cannot be mistaken when he says that his leg hurts any more than he could be mistaken when he says "ooow." Put another way, it makes no sense to say either that a person knows or that he doubts that he is in pain, for knowledge claims call for evidence, and there is none in the case of one's own sensations. "I know I am in pain" just means "I am in pain."

Wittgenstein's analysis has an interesting twist to it, a twist that goes counter to solipsism and seems to flow from dualism. The twist is that instead of saying that I can only know about my own pains, Wittgenstein seems to say that I cannot know that I am in pain; I can only have pain. If anything can be known with regard to sensations, it is the sensations of others, and this is the criteriological view.

The expression theory runs against the current of both dualism and behaviorism. It is in opposition to dualism because it claims that one cannot know one's own sensations, and it is in opposition to behaviorism because it claims that there is a distinction between pain and pain-behavior.

CRITERIOLOGICAL VIEW

As pointed out earlier, the criteriological view works if and only if the expression theory does. The statements "I am in pain" or "It hurts" are incorrigible because they replace a natural expression of pain which is incorrigibile. It is this incorrigibility which makes it possible for them to be critera of pain. That is, "ooow" or "I am in pain" are criteria of pain because they are incorrigibile, because a person cannot be mistaken when he utters such expressions. Put another way, we take a person's word when he says "I am in pain"; it makes no sense to ask him "Are you sure that you are not mistaken?"

Pain-behavior such as the expression "I am in pain" is a criterion of pain because it establishes beyond a doubt that a person is in pain when it is uttered in certain circumstances. When "I am in pain" is uttered in certain circumstances, it makes no sense to doubt the person's word, for that person cannot be mistaken in his utterance.

The criteriological view coupled with the expression theory, even though they are not monistic theories, do offer a possible solution to problems raised by dualism. The mind-body problem is handled by showing that the relationship between pain and pain-behavior, for example, is that the latter is both an expression and criterion of the former. Given this, the problem of other minds falls right into place. We can know that another person is in pain because his pain-behavior is a criterion of his pain, and the pain-behavior can be a criterion of pain just because it is an expression of pain.

One of the objections that might be raised against the expression theory is that it explains only a small number of cases, those where "I am in pain" is an *expression* of pain. There are many instances where "I am in pain" is either a report or a description. This objection also holds against the criteriological view, for this view depends upon "I am in pain" being an expression. An objection to the criteriological view is that the relationship between pain and pain-behavior is difficult to spell out. It does not suffice to say that one is a criterion of the other.

CONCLUSION

In our discussion of the philosophy of mind we have considered several problems and some theories of mind which attempt to solve these problems. The main issue, simply, is whether or not there exist minds in the traditional sense of the word, that is, whether or not there exist mental substances or things in which mental events go on.

The dualist argues that there are minds, but then seems to be stuck with the two main problems in the philosophy of mind, namely the mind-body problem and the problem of other minds. Monists, on the other hand, materialists and behaviorists, argue that there are no minds in the traditional sense of the word. The former holds that minds are really just brains; the latter that minds can be accounted for in terms of behavior. In effect, both of the monists discussed deny the existence of minds and mental events and this, in essence, is their answer to the two main problems. There is no mind-body problem because there are no minds, and the problem of other minds is handled because both the brains and behavior of others can easily be observed.

Though they are not monistic, the expression theory and the criteriological view also attempt to solve the mind-body problem and the problem of other minds. The expression theorist argues that the connection among mind, pain, body, and pain-behavior is, in some cases, one of expression. Pain-behavior is the expression of pain. It is on this connection that the criteriological view rests; we can know that others are in pain because their pain-behavior, which is observable, is the criterion for their being in pain.

Most theories of mind, then, seem to be attempts to solve problems which have arisen in the philosophy of mind, though it might be argued that dualism gave rise to the problems, especially to the mind-body problem and the problem of other minds.

TOPICS FOR DISCUSSION

1. Can dualism be defended against the materialist? Against the behaviorist? If so, how?
2. Are there more sophisticated versions of dualism than that of Descartes? Spell some of these out.
3. Smart's version of materialism is just one among many. What are some of these other versions? Are they superior to Smart's?
4. What might B. F. Skinner have to say about some of the problems and issues raised in the philosophy of mind?
5. Is the universe a fit place for "spooks" and "ghosts"? What are some of the implications of allowing their existence?
6. What are some of the religious implications of theories like materialism and behaviorism?
7. Is there a way of explaining the place of mind in the universe which is neither dualistic, in the Cartesian sense, nor monistic? Look at Wittgenstein's two theories.

SELECTED BIBLIOGRAPHY

Primary Source

Aristotle. *De Anima.* In *The Basic Works of Aristotle,* edited by Richard McKeon. New York: Random House, 1941.
Armstrong, D. M. *A Materialist Theory of the Mind.* London: Routledge and Kegan Paul, 1968.
Descartes, René. *Discourse on Method and Meditations.* Translated by Laurence J. Lafleur. New York: Bobbs-Merrill, 1960.
Plato. *The Republic.* Translated by Benjamin Jowett. New York: Random House, 1957.

Ryle, Gilbert. *The Concept of Mind.* New York: Barnes and Noble, 1962.
Smart, J. J. C. *Philosophy and Scientific Realism.* London: Routledge and Kegan Paul, 1963.
Wittgenstein, Ludwig. *Philosophical Investigations.* Translated by G. E. M. Anscombe. New York: Macmillan, 1953.

Secondary Source

Borst, C. V., ed. *The Mind/Brain Identity Theory.* London: Macmillan, 1970.
Chappell, V. C., ed. *The Philosophy of Mind.* Englewood Cliffs, New Jersey: Prentice-Hall, 1962.
Flew, Anthony, ed. *Body, Mind and Death.* New York: Macmillan, 1964.
Gustafson, Donald F., ed. *Essays in Philosophical Psychology.* Garden City, New York: Doubleday, 1964.
Hampshire, Stuart, ed. *Philosophy of Mind.* New York: Harper and Row, 1966.
Hook, Sidney, ed. *Dimensions of Mind.* New York: New York University Press, 1960.
O'Connor, John, ed. *Modern Materialism: Readings on Mind-Body Identity.* New York: Harcourt, Brace and World, 1969.
Shaffer, Jerome. *Philosophy of Mind.* Englewood Cliffs, New Jersey: Prentice-Hall, 1968.

CHAPTER 5

Eastern Philosophy

WHAT IS EASTERN PHILOSOPHY?

Before we in the West can begin to understand what Eastern philosophy is, we must realize that it is not an Oriental version of Western philosophy. Even if we claim to know nothing about the subject, the very idea of "Eastern philosophy" presupposes several things which are questionable, if not downright false: that it is a branch of philosophy homogeneous in nature and that it is philosophical in the sense in which Westerners traditionally use the term. Eastern philosophy is not a branch of philosophy, but a complete intellectual and spiritual tradition in its own right, comprising many different systems of thought from different periods and geographical areas. Nor is Eastern philosophy just philosophy in the fairly technical sense in which we generally use the term. What we call the philosophies of the East are attempts to answer the ultimate problems of the universe and life in a way which collapses the distinctions *we* draw between philosophy, religion, morality, and politics. To paraphrase one of the greatest Buddhist thinkers, Nagarjuna (c. 200 A.D.), it is neither theoretical nor practical, scholarly nor personal, nor a combination of the two. Eastern philosophers do not fit Western cubbyholes. If we approach Eastern philosophy from the standpoint of our own conceptual framework, we will be led to ask, for example, whether Hinduism is a philosophical system or a religion or whether Con-

The authors wish to thank Professor Hsueh-li Cheng of the Ohio University Philosophy Department for his help in preparing this chapter.

fucianism is a religion or an ethical-social theory. Whatever answer we give is apt to be confusing, for we will be forcing Eastern philosophy into an alien and constricting Western straitjacket.

This sort of confusion is a potential danger in any cross-cultural investigation. Consider the question "Do tribal Africans worship idols?" The early missionaries thought so and as a result destroyed thousands of African wood carvings. Many of these same objects are now considered works of art (see Chapter 9) and have been preserved. Which are they, idols or works of art? From an African point of view they are probably neither, not because Africans feel they do not fall within these conceptual boundaries, but because they do not happen to have these particular concepts in the first place. Both "idol" and "work of art" are Western concepts, involving many cultural assumptions or implications which may be alien to a non-Western culture. An idol, for example, is a "graven image" of a god, but most African peoples do not appear to worship "gods" as we think of them. A work of art, on the other hand, is the sort of thing one hangs on the wall just to look at or to decorate, a practice very alien to tribal Africa.

It would be strange if the traditions and assumptions of different cultures were exactly alike. We should expect some differences, and to the extent that there are differences it will be misleading to apply Western words to non-Western cultural phenomena. In describing another culture, we use English words with Western cultural overtones, and we must be aware of the dangers involved in doing so. Any application of a Western concept to a non-Western culture, then, is like a metaphor which we must be prepared to understand in the sophisticated way we understand explicit metaphors. Do tribal Africans worship idols? Do they appreciate works of art? All such questions must be answered with a sophisticated "yes and no": yes in the sense that they produce objects which are something like what we know as idols or works of art; no in the sense that this is not precisely the way tribal members view them.

Eastern philosophy must be approached in the same manner. *Philosophy* is an English word for a Western concept which may not fit Eastern thought systems. The word *philosophy* is used in ordinary English in two ways. In an informal, popular sense, philosophy is general wisdom about the ultimate nature of the universe with the practical and personal goal of discovering how best to live. In a more formal, professional sense, philosophy is a rational analysis and critique of conceptual difficulties which arise out of other types of investigation, including problems which arise from informal philosophizing. When we look to the East we find something similar to both kinds of philosophical investigation. Most of what we call Eastern philosophy, and most of that which has attracted the interest of the West, is philosophy in the informal sense. The aim is *theoretically* to discover the ultimate nature of the universe, not for scholarly or academic reasons, but out of a practical concern, more moral and religious in nature, to find the path to salvation, or more simply, the right way to live. Ethical-religious concerns are not separate in any important respect from social and political concerns, as they usually are in the West. In the East, when one has discovered the ultimate nature of the universe, one has also found a religious answer to salvation, an ethical answer on how to live, and a socio-political solution to the best ordering of society. There are parallels in Western philosophy, especially in its earliest phases; Socrates, for example, was concerned with the foundation for the good life, both personally and collectively, and the source of justice both in the individual and in the state.

Most Western philosophy, however, is a systematic and rational reflection on conceptual problems. Philosophy, in the formal sense in which we have been using the term in this book, is a specialized and professional discipline directed toward moral, religious, social, and political concerns, but it is nonetheless distinct from them. Out of personal, moral, and religious concerns, issues arise which lend themselves to philosophical analysis, and this appears to occur in the East as well as in the West. The attempt to clarify religious concerns, for example, leads to metaphysical, logical, epistemological, or ethical analyses of a specialized philosophical nature. In Eastern thought one can find not only the general philosophical wisdom which is enjoying such broad appeal among people in this country today, but also, in men like Sankara, Nagarjuna, Seng-chao, and Hui-neng, the kind of technical philosophizing which has begun to attract the attention of professional philosophers in the West.

Let's consider a simple but important example of the relationship between moral-religious concerns and philosophical analysis in our own tradition in order to understand its parallel in Eastern philosophy. Suppose I ask a basically religious question, "What must I do to achieve salvation?" This is not an academic question, but a practical concern of immense personal importance. Now suppose I am told, "You must believe that Jesus was

God made into flesh and bones to redeem you from your sins." At this point I may get sidetracked from a religious quest onto a theoretical, conceptual puzzle. "Wait," I ask, "I thought God was a spiritual, immaterial being. So how can God become flesh and bones? And even if He could, was this materialization part of God or all of God, or what? And how, even if this did occur, does this help me, two thousand years later? How does it work?" This is not a religious dilemma, but an intellectual problem concerning conceptual difficulties of a metaphysical nature about identity and causality. Nonetheless, I am unable to resume my religious quest till I can somehow get this conceptual problem behind me. Now the philosopher comes along, in the form of a theologian, to help me dispose of this dilemma. In a sense, he says, Jesus and God are different, and in a sense they are one and the same. How so? Just as the same substance can have different properties without itself changing in any essential way, so the spiritual nature of God can take on material form without undergoing substantial change. God the Father and Jesus are different manifestations of the same underlying substance. Thus, a philosophical solution has been used to solve a philosophical problem arising out of a religious concern. And this is precisely how Aristotle was introduced in the twelfth and thirteenth centuries to straighten out various conceptual difficulties in Christian beliefs, and out of various religious practices and traditions a reasonably consistent philosophical system was developed.

With the philosophical problem solved, I can return to my religious quest. But there is a serious danger involved in this process. What if I should become more interested in the philosophical-theological statement than the religious belief, or, worse, confuse the two? If that should happen, then instead of removing a temporary metaphysical barrier to my religious salvation, the philosophical exercise would have permanently established that barrier as part of the accepted religion! As we will see, one of the most philosophically interesting aspects of Eastern philosophy, for the formal Western philosopher, is the attempt to keep Eastern religions clear of metaphysical impediments.

Westerners have looked to Eastern philosophy in an attempt to see if and how Eastern philosophy can answer Western problems! Thus Eastern philosophy has been examined largely from a Western point of view. This has obvious advantages as well disadvantages. We have absorbed certain aspects of Eastern thought and gained new insights, but there has been a widespread distortion of Eastern thought as it is bent to the point of view of Western concerns. In this chapter we will first try to understand why many people in the West, with an elaborate religious, moral, and philosophical tradition of their own, have turned increasingly to the East for help; briefly characterize the main philosophical doctrines which have captivated the imagination of the West; and finally examine in more detail the attempts to solve some of the philosophical problems arising out of the moral and religious doctrines.

WHY EASTERN PHILOSOPHY?

A widespread complaint of Western intellectuals since the end of the eighteenth century is the "crisis" or "bankruptcy" of the Western intellectual tradition. From the Romantics in the early nineteenth century to the existentialists in the twentieth (see Chapter 8) there has been a growing realization that Western thought has played itself out, exposing a hopelessly inadequate base on which human beings can meaningfully live. The existentialists especially reflect the belief that modern man is isolated and alienated from his world, his society, and himself. Western philosophical and scientific history begins with, and is inconceivable without, the sharp divisions between nature, man, and God. In *Genesis*, for example, God creates Nature as a separate entity and gives man "dominion over" it. What made science and rational philosophy possible was the ability to talk about nature in a secular, nonreligious way. Generally it was assumed that the more one could remove human and religious biases from one's description, the more one approached the hard core of objective truth. Since these naturalistic explanations were always framed in the highest rational, intellectual generalities and abstractions possible, this not only alienated man from nature but the individual man from mankind, and in so far as the individual was encouraged to understand himself in terms of generalities affecting all mankind, it succeeded in alienating the individual from himself.

Alienation from the world reduces the possibility of sympathetic understanding. The only human interest in the world left for man is power over nature, controlling nature to satisfy his own needs. Our basic attitude toward the world, then, is one of getting and grabbing; even when we seek to understand nature it is not to understand something we ourselves are a part of, but primarily to gain control over it. Consequently, we pin all our hopes for the future on man's collective achievement in rational, technological progress.

The resulting situation has in many ways become very sad. We are bored with our jobs, frustrated at the prospect of an endless rat race of achievement and spoiling our environment in the meantime, and, after the Nazis of World War II, Hiroshima, the threat of nuclear disaster, and Vietnam, our confidence in the inevitability of human progress based on the essential rationality of man has been thoroughly shaken. Though only a trickle at first, the protests and reactions to this crisis have become a torrent in recent years, and in this context it should not be surprising to find men and women of the West turning increasingly to the East for answers to distinctly Western problems!

Understandably, it is precisely those aspects of Eastern thought which appear to directly oppose the disastrous trends outlined above which have held out the greatest promise to people in the West. Over a span of some 5,000 years, there have been hundreds of religious, philosophical, moral, scientific, logical, mathematical, historical, and literary theories in the many countries we lump together as the "East" (well over half the world's population). Western intellectuals have interpreted later Hinduism, Buddhism (especially the later Chinese and Japanese schools), and Taoism in terms of what Aldous Huxley called the "Perennial Philosophy," which he even tried to expand to include Western equivalents! It is important to remember that the grouping together of these schools is the product of biased Western interest in Eastern thought, and any serious scholar of Eastern thought would be highly suspicious of such a vast oversimplification. Nonetheless, this is how it has come across to us, and this is therefore the place to begin.

What is the Perennial Philosophy of the East? The first premise is that man is not alienated from but is essentially identical with the objective reality of the world. Secondly, it holds that this reality is not alienated from but identical with the highest spiritual, religious forces. When we discover the innermost secrets of reality we have discovered ourselves; when we truly come to terms with ourselves we thereby come to terms with the ultimate spiritual reality of the universe. God, nature, man—all are one. In the classical formula of the *Upanishads*, "Tat tuam asi," "You are that." None of the intellectual abstractions we use to communicate with in daily life describe that basic reality, but only hide it. Words, concepts, and reasons are simply tools we use to point to the world; they can never be identical with it or mirror it exactly. When you point to the moon, as the Zen Buddhists say, be sure you don't mistake the finger for the moon!

In this context, anxiety over power and alienation disappears. If nature is not an alien object standing apart and separate from a person, then there is nothing to get out of the world. The illusion of getting and grabbing is as silly as a pound of sugar trying to borrow a cup of sugar from itself. It simply can't be done. Anxiety of continually trying to "get ahead" is also based on confusion. *Who* is getting ahead? A personal ego, which is pitted against the whole world. But in Eastern thought the real self is inseparable from the world's reality, and getting ahead is like a racehorse trying to beat itself.

A BRIEF HISTORY OF EASTERN PHILOSOPHY

What are some of the main currents of Eastern thought from which this Perennial Philosophy has been derived? Historically, it began with late Hinduism in India, from which Buddhism evolved, passed into China where it blended with Chinese Taoism and Confucianism, and then moved on to Japan.

Before we consider this historical development we must understand the central religious problem in the East to which these systems of thought were offered as answers. The one theme which unites the great traditions of Hinduism and Buddhism is the underlying assumption of karma and reincarnation. In most Eastern thought it is assumed that the individual ego is born over and over again into different bodies, sometimes as men and sometimes as lower animals, depending on the moral and intellectual quality achieved in one's previous life. Morality thus extends beyond this life; whether a person becomes a man or a mouse in the next life depends on how he lived this life. This principle of moral consequences is known as *karma*. It is interesting to note that Plato held a similar view (see Chapter 3), but by and large this position is in opposition to the Western tradition. This is nowhere more apparent than in the different attitudes toward life after death. In the West, where we place such value on the personal identity of the psychological ego (the "I"), most people desire that ego to continue beyond death and yearn for eternal life. In the East the problem is not how to attain life after death, but how to get rid of it! To the Easterner, life after death is a drag. The central religious problem for the East is how to end the continuous wheel of rebirth (samsara). This is what the Eastern religious devotee means when he asks, "What must I do to achieve eternal salvation?" Basically, most answers have come in the form of establishing an attitude of mind (vidya) which breaks the karma chain linking life and death (samsara). This releases (moksa) the ego by discovering its true identity, not as an individual, separate ego, but as "that"—the whole of spiritual reality. In the Eastern view, that thing which is born and reborn again and again is not me, I am *that*. A person is never a separate object; so he can't continue to be one, for the simple reason that there are no separate, individual objects! Unlike the theory-practice distinction in the West, the Eastern ideal is a perfect blend of knowledge and practical consequences. Unhappiness is caused by a false view of the independent existence of the self and the world, and salvation comes from a correct view of their identity.

The basic Eastern beliefs raise several serious philosophical problems. In what sense are there no objects, no multiplicity, no divisions? Does this mean that you and I, for example, are one and the same? Are you then responsible for my bills? Is there no difference between a classroom full of chairs and an empty classroom? This begins to sound strange, confusing, and disquieting. And if these things are illusions, what *is* really there? Nothing? That's scary. Am I *that*? How so? As we will see, there is no way to avoid these problems short of keeping our mouths shut and our pens still, for the problems arise out of the very form of words we use to describe the "way out" of the cycle of birth and death. As the twentieth-century Austrian philosopher Ludwig Wittgenstein said, the very words we use lead us into philosophical puzzles. But this is even worse in a religious context because these conceptual puzzles sidetrack the mind and inhibit spiritual progress toward what is at heart a simple and terribly important realization. So, while solving this sort of problem is not really a religious matter, we can see how important it became in the minds of Eastern religious thinkers in clearing the path toward religious release. In fact, it was the attempt to dissolve certain conceptual philosophical problems which led to each of the breakaway movements which make up the history and evolution of Eastern thought.

Each new movement in Eastern philosophy began as a housecleaning operation designed to clear away the accumulated intellectual rubbish from simple religious truths. Each new departure was an attempt to save the religious and practical matters from being obscured by metaphysical, logical, and verbal problems and debates.

Hinduism

Hinduism, an extremely rich, many-faceted religion, stretches far back into man's earliest recorded religious experience. The earliest text is the *Rig Veda* (2000–1500 B.C.). This is a collection of ceremonial hymns to various gods who, historically and evolutionarily, belong to the same family of gods as Odin, Zeus, and Venus worshipped by the ancient Greeks and pre-Christian northern Europeans. The hymns appear to have accompanied sacrifices, which, as in ancient Greece, was the chief religious function. The gods—Agni, god of fire; Varuna, god of sea and air; Indra, god of the thunderbolt, plus gods of sun, moon, and so on—demanded sacrifices and hymns of praise.

In sharp contrast, the *Upanishads* appeared some thousand years and several missing evolutionary stages later. In this work the gods requiring endless sacrifices have been replaced by two central concepts, Atman and Brahman, and the thesis that they are identical. Atman is the true self while Brahman is the underlying nature of the universe. The point of the *Upanishads* is that salvation is to be achieved through the realization that Atman is Brahman, "Thou art that." From the *Kena Upanishad*, for example,

> At whose behest does the mind think? Who bids the body live? Who makes the tongue speak? . . . The Self (Atman) is ear of the ear, mind of the mind, speech of speech. . . . Having given up the false identification of the Self with the senses and the mind, and knowing the Self to be Brahman, the wise on departing this life, gain final release. Him the eye does not see, nor the tongue express, nor the mind grasp. Him we neither know nor are able to teach. Different is He from known, and different is He from the unknown. . . . That which cannot be expressed in words but by which the tongue speaks—know that to be Brahman. . . . That which is not comprehended by the mind but by which the mind comprehends—know that to be Brahman. . . . He who realizes the existence of Brahman behind every activity of his being . . . he alone gains release.

Just as the *Rig Veda* gods resemble those of the Greeks, so the Brahmanic belief in one underlying eternal reality resembles the early Greek quest for the "ageless, deathless ground of reality" (see Chapter 1). While we in the West have moved very far from this monistic insight, Hindu thought has not.

However, in the *Upanishads* the old order of nature gods and sacrifices are not entirely repudiated but simply reinterpreted in a new light and reabsorbed in an ongoing, developing Hinduism. In this respect, Hinduism is very conservative. In general, any revolution in thought can be described either as a break with the past or conservatively as a reinterpretation of the past. Christianity appeared as a clean break with Judaism, though it grew out of Judaism and all its early spokesmen, including Jesus, were Jews. On the other hand, despite important changes, the Protestant movement was described (by the Protestants) not as a new religion, but as a reformation of true Christianity. Because of its extremely conservative nature, Hinduism has rarely rejected old thoughts and beliefs in favor of new views. Contemporary Hindu religious beliefs include Brahmanism (the identity of Atman and Brahman), sacrificial worship of specific theistic gods such as Brahma the creator (not to be confused with Brahman), Shiva the destroyer, Vishnu the preserver, and even Jesus, as well as many other lesser gods.

A good example of this synthesizing of apparently diverse elements is Hindu's second most important scripture, the *Bhagavad-Gita*, or "Song of God" (second century, B.C.). This is only a small part of a long epic poem, the *Mahabharata*, in which Krishna, a manifestation of the ancient god Vishnu, appears to persuade a dubious nobleman, Arjuna, to take up arms and fight the opposing armies ranged against him. Though never contradicting the Upanishadic position, an important element of theism (belief in a personal savior God) is presented. Although Krishna presents many arguments for Arjuna to consider, his main case is that Arjuna should put his faith and trust in Krishna. This view, known as bhakti theism, is nonetheless presented as perfectly compatible with the old doctrine of the *Upanishads* that since there is no real difference between slayer and slain, one should not worry too much about the necessity of killing or being killed.

> Arjuna, is this hour of battle the time for scruples and fancies? Are they worthy of you, who seek enlightenment? . . . Shake off this cowardice, Arjuna. Stand up. . . . The truly

wise mourn neither for the living nor for the dead. There was never a time when I did not exist, nor you, nor any of these things. Nor is there any future in which we shall cease to be.... That which is non-existent can never come into being, and that which is can never cease to be.... That Reality which pervades the universe is indestructible. No one has the power to change the Changeless. Bodies are said to die, but That which possesses the body is eternal. It cannot be ... destroyed. Therefore you must fight. Some say this Atman is slain, and others call it the slayer: They know nothing. How can it slay or who shall slay it? [*Bhagavad-Gita*]

The second major element of the *Gita* is an ethical position which effects an important compromise between the Upanishadic position that all goal-directed action has bad karma implications and the ordinary human sense of responsibility to act in certain situations. In the *Gita*, Krishna elucidates this position:

If you refuse to fight this righteous war, you will be turning aside from your duty.... Now listen to the method of Karma Yoga. If you can understand and follow it, you will be able to break the chains of desire which bind you to your actions. ... In this yoga, the will is directed singly toward one ideal. When a man lacks this discrimination, his will wanders in all directions, after innumerable aims.... [Such people] grow deeply attached to pleasure and power. And so they are unable to develop that concentration of the will which leads a man to absorption in God.... You have the right to work, but for the work's sake only. You have no right to the *fruits* of work. Desire for the fruits of work must never be your motive in working.... Perform every action with your heart fixed on the Supreme Lord.... To unite the heart with Brahman and then to act: that is the secret of non-attached work.

Basically, Krishna's position turns on a valuable distinction between a naive action attached to illusory goals and a knowing action fully aware that there is really nothing to be achieved and no one to achieve it. Viewed in this way, one need not retreat from an active life, but one should enter into life as into a game or a dance where there is nothing to be achieved but the game or dance itself. It is difficult to overemphasize how opposed this is to our Western bias toward "teleological," that is, goal-directed, purposeful action. Without this modification, the older Upanishad theory is suitable only for a priestly class devoted entirely to meditation ("upanishad" originally meant "to sit"). What is new in the *Gita* is a "democratic" element and the first of many attempts to solve an old problem—how to make salvation accessible to the average person, how to have the practical religious consequences without a prohibitively involved theoretical initiation. A similar problem was worked out in Christianity between priestly and lay approaches to the same religious goals. The attempt to synthesize the *Gita* with the *Upanishads* and the *Rig Veda* eventually culminated in Vedanta ("the end of the Vedas") in which the central doctrines of all three works are preserved in a form which has lasted virtually unchanged until the present day. This is the Hindu's theology and is largely the work of the great ninth-century scholar, Sankara.

Buddhism

Buddhism appeared at about the same time as the early Greek philosophers (sixth century B.C.) as a critique and reformation of late Hinduism. Early Buddhism resembles Vedanta, the underlying view of the *Upanishads* that life is full of fear and anxiety because of the wheel of rebirth (samsara) and that this is produced by false views of an ego-object dichotomy, goal-directed action (karma) which can only be broken (vidya) by realizing its falseness (moksha). How then does Buddhism differ from Hinduism and how did it come to be a distinct religion? The founder of Buddhism, Siddhartha Gautama (d. 544 B.C.), had been educated as a Hindu, and became dissatisfied with the problems created in trying to explicate the religious way to salvation. Born a prince, Siddhartha renounced all earthly power until he could discover his own path to salvation and teach it to others. Why did he reject the established Hinduism?

In the *Upanishads* Brahman is somehow identified with the world and Atman with the self, and the two are said to be eternally one and the same. This belief raises several conceptual problems. It appears as though there are many different, changing things in the world and many different, changing impressions going on inside a person's mind. What exactly are these things and how are they related to Brahman and Atman? Sankara, the great Vedanta scholar (800 A.D.), held that reality is one and there is no duality anywhere. But this very way of putting it suggests the duality of reality and appearance. To discount the apparent multiplicity of things in the world as we experience it, one must contrast the real with the illusory, a position which ends up admitting two things—reality and appearance. The Western philosopher Spinoza (1632–1677) held there was only one substance with many different modifications, or "modes," which simply introduced a dualism between the one substance and the many modes. It does no good to say that individual things don't exist; they are stubbornly there and must be accounted for somehow. Sankara maintained that these things can be said neither to exist nor not to exist, a statement similar to Plato's famous phrase that things "roll about between being and non-being." But, like quicksand, this just gets us in deeper and deeper.

We can call things "appearances" or "illusions" (Maya), if we like, but this raises the question as to how appearances are related to reality, and this is not a religious problem but a metaphysical one. Thus religion gets into the business of philosophy. From a religious standpoint, metaphysical issues are beginning to get in the way of religious concerns. As we saw earlier, the basic metaphysical solution to the relation of appearance and reality is to treat appearances as accidental properties of an underlying substance. Thus, in order to answer conceptual puzzles arising out of what were originally religious aspirations, Hindu scholars were led into a kind of scholarly philosophy not unlike the great Western tradition of Plato, Spinoza, and Hegel (though this is admittedly a Western way of putting it).

The ever-changing, multifarious world of sensations is, from the metaphysical standpoint, simply a modification of the basic underlying reality, Brahman, in the same way that clay figures of horses, dancing girls, and so on are modifications of a basic clay substance. According to the Hindus, underlying all our hopes, desires, plans, daydreams, thoughts, impressions, and so on is an unseen substance, Atman. Thus, there are two basic entities in the world, Brahman and Atman, related to everything else as substance is to mode or accident. Moreover, these two things are somehow one and the same thing! But what has this to do with salvation? Clearly, a practical, religious problem has become an intellectual problem.

How, for example, can we decide if the Hindu account above

is correct or not? Not by religious reflection or faith. These are philosophical statements which must be decided before the bar of reason. We must carefully examine arguments, analyze distinctions, criticize supporting evidence, just as we would in trying to choose between Descartes' view that there are three substances and Spinoza's that there is only one. What reasons are there, for example, for supposing that the tree outside my window is not a fully real entity in its own right? Vedanta scholars offer several reasons very much like those of Plato and other Western metaphysicians, that such things are too impermanent and too transient and perishable to qualify as stable objects. They are constantly changing; there is no period of time, however short, when they remain still long enough to "be" some definite thing. The second form of argument, again very like Plato and his followers in the West, is that material things are not consistent objects of thought, that they are shot through with contradictions and so cannot be truly real. A tree, for example, is at once a whole object (a tree), a part (of the forest), and a collection (of limbs, trunk, leaves, and so on); it is big (relative to a potato) and small (relative to a mountain). But how can there be anything which is one thing, a part of one thing, many things, big and small, all at the same time? There can't be such a thing, so the tree is not a truly real object in its own right. There is also the question, already familiar to us from Western metaphysics, of the dependence of these things on one another (the tree on water and soil, for example) and, more important, on human beings. It is only because of the analyzing mind with its distinctions and manifold conceptions, say the Vedanta writers, that the world appears broken up into bits and pieces of independent existence. Without the mind these distinctions would cease just as distinctions in a dream cease as soon as we wake up.

What about these arguments? How good are they? This obviously calls for a rigorous examination of the conceptual relations among "whole," "part," "is," "becoming," "concept," and "object." This is clearly a job for a philosopher, yet everyone must work out his own religious salvation. What if one doesn't happen to like philosophy or be particularly endowed with philosophical ability? The wheel of rebirth continues nonetheless to spin round and round. The problem facing Siddhartha was therefore to free the religious problem from its metaphysical trappings, but this is not as easy as it sounds.

Notice how the Buddha's solution appears to skirt metaphysics in his famous Fourfold Truth and Eightfold Path.

1. Existence entails suffering.
2. This suffering is caused by selfish craving.
3. Selfish craving can be destroyed.
4. It can be destroyed by the Eightfold Path:
    a. Right Understanding
    b. Right Purpose
    c. Right Speech
    d. Right Conduct
    e. Right Vocation
    f. Right Effort
    g. Right Alertness
    h. Right Concentration.

Aristotle himself could not ask for a more logically compelling argument, and yet it seems to require no commitment to doubtful metaphysical entities. Anyone of sane mind can understand and accept this basic reasoning. We know point 1 is true simply by being alive. Point 2 is too deeply embedded in Indian thought to be seriously questioned. Points 3 and 4 state the cure in practical terms we can all test for ourselves. Metaphysics is simply an irrelevant consideration. Whether Brahman is spiritually one and physically many, or essentially spiritual and accidentally physical, or whether the tree outside my window is part of existence or nonexistence, does not at all matter to the central task of attaining religious salvation and is therefore quite rightly left to one side. Or, at least, so it appears.

In one of the early Buddhist texts, *Majjhima-Nikaya*, a student of the Buddha, Malunkyaputta, pesters the Buddha again and again to answer some of the pressing metaphysical issues of the day.

> These theories which the Blessed One has left unexplained, has set aside and rejected—that the world is eternal, that the world is not eternal, that the world is finite, that the world is infinite, that the soul is one thing and the body another, that the soul and the body are identical, that the saint exists after death, that the saint does not exist after death, that the saint both exists and does not exist after death, that the

> saint neither exists nor does not exist after death—these the Blessed One does not explain to me. [*Majjhima-Nikaya*]

The Buddha's answer is not to answer! He does not say there are no answers, or that they are ridiculous questions; he simply points out that they are not essential to, and moreover get in the way of, the religious life.

> The religious life, Malunkyaputta, does not depend on the dogma that the world is eternal; nor does the religious life, Malunkyaputta, depend on the dogma that the world is not eternal. Whether the dogma obtain, Malunkyaputta, that the world is eternal, or that the world is not eternal, there still remain birth, old age, death, sorrow, lamentation, misery, grief, and despair. [*Majjhima-Nikaya*]

On the other hand, the Buddha insists that the central religious and practical problem concerned with the latter has been thoroughly explained.

> And what, Malunkyaputta, have I explained? Misery, Malunkyaputta, have I explained; the origin of misery have I explained; the cessation of misery have I explained; and the path leading to the cessation of misery have I explained. And why, Malunkyaputta, have I explained this? Because, Malunkyaputta, this is profitable, and has to do with the fundamentals of religion. [*Majjhima-Nikaya*]

Buddhism therefore appears to reject all metaphysics; it maintains silence in regard to supersensible entities like God or Brahman. From a Western point of view this seems a strange attitude for a world religion to strike. But the rejection is not of God and Brahman as such, but of the metaphysical attitude of mind which inhibits religious growth. This position is illustrated in a well-known Buddhist story about a man who has been shot by a poisonous arrow. Immediately there is speculation as to who shot the arrow, where it came from, and so on. While the debate is going on, the man is dying. The point of the story is not that metaphysics is nonsense, but that it is superceded by the more pressing need to settle the ultimate moral and religious problems of life.

This should have been the end of our story, but fortunately

or unfortunately, people can't stop talking and speculating, and this led to a gradual buildup of philosophical doctrines, puzzles, schools and debates within Buddhist ranks. Thus, Buddhism became divided into different historical schools. The main split was the Mahayana break with Hinayana in the second century A.D. Mahayana itself split in the third and fourth centuries A.D. into two major schools, Madyamika and Yogacara. The history of Buddhism, which we will examine briefly, therefore revolves around these three schools, Hinayana, Madyamika Mahayana, and Yogacara Mahayana. As we will see, this historical evolution turns on the philosophical interpretation of the ancient Buddhist texts.

While the Fourfold Truth was designed to counteract empty speculation on some unknowable supersensible reality such as Brahman, Atman, or God, it is not without a metaphysical slant of its own. The first statement that existence is suffering does not just mean that as a matter of fact pain and unhappiness occur in this world. It also implies, in direct contradiction to the *Upanishads,* that nothing is permanent, that all is changing and transient, and that in reality nothing substantial really exists. The second statement ties unhappiness to the failure to realize the impermanent character of things. Psychologically, suffering is caused by selfish craving, but epistemologically it is the result of blind desire attached to illusory objects. The assurance of the third statement, that this craving can be destroyed, is based on the metaphysical doctrine that everything has a cause and so can be *un*caused, that is, cured. Since the cause is ignorance, the cure is knowledge ("Right Understanding"). The Fourfold Truth is thus more metaphysically and epistemologically complicated than at first appears. Suffering is produced by the false view that there are permanent entities and is overcome by the correct view that all is impermanent.

HINAYANA. The first Buddhist school to appear (Hinayana) already has its metaphysical slant. While it rejects the unverifiable character of the supersensible nature of Atman and in that sense is antimetaphysical, its very rejection replaces this metaphysics with another—a positivist, empiricist, pluralistic, and dynamic metaphysics in place of an otherworldly, monistic, and static metaphysics of Atman. In one sense early Buddhist thought is a rejection of metaphysics, but in another sense it is simply another kind of metaphysics. Vedanta is the metaphysics of Atman, a doctrine that behind the visible world of appearances there is nothing in reality but one unchanging eternal entity, Atman. The Hinayana doctrine holds the *An*atman ("not Atman") position that the world is composed of a vast plurality of ever-changing entities–emptiness in place of substance, nothingness instead of reality.

The Buddha's refusal to answer Malunkyaputta's metaphysical questions is not an unqualified rejection of all metaphysics. In the history of Buddhism there have been three main interpretations of the Buddha's refusal which coincide with the three major historical divisions of Buddhism. The Hinayana position is that Malunkyaputta's questions cannot be settled by man because they lie beyond his range of experience, and that it is therefore pragmatically useless to speculate about them. But, as we saw, in attacking the Atmanic metaphysics, Buddhism developed into an opposite sort of Anatmanistic metaphysics. Though it contradicts Vedanta, Hinayana Buddhism is a logical development from Atmanic metaphysics. To prove that there is only one eternally unchanging reality, Vedanta scholars had to show that the ordinary world of our experience is in a state of constant flux and hence unreal. The Hinayanists accepted the changing order of appearance, but questioned the unknowable character of some other transcendent reality underlying experience. Like Western Empiricists, the Hinayanists place emphasis on direct experience. Their belief is that since we can't see the one metaphysical reality (Atman), we should maintain a sceptical attitude toward it. Nonetheless, by opposing the one unchanging reality (Atman), Hinayana began to defend the manifold, ever-changing nothingness (Anatman). The same thing happened to the Western Empiricists, who, in rejecting the unknowable metaphysical nature of both material and mental substance, unwittingly developed a pluralistic metaphysics of sensations!

Hinayana Buddhism created a complex metaphysics of its own, and the religious insight of Buddhism came to involve a rigorous process of initiation and meditation inaccessible to the average lay person. This blunted the popular appeal of Buddhism, and a revolt occurred within Buddhist ranks, somewhat like the Protestant split with the Roman Church, to bring Buddhism out of the metaphysical realm and back to the ordinary person. This resulted in a more popular, liberal, and flexible Buddhism which made considerable concessions to the situation in which the average person finds himself. The reformers called themselves the "Greater Vehicle" (Mahayana) in contrast to the older Buddhism which they rejected as the "Lesser Vehicle" (Hinayana). Hinayana spread into the countries of Southeast Asia while Mahayana moved to the Far East. Like the different Protestant denominations, Mahayana Buddhism split into two major schools before it left India—Madyamika and Yogacara.

MADYAMIKA MAHAYANA. The first Mahayana revolt (second century A.D.), known as Madyamika in India and San-lun, or Three-Treatise School in China, offered a more radical antimetaphysical interpretation of the Buddha's refusal to answer Malunkyaputta's questions. While the Hinayanists maintained that the questions asked of the Buddha were beyond man's capacity to solve and hence a waste of time, Madyamika scholars considered them completely unintelligible and hence neither true nor false. Madyamika more forcefully rejected metaphysics and the contemplative life and shifted the focus of Buddhism away from a discussion of reality (whether it is one or many, eternal or changing) to a concern with the relationship of words and concepts to reality, a concern which has also loomed very large in contemporary Western philosophy. Instead of emphasizing metaphysical speculation and the process of attaining "Right Understanding" through laborious meditation, Madyamika focused on the original pragmatic concern of the Buddha on the simplest and most straightforward way for the layman to break the chain of life and death and achieve as much salvation as he was intellectually and psychologically prepared for. But metaphysics is hard to stamp out, and another interpretation of the Buddha's refusal to answer Malunkyaputta's questions appeared in the third and fourth centuries A.D. The second school of Mahayana Buddhism, known as Yogacara in India and Fa-hsiang in China, was more compatible with metaphysical speculation.

YOGACARA MAHAYANA. According to Yogacara, the Buddha refused to answer the questions because of Malunkyaputta's limited capacity to understand. The Buddha understood and could answer all important religious questions. Such questions are not beyond the comprehension of all men, as the Hinayanists said, but they are beyond the capacity of men in limited stages of development. If a student of Buddhism has the intellectual capacity and is prepared to go the whole way, he can and should try to understand the answers the Buddha would have given. But Buddhism is for everyone, and if the student is not intellectually and psychologically prepared to understand the complete Buddhist answer, as Malunkyaputta apparently was not, he is free to accept whatever he is capable of comprehending. Yogacara is a more democratic form of Buddhism; the concession to a popular level of understanding is not disparaged, but simply seen as one stage along the way.

Yogacara Buddhism includes many diverse forms—the worship of gods and demigods, the strict observance of religious practices, and even, in Chinese Pure Land Buddhism, an afterlife of heavenly bliss for the faithful! Late Mahayana is so diverse that its followers refuse to define Buddhism as one thing or even to admit there is a single entity called Buddhism. Buddhism is what you make it. The main difference between Mahayana and the older Hinayana Buddhism is the greater liberalism of Mahayana. The central expression of this difference is the Bodhisattva, or saint, who gives up his own total salvation to help others achieve as much salvation as they are individually capable of and refuses final release until all sentient creatures are saved. Like the *Bhagavad-Gita*, this introduces an element of theism which is contrary to the early Buddhist refusal to accept supersensible entities like God. Theistic Buddhism realistically admits that the average person cannot achieve enlightenment on his own and must put faith and trust in the Bodhisattva to save him.

The central idea of Yogacara Buddhism is that everyone has within him the potential to become the Buddha, though some are closer to attaining that ideal in this life than others, and that everyone should be helped to proceed as far as he can in his own way. At the top of the scale the truly enlightened fully understand the metaphysical answers the Buddha would have given Malunkyaputta had he been sufficiently prepared for them. Thus, Yogacara Buddhism, especially as it evolved in China, gradually returned to the kind of monistic, spiritual pantheism (God is all and all is God) of Vedanta. Generally, the evolution of Buddhism is toward popularization at one end of the scale and metaphysical speculation at the other.

Because of its popular appeal Buddhism was successfully transported from India to neighboring lands, notably China (about the first century A.D.) where the great metaphysical imagination of India merged with the simple Taoist mysticism and practical Confucianist philosophy to create a Buddhism with a distinct Chinese flavor. When Buddhism arrived in China there was already a well-established philosophical tradition of Taoism and

Confucianism. And it is in terms of these Chinese traditions that Buddhism was interpreted and in association with which it survived.

Taoism

From the Western point of view, Taoism is part of the Perennial Philosophy. Reality is one and indivisible, identical with the self, and known not through words, concepts, and logic but by direct experience. Little is known of the origins of Taoism, but sometime during the Han dynasty (206 B.C.–220 A.D.) there appeared a collection of 81 religious poems known as the *Tao Te Ching* and attributed to Lao-Tzu. Taoism has a down-to-earth flavor in keeping with the practical orientation of Chinese philosophers, who have always been suspicious of otherworldly speculation. Compare Lao-Tzu's use of visual imagery, for example, with the more abstract metaphysical passage from the *Kena Upanishad* quoted earlier.

> The Way is a void,
> Used but never filled;
> An abyss it is,
> Like an ancestor
> From which all things come.
>
> It blunts sharpness,
> Resolves tangles;
> It tempers light,
> Subdues turmoil.
>
> A deep pool it is,
> Never to run dry!
> Whose offspring it may be
> I do not know:
> It is like a preface to God.
>
> [*Tao Te Ching*]

Taoist simplicity is not simplemindedness; it reflects a sophisticated conception of human freedom based on naturalness which has had a marked effect both on Confucianism and later Chinese and Japanese schools of Buddhism. The Taoist view of freedom is in direct contrast with the Western conception and deserves our attention. In the West (see Chapter 1) freedom is seen in opposition to causal determinism. According to Determinism everything has a cause and this is understood to mean that nothing is free. Thus, a free act is defined as one which is uncaused, at least by factors outside the agent's control. As long as I can determine all my acts, I am free. The problem is that the springs of action, the ultimate motivation, do not seem to be in my control, and this suggests that I am not free. I am free to choose a medical career and having decided on that, I am free to choose what university to attend, and so on. But why do I want to become a doctor? Because I want to be rich and respected. Why do I want that? Did I choose that? Is that something I have control over or is it something outside my control, something I was born with or had instilled in me by the time I was able to think about it? As we trace the causal chain of actions back in time, we inevitably reach a point where the desire or motivation is simply given, not chosen. Looked at in this way, freedom is merely an illusion; there is the appearance of freedom in the short run, but in the final analysis we are not free. It is this conception of freedom which creates anxiety over trying to control everything.

The Taoist approach is quite different. They say that the anxiety to control is precisely what is not free or spontaneous, but awkward and fumbling. You are most free when you are not clamping a tight control on every syllable you utter, but letting it flow. Similarly in playing a sport. As soon as you become self-conscious and try to control each move you become awkward and inept. The freest and most spontaneous exercise is when you have the confidence in your inner workings to just let go and do it. The springs of action are in you and a part of you, often the product of practice and training, but they are not subject to conscious control. Nor do they need be. There is a place for conscious control, as we suggested in Chapter 3 in our discussion of Ryle and Dewey, where special problems arise within the activity, but the activity as a whole cannot be consciously controlled. But for the Taoist, this does not mean that we are determined, but that we are free. It does imply loosening the sharp distinction we cling to between me and the rest of the world. The springs of action go far back beyond my own existence, perhaps into the dim recesses of our evolutionary past. Perhaps the reason I want to be rich and respected is traceable to a survival instinct which I share with the entire animal kingdom. In that case, my confidence in myself is a confidence in the bond I share with the rest of the world.

After all, I did not create myself. When rational thought first appears it is to articulate feelings and instincts which precede it and over which it has no final control. The Taoist message, then, is to trust in your own nature and its origins in the nature of the universe. Just let it be.

"If you sin against heaven you have noone to save you." Confucius.

Confucianism

Confucianism, the most important philosophy in China, has been largely ignored in the West primarily because it does not fit in with the Perennial Philosophy. Confucianism has always been the dominant intellectual force in China, and it continues to exert a major influence in China today. The first thing to note about Confucianism is that, contrary to many Western interpretations, it is not a religion. When Confucius was asked how to serve God, he replied, "We do not yet know how to serve men; how can we know about serving God?" When he was asked about life after death, he replied in much the same way, "We do not know yet about this life; how can we know about life after death?" His attitude was not hostile to religion as such, but simply a sense of "first things first." The priority in Confucius' mind was on man and this world, and in this sense Confucianism is strongly humanistic. Like the early Hinayana Buddhists, Confucianism is suspicious of all metaphysical speculation on supersensible, otherworldly matters. This mood prevailed in China even after the introduction of Mahayana Buddhist metaphysics (first century A.D.). In the eight and ninth centuries a Confucian revival occurred which modified the Buddhist impact on Chinese thought.

Confucius (557–479 B.C.) devoted his life to moral and social reform. He traveled widely throughout China, offering his social and moral doctrines to various local rulers. Although his ideas for reforming society were never put into effect, his concern for moral reform made a great impact on the Chinese people. Confucius' main concern was with the correct social and political ordering of human society. Social reform, he argued, could not come from above or without, but had to spring from the human heart. Like the Taoists, he was optimistic about human nature. If each man could uncover his own inner potential for good, society would right itself. This was the hope of many people in this country a few years ago as expressed, for example, in Reich's *The Greening of America*. The revolution, Reich argued, would not come from force of arms, whether by a leftist overthrow or a right-wing program of "law and order," but quietly from within a growing number of young people who were working out a life style based on their own inner resources. Today Reich's book appears overly optimistic, but it is not unlike Confucius' attitude toward social change. Morality cannot be legislated, in Confucius' view; it must come from within, and this is possible because human nature is moral.

The foundation of morality, according to Confucius, is *jen*, which is translated roughly as goodwill to men or love and is expressed in a Chinese version of the Golden Rule. This principle can be realized by man because it is within him if only he will recognize and accept it. Human beings are not isolated individuals but social creatures with an inborn concern for others. This begins in the family and can be extended to larger and larger social units.

The second most important Confucian moral principle is *yi* which holds that the ultimate justification for an action is not expediency but inner rightness. In the 1940s Mao Tse-tung appealed to this principle by depicting capitalism as based on selfish expediency in contrast with communism which is based on *yi* and *jen*, the sacrifice of the individual for the greater good of his fellow human beings. This is not to say that Confucianism and Communism are one and the same, but the acceptance of Communism by the Chinese people sprang from an understanding of it in terms of the Confucian tradition, which in turn gave Maoist Communism a distinctly Chinese character. Indeed, the Chinese problem in understanding and assimilating Communism is just like our problem in understanding Confucianism—how can any group of people understand another culture except in terms of their own? Like the development of Chinese Communism, no philosophical or religious system of thought was imported into China without considerable modification by the indigenous Chinese schools of Taoism and Confucianism. This is especially true of Buddhism. From our point of view the most interesting fruit of the synthesis of Indian Buddhism and Chinese thought is Ch'an, or Meditation Buddhism (known in the United States after the Second World War primarily by its Japanese designation, Zen). Actually Ch'an is only one fairly minor sect in the evolution of Chinese Buddhism, but from our admittedly biased point of view it takes on a magnified importance.

THE FINGER AND THE MOON

The central motivating force of Zen is to purify the basic religious doctrine and to clear away metaphysical problems. It became clear that even in traditional Buddhism many philosophical problems remained obscure because of the language used to describe the path to salvation. For example, the Buddhist texts stated that men should not seek to gain anything from activity. Did this mean that men should want to stop wanting anything? That sounds very difficult. "Don't try so hard" is good advice but hard to follow. The traditional Buddhist texts presented intellectual puzzles. The terms and language in which ideas were expressed resulted in conceptual problems. The scriptures said that everything is Buddha and that one should try to become Buddha, and that we are free and should become free. If everything is Buddha, then each of us is Buddha, so why should anyone train for 25 years or more to achieve Buddhahood? A state of enlightenment (vidya) was contrasted with a state of ignorance (avidya), yet all dualistic thinking was emphatically rejected. If there is no difference between the two, then why should anyone spend hours of meditation trying to give up one in order to achieve the other? The texts also said that there were no things existing in the world except the Buddha reality (sometimes referred to as Mind). Did that mean there was only one thing existing, namely the Buddha Mind? If so, what sort of thing is that mind? Is it a gigantic consciousness with no body? Assuming it is mental in nature, is it like the dreaming state or the waking state of mind? Does it think different thoughts in succession, or does it just stare at one thing only (and what would that thing be)? The questions are obviously endless, and the debate, though philosophically interesting, is religiously beside the point.

The Doctrine of Emptiness

A good example of this kind of metaphysical worry is found in the sixth-century Tien-tai, or Lotus school interpretation of Nagarjuna (c. 200 A.D.), founder of the Madyamika school of Buddhism referred to earlier. Nagarjuna taught the doctrine of Emptiness: all is empty, there is no real existence anywhere. He did not mean that reality is literally a void; in fact he expressly rejected the annihilation of anything. "Matter is empty in and of itself," he said; it doesn't have to be wiped out. What he meant was that reality is beyond linguistic and conceptual predication. We cannot say reality exists, not because it doesn't exist, but because "existence" is a word and words have no absolute fix on reality. Nor can we say it is empty or void, because *empty* and *void* are also human concepts which have only a rough application to reality. Thus Nagarjuna's doctrine of Emptiness is not a metaphysical theory that reality is void, but an analytical or linguistic doctrine about the relationship of words to the world.

Nevertheless, Chih-k'ai, the founder of Tien-tai, interpreted Emptiness metaphysically. He took Nagarjuna to mean that since everything is empty, everything is the same—one-in-all and all-in-one. The ultimate reality (called Buddha) is to be found in everything, and indeed, everything is this ultimate reality. All distinctions are collapsed and the net result is a kind of monistic pantheism, not unlike the ancient Upanishadic monistic doctrine of the one Atman substance. Just as the *Upanishads* said "you are that," so Tien-tai said "everything is that." It maintained that every particular object in the phenomenal world of space and time is the ultimate reality, which is empty. But this is the one substance metaphysics all over again! As we have seen, the metaphysical impulse arises again and again; and the need to put it down also appears time and again, first in Hinduism, then in Nagarjuna's Madyamika, and finally in Ch'an, or Zen, in the sixth and seventh centuries A.D.

Zen Buddhism

In many ways, Zen was an attempt to finish a job begun hundreds of years earlier. Though less metaphysical and conceptual in nature, it is this school of Eastern philosophy which has recently attracted the attention of professional, academic philosophers in the West because of their concerns with the relation of words to reality.

The goal of Zen, like that of other Buddhist schools, is to discover the Buddha nature within oneself. It is the Zen methods for achieving this which are different, and particularly its solution to the recurring problem of metaphysical speculation. The Zen solution, which has so intrigued contemporary Western philosophers, is to use philosophy to overcome philosophy. This is very much the view of Ludwig Wittgenstein (1889–1950), the founder of the Anglo-American movement of "Analytic Philosophy." Wittgenstein said that philosophy is a disease which only better philosophizing can cure. Basically, he said, the cause of the disease is a faulty view of the role of language in relation to the world, and the cure is, accordingly, a more accurate theory of language. The very form of words we use causes what Wittgenstein called "mental cramps," and the only way to relieve these cramps is to analyze the misuse of language which has led to them. The Zen approach is very similar. Wittgenstein said that philosophy is like a ladder which we must use to get ourselves out of the hole philosophy has gotten us into—a ladder we promptly discard once we are out, having no further use for it. Zen, borrowing a line from the Taoists, puts the point more succinctly: "Once the fish is caught, what further need have we of the trap?"

The Zen solution to this "metaphysical disease" is ingenious. Rather than asserting one metaphysical position against others or, as Siddhartha Gautama supposedly did, simply refraining from metaphysical discussions, the Zen masters explained away all metaphysical problems as linguistic problems arising out of a primary misunderstanding of the relation of thought to the world. This approach eradicates the problem by going straight to its source. Discussing metaphysics simply encourages it and avoiding it just puts it temporarily to one side. The Zen approach "dissolves" the problem away, as Wittgenstein said in another context, rooting it out completely.

The seeds of this solution go far back in the history of Eastern thought. In the Upanishadic tradition, the illusion of thinking that there are distinct existing things (rupa) is traced to the human invention of words, concepts, and names (nama). Multiplicity comes about through a tempting but unjustifiable extension of language. The assumption, as Western scholastic philosophers put it, is "unum nomen, unum nomenatum" (one word, one thing named), an "ontological" object for every "grammatical" object (see Chapter 3). As contemporary Anglo-American language philosophers are fond of saying, the very language we speak can play tricks on us, leading us unsuspectingly into metaphysical dilemmas of our own making. Thus, we are led to look for a real object for every noun, a real distinction behind every linguistic distinction, a real category or type for every linguistic classification.

Plato reasoned that if we talk about triangles, there must *be* triangles; and since triangles are not material objects, they must be immaterial objects. This leads to the task of defining "immaterial object." Plato also reasoned that since we talk about general features of trees, there must be, in addition to all the individual trees, some general, abstract Treeness or Treehood; since this can't be physical, it must exist outside space and time. The problem is one of our own making, "a learned dust," as Berkeley said, we have raised ourselves.

The Vedanta approach is to treat this metaphysical disease as a linguistic difficulty, confusing "nama" with "rupa." But the cure did not go deeply enough into the heart of the matter, and as in the West, the half-hearted cure leads to Idealism, the view that these supposedly physical things are really mental things. We learn that the notion of distinct physical objects depends on our thinking selves, that is, on our thoughts, words, concepts, and so on. As distinct, independent entities, objects exist only in our minds, not in reality. But this doesn't eliminate metaphysics, it just shifts its ground from physical reality to mental reality. The same type of metaphysical worries occur all over again: Are there many individual mental appearances? Is there a substratum holding together and underlying all these different illusory thoughts? Is there an external cause of such mental phenomena (maya)?—and so on. The cure, if it is to work at all, must be applied completely, and this means leaving aside all metaphysical problems as linguistic confusions.

Early Hindu and Buddhist scholars applied linguistic analysis to dissolve the distinctions which appear to us in the ordinary world of sense experience, but not to the underlying relations between reality and appearance, knowledge and ignorance, one and many, existence and nonexistence—in short, not to the metaphysical language of their own theories. In this respect Zen completes the job. Zen is neither another metaphysics nor a refusal to play metaphysics, but a thorough diagnosis of metaphysical worries of all kinds as linguistic excesses.

Consider, for example, the Buddhist assertion that reality is empty, that nothing really exists in the world. Metaphysically understood, this means that the world is void of objects, like empty space, empty in the sense in which a clear sky contains no objects or differentiation. This is hard to swallow. But understood as a piece of conceptual analysis, the statement begins to make sense. It means that there is nothing in the world corresponding exactly to human concepts and categories of thought, that thoughts are not identical with the objects they denote and the objects denoted are not exhausted by but transcend the words we use to describe them. The eighth-century Zen master Nan-ch'uan puts it,

> During the period before the world was manifested there were no names. The moment Mind arrives in the world there are names, and so we clutch hold of forms. . . . If there are names, everything is classified in limits and bounds. [*Sayings of Ancient Worthies*]

This is less a metaphysical assertion about the nature of reality (that it is void) than a statement of the limitations of language. It is a denial not of the existence of things, but of the objectification of our concepts into things. It is less a theory of reality than a theory of language. Huang-po (d. 850) is aware of this when he writes,

> Men are afraid to forget their own minds, fearing to fall through the void with nothing on to which they can cling. They do not know that the void is not really the void but the real realm of things. [*The Teaching of Huang-po*]

Naturally, when you tell someone that his individual mind, with all its particular thoughts, and all physical things which he can see and touch are unreal, he understands these words metaphysically and becomes terrified, as though the truth of the statement would wipe out the whole of existence! Huang-po says that, properly understood, the assertion of emptiness is not a denial that things exist in the world, but an assertion of the emptiness of these things. It is not an attempt to wipe them out, but to point out something about them, namely, that they are in themselves distinct from the meanings we as human beings attach to them, and in this sense, empty. Human concepts, in other words, are not attached to objects as properties or labels. Huang-po maintains that emptiness is a condition of the world: "Who told you to eliminate anything? Look at the void in front of your eyes. How can you produce it or eliminate it?" If the world *is* empty, it doesn't make any sense to advise people to empty it, for this implies that it is full and needs emptying. But this is precisely what students of Buddhism were taught, or at least this was the most literal and therefore simplest way for them to understand what their instructors required them to do.

The task Huang-po faced as a Zen master was the problem of textual interpretation in the instruction of young Buddhist monks. The sacred Buddhist texts typically asserted that things were unreal, empty, and void and that all duality was illusory; they then went on to prescribe various techniques for eliminating all discriminating thought—"polishing the mirror" of the mind, as it was called, so that it would reflect everything and retain nothing. Understood in a literal way, as a metaphysical theory of reality, such assertions are nonsense and lead to a state of self-hypnotic tranquility or pretense that all those things wiped out of the mind weren't really there in the first place. The way to correct this constant source of misunderstanding was to interpret the emptiness of things as the emptiness of objectified concepts, to realize the interpreting nature of thought without changing it. In other words, don't try to change either your thoughts or the world, but just your mistaken theory about those thoughts and how they relate to a world. As the San-lun scholar, Seng-chao (384–414 A.D.) had written earlier,

> When we say that there is neither existence nor nonexistence, does it mean to wipe out all the myriad things, blot out our seeing and hearing, and be in a state without sound, form or substance before we can call it absolute truth? Truly, absolute truth is in accord with things as they are and therefore is opposed to none. . . . Not being existent and not being nonexistent do not mean that there are no things, but that all things are not things in the real sense. As all things are not things in the real sense, what is there in relation to which a thing can be so-called? Therefore the scripture (of Nagarjuna) says, "Matter is empty by virtue of its own nature; it is not empty because it has been destroyed."
> [*The Emptiness of the Unreal*]

In Seng-chao's view there are things and they are empty. In so far as we interpret the world, there will be a diversified collection of objects and multiple distinctions. We are not to deny or destroy this world, but it must be recognized that it is an interpretation, that in themselves there are no conceptual categories exactly corresponding to and exhausting reality, and that concepts are human labels used to package the world into convenient, self-contained units.

Another group of contemporary Western philosophers to whom these views will sound familiar is the phenomenologists, notably the German philosopher, Edmund Husserl. In Husserl's analysis of the "world from the natural standpoint," he seeks to observe without criticizing or correcting the ordinary man's everyday view of things. As he observes, we normally take the world as given, that is, we do not normally recognize any distinction between our concepts and the objects to which those concepts are directed. Not distinguishing them, we confuse the two, "mistaking the finger for the moon." As we will discuss further in Chapter 8, we ordinarily suppose, naively, that our words, names, concepts attach themselves to objects, belong to them inherently, like labels or properties. The naivety of this "Naive Realism" was also recognized by nineteenth-century Western Idealists who saw this, however, like certain Hindu and Buddhist thinkers, as a mistake which had to be corrected by a better and more sophisticated metaphysical theory. What this shows, they argued, is that our view of the world is dependent on us and our thinking and linguistic apparatus. Therefore these supposed physical things are really mental things (appearances, illusions, phenomena). The world is my idea, as Schopenhauer boldly said; nothing exists but minds and their thoughts. Naive Realism is thus replaced by a sophisticated Idealism.

But this is just the other side of the metaphysical coin. Like Zen, Husserl is not trying to change or correct the way the world ordinarily appears to us, or to make us think this is all a big mistake, except to make us aware of how this takes place. It's like becoming aware that you are hiccupping; you don't stop hiccupping, but simply realize what you are doing. All that changes is that we are no longer naively swallowing a false view of the relation of language to the world. We do what we have always done, though this time we know what we are doing. So long as there are people there will be linguistic and conceptual interpretations of the world, and so there will be objects, properties, divisions, and so on. The only mistake in all of this is a failure to realize our own responsibility for this arrangement, the recognition that in themselves things are empty of the labels we project onto them.

The point is made in a telling way in a story about the selection of Hui-neng (637–713 A.D.) as the Sixth Zen Patriarch. His predecessor, Hung-jan, decided to bestow the honor on the monk who could write the best poem on the nature of Buddhism. One night a young contender, Shen-hsiu, posted the following poem on the temple walls.

> The body is the Bodhi Tree;
> The mind like a bright mirror standing.
> Take care to wipe it all the time,
> And allow no dust to cling.

Publicly Hung-jan praised the poem, but when Shen-hsiu came to him privately, the Fifth Pariarch was critical. The next day another poem appeared in place of the first which everyone understood could only have been written by Hui-neng.

> There never was a Bodhi Tree,
> Nor bright mirror standing.
> Fundamentally, not one thing exists,
> So where is the dust to cling?

This expressed better the nature of Buddhism and so Hui-nèng was named to succeed Hung-jan. By analogy with wiping the mirror, Shen-hsiu's poem suggests, rightly enough, the emptiness of phenomenal reality, but it also suggests another underlying reality which is just as damaging to religious insight, that of minds, illusions, existence, and nonexistence.

In a similar exchange, to Wo-luan's poem,

> I, Wo-luan, know a device
> Whereby to blot out all my thoughts:
> The objective world no more stirs the mind,
> And daily matures my Enlightenment!

Hui-neng responded with one of his own:

> I, Hui-neng, know no device,
> My thoughts are not suppressed:
> The objective world ever stirs the mind,
> And what is the use of maturing Enlightenment?

Similarly, when Huang-po writes, "There is no 'self' and no 'other.' There is no 'wrong desire,' no 'anger,' no 'hatred,' no 'love,' no 'victory,' no 'failure,' " we must be careful how we understand him. In one sense the assertion is true; but in another sense it is quite false. Of course, there is hatred, love, and failure in the world. If our understanding of language views words like "hatred," "love," and "failure" as illuminating certain genuine aspects of the world from different human standpoints, then it is obviously true to say that there is hatred, love, and failure. But if we view language as naming inherent properties, literally corresponding with objects, then it would be false to say that hatred, love, and failure exist in the world. Huang-po's assertion that there is no hatred or failure means that hatred and failure are to be viewed not as things in the world but as concepts we use with varying degrees of success to illuminate aspects of the world.

Since religious instruction, like all instruction, must rely on linguistic media, there is a persistent and permanent danger of confusion which much Zen writing is designed to correct. The difficulty is unavoidable insofar as it is built into the very nature of language. To express the fact that men mistake concepts for reality, classical Buddhist texts contrasted ignorance with enlightenment, the emptiness of reality with the fullness of things in the ordinary world of appearances. This view suggests some special state of mind to be achieved, namely Enlightenment, and that this Enlightenment consists in the realization that the world is utterly empty! However, this is the very way of thinking the texts were trying to overcome!

Some of the most puzzling and yet philosophically interesting comments in Zen literature are concerned with eliminating this linguistic source of misunderstanding. As Huang-po says,

> There *are* no Enlightenment men or ignorant men, and there *is* no oblivion. Yet though basically everything is without objective existence, you must not come to think in terms of anything nonexistent; and though things are not nonexistent, you must not form a concept of anything existing. For "existence" and "nonexistence" are both empirical concepts no better than illusions. [*The Teaching of Huang-po*]

It is not a question of asserting or denying objects or properties in the world; the question is primarily how we understand the words we do use to describe the objects which we do experience. *Oblivion* and *emptiness* are concepts we use to suggest the interpretive nature of human thought and the open-ended character of things in the world of ordinary experience. These terms are useful devices and properly understood lead to true assertions about reality, but contrary to their intended meaning, they also suggest the false position that there exists a special state of mind in which reality is apprehended as blank oblivion.

There is a similar situation in the "negative way" of many mystic writers. Reality, they say, is not A or B or C or anything else you care to mention. If we understand such expressions as denying these features of reality in the ordinary naive way, we arrive at the preposterous interpretation that reality is a formless void in the light of which our ordinary experience is an utter hoax. But if we view such statements as putting forward one view of language at the expense of another, then they begin to make sense. Reality is not A in the sense that A does not fix or exhaust reality; A is simply a human interpretation which clarifies for us certain facets of reality from a given point of view. As Huang-po puts it, reality

> is not green nor yellow and has neither form nor appearance. It does not belong to the categories of things which exist or do not exist. . . . It is neither long nor short, big nor small, for it transcends all limits, measures, names, traces and comparisons. It is that which you see before you—begin to reason about it and at once you fall into error. It is like the boundless void which cannot be fathomed or measured. [*The Teaching of Huang-po*]

The point is not that we can't meaningfully and truly make comparisons and draw distinctions, which we obviously can, but that reality "transcends all measures and comparisons." The error is in objectifying concepts, that is, naively projecting our concepts onto the world without knowing we are doing so. At first when Huang-po says that reality does not belong to any of our categories, that it transcends all limits, and so on, we may begin to think of some gigantic, mystical stuff underlying everything, encompassing all. But when he goes on to say that "it is that which you see before you," we are brought back to earth once more. It is not Reality (with a capital R) which transcends our categories, but simply things like the book you are holding in your hand. "Book" is an English word which designates a class of things of which this object is a member. But this is a very general description. This thing is not just "a book," but an individual, existing thing in its own right. No matter how detailed your description of it is, it never exhausts the simple object in your hands, both in the sense that that description could apply to another book and in the sense that you could, if you had the time, think of other true things to say about this object.

This is why many religious thinkers prefer to express themselves in terms of nonduality: "It is neither X nor non-X, nor is it neither X nor non-X, nor both X and non-X; but we use the term 'X' to call attention to it." As Nagarjuna put it,

> It cannot be called void or not void,
> Or both or neither;
> But in order to point it out,
> It is called "the Void."
> [*Madhyamika Karikas*]

This overcomes the metaphysical tendency by literally wearing it out. Every metaphysical possibility is carefully and systematically exhausted. If it's not X then it's non-X, right? Wrong. Well, then, it's neither X nor non-X, right? No. Both? No. Hmmmm. Putting it this way attacks head-on the literal, metaphysical understanding of the relation of word to object, frustrating it and putting it, at least temporarily, in abeyance, so that one is prepared to understand in a radically new way the idea that we "use the term 'X' simply to call attention to it." As Huang-po said, "It is *like* the boundless void." We use the idea of the void, not to deny the multiplicity of things in our experience, but to call attention to the fact that the lines of demarcation between things are lines we have traced from our own point of view for our own purposes.

> So let your symbolic conception be that of a void. . . . Eschew all symbolozing whatever, for by this eschewal, is "symbolized" the Great Void in which is neither unity nor multiplicity—that Void which is not really void, that Symbol which is not a symbol. [*The Teaching of Huang-po*]

This statement of Huang-po should rank in profundity and brilliance with the poems of Hui-neng. Really there is no Great Void and no giving up of symbolizing, but these are two symbols we use to point to the same thing. To encourage us to give up symbolizing in the wrong way we speak of the Great Void, then, when the metaphysical impulse is in danger of converting that symbol into a new metaphysics of Nihilism, we explain the Great Void as a way of getting people to give up symbolizing in the wrong way. But they're all symbols, including the symbol "symbol"!

It is like trying to draw a picture of a tree. There are many aspects of the tree which may interest us and which we can convey with varying degrees of success by lines drawn on paper. We may be impressed with the overall configuration of the leafy section of the tree which we translate as a single linear outline. Or we may be interested in the relation of light to darker areas which we transcribe onto paper as black and white patches. These aspects are there to be drawn, but it is we who emphasize them by drawing them, calling attention to them. There *is* a shape to the tree which some outlines convey better than others, but no single continuous line tracing this. There *are* lighter and darker areas, but no patches of black and white. The point is made clearly in the Buddha's reply to his students' speculation about the nature of ultimate reality in the Hinayana parable of the elephant (in the *Udana* scripture):

> In former times a Raja sent for all the blind men in his capital and placed an elephant in their midst. One man felt the head of the elephant, another an ear, another a tusk, another the tuft of its tail. Asked to describe the elephant, one said that an elephant was a a large pot, others that it was a winnowing fan, a ploughshare, a broom. Thus each described the elephant as the part which he first touched, and the Raja was consumed with merriment. "Thus," said the Buddha, "are those students who, blind, unseeing, knowing not the truth, yet each maintain that it is thus and thus." [*Udana*]

Another stratagem devised by Buddhist writers to get around such misunderstandings was to interpret the classic texts as tools or devices for getting the uninitiated from a naive way of looking at things to a more sophisticated standpoint. The implication is that once we have made the step up, we no longer accept the tool (the words) at face value. Once we're out of the hole, who needs the ladder; once the fish is caught, who needs the net? According to Chi-tsang those on the first level ordinarily suppose, like those who view the world "from the natural standpoint" (Husserl), that objects exist just as they appear to us, and the classic texts, Chi-tsang says, addressing themselves to this level of thought, begin by showing reasons why these objects do not exist in this way.

The Finger and the Moon   195

These arguments, as we have seen, lead to a kind of idealism or nihilism in which ordinary objects of experience are said to be unreal and mind-dependent. But this second stage of awareness is only intended as a device to get initiates away from the first stage of naive absorption in things; it is not meant to characterize the final Buddhist position. And so we come to the final stage in which it becomes clear that all these terms, "reality," "emptiness," "duality," are simply devices for overcoming a false view of the relation of thought and language to reality. As Chi-tsang puts it,

> Ordinary people say that things . . . possess being, without realizing that they possess nothing. Therefore the Buddhas propound to them the doctrine that things are ultimately empty and void. When it is said that things possess being, it is ordinary people who say so. This is worldly truth, the truth of ordinary people. . . . Next comes the second stage, which explains that both being and nonbeing belong to worldly truth, whereas nonduality (neither being nor nonbeing) belongs to absolute truth. . . . Next comes the third stage in which both duality and nonduality are worldly truth. [*Essay on the Double Truth*]

Further on in the essay he writes,

> The idea of nonexistence is presented primarily to handle the disease of the concept of existence. If that disease disappears, the useless medium is also discarded. . . . We are forced to use the word "correctly" in order to stop the perverseness. Once perverseness has been stopped, correctness will no longer remain.

At that point we no longer need Wittgenstein's ladder or the Zen fish trap. In the famous *Chung Lun* text,

> The Great Sage preached the law of Emptiness
> In order to free men from all views.
> If one still holds the view that Emptiness exists,
> Such a person the Buddhas will not transform.

On the final level, then, one sees assertions about the being of Nirvana, Buddha, and so on, and the nonbeing of duality, objects, and so on, as statements about the nature of thought and language and their relation to reality. If we are aware that thought and language are the projections of human concepts and meanings, then, coming full circle, there is no danger and hence nothing false in saying that the world is full of different individual things. There is no denial of anything in the world, only various attempts to correct inadequate ideas as to how we stand toward things in the world. The important thing is to see what words can and cannot be made to do. As Huang-po says,

> Even Enlightenment, the Absolute, Reality, Sudden Attainment, the Dharmakaya and all the others . . . are—every one of them—mere concepts for helping us through samsara, they have nothing to do with the real Buddha-Mind.
>
> "Studying the Way" is just a figure of speech. . . . Studying leads to the retention of concepts and so the way is entirely misunderstood. . . . The first step is to refrain from knowledge-based concepts. . . . You must not allow this name ("Way") to lead you into forming a mental concept of a road. [*The Teaching of Huang-po*]

Are there objects and properties in the world? In one sense, according to one view of language and meaning, yes; in another sense, according to another view of language and meaning, no. The wisdom of Zen writing is its keen awareness of this ambiguity. In the end, as Wittgenstein also said, nothing is denied, everything is "given back," and in a sense we simply return to the beginning—but with an important difference we will discuss in Chapter 8. Ching-yuan (d. 740) states it perfectly.

> Before I had studied Zen for thirty years, I saw mountains as mountains, and waters as waters. When I arrived at a more intimate knowledge, I came to the point where I saw that mountains are not mountains, and waters are not waters. But now that I have got its very substance I am at rest. For it is just that I see mountans once again as mountains, and waters once again as waters. [Ch'uan-teng Lu, *Record of the Transmission of the Lamp*]

These are the various stages referred to in Chi-tsang's statement above. We begin by supposing that objects are simply identical with our way of describing them (Naive Realism, or the world from the natural standpoint). Later we see that these descriptions are our own projections and this leads to the idealist denial that there are any mountains and the like in reality. But this is simply the opposite side of the naive realist position, equally sunk in all its half-digested assumptions. And so we are led to a final assessment which neither denies nor affirms, but simply takes note of the interpretive nature of thought and language. Naively, mountains just are mountains. But this naive view is wrong; mountains are not simply mountains, that is, reality is not exhausted by but overflows our concept of a "mountain," and in this sense, mountains are not mountains. But once we have got beyond this naive view of things, we are free to say once again that in the sense that "mountain" does illuminate a perceptible aspect of the world from a certain point of view, mountains are mountains. In the end we are brought back to the everyday world of sense experience.

What is so remarkable about Zen is that it is not directed to mysterious or supersensible entities which transcend ordinary sense experience, but to the rich, beautiful, confusing world of everyday experience. This is one of the reasons Zen is so closely allied to the arts. Art is concerned with objects of sense, either representing certain aspects of perceptible objects or creating new objects of sight and sound. In most religions the objects of worship, God and so on, are not physical, perceptible objects and therefore can only be represented symbolically. Often in the history of these religions there is an underlying hostility between art (concerned with the here and now) and religion (concerned with a transcendent reality beyond time and space). In Zen there is no such tension, and many of the most telling expressions of Zen are poems (haiku) and ink-wash drawings. Here art and religion combine with an earthy quality to form a unique blend.

> Weeds in the rice-field,
> Cut and left lying just so—
> Fertilizer!

> On a withered branch
> A crow is perched,
> In the autumn evening.

> With the evening breeze,
> The water laps against
> The heron's legs.

> In the dark forest
> A berry drops:
> The sound of the water.
>
> Leaves falling,
> Lie on one another;
> The rain beats on the rain.
>
> A trout leaps;
> Clouds are moving
> In the bed of the stream.
>
> The sound of the scouring
> Of the saucepan blends
> With the tree-frogs' voices.

Metaphysics seems at last to have been left far behind!

CONCLUSION

Today Buddhism, Confucianism, and Hinduism continue to exert enormous influence on the practical day-to-day affairs of millions of people in the East, and Eastern thought continues to have a powerful effect on the Western imagination trying to solve its own problems. But changes are also occurring. Modernization in India, China, and Vietnam brings with it the same process of secularization we have experienced in the West and a corresponding dimunition of religious thinking in the affairs of those countries. And in the West our attitude toward Eastern thought is becoming more mature and less biased. More and more we are making the attempt to understand Eastern philosophies on their own terms without rewriting them in Western concepts. Hopefully, this will improve the growing dialogue between philosophy East and West.

TOPICS FOR DISCUSSION

1. What are some of the differences between philosophy and religion? Why are Eastern religions more philosophical in nature than Western religions?
2. Is contemporary Chinese Communism a refutation of its philosophical past?

3. Do Eastern religions believe in God?
4. If, according to Hinduism, goal-directed action is bad, what are we supposed to do, sit back and do nothing?
5. What is freedom according to Taoism? Are you free in this sense?
6. Did the Buddha think reality was one or many, eternal or changing?
7. Why are Eastern religious practices so popular in this country today?
8. What is the point of Hindu or Buddhist meditation?
9. In what sense is Eastern philosophy philosophical; in what sense is it not?
10. In what sense is everyone already a Buddha; in what sense have some people failed to achieve Buddhahood?
11. How does religious belief differ from metaphysical belief?

SELECTED BIBLIOGRAPHY

Primary Source

Burtt, E. A., ed. *The Teachings of the Compassionate Buddha.* New York: The New American Library, 1957.

Chan, Wing-tsit, trans. *A Source Book of Chinese Philosophy.* Princeton: Princeton University Press, 1963.

Edgerton, Franklin, trans. and ed. *The Bhagavad-Gita.* 2nd century B.C. New York: Harper and Row, 1968.

Henderson, Harold, trans. and ed. *Haiku.* Garden City, New York: Doubleday, 1958.

Huang-po. *The Teaching of Huang-po.* 9th century. Translated by John Blofeld. New York: Grove Press, 1959.

Husserl, Edmund. *Ideas.* 1913. Translated by Boyce Gibson. New York: Macmillan, 1969.

Huxley, Aldous. *The Perennial Philosophy.* London: Harper and Row, 1945.

Lao-Tzu. *Tao te Ching.* 3rd century B.C. Translated and edited by Wing-tsit Chan. New York: Bobbs-Merrill, 1963.

Macnicol, Nicol, ed. *Hindu Scriptures.* New York: Dutton, 1957.

Radhakrishnan, Sarvepalli, and Charles Moore, eds. *A Source Book in Indian Philosophy.* Princeton: Princeton University Press, 1957.

Swami Prabhavananda and Frederick Manchester, trans. *The Upanishads.* c. 600 B.C. New York: New American Library, 1957.

Wittgenstein, Ludwig. *Philosophical Investigations.* Translated by G. E. Anscombe. New York: Macmillan, 1953.

Secondary Source

Barry, William de, ed. *The Buddhist Tradition.* New York: Random House, 1969.

Blyth, R. H. *Zen in English Literature and Oriental Classics.* 1942. New York: Dutton, 1960.

Earhart, H. B. *Japanese Religion.* Encino, California: Dickenson, 1969.

Fung Yu-lan. *A Short History of Chinese Philosophy.* Edited by Derk Bodde. New York: Macmillan, 1966.

Herrigel, Eugene. *Zen in the Art of Archery.* Translated by R. F. C. Hull. New York: Pantheon, 1953.

Hick, John. *Philosophy of Religion.* Englewood Cliffs, New Jersey: Prentice-Hall, 1963.

Hopkins, Thomas. *The Hindu Religious Tradition.* Encino, California: Dickenson, 1971.

Humphreys, Christmas. *Buddhism.* Harmondsworth, England: Penguin, 1954.

Organ, Troy. *The Hindu Quest for the Perfection of Man.* Athens, Ohio: Ohio University Press, 1970.

Otto, Rudolf. *Mysticism East and West.* 1932. New York: Meridan, 1957.

Reich, Charles. *The Greening of America.* New York: Random House, 1970.

Robinson, R. *The Buddhist Religion.* Encino, California: Dickenson, 1970.

Suzuki, D. T. *Zen Buddhism.* Edited by William Barrett. Garden City, New York: Doubleday, 1956.

Watts, Alan. *The Way of Zen.* New York: Pantheon, 1957.

Wienpahl, Paul. "Zen and the Work of Wittgenstein." *Chicago Review,* Summer 1958.

Zimmer, Heinrich. *Philosophies of India.* 1943. Edited by Joseph Campbell. New York: Meridan, 1957.

CHAPTER 6

Ethics

The Philosophy of Morality

WHAT IS ETHICS?

Ethics, simply put, is moral philosophy. It is generally divided into two areas: (1) normative ethics and (2) metaethics. Moral philosophy is the branch of philosophy which deals with moral judgements, issues, and problems.

Normative ethics is concerned with moral judgements and considers such questions as "What action is right?" and "How is the moral man to be recognized?" There are basically three kinds of moral judgements. First, there are judgements of moral obligation. These are judgements about the rightness or wrongness of actions. Saying that a certain action is right is a judgement of moral obligation. Secondly, there are judgements of moral value. These are judgements about the goodness or badness of persons. Finally, there are judgements of nonmoral value. Such a judgement is made, for example, when someone says that a particular kind of car is good. The main intention here is to commend the car, not to praise it as being moral. There are several different types of normative ethical theories, and they can be categorized in terms of these three kinds of judgements. The main task of normative ethics is to discover criteria with which moral judgements can be made. That is, normative ethics has to make clear just what norm or standard is being used when an action is judged right or a man good.

Metaethics, on the other hand, is not concerned with norms and standards. Metaethical issues include, for example, the meaning of the words "right" and "good" and the distinction between facts and values. We often cannot answer normative issues without also answering certain metaethical issues. For example, to determine the rightness or wrongness of actions we must first determine just what "right" and "wrong" mean. Metaethics has come into its own only in the twentieth century, and it goes beyond traditional ethics, which was primarily normative, by considering problems which had not traditionally been thought to be part of ethics at all.

The moral problems themselves (abortion, for example) which generate the debate within these two main areas of ethical consideration are, of course, another important aspect of moral philosophy. Both normative ethics and metaethics try to solve these moral problems, not keep them in the realm of the general and theoretical. If they did not approach the problems this way, ethics would not be the practical enterprise that philosophers consider it to be.

Before a moral problem can be adequately treated and answered, there are certain philosophical tools which must necessarily be acquired. These tools are best acquired through a basic understanding of normative and metaethical theories. Thus, even though moral problems may be said to generate ethical theories, knowledge of the ethical theories themselves is necessary in order to adequately solve the problems.

NORMATIVE ETHICS

Relativism

Before discussing normative theories which put forth objective criteria for right and wrong, let us look at *relativism*, a theory which does not have such criteria. Relativists maintain that no action can be judged right or wrong, good or bad, by a standard that applies to all people at all times; rather they claim that all ethical standards must be regarded as relative to and dependent on the individuals and societies holding them. Many sociologists and anthropologists have been relativists. Relativism is a moral theory which seems to justify any action. If a moral theory can justify any action, however, then it is no moral theory at all for it denies any distinction between right and wrong.

Relativists usually begin with the basic premise that ethical beliefs or standards are different for different societies and people.

From this premise some relativists conclude that since there appears to be no way to tell which ethical standards are universally valid or applicable, there are therefore no objective criteria on which to establish ethical beliefs and judgements at all. Normative relativism takes a less extreme view, maintaining that what is right for one group or society is not necessarily for another. Most philosophers argue that normative relativism is not a true ethical theory, for ethical theories must all be based on a principle of universality, that what is right for one individual or society is necessarily right for another. Nonetheless, normative relativism is the most popular relativist position.

The following is a general formula for normative relativism: " 'X is right' means 'Y ——— X is right,' " in which X represents any action whose rightness or wrongness we are trying to determine; Y represents any individual being or group of beings and could be replaced with "I," "you," "society," "the gods," and so on; and the blank is to be filled in with any feeling or attitude, such as "thinks that" or "does not believe that." A normative relativist might make the following claim: Helping others is right because I think or feel that it is right or helping others is right because my peers think or feel that it is right. The rightness or wrongness of actions thus depends on the attitudes and feeling of persons.

It is this theory of ethics which makes people say that what is right for me is not necessarily right for you, or that what is right for one society or nation is not necessarily right for another. For example, it might be right for one society to practice infanticide and yet not right for another to do so. What makes this possible is the fact that right and wrong have to do with attitudes, not objective criteria. Infanticide is right for one society because that society believes that it is right, while it is wrong for another society because that society believes that it is wrong. Both societies are correct in their ethical beliefs or judgements precisely because such judgements are attitudinal in nature.

Such an ethical theory has some very obvious shortcomings. According to this theory, an action may be both right and wrong at the same time or right at one time and wrong at another —"X is right" and "X is wrong" may both be true. A relativist must admit, then, either that his theory involves a contradiction or that even though there seems to be a contradiction there actually is not for right and wrong really do depend on how people feel, think, believe, and so on. The first alternative is not philosophically tenable. A theory which involves a contradiction is no theory at all. The second alternative gets the relativist into even deeper trouble. If right and wrong really do depend on feelings, beliefs, and so on, then the most heinous of crimes might be justified on the relativist's grounds. For example, a society might justify mass murder of a minority within that society on the grounds that the majority feels or believes that such an action is right.

Probably the strongest argument against relativism is that it leads to an infinite regression. The relativist argues that "X is right" means "I feel that X is right," for rightness is defined in terms of feeling. It might be asked what the "X is right" in "I feel X is right" means. The relativist would answer that it means "I feel X is right." If the same question is asked of the reply, the same answer must be given, ad infinitum. We are never really told what "right" means; all we are told is that someone has a certain attitude toward an action.

Relativism does not give any objective way to judge an action's rightness or wrongness. We can come to know how people think or feel about certain actions, but we can never come to know whether these actions are right or wrong. Thus, as an ethical theory, relativism has no merit at all. Yet as a theory of taste it might have some. It is possible for certain practices to be right in a nonmoral sense for one group or society and to be wrong in a nonmoral sense for another. For example, among certain segments of the American population, long hair on males is considered wrong, yet among other segments it is considered not only right but desirable as well. Tastes are not universal, ethical truths are. Let us now turn to some normative ethical theories which do claim to have objective criteria and universal validity, that is, theories which claim that rightness and wrongness are independent of how people feel or what they think.

Teleological Theories

Teleological theories are ethical theories in which the objective criterion for the rightness or wrongness of an action is the amount of nonmoral good brought into being by that action. "Teleological" is derived from the Greek word *telos*, which means "end," and teleological theories determine the rightness or wrongness of an action by looking to the end of the action.

If in the end an action produces a greater balance of good over evil than any other possible action, then that action is right. If the action does not produce the greatest possible balance of good over evil, then it is not right.

There are two main considerations in teleological theories. One is the person or persons for whom the good is produced. If the good produced is only supposed to benefit the agent of the action, then *egoism* results. *Utilitarians*, on the other hand, argue that the good produced must be for the greatest number of people; possibly excluding the agent of the action. The second consideration is how "good" is to be interpreted or defined. There are many theories of good; hedonism and the perfection theory are two of the most common. The theory of hedonism claims that good is simply pleasure or happiness and that evil is the lack of pleasure or happiness. The perfection theory claims that good is perfection: the more perfection the more good, the less perfection the less good. In our discussion of egoism and utilitarianism, we will concentrate on two important and well-known English hedonists: Thomas Hobbes (1588–1679) who is a hedonistic egoist, and John Stuart Mill (1806–1873) who is a hedonistic utilitarian.

EGOISM. An egoist is one who claims that the criterion for the rightness of actions is the amount of good produced for the agent of the action. According to egoism, an individual has only one basic moral obligation: to produce for himself the greatest amount of good possible, or rather, the greatest possible balance of good over evil. It follows from this that even in making second- and third-person judgements of moral obligation, an ethical egoist must use as his criterion what is to his own advantage.

For an ethical egoist, then, first-, second-, and third-person moral judgements are to be made in terms of the advantages produced for him. For example, as an egoist I would say that an action I am doing is right if and only if it is advantageous to me. Furthermore, if, as an egoist, I say that an action which you are doing is right, I still would mean that that action is right if and only if it is to my advantage, not necessarily to yours. In other words, an egoist judges his own or another person's action to be right if and only if it produces the greatest possible balance of good over evil for himself.

It might well be asked why ethical egoism should be adopted instead of the moral point of view which is usually considered to be the disinterested view. The interested, that is, self-interested point of view (egoism) is usually thought not to be a moral point of view. The disinterested view is considered moral because morality, ethics, has to do with our actions toward others and thus with the interests of others, not just our own interests. In response it is often argued that ethical egoism should be adopted because it is human nature for each person to seek his or her own good advantage. This position is called psychological egoism because it maintains that people are psychologically constructed in such a way that they can only seek their own interests. Thus, it is argued that we ought to seek our own good because it is natural for us to do so.

The seventeenth-century British philosopher Thomas Hobbes held a similar view. Hobbes was a philosopher in the broadest possible sense of the word and his studies ranged from political philosophy to science. He is most remembered for his book *Leviathan*, which contains his civil and political philosophy as well as his ethics. According to Hobbes, each man has the liberty (the absence of external impediment) "to use his own power, as he will himself, for the preservation of his own nature; that is to say, his own life; and consequently, of doing anything which in his own judgement and reason he shall conceive to be the aptest means thereunto."[1] Hobbes calls this liberty "the right of nature." The right of nature prevails only in what Hobbes calls the natural state of man, the state of nature. In this state, the original human condition, there is no common power over all people; rather every person is against every other person. Further, in the state of nature there is no law and no justice, and each person may make use of whatever he must to preserve his own life. Life in this natural state was, according to Hobbes, solitary, poor, nasty, brutish, and short. When each person serves only his own self-interest and finds every other person a possible impediment to this self-interest, life is not, indeed, a pleasant experience.

Man soon discovers that in the state of nature there can be no security for anyone and "that every man ought to endeavor peace, as far as he has hope of obtaining it; and when he cannot obtain it, that he may seek, and use, all helps and advantages of war,"[2] of the state of nature. That is, man soon discovers,

---

1. Hobbes, Thomas, *Leviathan* (New York: Collier Books, 1962), p. 103.
2. Ibid., pp. 103–104.

through reason, that the state of nature is a state of war in which every person opposes every other person. The only way to insure against this condition is to seek peace. Man discovers that he must lay aside the right of nature, his right to do anything to survive or to preserve his life, to insure peace and his own security. This discovery is the discovery of a law of nature. A law of nature is "a precept or general rule, found out by reason, by which a man is forbidden to do that, which is destructive of his life, or taketh away the means of preserving the same; and to omit that, by which he thinketh it may be best preserved."[3] The right of nature differs from a law of nature in that the former is the liberty of each person to do or not to do what he must to preserve his own being, whereas the latter is the obligation of each person to do or not to do what he must to preserve his own being. The laws of nature, in effect, override the right of nature because the natural condition iself is not conducive to the preservation of the individual. Thus, the right of nature says that man naturally does anything that he must to survive in the natural state, whereas the laws of nature say, in effect, that the state of nature itself is not conducive to survival and that man must therefore seek a civil state. Both right and law address themselves to the preservation of the individual and are, therefore, egoistic.

Hobbes is an egoist, then, because he argues that judgements of moral obligation are to be made in terms of what is good for the individual, namely the individual's preservation. Hobbes does not talk of the greatest amount of good for the greatest number of people, as we will see Mill does, but rather of the greatest amount of good for the individual.

Egoism, like relativism, has many shortcomings. It lacks what most moral theorists argue is an essential ingredient of any good moral theory, namely a universality with regard to obligation. Egoism is based on self-interest rather than disinterest, the latter being the moral point of view. This leads to one of the shortcomings. As has been stated earlier, ethical egoism is often justified on the grounds that psychological egoism is true. However, it is highly questionable whether psychological egoism is true, for there are many instances of persons acting out of an interest for others and not out of their own self-interest. Further, even if psychological egoism is true, even if people do always act out of their own self-interest, ethical egoism does not follow.

3. Ibid., p. 103.

What follows is that there can be no morality, for morality requires the freedom to act in various ways.

There are also some serious flaws in ethical egoism itself. It might be asked whether the promotion of self-interest and obligation always coincide. Are there right actions, for example, which do not promote our own self-interest? The answer seems to be yes.

Ethical egoism is also going to have difficulty with such concepts as judging and advising. If a judge were an ethical egoist, then his decision would have to be rendered on the grounds of what is good for him, hardly an objective and impartial way to make decisions. The concept of advice is no more well handled by the egoist. When giving advice, the egoist has to do so on the grounds of what would be good for him. Again, this is hardly objective or impartial.

UTILITARIANISM. Utilitarian theories are teleological in that the criterion for the rightness or wrongness of an action is the nonmoral value brought into being as an end result of that action. Nonmoral values are simply those values which have no direct moral value, as in the example that a car may be good, but it is not morally good. Utilitarianism differs from egoism by maintaining that the amount of good brought into being must be for the greatest possible number of people, whereas egoism holds that such good need be only for the agent of the action.

John Stuart Mill was a nineteenth-century British philosopher who is remembered today as one of the early utilitarians, though his interests covered a broad spectrum of areas within philosophy. Mill expounds his version of utilitarianism in what has come to be one of the most influential short essays in all of philosophy, *Utilitarianism*. The first principle of utilitarianism is, according to Mill, the utility or greatest happiness principle which "holds that actions are right in proportion as they tend to promote happiness; wrong as they tend to promote the reverse of happiness."[4] Actions are right if they promote happiness, a nonmoral good, and wrong if they promote unhappiness, a nonmoral evil.

In his essay, Mill examines the two main considerations of teleological theories mentioned earlier—for whom the good is to

---

4. John Stuart Mill, *Utilitarianism* (New York: Bobbs-Merrill, 1957), p. 10.

be produced and what this good is. He argues that the good produced is not the agent's own happiness; rather it is the good produced for the greatest number of people. The nonmoral good which is to be brought into being is happiness or pleasure; the nonmoral evil which is to be avoided is unhappiness or pain. Thus, Mill's first principle is that an action is right if it produces the greatest amount of good, or pleasure, for the greatest number of people, and is wrong if it produces a great amount of evil, or pain, for a great number of people.

But just what kind of pleasure is Mill concerned with? For example, is an action which produces a great amount of sensual pleasure for a great number of people better than one which produces intellectual pleasure for a relatively small number of people? Is pinball better than poetry? Mill answers that not only the quantity of the pleasure produced but also the quality must be considered. There are higher and lower pleasures, qualitatively. Intellectual pleasures such as poetry are higher than sensual pleasures. Mill argues that intellectual pleasures are higher pleasures because these are the ones chosen by a competent judge who has experienced both higher and lower pleasures. A competent judge is one who has experienced both intellectual and sensual pleasures and assigned the former to a higher plane and the latter to a lower plane. In effect, Mill argues that human (meaning intellectual) pleasures are better than animal (meaning sensual) pleasures, a position summed up in his famous statement "It is better to be a human being dissatisfied than a pig satisfied; better to be a Socrates dissatisfied than a fool satisfied."[5]

The questions might be raised as to how Mill arrived at his first principle of morality and how he proved this principle. First principles are usually not thought to be provable. Mill himself argues that such principles are not amenable to direct proof and that ultimate ends, in this case good, cannot be directly proven. It can further be argued that if a first principle were itself always provable, an infinite regression would be generated. However, Mill argues that his first principle can be given a proof, though not a direct or deductive one, and this proof in turn gives the reasons for accepting or rejecting the first principle of utilitarian ethics.

Mill begins the proof of his first principle with what he calls a "theory of life." The theory of life is hedonism which

5. Ibid., p. 15.

claims "that pleasure and freedom from pain are the only things desirable as ends; and that all desirable things [which are as numerous in the utilitarian as in any other scheme] are desirable either for pleasure inherent in themselves or as means to the promotion of pleasure and the prevention of pain."[6]

This hedonistic theory of life is, in actuality, a psychological theory. Mill makes an empirical claim that all people desire or seek pleasure and avoid pain. It is a claim about how people are, how they are made up, how they are built, and Mill claims they are built to desire that which is instrumental to happiness or is happiness itself.

Hedonism is the foundation of Mill's proof. Mill seeks to prove that happiness is desirable, that is, that happiness ought to be desired. This is, of course, just the first principle restated, which Mill proves in the following way: he argues that "the sole evidence it is possible to produce that anything is desirable is that people do actually desire it. . . . No reason can be given why the general happiness is desirable, except that each person . . . desires his own happiness."[7]

At first glance, it seems that Mill has given a direct proof of the first principle. He seems to have argued that from the fact that happiness and happiness alone is desired as an end, it follows that happiness and happiness alone is desirable or good as an end. It might be argued that Mill's proof is invalid because the term "desirable" appears in the conclusion but not in the premise. This poses no difficulty, for all that is needed is another premise. The proof would then look like this.

> Happiness and happiness alone is desired as an end.
> Only what is desired as an end is desirable as an end.
> Happiness and happiness alone is desirable as an end.

The proof is now valid but subject to objections. It might be objected, for example, that when Mill proves the first principle in the above manner, he is guilty of defining values in terms of facts, that is, of defining ethical characteristics ("is desirable") in terms of nonethical ones ("is desired").

There is an interpretation of Mill's proof which avoids the problem that a direct proof does not. If the first premise above is

---

6. Ibid., pp. 10–11.
7. Ibid., p. 44.

assumed to be true, then it can be argued that it would be absurd to deny the truth of the conclusion. That is, if happiness is desired, it is absurd to argue that it is not desirable. If human nature is so constituted as to desire happiness, then it is absurd to say of people that they ought not desire it. This interpretation of the proof of the first principle is perfectly consistent with Mill's claim that the only reason which can be given that happiness is desirable is that happiness is desired.

As was stated earlier, judgements of moral obligation and judgements of moral value are different. The former has to do with the worth of actions, the latter with the worth of agents or persons. Upon what criteria does the worth of agents depend? How are we to tell the moral worth of a person, whether a person is good or bad? It might seem at first glance that the worth of an agent depends upon what he does: a person is good if he does right actions. And yet it is possible for an evil person to act rightly. It is also possible for a good person to do something wrong. If this is the case, then there seem to be two criteria involved. Mill argues that actions are right if they produce good consequences and that the motive of the agent has much to do with the worth of the agent. Thus, a person might have good motives and thereby be a good person, even though what he does has bad consequences and is therefore wrong. Conversely, an evil person might have bad motives even though what he does has good consequences. It seems, then, that motive has nothing to do with the worth of actions and consequence nothing to do with the worth of agents. This account is attractive and simple, but it is too simple. It may be true that motive has nothing to do with an action's worth, but it is not true that consequence has nothing to do with an agent's worth. Take a case, for example, in which an agent repeatedly claims to have the best of motives but nevertheless continually does actions which produce bad consequences. Are we to believe such a person when he says that his motives are good? Are we to believe that such a person is a good person? At what point do we refuse to believe any longer? There is a popular saying that the road to Hell is paved with good intentions. It seems that the rightness of actions, and thus consequences, must have something to do with judging the worth of an agent. An agent who claims to have the best of motives but continually does the wrong thing must, after a certain point, no longer be believed. Such an agent is not a good person. Thus the worth of agents, judgements of moral worth, depend not only on the motive of the agent but also on the kinds of actions the agent repeatedly does.

Like any moral theory, utilitarianism has some debatable points or shortcomings. One objection to utilitarianism is that it seems to be a theory in which the end justifies the means. For example, there might be two actions which produce the same balance of good over evil, and yet one might involve a serious wrong. That is, two actions, X and Y, might both produce the same balance of good over evil, and yet X might involve killing. According to the utilitarian, both actions are equally right, though intuitively Y would appear to be the right thing to do for it is just as right as X and yet does not involve killing.

Another objection to utilitarianism is that the phrase "the greatest amount of good for the greatest number" is somewhat ambiguous. That is, it is not clear what the greatest amount of good for the greatest number comes to. For example, in a universe with one hundred beings and one hundred increments of good to be distributed, it is not clear just how to proceed with the distribution. Are we to give each being one increment of good, or two to forty and one to twenty, and so on? The first principle does not instruct us on this distribution. What is needed is a principle of justice.

A final objection to Mill's theory of ethics is an objection more to hedonism than to utilitarianism. Mill's hedonism or theory of life is that people seek pleasure and avoid pain. Implicit in this theory is the view that pleasure and pain are different sensations on the same continuum: pleasure is at one end of a continuum, pain is at the other, and both cannot be had at the same time. The objection is that both pleasure and pain are not sensations; only pain is. This might be argued in the following way.

Pleasure and pain have different sets of characteristics and are, therefore, different. Pain, for example, can be located. The statement "The pain is in my right big toe" makes sense, but what sense are we to make of "The pleasure is in my right big toe"? Also, pains can be of long duration, but pleasures cannot; a person may be in pain for many hours, but pleasure is not measurable in this way. Moreover, pain can be, and usually is, the result of a physical stimulus. Pain can be caused by a hammer hitting a toe for example. Pleasure is not the effect of any such stimulus.

What all of this points to is that pain is an event which

has location, duration, physical cause, and so on, while pleasure is not an event, not a going-on. Pleasure is, rather, more like a state of affairs. Pain is a sensation; "pleasure" belongs to the family of concepts that have to do with liking, enjoying, and so on. Nothing belonging to this family of concepts is locatable, of any duration at all, or caused by physical stimuli. As Ryle might have said, to put "pain" and "pleasure" in the same family of concepts is to make a category-mistake.

As stated earlier, to object to hedonism is not necessarily to object to utilitarianism. It is possible, that is, to be a utilitarian without being a hedonist. A utilitarian may adopt a theory of good other than hedonism. This has been done in the twentieth century by a well known British philosopher, G. E. Moore. Moore thus avoids the arguments against hedonism, but whether he avoids the arguments leveled against utilitarianism is a different issue.

Deontological Theories

Deontological theories deny precisely what teleological theories affirm, namely that judgements of moral obligation depend on judgements of nonmoral value. That is, deontological theories do not claim that rightness depends on nonmoral goodness. A deontologist would never argue that the way to tell whether an action is right or wrong is to look at the consequences produced by that action. Rather, a deontological theorist would argue that the rightness or wrongness of actions depends on certain formal moral criteria such as rules or principles. The rules and principles, in turn, are not dependent on empirical considerations of the consequences of obeying such rules and principles. The deontologist must, then, formulate the moral rules and principles of his theory in a nonempirical manner. This will become clearer when we discuss Immanual Kant's deontological theory.

There are, basically, two kinds of deontological theories: (1) act deontology and (2) rule deontology. Act deontology, as the name implies, cannot have as a criterion of rightness either consequences or rules. It cannot have consequences, for then it would be a teleological theory; it cannot have rules, for then it would be a form of rule deontology. Act deontologists claim that each individual situation must be decided separately without the benefits of rules or consequences. What, then, according to the act deontologist, is the criterion of rightness? There is no particular criterion for rightness, each situation calls for either an intuitive or an existential decision, and these decisions can be made only by a particular person in a particular situation. They cannot be made by anyone else. Like relativism and egoism, such an ethical theory denies that there are universal criteria for rightness which apply equally to all people. In other words, act deontology denies what most ethical theories affirm.

Rule deontology does not deny that there are universal criteria which apply equally to all rational beings. On the contrary, rule deontology is one of the theories which argue most strenuously for this position. Rule deontologists argue that there are universal standards of right—rules or laws which are applicable to all rational beings. Let us now turn to Immanuel Kant (1724–1804) and examine his ethical theory which is a form of rule deontology.

KANT'S ETHICAL THEORY. For Kant, ethics is a branch of rational knowledge which, strictly speaking, has no empirical aspect at all. If ethics has any empirical aspect, it is anthropology. Ethics or morals is metaphysical, according to Kant. Kant wants to separate anthropology, which is empirical in nature, from ethics, which is metaphysical in nature, for this will allow him to ground obligation a priori in reason. This will give Kant's ethics a universality and necessity not found in an ethical theory grounded empirically. To put it another way, Kant's ethical theory, specifically his theory of obligation, is not dependent on any empirical factors such as consequences. Kant argues that the rightness of actions is discoverable in a nonempirical way; the rightness of actions is grounded a priori in reason. Ethical theories which are grounded empirically do not have the force, at least theoretically, of those grounded metaphysically; the principles of the former can, at best, be only particular and contingent while those of the latter are universal and necessary.

One of the most well known statements in all of ethics is Kant's claim that "nothing in the world—indeed nothing even beyond the world—can possibly be conceived which could be called good without qualification except a good will."[8] The claim is basically that the only unqualified good is the good will. If all

---

8. Immanuel Kant, *Foundations of the Metaphysics of Morals*, trans. Lewis White Beck (New York: Bobbs-Merrill, 1959), p. 9.

of the ramifications of this claim are understood, then Kant's ethics is understood.

Kant claims that the good will is not good because of what it accomplishes or because it has a certain inclination to do what is right or because it acts out of self-love. Kant dismisses utilitarianism, relativism, and egoism as totally inadequate ethical theories for they cannot make any claims to unqualified good. The good—or right—about which these ethical theories are concerned is always qualified by consequences, by inclination, or by self-love. Kant's ethical theory is concerned only with unqualified good.

Why, then, is the good will good? Kant's answer is both disarmingly simple and subtly complex. The good will is "good only because of its willing; it is good of itself."[9] The good will is, according to Kant, good in and of itself; it is an intrinsic or unqualified good. What makes the good will good is its very willing, not its willing of consequences or anything else of that kind. To put it another way, the good will is good because it acts for the sake of duty. Duty, for Kant, is just the necessity of acting out of respect for moral law. Thus, the good will is good because it acts out of respect for law itself, because it has as its principle of action the universal conformity of the action to moral law. In short, the good will is the will which acts in such a way that its principle of action (what Kant calls a maxim or subjective principle of volition) can be made into a practical or moral law (what Kant calls an objective principle of morality).

For Kant, the will itself is the faculty of choosing that which is good, that which reason recognizes as necessary. Will is just practical reason, for will is the capacity of acting according to the concept of law and reason is required for the subsumption of actions under laws. Kant speaks as if reason determines will; this, of course, just means that reason determines itself. According to Kant, reason may determine will in two ways, either infallibly or fallibly. The will which is infallibly determined by reason is a holy will. This will chooses only that which reason recognizes as practically necessary, that is, as good. In other words, the holy will cannot help but be good. The will which is fallibly determined by reason is not always good. This will may, and does, choose that which reason does not recognize as good. The will which is fallibly determined is the human will; it, of

---

9. Ibid., p. 10.

course, is subject to error and thus must be constrained and commanded by reason.

The holy will, then, is the will which has as its subjective principle of volition, as its maxim, an objective principle of morality, a moral law. This will is an infallibly good will. The human will is not infallibly good. It does not have as its subjective principle of volition an operative principle of morality in every case. When it does, then it is, of course, a good will, though only fallibly good.

The holy will cannot be constrained by objective laws, or moral laws, because it acts simply through the conception of such laws and for no other reason. This is just another way of saying that the maxims of the holy will are moral laws. The holy will need not be commanded by reason, for its volitions or maxims are always necessarily in unison with moral law. Only an imperfect will needs to be commanded by reason, to be constrained. According to Kant, "the conception of an objective principle, so far as it constrains a will, is a command, and the formula of this command is called an imperative. . . . All imperatives are expressed by an 'ought' and thereby indicate the relation of an objective law of reason to a will which is not in its subjective constitution necessarily determined by its laws."[10] The holy will, then, need not be told that it ought to do a certain action, while the human will does need to be told that it ought to. Only human wills need listen to the imperatives of reason.

CATEGORICAL IMPERATIVE. All imperatives, Kant argues, command either hypothetically or categorically. Hypothetical imperatives present actions as means to some other end. For example, the imperatives of a teleological theorist would, according to Kant, be hypothetical. Categorical imperatives do not present actions as means to any other end; actions are presented as objectively necessary in and of themselves. The categorical imperative commands a certain action without making its condition some purpose to be achieved by it. Kant holds that there is only one categorical imperative; it is: "Act only according to that maxim by which you can at the same time will that it should become a universal law."[11] This imperative contains both the universal or moral law and the necessity that maxims con-

10. Ibid., p. 30.
11. Ibid., p. 39.

form to this law. It sounds much like the golden rule and says that the good will must have as its maxims only that which can be willed to be moral law.

We are now in a position to articulate Kant's criteria for the rightness of actions and the worth of moral agents. An agent has moral worth, or a will is good, only when that agent, or will, has as a principle of action or maxim that which can be made into an objective or universal or moral principle. Thus, an agent is moral when that agent obeys the commands of reason, when the categorical imperative is obeyed. Further, an action is right when the maxim of the action can be made into a universal or moral law. Thus, the worth of agents and the rightness of actions depend on one and the same criteria, namely the categorical imperative. Whereas Mill argued that judgements of moral obligation and judgements of moral value have two different criteria, Kant argues that they both have the same criterion. For Kant, an action is right for the same reason that an agent is good. This is possible for Kant precisely because the rightness of actions does not depend on the end brought about by them.

Kant's first principle of morality is, then, the categorical imperative. How is this principle to be proved? As we saw earlier, ethics is not merely descriptive for Kant. Ethics does not merely tell us how men do act; it tells us how men ought to act. Anthropology tells us how men do act, but from this information we cannot deduce how they ought to act. Thus, how men do act is of no help to us in ethics. In short, first principles in ethics cannot be proved empirically.

The categorical imperative does not tell us how men do act but how they ought to. This imperative is a priori in that it is universal and necessary, that is, it is binding for all rational beings. The categorical imperative is formulated by pure reason from the concept of obligation itself: we are to discover how men ought to act by looking to the concept of obligation. This concept, according to Kant, contains the universality and necessity found in the categorical imperative. The concept of obligation dictates to us the criterion for our obligations, namely the categorical imperative.

Thus, Kant's first principle of ethics is proved a priori, in a nonempirical manner, by reason. The concept of obligation is found to contain, a priori, universality and necessity. This universality and necessity is expressed by the categorical imperative. This imperative is our criterion for deciding what our obligations are. According to the categorical imperative we are obligated to act in such a way that the maxims of our actions could be made into universal laws, laws which necessarily bind all rational beings. If our maxims can be made universal, then our actions are right and we are good.

Many objections have been leveled against Kant's deontological theory. For example, it has been objected that this theory is not equipped to handle situations where conflicts of duties arise. Suppose a conflict arises between duty X and duty Y and we find ourselves in a situation where it is possible to do either X or Y but not both. If both are equally our duties, then it seems that deontological theories give us no way to decide between the two.

Another objection to Kant's ethical theory is that it seems to confuse judgements of moral obligation and judgements of moral value. More specifically, it seems to run the two different kinds of judgements together. It is entirely possible, for example, for a man to have the most horrible motives and yet for the action he does to be right. This is possible because the rightness of actions is independent of what the agent intends. In other words, there is a distinction between the agent's intentions and the action's consequences. It is just this distinction which is important for showing the difference between judgements of moral value and judgements of moral obligation. The agent's intention is the criterion used in making judgements of moral value and the action's consequences the criterion used in making judgements of moral obligation.

A final objection is that Kant's theory allows for no exceptions, and it is common knowledge that all laws have exceptions. For example, Kant seems to say that all promises ought to be kept, but it is not difficult to imagine a situation where this is not the case. Kant's ethical theory, then, is too inflexible for it cannot account for cases where exceptions have to be made.

METAETHICS

Metaethics deals with issues and problems much different from those of normative ethics. Whereas normative ethics is concerned with the criteria for right and good, metaethics is concerned with clarifying so-called ethical terms used in ethical theories and with the advantages and disadvantages of competing ethical theories. Metaethics is not concerned with the norms and standards of normative ethics.

Act and Rule Utilitarianism

John Stuart Mill's *Utilitarianism* gives rise to at least two different kinds of utilitariansim, act and rule. Mill himself probably did not know or realize the differences between act and rule utilitarianism. In some places he seems to support one view, and in others he seems to support the other view.

Act utilitarianism is the view that each particular action is to be weighed directly against the first principle in order to determine its rightness or wrongness. Thus, an action is right if it produces good consequences and wrong if it produces bad consequences.

Rule utilitarianism, on the other hand, is the view that the rightness or wrongness of actions is to be determined by weighing them against secondary principles which, in turn, must be weighed against the first principle. In other words, rule utilitarianism has an intermediate step which act utilitarianism lacks.

There are two major differences between these competing views. According to act utilitarianism, it is never right to do an action when some alternative action would produce a greater balance of good over evil. On the other hand, according to rule utilitarianism, it may sometimes be right to do an action even though some alternative action might produce more good. Suppose there are two alternative actions, X and Y. X is lying and Y is telling the truth. Now suppose also in this situation where X and Y are the two possible alternatives that doing X produces more good than doing Y. An act utilitarian will, of course, opt for X. But a rule utilitarian may not, especially if the secondary principle he is weighing the alternatives against is "Do not lie." Thus, even though Y does not produce as much good as X, a rule utilitarian may be forced to opt for Y on the grounds that lying in general does not produce good.

The second major difference between the two views explains the first, to some extent. According to act utilitarianism, the rightness of an action is determined by its actual consequences, while according to rule utilitarianism, the rightness of an action is determined by hypothetical consequences.

The act utilitarian argues that an action is right if its actual consequences are good, action X in the above example. The rule utilitarian, on the other hand, argues an action is right only if it is rule-like, or generalizable, action Y above. In other words, the rule utilitarian asks the question "What if everyone did X?" and worries about the hypothetical consequences.

Each interpretation of Mill's utilitarianism has, of course, advantages and disadvantages. The greatest strength of rule utilitarianism is that in this theory actions are governed by moral rules, secondary principles. However, this strength is also what causes the theory difficulty. Rule utilitarianism seems to lead to the paradoxical position of secondary principles, which are supposed to be corollaries of the first principle, contradicting the first principle. Let us again look to the example given above to see how this occurs. Doing X may produce good consequences, better than those produced by doing Y at any rate, in which case it is the right thing to do according to the first principle. The difficulty is that doing X involves disobeying a secondary principle. The paradox is that on rule utilitarian grounds one must not always do that which leads to the greatest good. This conclusion is certainly paradoxical for a utilitarian of any sort.

Act utilitarianism's lack of rules allows it to escape the paradox inherent in rule utilitarianism. However, the greatest weakness of act utilitarianism is that it does exclude rules and by so doing seems to deny one of the basic tenets of traditional ethical theories, namely that moral activity is rule-like activity.

The Ought-Is Controversy

Philosophers have for some time been arguing about the differences between "ought" and "is." Some have argued, that an "ought" can be derived from an "is." Most, however, argue that an "ought" cannot be derived from an "is," that is, ethical propositions cannot be derived from nonethical ones. The attempt to do so is one version of what has come to be called the *naturalistic fallacy*. Another version of the fallacy is the attempt to define ethical characteristics in terms of nonethical ones.

It has been argued that John Stuart Mill committed the naturalistic fallacy. Mill, it seems, attempted to derive an "ought" from an "is." It has been argued that in Mill's case, "desirable" was derived from "desired." In other words, Mill attempted to derive an ethical proposition from a nonethical one. As you will remember, the proof went something like this. From the premise "Happiness and happiness alone is desired as an end" Mill seems to conclue that "Happiness and happiness alone is desirable as an end." Put another way, Mill seems to conclude that from the fact that all men seek or desire pleasure it follows that pleasure is good or desirable. The argument in its present form is certainly fallacious, for an ethical term appears in the conclusion and not the premise. But, this is easily remedied, as we have seen, by the inclusion of another premise, namely "Only what is desired as an end is desirable as an end." Now the argument is perfectly valid and no fallacy is involved. Thus, even if Mill did argue in such a manner, his argument is not fallacious. Ethical propositions are, in a straightforward way, derivable from nonethical ones. All that is needed is a proposition, a second premise, which defines ethical characteristics in terms of nonethical ones. If the second premise is supplied, then the argument is not fallacious. This brings us to the second version of the naturalistic fallacy, the attempt to define ethical characteristics in terms of nonethical ones.

The second version of the naturalistic fallacy essentially involves treating two properties or characteristics—one ethical and one nonethical—as one, for example, "goodness is that which is desired." In other words, the second version of the fallacy is a confusion or identification of two characteristics. But are these two properties being confused or identified? One philosopher might argue that they are, for "good" is not definable and any attempt to define "good" results in committing the naturalistic fallacy. Another philosopher, on the other hand, might argue that the properties are not being confused because "good" is definable and definable in naturalistic or other nonethical terms. In effect, the first philosopher argues that the definition "good is that which is desired" is fallacious because there are really two characteristics, namely "good" and "that which is desired," and these two are being confused or identified. The other philosopher can, of course, retort that there is really only one characteristic for which there are two names, namely "good" and "that which is desired." It appears, then, that to define "good" as "that which is desired" does not necessarily result in a fallacy.

Neither of the versions of the naturalistic fallacy which we have discussed seems really to be a fallacy. That is, neither deriving an "ought" from an "is" nor defining an "ought" in terms of an "is" is fallacious. The real issue at stake in this controversy appears to be whether an "ought" can be derived from or defined in terms of an "is," and why or why not. The controversy is not settled by labeling the two attempts as fallacious.

MORAL PROBLEMS

Abortion and pacifism are two moral problems which have been discussed a good deal in the last ten to twenty years. In this section we will examine these problems in order to see how philosophical thinking in general applies to issues which arise in our everyday lives and how we can use the ethical theories in particular which we have discussed in this chapter to confront these issues.

Abortion

Traditionally, abortion—the expulsion of the human fetus from the uterus—has been considered only in those cases where there is a mortal conflict between mother and fetus. There are three such cases: (1) the case in which only the mother can be saved by the abortion of the fetus, and both the mother and the fetus will die if nothing is done; (2) the case in which either the mother or the fetus can be saved, but not both, and both the mother and the fetus will die if nothing is done; and (3) the case in which either the mother or the fetus can be saved, but not both, and only the mother will die if nothing is done. In all of these cases, the mortal conflict is that only the mother or the fetus, but not both, can live. A fourth case in which abortion has come to be considered has developed in the last few decades. It is a case in which there is no mortal conflict, namely abortion on demand.

Abortion in the first and second cases has sometimes been justified by the "doctrine of double effect." The doctrine says that it is sometimes morally permissible to bring about something which is foreseen (indirectly or obliquely intended) where this something is neither the intended end nor a means to this end (directly intended). The "double effect" refers to the two effects, the indirectly intended and the directly intended. It is argued that the abortion is justified in the first two cases because the death of the fetus is not directly intended; it is only a foreseen consequence of saving the mother's life. The fetus's death is not the end aimed at by the physician when he saves the mother's life, though the physician does know that there is a good chance that the fetus will die. Put another way, the fetus is allowed to die as the mother is being saved.

However, the doctrine of double effect will justify abortion only in certain instances even within the first two cases. If, for example, positive steps have to be taken to kill the fetus to save the mother in either of the first two cases, the doctrine of double effect will not justify abortion for now the death of the fetus is directly intended.

In the third case, abortion will not be justified by the doctrine of double effect because, again, something positive must be done to kill the fetus. If nothing at all is done, the mother will die, though the fetus will live. It is similarly true with regard to the fourth case of abortion, abortion on demand. The fetus cannot be allowed to die for it will not die if nothing is done. In this case, moreover, neither will the mother.

Thus, if the doctrine of double effect justifies abortion at all it does so only in certain instances of the first two cases. In any case where certain action to kill the fetus has to be taken, the doctrine of double effect will not justify abortion.

There is something counterintuitive about the doctrine of double effect. Why is it, for example, that certain instances within the first two cases of abortion are justifiable and others are not? If both the mother and the fetus will die if nothing is done, why is it justifiable to allow the fetus to die but not justifiable to kill it? What is the difference between allowing to die and killing?

The doctrine of double effect depends on the distinction between allowing the fetus to die, indirect intention, and killing the fetus, direct intention. It will not do to argue that it is right to allow the fetus to die but wrong to kill it for in many cases allowing something to happen is certainly wrong. For example, allowing a child to drown when it could have been saved very easily is morally wrong. In a like manner, allowing a fetus to die when there is any chance of saving it may be wrong, just as wrong in some cases as killing it. Further, the doctrine of double effect seems to equate indirect intention and allowing something to happen and direct intention and doing something. But surely this is also a mistake for one may intentionally allow something to happen. For example, a doctor may allow a fetus to die and he may do this intentionally: his direct intention may be to allow the fetus to die. Thus, the distinction between oblique or indirect intention and direct intention does not hold up in the way those who hold the doctrine of double effect want it to. With this collapse of the distinction goes the collapse of the doctrine of double effect.

Let us turn to the fourth case of abortion again, the case where abortion is done on demand. If this case of abortion can be justified, then, of course, all the other cases will also be justified. Abortion on demand might be justified by arguing that the fetus, up to any number of months, is not human or human-like enough to have any rights, certainly not the right to live. One could argue that sensations, thinking, and so on are just brain processes and nothing more. If this is true, then it might be argued that the fetus does not exhibit any of these processes in a sophisticated enough manner to warrant being called a human being. In other words, it might be argued that the brain processes of a fetus are not complex enough to be called the brain processes of a human being. If we deny that the fetus is a human being on these grounds, then killing it poses no problem at all.

The problem of whether abortion is or is not justifiable is a complex one, and we have hardly begun to cover all of the aspects of the controversy. To do this would require a good deal of time and space. Our discussion here has been only introductory in nature, a beginning point.

Pacifism

Pacifism is the position that all violence is morally wrong or evil. It is a moral position and thus is supposed to hold for all people, not just pacifists. Pacifism depends, in large part, on just how violence is to be understood. For the purposes of our discussion, we will understand violence to be physical violence, the physical violation of a person. Some pacifists might want to extend the concept of violence to cover psychological violence. The position of pacifism then becomes much broader, but it also becomes harder to defend.

The position that all violence is morally wrong entails the position that it is also morally wrong to prevent, resist, or punish violence. Thus, according to the pacifist, it is wrong to try to prevent violence or to resist it either if it is about to occur or is occurring. Further, once violence has occurred, it is wrong to punish it. Self-defense, helping others by preventing violence, and punishing those who commit violent acts are, on the pacifist's grounds, wrong. It is wrong on pacifistic grounds to do things which most moral theories would certainly justify.

Pacifism, it might be argued, is logically untenable for it denies precisely that which it wishes to affirm. The pacifist argues, in effect, that it is everyone's right not to have violence done to him. Having a right involves having the right to be defended against breaches of that right. If all people have the right not to have violence done to them, then they also have the right to do whatever may be necessary to prevent infringements of that right, even to the point of violence. This position is, of course, contradictory for it holds both that everyone has the right not to have violence done to him and that everyone also has the right to defend that right, even violently. The pacifist's position is, then, untenable if it is argued that pacifism is a moral position. If it is not a moral position, then it is weakened considerably.

CONCLUSION: EXPEDIENCY VERSUS RIGHTNESS

The issue of expediency versus rightness has been fought for a long time by ethical theorists. Almost every ethical theorist argues that expediency alone is not enough to justify an action. That is, most ethical theorists argue that expediency and rightness are independent of one another. Certainly an action may be both expedient and right, but it is not right because it is expedient.

Several of the ethical theorists discussed in this chapter, though, would be able to justify an expedient action as right. Both relativists and egoists would, on the basis of their theories, be able to justify a burglary, for example. The former would do so on the grounds that the burglars thought that the action was right. The egoist, on the other hand, would be able to justify the burglary on the grounds that it was in his own self-interest. As we saw earlier in this chapter, both relativism and egoism seem to lack the one ingredient that makes an ethical theory what it is, namely a principle of universality. Neither theory provides for the rightness of actions to be judged in terms of how all persons should act. In short, both theories would be able to justify as right the action that is merely expedient, for both theories do not require right actions to be the kind of actions that they would have others do. Relativism and egoism, rather than being genuine ethical or moral theories, seem to stand in opposition to such theories.

Teleological and deontological theorists would agree that an action is wrong if it is merely expedient, for both would agree that expediency alone justifies nothing in the moral realm. These two ethical theories would not justify any action merely on the grounds that the action was conducive to the advantage or interest of an individual or group of individuals.

John Stuart Mill, one of the teleological theorists discussed in this chapter, tries to show in his book, *Utilitarianism*, that expediency and utility do not have the same meaning. He argues that expediency is a branch of the hurtful rather than of the useful because that which is expedient is expedient for the interests of an individual while that which is useful produces the greatest amount of good for the greatest number. In short, Mill argues that an action to be right must have utility.

Kant, a deontological theorist, would also argue that an action which is merely expedient is not right. For Kant, an action is right only if the principle of the action can be made a principle of action for all rational beings. Actions for which the principle is expediency cannot be right because the principle of expediency cannot be made a principle of action for all rational beings. Expediency can be the principle of action only for an individual or a group of individuals.

Thus both Mill and Kant, the representative teleological and deontological theorists discussed in this chapter, would agree that merely expedient actions are not right actions. Expediency alone cannot stand as the criterion of the rightness of actions. Most moral or ethical theorists would agree with Mill and Kant.

TOPICS FOR DISCUSSION

1. What recommends the moral point of view against a more self-interested view? That is, why be moral at all?
2. Might not relativism be defended in a sophisticated way so that it is moral to act in any way that an individual deems best?
3. Of the two general types of moral theories, teleological and deontological, which one is superior to the other? Why?

4. How are religion and ethics related? Is there any relation between the two at all? Can a person be moral without being religious?
5. Investigate and discuss some metaethical issues and controversies which have not been discussed in this chapter.
6. How well equipped is ethics to handle the moral problems which might face us in our everyday life? What are some of these problems? How are they to be solved?

SELECTED BIBLIOGRAPHY

Primary Source

Aristotle. *Nicomachean Ethics.* In *The Basic Works of Aristotle,* edited by Richard McKeon. New York: Random House, 1941.
Kant, Immanuel. *Foundations of the Metaphysics of Morals.* Translated by Lewis White Beck. New York: Bobbs-Merrill, 1959.
Mill, John Stuart. *Utilitarianism.* New York: Bobbs-Merrill, 1957.
Plato. *The Republic.* Translated by Benjamin Jowett. New York: Random House, 1957.

Secondary Source

Baier, K. *The Moral Point of View.* New York: Random House, 1965.
Flew, A. G. N., ed. *The Is/Ought Question.* London: Macmillan, 1969.
Foot, P., ed. *Theories of Ethics.* Oxford: Oxford University Press, 1967.
Frankena, William. *Ethics.* Englewood Cliffs, N.J.: Prentice-Hall 1963.
Hare, R. M. *The Language of Morals.* Oxford: Oxford University Press, 1964.
Moore, G. E. *Principia Ethica.* Cambridge: Cambridge University Press, 1968.
Rachels, J., ed. *Moral Problems.* New York: Harper and Row, 1971.
Stevenson, C. L. *Facts and Values.* New Haven: Yale University Press, 1963.
Taylor, P. W., ed. *Problems of Moral Philosophy.* Encino, California: Dickenson, 1972.

CHAPTER 7

Social Philosophy

WHAT IS SOCIAL PHILOSOPHY?

There are some problems which call for analysis but which do not seem to be the appropriate object of study for either ethics proper or political theory. As was maintained in Chapter 6, the principal task of ethics is to analyze moral terms such as "right" and "good" and to set forth criteria by which moral judgements can be made. Political theory is mainly concerned with evaluating political power and the institutions which go to make up this power. Insofar as it examines the criteria for moral evaluation of political power, political theory can be regarded as a branch of ethics.

Social philosophy is also a branch of ethics in that it, too, is concerned with moral evaluation. But, as with political theory, social philosophy is primarily concerned with nonnormative analyses. Social philosophy considers those concepts and issues which arise out of the social milieu but which are not directly moral or political in nature, though, of course, these concepts have both moral and political overtones. The lines of demarcation among moral, political, and social concepts are often poorly drawn.

As a branch of ethics, social philosophy is the application of moral criteria and principles to those issues which fall within its domain. First, however, social philosophy must give clear and precise analyses of the social concepts and issues themselves. Thus, social philosophy must carefully define and examine certain concepts and issues as well as apply moral criteria to them.

For example, the concept of violence, which lies within the domain of social philosophy, must be clearly analyzed and understood before the question of its justification can be answered—we must know just what violence is before we know when, if ever, it is to be justified. The justification of violence, then, depends on our definition of violence. In this chapter, our primary concern will be with the clarification of social concepts and issues, though moral justification will be discussed briefly when it is pertinent.

Until very recently, social philosophy was largely ignored by philosophers in the Anglo-American tradition. Especially during the first half of this century, philosophers have concentrated on ethics, philosophy of mind, metaphysics, and epistemology. Social philosophy was at best treated peripherally. The reason for this may have been that philosophers were first sharpening their philosophical tools, disciplining themselves in traditional philosophical methods. It might be argued that only afterwards could the concepts and issues with which social philosophy is concerned be clarified. Throughout the history of intellectual thought, the best social philosophers have invariably been those with good tools and rigorous discipline. A person aspiring to be a social philosopher might do well to study logic, mathematics, and science before directly attacking a particular social problem without any previous study, for it is precisely such disciplines that develop the proper philosophical tools and rigorous thought. Without these it is almost useless, and sometimes even worse than useless, to attempt to confront and solve a problem.

FREEDOM

Mill's essay *On Liberty* has become a classic treatise in social philosophy. Its fame rests on its precise and reasonably clear manner of setting forth many of the issues at stake in political freedom. One of the most important of these issues is the freedom of the individual. For Mill, the freedom of the individual is concerned with which actions an individual in society ought to be allowed to do. In our discussion, we will closely examine Mill's arguments for the freedom of the individual and then evaluate them, drawing the fundamental distinction between "freedom from" and "freedom to."

Mill's basic claim in *On Liberty* is that "the only part of the conduct of any one, for which he is amenable to society, is that which concerns others. In the part which merely concerns himself, his independence is, of right, absolute. Over himself, over his own body and mind, the individual is sovereign."[1] This claim is really twofold: (1) in matters regarding others, external matters, society may interfere with the individual; (2) in matters regarding only oneself, internal matters, the individual is guaranteed noninterference.

Thus, when Mill speaks of the freedom of the individual, he argues that the individual ought to be free to do as he chooses only in those matters which are internal. In external matters the individual must be guided, in part, by the right of others. Further, Mill argues that the distinction between the inner and outer spheres of interest will hold up. But will it?

There is another argument which Mill gives for the freedom of the individual. He argues "that it is only the cultivation of individuality which produces, or can produce, well-developed human beings ... what more or better can be said of any condition of human affairs, than that it brings human beings themselves nearer to the best thing they can be ..."[2] Mill claims that in internal matters the individual ought to be left alone for only in this way will he become a well-developed human being. In other words, the well-developed human being is likely to be the individual with whom society has not interfered. The individual, not society, is the best judge of his own interests, those interests which concern only himself. The question here, of course, is whether it is true that human beings are or can become well-developed when they are left alone in those matters which concern only themselves. Are individuals always the best judge of their own interests?

These are the two claims which compose Mill's view on the freedom of the individual. His argument, in short, is that there are two spheres of interest, the inner and the outer, and that the individual is the best judge of those matters in the inner sphere of interest. Let us now see if either of these two claims is valid.

For Mill, the distinction between the inner and outer spheres of interest is made on purely empirical grounds. A matter belongs to the inner sphere if it affects only the individual concerned, or

---

1. John Stuart Mill, *On Liberty*, in *Essential Works of John Stuart Mill*, ed. by Max Lerner (New York: Bantam Books, 1961), p. 263.
2. Ibid., p. 312.

possibly that individual and a few others. A matter belongs to the outer sphere if it affects more than a few others. This line is notoriously fuzzy. It is not clear just how many a few others or more than a few others is. Therefore, the distinction between the inner and the outer spheres must be not one of kind but one of degree. One sphere involves a few others and the other more than a few others. Further, a specific matter may, in some instances, be in the outer sphere. The deciding factor is an empirical one, how many persons are affected. In other words, for Mill there is thus no real empirical distinction between the inner and the outer spheres of interest.

Even though Mill cannot make the distinction between the inner and outer spheres of interest on empirical grounds, this is not to deny that the distinction can be made. If the distinction is to be made at all, it must be made on normative grounds. It might be argued, for example, that a person has the right to control certain matters because it is a right which all persons have, but not because that matter affects only a few. That is, there may be certain matters which fall within the so-called inner sphere of interest, but they do not do so just because they affect only a few other persons.

Given this new interpretation of an inner sphere, is the individual always the best judge his own interests? Does the individual always know what is best for himself? Mill's answer is yes. But is this the case? There are many examples where an individual does what seems to be worst for himself. Continually shooting heroin, for example, might be a matter which falls within the inner sphere of interests because it affects only the individual taking the drug. Even if the individual taking heroin wants to take heroin, and says so, surely it can be argued that this individual does not know what is best for himself. In cases like these, other persons may be in the best position to know what is best for an individual. There can be no guarantee that an individual is always the best judge of what is good for him.

Mill's two claims which back up his view on individual freedom do not seem to hold up under close analysis. Put another way, even if there is a sphere of interest over which the individual is sovereign, it is not always the case that the individual is the best judge of what should go on in this sphere. This last matter might be rephrased as it was earlier. Is noninterference a necessary condition of being well-developed, as Mill seems to think it is? Again, the answer seems clearly to be no. In fact, in many cases interference from society seems to be a necessary condition for an individual's developing well.

Mill's doctrine of noninterference with the individual seems to fall down. The kind of freedom which Mill articulated is really a "freedom from." It guarantees each individual a certain amount of noninterference, but it guarantees very little else. What is needed is a concept of freedom to compliment the freedoms from. To illustrate this, let us look briefly at two documents: the Constitution, and the Universal Declaration of Human Rights and the Covenants on Human Rights.

The freedoms set forth in the first ten amendments to the Constitution are freedoms from. Many of them are stated negatively and guarantee an individual noninterference from outside sources.

The freedoms set forth by the Universal Declaration of Human Rights and the Covenants on Human Rights are both freedoms from and "freedoms to." The latter are put positively and guarantee an individual more than noninterference. They guarantee an individual certain options in life. Included in the freedoms to are the right to education, the right to an adequate standard of living, and so on. These freedoms go a long way toward ensuring that each individual has a chance to gain autonomy and experience dignity.

As with most important social concepts, the way the concept of freedom is articulated is crucial. For example, if by freedom is meant freedom from, then it might be the case that everyone in the United States is equally free. But if by freedom is meant freedom to, then it is not the case that everyone in the United States is equally free. Some Americans are more free than others. Those who have the most options in life are the most free. For example, a black person living in a ghetto may enjoy most of the freedoms from set forth in the Constitution and yet have very few real options in life. In other words, a ghetto black may have the freedoms from but not the freedoms to. Thus when a middle-class white says that America is a free country and a ghetto black says that it is not, they are disagreeing not only about whether America is free but also about exactly what constitutes freedom. That is, they both have a different concept of freedom.

Just how important it is to clarify a concept like freedom is obvious. If a person thinks that freedom is simply freedom from, then he may wonder why there is such a great disparity among people, why some people seem to do so well in life while others do not do well at all. This person may even come to think that since all people are free, that is, they all enjoy the freedoms from, the disparity can be accounted for by showing that some people are lazy, do not really wish to work or succeed, like to live on welfare, and so on.

A more reasonable way to account for the disparity among people under the conditions created by the freedoms from is that such freedom does not allow many persons to achieve any kind of self-realization. Again, this is just another way of saying that interference is needed if more than a few are going to become well developed. The concept of freedom must be extended to include the freedoms to, the freedoms which allow, as much as possible, each individual to achieve self-realization. An individual may enjoy all of the freedoms from, that is, he may be guaranteed the right of noninterference, but unless that person is given certain options, guaranteed certain freedoms to, he will, in truth, have little freedom.

VIOLENCE

A discussion of violence is a good illustration of the importance of clarifying and defining a social concept before attempting to evaluate it. If violence is considered only as "crime in the streets"—murder, robbery, rape, and so on—then to many people it seems clear how violence should be treated. What is needed is more police, more respect for property, and so on. On this analysis of violence, those who commit violent acts are thought to be entirely at fault. It might be argued, though, that so restricting the concept of violence is too simplistic and that the concept must be extended to cover many other cases. If the concept is extended to psychological and institutional cases of violence, then the cure for violence is neither the same nor so simple. Further, those who commit these types of violence often are not seen to be entirely at fault, or, at least, their position can be understood and possibly justified or excused. How the concept of violence is defined, then, is critical, for this definition will be reflected in the moral evaluations of violent acts.

"Violence" is almost always defined in terms of physical force, but as we have seen, this definition is too narrow. More broadly, "violence" may be defined as the violation of a person.

There are several ways in which a person may be violated: a person's body may be violated, as may his "mind," his autonomy, or his property. Furthermore, this violation may come at the hands either of another person or of an institution. With this in mind, it may be seen that violence can be categorized into certain types: (1) personal physical, (2) personal psychological, (3) institutional physical, and (4) institutional psychological. Let us look at each one of these four types individually.

Personal physical violence includes murder, rape, mugging, assault, and possibly robbery. This kind of violence is personal because it is done to one individual by another individual, and it is physical because it is the violation of body or property. It has been argued by many that personal physical violence can be stopped by the use of more police. It might be argued, however, that this will treat only the symptoms and effects but not the underlying cause of the problem. In fact, more police might make the problem worse rather than better. Police may be needed to help quell this kind of violence, but other methods of control, especially those which attack the cause, must also be found.

The second type of violence, personal psychological violence, is more subtle than the first. This may explain why it has often been left out of explanations of violence. This kind of violence is nonphysical. For example, a girl being told repeatedly by her teacher that she should be more feminine and not compete with the boys in the class might constitute a case of personal psychological violence. Psychological brutalization of one individual by another is a fairly common occurrence. In some instances, this kind of violence may be a cause of personal physical violence. Often a person may strike out physically at another person because he cannot combat the other's psychological abuse any other way. If personal psychological violence could be curbed, it is probable that much of the so-called crime in the streets—personal physical violence—would cease.

It might be that personal psychological violence is not often treated because it is so difficult to detect and treat. Even if this type of violence is one of the causes of personal physical violence and even if treating the former would go a long way toward halting the latter, the latter is more often treated because it is fairly simple to detect and treat. Thus, even though it is best to treat the cause, it is often quite difficult to do so; this results in only the symptom or the effect (personal physical violence) being treated. But until the full causes of crime in the streets are found, articulated, and dealt with, this kind of violence will continue to be with us. A large police force or other deterrent is not sufficient to handle the problem.

The fourth kind of violence mentioned above may also contribute to acts of personal physical violence. There are many examples of institutional psychological violence. Slavery, prejudice, minority oppression, and discrimination in school systems are a few of the institutional ways a person can be psychologically violated. Of all the types of violence, this may be the most difficult to combat. Whereas it is relatively easy to prevent rape, it is notoriously difficult to stop prejudice.

There is one common denominator which ties all types of institutional psychological violence together. This is the violence which systematically and methodically determines for a person what kinds of choices and options he will have in life. A person living in a ghetto, for example, does not enjoy the same options as does a more affluent person living in suburbia. It may be realistic for the suburban child to choose and expect to go to college. This may not, however, be a real option for the child who lives in the ghetto.

Institutional psychological violence is perhaps the most subtle and injurious type of violence. It is the kind of violence which affects a person's autonomy and dignity. If this kind of violence could be curbed, an admittedly enormous task, then much of the personal physical violence would probably cease.

The third type of violence, institutional physical violence, is not at all subtle and is discussed in most analyses of violence. Included in this type of violence are wars, riots, and the like. Though there are many instances of personal physical violence in war, war itself is not another instance of personal physical violence. War is institutional because it is not waged by one individual on another.

The way violence is defined may be crucial in many ways. If a black ghetto-dweller says that the United States is a violent country, he may not be referring to crime in the streets. He may, instead, be referring to the living conditions in the ghetto, or to the way he has been systematically denied certain options in life. On the other hand, when a white suburbanite says that the United States is violent, he may be referring to crime in the streets. When the black person above says that violence needs to be curbed, he does not mean that more police are needed or that the police need bigger and better weapons. He would most likely argue that what is needed is social reform to clean up the ghettos and to give black people more options in life. The suburbanite, on the other hand, would probably argue that violence can and should be stopped with more deterrent force.

The difference in opinion between the ghetto black and the suburban white illustrates how difficult it may be for people to agree on just what violence is and, thus, on how it is to be curbed. This issue has far-reaching political, ethical, and social ramifications.

Before we leave the concept of violence, let us look briefly at whether or not it is ever justifiable, or excusable. Violence is not inherently evil; we cannot decide on a priori grounds that violence is always wrong. Violence does need, however, either a justification or an excuse. There are numerous examples where violence can be justified. Self-defense, certain wars, and certain kinds of psychological indoctrination are a few instances when violence may be justifiable. Each case must be taken individually and looked at carefully before it can be judged to be justified or not. There is no easy way to do this.

REVOLUTION

It is quite natural to discuss the concept of revolution after discussing freedom and violence, for revolutions are often violent and done in the name of freedom. Revolutionaries justify violence and revolution by showing that they are necessary to ensure the freedom of the masses. But before discussing the justification of revolution, let us turn to the concept of revolution.

Probably one of the best definitions of "revolution" was that given by Eugene Kamenka: "Revolution is a sharp, sudden change in the social location of political power, expressing itself in the radical transformation of the process of government, of the official foundations of sovereignty or legitimacy and of the conception of the social order."[3] The most important characteristics of revolution is the sharp, sudden change in the social location of political power. This is precisely what makes revolutions differ from

---

3. Eugene Kamenka, "The Concept of a Political Revolution," in *Revolution, Nomos VIII*, ed. by C. J. Friedrich (New York: Atherton Press, 1966), p. 123.

coups d'etat, rebellions, and the like. Coups d'etat, for example, usually result in a change of leaders, but the new leaders usually come from the same class as the old leaders. Thus, there is no change in the social location of political power. The social location remains the same, most commonly with the upper class or the military.

In a revolution, on the other hand, the social location of political power does change. In the Russian revolution, for example, the social location of power changed dramatically. This change in the location of power was accompanied by a transformation in the forms of government: a monarchy was replaced by a communist form of government. Also, the official foundations of sovereignty were altered, as was the conception of the social order. Sovereignty after the revolution was rooted in the people, not the Czar; the social order was no longer conceived as hierarchical.

The American revolution also seems to fit Kamenka's definition. The social location of political power changed from a ruling class to the citizenry. A monarchy was replaced but in this case by a democratic form of government. Rejecting the King of England, the people became their own sovereigns, and the concept of a ruling class was no longer tolerated.

Now we might ask, When is revolution justified? To answer this question we will have to include in our discussion some of what was said earlier about freedom and violence.

One of the answers given to this question is the following: "That whenever any Form of Government becomes destructive of these ends [Life, Liberty and the pursuit of Happiness], it is the Right of the People to alter or to abolish it, and to institute new Government . . . when a long train of abuses and usurpations, pursuing invariably the same Object evinces a design to reduce them under absolute Despotism, it is their right, it is their duty, to throw off such Government . . ." This answer would be called radical by some people. It is, of course, the answer given in the Declaration of Independence. In short, the Declaration of Independence claims that revolution is justifiable when the people are oppressed and their freedoms are abridged. Further, not only is revolution justifiable, it is the duty of the people to revolt under these circumstances.

Now we might see how the earlier discussions of freedom and violence fit in here. If a certain segment of a population is being systematically violated and denied its freedoms, then this segment seems to be justified in revolting. This is the justification that some present-day radicals give for revolution; it is also the justification given by those earlier-day "radicals" who wanted the Colonies to be free and independent states. This analogy illustrates that revolution is most often justified on the grounds that people are being violated and denied their freedom. What is crucial to this matter is how "violence "and "freedom" are defined.

THE LAW AND CIVIL DISOBEDIENCE

Two positions have been traditionally argued concerning obedience to the law: (1) that the law ought never be disobeyed, and (2) that there are certain conditions under which disobeying the law is justified. Socrates in the *Crito* argues the first position, while others, among them Thoreau, have argued the second.

In the *Crito*, Socrates is in prison preparing for his death. He has just been condemned to die and is being visited by various friends, one of whom is Crito. Crito tries to persuade Socrates to escape, but Socrates will do nothing of the sort. In his dialogue with Crito, Socrates has, in effect, a dialogue with the laws of Athens. In this dialogue, Socrates argues that it would be unjust for him to escape because to do so would involve breaking the laws of Athens.

Socrates sets his argument up very carefully. It goes something like this: one ought never to act unjustly; it is unjust to break agreements; one has certain agreements with the state; escaping would break an agreement with the state; it is unjust to escape. In short, Socrates argues that it is unjust to escape because to escape would be to break Athenian law, and to break such law is never right.

But is Socrates not justified in breaking the law if he was unjustly convicted and condemned to die by it? Socrates' answer is a resounding no, two wrongs never make a right. Further, Socrates argues that he will die the victim of the injustice not of law but of men. In other words, Socrates holds that it is men, not laws, who have let him down.

So far we have avoided the main issues. What would Socrates do if the law had let him down, if he were the victim of the injustice of a law? Even in this case Socrates would still not escape, for he argues that a citizen owes allegiance to his state and does so by the very fact of remaining in that state voluntarily. Further, one does not show one's respect of the law by breaking it. Thus, even if Socrates were the victim of a bad law or two, breaking still other laws would not be justified, for they are laws that he has contracted to obey by being a citizen. To put it another way, Socrates was probably one of the earliest to draw the distinction between the spirit and the letter of the law. Even if he were the victim of a bad law, the law as such had treated him well.

Socrates is committed to obeying the law for several other reasons. He had argued all of his life that the law ought to be obeyed; how would it look if he now broke it? Further, the law binds a society together, and Socrates would set a very bad and dangerous example if he, one of the most well known citizens in all of Athens, broke the law.

In light of the above, Socrates argues that if one disagrees with a particular law or with the law in general, one has only three alternatives, one of which is not disobeying it: (1) obedience, (2) persuasion, or (3) exile. That is, a person may obey the law even though he disagrees with it; he may try to persuade the state to change the law; or he may leave the state.

With the complex legal systems of modern states coupled with the diverse natures of the state's citizenry, Socrates' position does not seem to be adequate any longer. There are too many cases in which certain laws seem to be unjust. Thus, it is argued that in certain instances it is justifiable to break the law. As we will see, this position agrees with that of Socrates on one point—the spirit of the law must never be violated. Let us now examine this position, which is called civil disobedience.

Civil disobedience is just what the name implies—the disobedience of a law in a civil, that is, nonviolent manner. Such civil disobedience is, indeed, law-breaking and as such differs from boycotts, conscientious objection, and the like. Conscientious objection, for example, is not a case of law-breaking because it is perfectly legal. It is, in fact, built right into the legal system. Civil disobedience must be nonviolent for only in this manner can it be directed at a particular law. If disobedience becomes violent, then it challenges the system of authority as a whole and becomes revolution.

Persons who are civilly disobedient often argue that they have more respect for the legal system than those who blindly obey all laws, even bad ones. This is argued on the grounds that civil disobedience is not aimed at changing a system but rather at changing a law or several laws. Civil disobedience challenges individual laws, the letter of the law, and not the spirit of the law itself. In fact, civil disobedience can take place only within an established framework of law, for if no such framework existed, no law could be changed. Thus, those who commit civil disobedience seek to strengthen the legal system by ridding it of bad laws.

Civil disobedience differs from other kinds of law-breaking in that it is done publicly, and those who commit it must be willing to accept punishment. These two conditions are vital because they help ensure that the law which is being protested will be either changed or stricken from the books.

When, if ever, may a law be justifiably disobeyed? The answer is both simple and extremely complex. A law may be justifiably disobeyed when it would be wrong to obey it. This seems quite simple. The difficulty lies in knowing when it is wrong to obey a law. There is no easy way to determine this, though there are certain relevant considerations. We need to know just how wrong the law is, for example. If the law is trivial, then civil disobedience might be disproportionately dramatic. Such a law might be better ignored. Further, we need to know what the foreseeable consequences of the act of civil disobedience might be. These could be determined by asking such questions as: Will the act succeed? What risks are involved? What are the personal consequences? Another consideration is the availability of alternative actions. If a law can be changed without having to be protested, then civil disobedience might be a case of overkill. If there are legal or political ways to change a law, they ought to be pursued and exhausted before civil disobedience is committed.

The above are just some of the relevant considerations which help us to know when civil disobedience is justified. Each case must be decided on its own merits or lack of them. The important point to remember is that obeying a law is never a guarantee of following the right action. There is a difference between legality and morality.

TOPICS FOR DISCUSSION

1. What is Mill's view on liberty, that is, on freedom? How does this position concern society and the individual's place in it? Is this position adequate? Why or why not?

2. Why is it important to articulate social concepts? How does the way these concepts are handled affect society? Discuss these questions with respect to violence.
3. What is the difference between revolution and civil disobedience? Is either ever justified? If so, spell out the conditions. If not, why not?
4. How does legality differ from morality? Does obeying the law guarantee that you are acting morally? Why or why not? Give examples.
5. Is civil disobedience really nonviolent? Discuss this question with respect to a broadened concept of violence.

SELECTED BIBLIOGRAPHY

Primary Source

Mill, John Stuart. *The Essential Works of John Stuart Mill.* Edited by Max Lerner. New York: Bantam Books, 1961.

Secondary Source

Burr, John R. and Milton Goldinger, eds. *Philosophy and Contemporary Issues.* New York: Macmillan, 1972.

Dewey, Robert E. and James A. Gould, eds. *Freedom: Its History, Nature and Varieties.* New York: Macmillan, 1970.

Hart, H. L. A. *Law, Liberty and Morality.* London: Oxford University Press, 1963.

Held, Virginia; Kai Nielsen; and Charles Parsons, eds. *Philosophy and Political Action.* New York: Oxford University Press, 1972.

Leiser, Burton M. *Liberty, Justice and Morals: Contemporary Value Conflicts.* New York: Macmillan, 1973.

Shaffer, Jerome A., ed. *Violence.* New York: David McKay, 1971.

Wasserstrom, Richard A. *Morality and the Law.* Belmont, California: Wadsworth Publishing, 1971.

CHAPTER 8

Existentialism

The Philosophy of the Absurd

WHAT IS EXISTENTIALISM?

Strictly speaking, existentialism is not a philosophy at all! Much of it appears in the form of novels, plays, and essays, not in philosophical treatises. It might justly be called antiphilosophy, for it is primarily a rebellion against all those things philosophers have traditionally stood for: objectivity, rationalism, and universal norms of behavior. It is, in short, a revolt against reason.

Nonetheless, existentialism belongs in a philosophical discussion for two reasons. In its earlier phase, the nineteenth century work of Kierkegaard and Nietzsche, it was directed against philosophers, and expressed in terms of philosophical issues. In its later stages, the twentieth century work of Heidegger and Sartre, it provided the major themes and concerns of phenomenology, a branch of philosophy. Existentialism can be seen as an emotionally concerned critique of the most important assumption of philosophy—reason itself. The best approach to existentialism is to try to understand what the existentialists were rebelling against.

The Rational World

From Plato to the present day, Western thought has been dominated by what may be called, in a very broad sense, *rationalism*; the belief that the universe is rationally ordered; that it follows clearly formulated laws, that it is comprehensible to human reason and intellect, that man is rational in his affairs (or at least could and should be) and occupies an intelligible place in this rational world. Irrational factors—human passion, madness, and chaotic situations—were recognized, but these were perceived as illusions, as evils to be overcome or areas of ignorance which the light of reason had not yet penetrated. Philosophy grew out of the great fear of the dark irrational side of life and the need to explain the irrational aspects of the world. Irrationality was admitted, but only as an appearance of an underlying rational substratum. Basically, the world was all reason and light.

In ethics, we derive by logical deduction the universal norms of behavior from our common human nature. In *The Republic*, for example, Plato says that we ought to be just because justice is allowing reason to control passion and this is what man's rational nature dictates. If man is by nature rational, then his reason ought to control his passions, and if I am a man this is what I ought to do. Thus an individual person infers what he ought to do from the general moral laws governing all mankind. As Kant pointed out, if something is wrong for one person to do, it is wrong for everyone.

The Rebellion Against Rationalism

For the existentialists, the most glaring inadequacy in the rational view of man and the world is the rather small and inconsequential place afforded the individual person. The individual is not entirely ignored within a rational system; but he is regarded simply as a member of the human species, one of many of a kind we call human beings. You and I, for example, are more or less interchangeable—we are both people. But what about the differences between us? As an instance of the class I understand myself just as I understand you, in terms of the rational definition we have of the class of "human beings." What is left out of this account is the *individuality* of the individual, the way I regard myself and the way you regard yourself as distinct and unique. The Danish philosopher Søren Kierkegaard rebelled against this, saying, "I refuse to be a paragraph in a system."

We can intuitively sympathize with Kierkegaard's objection. But this represents a completely irrational way of thinking. As pointed out in the essence/existence problem, there is no way to think or talk about the unique individual. You can never explain what you are except in general terms. Indeed, we can't explain anything except in general terms. This is the way reason and intellect work, and to a large extent this is the way language works. Whatever you can say reasonably, intelligibly, and rationally about yourself will necessarily apply, at least potentially, to someone else. You are not just a human being, let us say, but a woman, but there are lots of women. You are not just a woman, but a dark-haired woman, but again there are lots of dark-haired women. Well, you are a slim, dark-haired woman, or a young, slim, dark-haired woman. But you still haven't, and never can, logically and conceptually put your finger on the unique creature you are. We all know what it is to be an individual, but we can't express this rationally. To place the emphasis on you as you feel yourself from inside is, in a sense, to disconnect you from the rational world and to renounce reason, universality, and objectivity in favor of privacy, particularity, randomness, and subjectivity. This is why the best expressions of existentialism have come from novelists and artists, rather than academic scholars. Although philosophers, especially the phenomenologists, have tried to provide a "second-order" account of the existentialist pleas for individuality and subjectivity, the pleas themselves are more like a cry from the heart than an intellectual position to be defined.

The existentialists were not the first to rebel against rationalism in this broad sense. While rationalism has been the predominant preoccupation of Western intellectual thought, there have also been persistent antirationalist theories. Antirationalism has always taken second-place to rationalism and been looked upon as antiestablishment. Tertullian, for example, in the third century saw the danger of rationalism for the distinctly personal character of religious experience. "I believe," he said, *"because* it is absurd." The Gnostic tradition of the East was outlawed by the early Christian philosopher-theologians, but it was never completely wiped out and continually reemerges in occult practices —astrology, mysticism, witchcraft, vampirism, Satanism, and so on which are enjoying an especially popular revival today. Socrates and the sixteenth-century French philosopher Blaise Pascal are also honored as forerunners of existentialism, and the nineteenth-century Romantics, Coleridge, Wordsworth, and Schelling, can easily be seen as belonging to this underground, antiestablishment tradition. But it is primarily Nietzsche and Kierkegaard who figure as the great existentialist thinkers who set the themes and problems for the later existentialist-phenomenologists as well as the Absurdist literary movement of the 1950s. The existentialist thinkers posed the problem in a radically personal way which the phenomenologists later tried to clarify and answer in a philosophically rational and systematic format, and which Absurdist writers, like Camus, Beckett, and Ionesco, transformed into art.

KIERKEGAARD AND NIETZSCHE: THE PROBLEM STATED

One of the central existentialist themes is the critique of objectivity, and the central spokesmen of this critique are Nietzsche and Kierkegaard. Søren Kierkegaard (1813–1855) was a Danish philosopher and theologian generally recognized as the founder of existentialism. Friedrich Nietzsche (1844–1900) was a brilliant young German philosopher and philologist who wrote a number of widely read books emphasizing the supremacy of human will over reason. Both men were bitter critics of the society of their day—Kierkegaard lambasting the hypocrisy of the established church in Denmark, and Nietzsche attacking the smug Lutheran morality of his boyhood. Although both Nietzsche and Kierkegaard lived and wrote during the nineteenth century, they are recognized today as major prophets of the twentieth century. Both men focused their attack on the universal belief in rationality and objectivity. The goal of scientific knowledge is complete objectivity —that is, removing all personal biases or prejudices to get an honest look at things as they really are in themselves. Nietzsche argued that this was impossible and Kierkegaard objected that it would be worthless even if it were possible.

Nietzsche: Truth as a Human Value

Nietzsche criticized the traditional view of truth as an ideal standing apart from human needs and aspirations toward which men ought to devote themselves. Nietzsche stressed the role of truth as the expression of human needs. It is not we who must conform to "Truth," but truth which must prove its usefulness in human affairs. Why should we be truthful, to put the question in a moral context? What disadvantage would we suffer if we were not truthful? Imagine a society in which everyone always told lies whenever it suited him. What would happen? Obviously we could never trust anyone. And if we never trusted anyone, the ordinary exchange of information would be impossible. For example, it would make no sense to ask the grocer for the price of eggs or to promise to meet someone at an appointed time and place. Without a general commitment to truthfulness these activities would make no sense. But then look at how much of the ordinary affairs of any society would be jeopardized. We can begin to see why we *need* truthfulness; we begin to appreciate its social utility. Knowledge and truth are relative to men; as the Greek Sophist Protagoras put it, "Man is the measure of all things."

Nietzsche maintained that truth is a human value; it is not some external goal which we try to achieve. We can never step outside our own skins to distingiush absolutely what is "True" from what we only think is true. We should be as objective as we can, perhaps, but we can never see things as they are in themselves, as opposed to how they appear to particular human beings looking at the world from some particular human standpoint. Objectivity is a human value to be accepted or rejected, and knowledge is also a human achievement representing certain interests we take in the objective world. We can never view things just as they are, but only as they appear from our own limited point of view. It is the human predicament, so to speak, not to be able to completely transcend this subjectivity. I cannot understand Shakespeare or the French Revolution from the point of view of a contemporary of Shakespeare or Robespierre. However much I may try by an intensive study of history, my only point of view is that of someone living in the twentieth century and, moreover, that of someone in a particular country, race, class, and so on. Even scientific facts are meaningless unless they strike someone as puzzling or problematic. As you probably know from your own experience, learning can be a bore until you get involved in it. This is how Kierkegaard understood Socrates' method of questioning people, forcing them to confront issues face to face. Without human involvement, there is no truth.

Kierkegaard: Subjective Truth

In Kierkegaard's phrase, "Truth is subjectivity." This does not mean there is no relatively common ground on which we all more or less agree. It means that the only truth which is ultimately important is the truth which an individual has been able to absorb in his own way, that which he has been able to make

Kierkegaard and Nietzsche: The Problem Stated 247

his own. In a religious context, for example, it does no good for me to deduce from the general fact that because all men are by nature sinful, that I am therefore sinful. This type of knowledge simply adds one more bit of information to my existing store of ideas, neatly sorted, classified, and filed away for future reference. It has no direct impact on me as an individual. It is a different experience, however, when a religious person comes to see for himself the inadequacy of his own life.

In a curious way, a similar distinction exists in psychoanalysis between objective and subjective truth. A psychiatric patient will often spend years and thousands of dollars trying to make subjective a kind of objective knowledge about himself which he already has. Suppose on my first trip to the psychiatrist I am told that I am suicidal. Now, since I trust the doctor and believe him to be knowledgeable and truthful, why can't I just accept the truth of this diagnosis and save myself the expense of more $50-an-hour sessions? I know I am suicidal from the outside, but not from the inside. While I accept the fact that I am one of those 4.7 percent Americans who are suicidal, I have not yet admitted to myself the full personal ramifications of this fact. It may take me many painful years to understand myself in this sense. Only then will this diagnosis be useful to me in changing my life. In much the same way, any ultimate religious truth is apt to prove trite and trivial when understood objectively. Perhaps you have had the frustrating experience of finding the breathtaking insight you reached at 3 A.M. embarrassingly hollow over coffee the next morning. Thoughts which subjectively—from the inside—seem highly profound one moment, may turn out to be flat and stale when judged objectively.

It is necessary for the individual to make public forms of information personal. This is what much of adolescent rebellion is about. We are told in general terms by those in charge what we are supposed to think and become, how we are supposed to act, and conform. The problem is how to fit oneself into these pigeonholes. It is not primarily a question of the objective rightness or wrongness of these social standards; it is primarily a question of making what is a social standard a personal standard. Even if the standard is legitimate, I must make it my own. If I am successful, then when I later "take my place" in society it has become *my* place, even though, from the outside, I appear to be doing what everyone else is doing!

The clearest statement of "subjective truth" is Kierkegaard's discussion in *Fear and Trembling* (1843) of Abraham's planned sacrifice of Isaac. Kierkegaard invites us to see how ridiculous this is in terms of the rationalist tradition. Reason dictates that a man should act in accordance with general rules applicable to all people at all times (see Chapter 6). But clearly, killing one's kids cannot be an example of such a morally praiseworthy law! Surely God doesn't mean that it is always good to murder our sons. It is good only in this particular case. But, one might object, such an action is always good if God commands it. But how does Abraham know that God has commanded it? What is the test for a divine command? Suppose you heard a disembodied voice or saw some unusual phenomenon, such as a burning bush which was never consumed. Is this always necessarily a sign from God? Isn't it possible you were simply dreaming or hallucinating all this? How could you be sure? You might consult a religious authority. But how does he know? And how do you know that his advice is reliable, and how can you tell when he is right and when he is not? If two authorities disagree, as they often do, whose advice will you take? Ultimately, the decision is yours; the responsibility rests squarely on your shoulders. In the final analysis Abraham acts entirely alone, and the responsibility is all his.

THE PHILOSOPHY OF EXISTENCE: SARTRE AND HEIDEGGER

The early existentialists, Kierkegaard and Nietzsche, stated the human problem in painfully personal terms. For them, philosophy was an agonizing way of life. Half a century later this early expression of existentialist themes became the basis for a more systematic analysis of the human situation which converted existentialist thinking from a tormented affirmation of individual values to a more sober theory of human nature. The philosophical underpinning for this philosophy of man was the phenomenological theories of Edmund Husserl (1859–1938). Husserl developed a philosophical technique, known as "phenomenology," whereby all presuppositions could be set aside (or "bracketed") in order to perceive directly the basic character of human experience.

One of Husserl's most influential students was the contemporary German philosopher Martin Heidegger (1889–   ), whose theory of man was adopted in large measure by the leading existentialist Jean-Paul Sartre (1905–). Heidegger subjected the existentialist themes introduced by Kierkegaard and Nietzsche to Husserl's phenomenological analysis, making dread, anxiety, and alienation the key to understanding man. Sartre, one of the most versatile figures in the twentieth century, is also an example of a third kind of existentialist writer, those who after the Second World War expressed existentialist themes in works of fiction.

Sartre: The Individual and Responsibility

Sartre presents the existentialist theme of the loneliness of freedom and moral responsibility in a mundane context. In his essay "Existentialism and Humanism" (1946), Sartre argues that the individual can never derive his moral duty from general rules or norms supposedly derived from a universal human nature. Responsibility for an act rests with the individual, not with humankind. Sartre offers the example of a young man torn between his duty to join the army and defend his country from the Nazi armies and his duty to stay and care for his aged and dependent mother. There are good reasons for doing both, and excellent advisors can be found to counsel either course of action. In general men should defend their countries *and* their parents. But these rules are worthless to this particular young man in this particular situation. He cannot perform both actions and there is no rule for sorting out which is his higher obligation. If he decides to seek the advice of an expert, he must then decide which expert—an uncle in the army or a priest. And, of course, he alone must decide whether to take whatever advice is offered. In Sartre's analysis the man is not constrained by anything; he is infinitely free and totally responsible. But if Sartre is right, then this is the situation in which we all find ourselves all the time. It is no good for the Watergate defendant or the Nazi Party subordinate or the private in the Vietnam War to plead, "They told me to do it." We all follow orders or rules laid down by other people. But this does not absolve us from responsibility for our actions, since we are free and therefore responsible for accepting those orders and rules in the first place.

In Sartre's famous phrase, "Existence precedes essence." In other words, the individual does not derive what he is and does from the general norm or rule, but rather he becomes what he is by his own decisions and of his own free will. Rules and laws are human achievements, and it is our responsibility to accept or reject them. Even scientific theories about human nature are ours to consider. We are free to choose whether we accept them on authority from those we trust or to maintain a critical attitude, and therefore we are responsible. Sartre particularly attacks the Humanist idea that we can derive all our actions from the definition of human nature. He argues that there is no human nature standing over and above individual human beings, as many philosophers have thought. There are only certain common features which might or might not be important, depending on what those of us who are framing the definition are interested in (see Wittgenstein's attack on essentialism, Chapter 9).

As we saw earlier, facts do not group themselves according to similarity and difference. Everything is like and unlike everything else, and it is up to us to pick out those similarities we think are important. This can obviously result in different definitions of human nature, and the selection of one of these over the others requires a responsible decision on our part. Sigmund Freud said that men are basically aggressive; Eric Fromm said that they are basically loving. Who is right? Both theories are hypothetical constructions from the same facts: people are both aggressive and loving in different degrees and at different times. Neither Freud nor Fromm deny these facts; they just explain them differently. Both dismiss all counterexamples to their theories as cases of a thwarted human nature. Acts of love display a sublimated aggression according to Freud, while for Fromm they display our true nature; acts of aggression reveal one's true nature for Freud, while for Fromm they are a perversion of that nature. Some thinkers, like the existentialists, claim there is no human nature; others, that there is, though they disagree among themselves as to what it is and whether it is unchangeable or changeable. The point is that there is no law, fact, or nature about people which is not a matter of conjecture requiring some decision on our part, and the responsibility for making that decision rests ultimately on each individual. There are reasonable grounds for making such a decision, and it is our responsibility to weigh that evidence. We don't have to be rational; we are free to ignore the evidence if we like. Whether I choose to flip a coin or trust my teacher or some other authority is my decision, for which I bear the full consequences. If I refuse to bother about it, that is also my choice. In the nineteenth century many people found it convenient to accept the authority of those scientists who said that people were divided into "races," some of which were naturally inferior to others. They were nonetheless responsible for the colonial and slave policies which these theories were used to justify.

Sartre contends that there is no objective human nature, but only individual men with certain similarities and differences and various definitions of "man" which different people have proposed. How many races of man are there in fact? As many as there are inherited physical differences. But this is like asking how many colors there are in the color spectrum—as many as you like. Blonde, brunet, blue-eyed, brown-eyed, stocky, slim, all are inherited physical differences. These do not represent different racial types because we have no interest in making divisions along these lines, and this is a decision which we have made. The only thing we are not free to do is avoid our responsibility. As Sartre puts it, we are condemned to be free!

According to the existentialists, a man faces the world alone with no outside support. This is the human situation or predicament, and that factor of human life called "existence"; each man is responsible for himself and for his view of the world and other people, and he is thus separate from the rest of the universe. This analysis of existence presupposes a fundamental and sharp dichotomy between the being of man, that is, the way men exist, and the being of everything else. This basic existentialist position is fundamentally opposed to the entire Western intellectual tradition stemming from Aristotle (see Chapter 2) which considers reality only as the reality of objects and knowledge as knowledge of the essence of the kind of object in question. In particular existentialism is opposed to the eighteenth-century Humanist view that man is just one more kind of thing with its own essence or nature, in terms of which each man is judged and to which he is responsible.

Heidegger: Inauthentic Existence

Like rationalism, Humanism places man in the larger context of the natural world. Man is just one of many different kinds of things in the world; a grand and profound thing, perhaps, but a thing of a kind nonetheless. For the existentialists, this fails to capture the peculiar way in which men actually exist. Man is unique in his responsibility for himself and his view of the world. But this is not a particularly comforting thought. Always alone,

252 Existentialism—The Philosophy of the Absurd

I can never relax and accept things "as they are," or be sure I am right. Instead of a fixed and abiding human nature, what characterizes human existence for the existentialist is anxiety, dread, and alienation. In compensation, we try to shift some of this responsibility onto the shoulders of society, experts, authorities, and scientific "laws." Normally, as Heidegger puts it, we live and think in a collective way in terms of what "people say" and "everyone does." "Society," we say, "makes us think and act this way; there's nothing the individual can do." Heidegger characterizes this frequent sort of cop-out as *inauthentic existence*, not because it is wicked or naughty, but because it fails to own up to its own existential nature. A man lives inauthentically when he is not true to himself, turning his back on his responsibility by losing himself in external affairs, becoming absorbed in an "objective world." However, one cannot fully cast off responsibility and freedom. A person can pretend to but this never really works, according to Heidegger. The harder you try to forget, the more you remember. You can't completely accept the situation and you can't completely forget it. You are caught in the middle, and the net result of this inauthentic pretense is a dull anxiety, vaguely aware of its dishonesty but unable to come clean.

The existentialists recognize that inauthentic existence is in fact the normal state of human existence. But there are certain situations which recall us from this inauthentic mode of existence, and these are recurring themes in existentialist literature. One is the situation in which a person finds himself completely alone, without friends, without precedents, objectively in the wrong, like Abraham. The situation which has the most impact on people and which affects everyone is death—not death in general, but each man's death. Everyone knows he is going to die, but in a personal sense, he doesn't really recognize the fact. Objectively, I know that all men are mortal. I also know that I am a man. And I understand enough logic to infer from this that I am therefore going to die. But the full impact of this rarely hits me full blast, and when it does it is a very different kind of knowledge—the subjective truth Kierkegaard talks about. In "The Death of Ivan Ilyich" Tolstoy tells the story of a very ordinary man who knows he is dying. Gradually the full significance of this dawns on him and for the first time he is forced into an authentic reflection on his life. Similarly, in "The Wall," Sartre's story of a man about to be executed before a firing squad, it is death which recalls the man from an inauthentic existence. Existentialist literature in general deals with dreary and unpleasant themes—alienation, anguish, absurdity, dread, death, and a terrible and lonely freedom and responsibility—because these are the ways in which man's true existential character comes to light.

MEANING AND MEANINGLESSNESS

The most important existentialist theme and the one which has preoccupied many philosophers and writers of fiction is the meaningless absurdity of life. For this reason, existentialism is often called the "Philosophy of the Absurd." All of us at times feel that things are meaningless. Perhaps our job is pointless or school seems senseless, or we are involved in a meaningless relationship with someone of the opposite sex, or the social rat race of our parents strikes us as absurd. Presumably, in this context "meaninglessness" refers to the absence of meaning. But what kind of meaning; meaning in what sense? Some contemporary analytic philosophers think that meaning is simply a feature of language—that is, the linguistic meaning of words and sentences and definitions. In the philosophical tradition, a word gets its meaning from the essential nature of what is being referred to (for example, justice), an essence which is perceived as an idea and expressed as a definition. But the meaninglessness of one's work is not meaningless in that sense, and thus it is necessary to look at other kinds and senses of "meaning" before we can adequately characterize that painfully personal experience of meaninglessness which has emerged as a major sociological phenomenon of our times.

We use words like "means" and "meaning" in a variety of ways. Consider the following examples of ordinary English.

1. I mean to help if I can.
2. It was never meant to be.
3. Keep off the grass. This means you.
4. He meant more than met the ear.
5. He means well.
6. Buzzing means bees and bees mean honey. (Winnie-the-Pooh)
7. Money means little to me.
8. Procrastination means putting things off.

Of the 8 only the last has to do directly with the meaning of words and sentences.

To clarify the issue of meaninglessness we need to reduce this variety by classifying the different uses of the word to a few broad headings. Most recent attempts at classification seem to agree on the following as the main senses of "meaning," only one of which, the last, is the standard dictionary definition of words. The following senses of "meaning" correspond to the examples above:

1. to intend
2. to design something for a specific purpose
3. to intend a remark to have a particular reference
4. to intend to convey an individual thought or feeling by a standard form of speech
5. to be well-intentioned
6. to lead to or be somehow connected or associated with
7. to have a specified degree of importance to someone
8. linguistic meaning, that is, the standard dictionary meaning of a word

What emerges as the dominant idea of "meaning" is that of *purpose* and *intention* and the purposeful *connections between things*. Meaning is not some objective Platonic essence standing over and above mankind, but, like truth, it is a human achievement.

Meaning and Purpose

The modern sense of "meaning" appears to include the following: the sense of being designed (for a certain purpose), linguistic meaning (the intentional use of words and language to communicate), the quasi-intentional association of one thing with another (money "for the sake of" happiness, clouds "in order to" warn of rain, bees "for the sake of" honey), and the purposively described place of X in a system of things (the heart "in order to" pump the blood, the veins "in order to" carry the blood, the eye "for the purpose of" seeing). Dark clouds mean rain and bees mean honey, but rain doesn't mean dark clouds, nor does honey mean bees because in terms of human purposes the relationship works the other way round. Pooh wants honey; that's why he is interested in the bees. The bees mean honey in the sense that they lead him to honey. I am interested in rain for my own purposes: I want my cabbage plants to get wet but not myself as I walk to work. I interpret dark clouds as a forecast of rain and make my plans accordingly. Basically, then, it is people who *mean* because it is people who intend and plan purposefully. Once a group of people have decided on a standard means to convey their intentions, such as language, the sense of meaning is gradually transferred from the people to the intention and to the words used to convey that intention. Similarly, we speak of what a book says as a way of describing what the author says in the book. Nonetheless in the primary sense it is people who mean just as it is the author who speaks. Because people purposefully intend, they see the world in terms of intentional links, and in a secondary sense the web of purposeful links gives meaning and structure to the world as human beings experience it.

Contextual Meaning

When we examine recent empirical investigations into meaning we find much the same intentional, nonlinguistic story. Contemporary anthropological studies, for example, view meaning as the place of an action or remark in a particular social context. According to a number of leading anthropologists like Evans-Pritchard and Levi-Straus, the meaning of a social form of behavior lies in its "social syntax," that is, in the functional interdependence between it and different forms of behavior within a specified area. For example, an anthropologist may want to explain the meaning of the following behavior. A group of men are seated in a circle around a container of small stones. One man removes several handfuls, placing them in a separate pile. A second man then takes some of the stones from the second pile and puts them back in the original container. The first man repeats his original action, transferring a smaller amount of stones to the second pile, and so on, until neither man moves any more stones from one pile to the other. What does this mean? To find out the anthropologist tries to locate this behavior within a larger pattern of social interaction. He will note that the men belong to two families and that the second man brought the stones to the house of the first man. He will also observe that following this activity, men from the second man's family brought exactly the same number of goats to the house of the first man as the final number of stones in the second pile, and shortly thereafter a ceremony took place which the anthropologist already understands as the marriage of the second man to the daughter of the first. Knowing this, the meaning of the original activity becomes clear: the men were bargaining over the "bride's price," the meaning of which we have come to understand by seeing its relation to other activities in the broader "social syntax." The meaning of the bride-price itself could be made more intelligible by seeing its place within the broader spectrum of tribal marriage, divorce, family life, and so on.

Meaning, then, in one important sense refers to functional interdependence, the intended place of X in a socially-understood system of things. Knowing the meaning of X in this sense is not necessarily an explicit, conscious understanding as our understanding of linguistic meaning is generally thought to be. An outsider to a given society, such as an anthropologist, understands the meaning of X by seeing explicitly its relation to Y and Z, but a member of that society knows the meaning of X without this explicit understanding. He simply has a sense of being at home in this system, knowing his way around, experiencing no surprises or confusion. Ironically, the system as such becomes apparent to him only if and when it begins to break down or when he views it from an alien perspective. In other words, a native knows the meaning without understanding it *as* such.

Traditionally, meaning is an articulate, expressible thing which words have—their definition. If we insist on thinking of meaning exclusively as dictionary definitions, then we will probably hesitate to say that the interrelatedness of things in a social system constitutes meaning. Instead we may want to say that functional interdependency is that which makes meaning possible, or that in terms of which we understand the meaning. But dictionary meaning is one kind of meaning; the interrelatedness of things in a system is another. When we say a social system has meaning or has lost meaning, all we understand that it has or has lost is this interconnectedness of things. Similarly, when we say we understand the meaning of an action in its broader social context, we are understanding the place of X in its social context in relation to Y and Z. What we cannot do is express the meaning in words. We do not say a social system has *a* meaning, which invites the question, "what meaning?" We say that it has meaning, that it is meaningful. The question of the translation meaning of words and sentences is simply out of place here. Indeed, as we will see, in the final analysis linguistic meaning must be understood in terms of such nonlinguistic forms of meaning as functional interdependency.

At any rate, it is this sense of contextual meaning we have in mind when we wonder about the meaning of life, or our job, or our relationships with people—that is, whether the individual parts of our lives hang together in a purposeful web, or whether there is any overall purpose for our life or human life in general. As Sartre says, we tend to transfer our concept of the human purpose for which we make and do things to the purpose for which we, ourselves, were created.

> If one considers an article of manufacture—as, for example, a book or a paper-knife—one sees that it has been made by an artisan who had a conception of it . . . and . . . pre-existent technique of production which is a part of that conception and is, at bottom, a formula. Thus the paper-knife is at the same time an article producible in a certain manner and one which, on the other hand, serves a definite purpose, for one cannot suppose that a man would produce a paper-knife without knowing what it was for. . . . Here, then, we are viewing the world from a technical standpoint. . . . When we think of God as the creator, we are thinking of him . . . as a supernatural artisan. Whatever doctrine we may be considering, . . . we always imply that the will follows, more or less from the understanding or at least accompanies it, so that when God creates he knows precisely what he is creating. Thus, the conception of man in the mind of God is comparable to that of the paper-knife in the mind of the artisan: God makes man according to a procedure and a conception, following a definition and a formula. [Sartre, "Existentialism and Humanism"]

Even where we no longer accept the existence of God, the idea of a divine plan lingers on in a quasi-intentional or purposive manner as the idea of a fixed and abiding human nature.

Despite the contemporary bias in favor of linguistic meaning as the primary sense, both Wittgenstein and Heidegger, who provide the conceptual foundations for most contemporary discussions of meaning, regard nonlinguistic meaning as basic. Meaning for both Heidegger and Wittgenstein is ultimately the place of things in a humanly-interpreted world—the world as a system of relationships seen from a human point of view. For Heidegger, as for Pooh, this involves regarding everything as though it were designed to serve our own needs; a pencil to write with, a chair to sit on, bees to give us honey, and the forest as firewood, timber, potential farmland, recreation, or wilderness. Man is a purposive creature and the world hangs meaningfully together because he projects that sense of purposefulness into the world. Although the defining of concepts remains the most familiar concept of meaning philosophers are coming to realize that linguistic meaning, and the possibility of linguistic meaning, can only be understood against such an anthropological background of contextual, nonlinguistic meaning. Certainly, it is only the loss of some nonlinguistic meaning which can explain the modern sense of meaninglessness. We can begin to understand the experience of meaninglessness in terms of the loss of meaning in one or more of the nonlinguistic senses already discussed—meaningless, for example, as the lack of purpose or reason (the sense of absurdity), or the loss of a pattern or structure holding things together (the sense of things falling apart, or of our being lost in a maze), the lack of any recognizable shape or form (a sense of strangeness, alienation), the loss of importance, savor, zest (the sense of being dead to life or love), the loss of a sense of the consequences of one's actions (the sense of impotence, hopelessness).

Being-As

The problem with nonlinguistic meaning is that it is not perceived explicitly and self-consciously *as* meaning, and this makes it difficult to analyze. The main difficulty with this type of meaning is our inability to say *what* an event, action, or phenomenon means. Because of the environment in which I was brought up, a chair is a "meaningful" item in my experience in a way it would not be for someone who had never seen European furniture. I see it and recognize it *as* something to sit on, rest in, and so on. But if the chair has meaning, one could ask, what exactly does it mean? Well, nothing—or rather, nothing we consciously or explicitly understand and could put into words. The meaning does not appear *as* meaning; it consists simply in my having an ordered, systematic perceptual experience, in which everything fits together. Let us call this type of meaning *being-as*, which is a play on the psychologist's term *seeing-as*. The world we know is "concept-laden." In the world as I experience it there are no mere things but only things of a certain kind. To see a thing is therefore to see it *as* this or that, a pencil or a grasshopper or whatever. As Aristotle put it (Chapter 2), substance is essence. I can't see X without seeing it as a member of a conceptual class or kind; I don't just know its classification, I actually see it that way. Hence the tacit familiarity and implicit identity of things to the native speaker. He doesn't realize that he is seeing the world in terms of conceptual categories; things just look like that to him. He would not say, "I see that *as* a chair," precisely because he does see it that way. The seeing-as is so successful, in other words, it never occurs to him it could be anything else. *Being-as* is the mute recognizable identity of things which makes the world a familiar place.

It is undeniable that situations, events, actions, and phenomena are commonly regarded in everyday speech as meaningful or meaningless, and it would therefore seem a mere laziness or timidity on the part of the philosopher to avoid altogether the theoretical investigation of this important type of meaning. Besides, being-as is not an utterly sterile notion. We can indicate, though in a roundabout way, what the chair means. We simply have to suggest or imagine an alternative, that is, what it would be like if the chair were not recognized as a chair. We could do this by an imaginative contrast with the Australian aborigine's first experience of a chair (is it a god or a weapon?), or that of a child; we can discuss it in terms of our own behavioral anticipations and expectations (how sad and empty, for example, a room looks without any furniture, or how strange chairs would look hung from the walls like paintings, or neatly arranged in the middle of a superhighway), and so on. In this sense we can, and just did, put into words what the chair means, but not "just like that," as in a dictionary, just as we can, in a sense, say what a work of art means (see Chapter 9), though not in the sense of an adequate translation identical with and substitutable for the work of art.

From our analysis of meaning four primary senses of meaning have emerged:

1. linguistic (translation equivalence)
2. being-as (recognizable identity)
3. interrelatedness of things in a pattern (contextual meaning)
4. intention and purpose.

The importance of this division lies in the relationships it provides between these four types of meaning. Linguistic meaning presupposes and would be impossible without being-as; being-as presupposes the systematic interrelatedness of things; and this presupposes human purpose and intention. Knowing what the word "table" means presupposes the ability to know and identify an object *as* a table; but this depends on an understanding of the place that thing occupies in a system of socially-intelligible relations (seeing it as something to write on, eat off of, put flowers on, and so on). This type of understanding would be impossible without our ability to assign purposeful or intentional relationships to things (tables designed for the purpose of eating off of, writing on, and so on).

Imagine you are trying to explain to someone of a totally different culture what "chalk" means. First you point to a piece of chalk. The person will not understand unless he knows what chalk is and what it is for. How can you explain that? Chalk is used for writing. Writing, what's that? Writing is for the sake of communication, like talking. Then why not just talk? We write to communicate to a broader audience than those who happen to be within earshot. But why? Ultimately the foreigner would have to understand our whole way of life. Now imagine the reverse problem which would confront you trying to figure out the meaning of a Yoruba woman wearing a small Ibije figure round her waist. The figure represents her twin brother. But why wear it? To keep her brother's spirit from possessing her. Why would it do that? And so on. We can't understand this until we understand the total Yoruba conception of man and the universe. To take a simpler case, imagine your first day at work in a large factory. The layout of the plant is strange, incomprehensible, and you feel uneasy. Six months later, as you learn your way around, everything falls into place, the individual pieces of machinery loose their alien, threatening look and you feel at home working among them.

We are now in a better position to understand meaninglessness as the absence of meaning in these four senses, with the exception of linguistic meaning. Meaninglessness we now see as:

2. the loss of recognizable identity (being-as), the frightening strangeness and repugnant otherness of mere things devoid of meaning, feeling unwanted, not at home in an alien world, estranged and alone,
3. disconnected, uprooted, lost in a maze, in a thoroughly Catch-22 world, and

4. the purposelessness, irrational absurdity and pointless futility of life.

This is a reasonably faithful characterization of our ordinary experience of meaninglessness, and it accords very well with the existentialist literature.

The Absurd

If existentialism is a revolt against reason, systems, and so on, how can there be a systematic theory of the existential nature of man? As we suggested at the beginning of the chapter, there is indeed a kind of contradiction in the idea of an existentialist philosophy. Sartre and Heidegger are primarily phenomenologists directing their philosophical attention to existentialist themes. They are analyzing dread from a philosophical point of view, not suffering it.

For this reason, some of the best examples of existentialist writing come from a literary movement, known as the "Literature of the Absurd," which centered in Paris after the Second World War. Albert Camus (1913–1960) was a French Algerian, Eugene Ionesco (1912–   ) is a Roumanian, Samuel Beckett (1906–   ) is an Irishman, Arthur Adamov (1908–   ) is a Russian, but during the 1940s and 1950s they all lived in Paris and wrote novels and plays in French on the absurdity of the human condition.

In their writings we find two main existentialist senses of "absurd": (1) that the *world* is absurd because it is unreasonable, irrational, inexplicable (that is, without the interconnectedness of meaning-3 or the purpose of meaning-4), and (2) that *things* are absurd because they have been stripped of the meanings we as human beings assign to them (that is, without being-as in meaning-2). Absurdity refers either to a world without reason or to things without sense.

A WORLD WITHOUT REASON. When we speak of things being reasonable, we usually mean that there is a purpose for their being there, or that they can be related together in a system or pattern which can be perceived in terms of purposes. Your friend from an alien culture sees a man running to catch a bus and asks you why he is running. How can you explain this to him? He is running in order to catch the bus. But why? This must be related to many other purposes in order to become intelligible to your friend. Why doesn't the bus wait for him? Because it is tied to a schedule. Why? So that other people can rely on it. But if there are other buses why not wait for the next bus? He wants to be on time. Why? Because he has a job. What's that (that is, what is it like to be employed by another person for cash wages)? Children, who are, in a sense, also culturally alien, frequently ask such a maddening string of questions. As in a jigsaw puzzle, the individual piece makes no sense until all the pieces have been put together into a total picture. "Absurd" originally meant musically out of harmony, and from this it has come to mean out of harmony in the broader sense.

ALBERT CAMUS. A world without purpose and purposeful links is therefore a world without reason, which is precisely how the French existentialist novelist and playwright Albert Camus (1913–1960), describes absurdity. In *The Myth of Sisyphus* (1955), Camus carries this idea of absurdity to its logical conclusion, the problem of suicide. "Does the lack of any reason for living logically demand or morally sanction suicide?" Camus' answer is "no," but we are concerned with his statement of the problem rather than his answer to it. The main feature of absurdity, for Camus, is its irrationality.

> You continue making the gestures commanded by existence for many reasons, the first of which is habit. Dying voluntarily implies that you have recognized, even instinctively, the ridiculous character of that habit, the absence of any profound reason for living, the insane character of that daily agitation, and the uselessness of suffering. [Camus, *The Myth of Sisyphus*]

Camus contends that in such a world nothing is explainable or accountable; hence nothing is familiar, everything is strange, alien.

> A world that can be explained even with bad reasons is a familiar world. But, on the other hand, in a universe suddenly divested of illusions and lights, man feels an alien, a stranger. . . . This divorce between man and his life, the actor and his setting, is properly called the feeling of absurdity. [*The Myth of Sisyphus*]

Of particular interest is Camus' analysis of the stages by which absurdity reveals itself. The first stage is the awareness that the connecting links holding things together in a coherent world are breaking up, that things are falling apart.

> That odd state of the soul in which the void becomes eloquent, in which the chain of daily gestures is broken, in which the heart vainly seeks the link that will connect it again, then it is as it were the first signs of absurdity. *[The Myth of Sisyphus]*

From this point the isolated, disconnected pieces take on an alien strangeness.

> A step lower and strangeness creeps in: perceiving that the world is "dense", sensing to what degree a stone is foreign and irreducible to us, with what intensity nature or a landscape can negate us. At the heart of all beauty lies something inhuman, and these hills, the softness of the sky . . . at this very minute lose the illusory meaning with which we had clothed them. *[The Myth of Sisyphus]*

The absurd world is alien because it is inhuman, and it is inhuman because it is devoid of human reasons, explanations, and concepts.

> The mind's deepest desire . . . is an insistence upon familiarity, an appetite for clarity. Understanding the world for a man is reducing it to the human, stamping it with his seal. . . . The mind that aims to understand reality can consider itself satisfied only by reducing it to terms of thought. *[The Myth of Sisyphus]*

Without purposeful, rational links between things, the individual pieces of our lives appear disjointed, and hence pointless, senseless, and absurd. I may feel, for example, that my job in a pickle factory is alien and unrelated to my own personal goals and self-image. But in another sense meaninglessness may appear as the irrational pointlessness of things as a whole. Even if I begin to see how the various facets of my life and that of the larger society hang together, I may still wonder what all this is for, why human beings exist at all! This view of the world arises primarily from the stance of the man who looks at things *sub specie aeternatatis*, from the absolute standpoint of "What will it matter 5000 years from now?" From the aspect of eternity everything seems contingent, futile, pointless, and scarcely worth the effort. If it's not going to make a difference 5000 years from now, in the grand scope of things, then does it really matter now? From this absolute perspective meaninglessness refers to the insignificance of man and the futility of his action when seen against the backdrop of infinite space and time.

One of the earliest and certainly one of the best expressions of this view of absurdity was given by the seventeenth-century French mathematician, Blaise Pascal (1623–1662). Pascal was one of the first to articulate the painful contrast between the relative worth of man in a scientific framework and the absolute hope for man within a religious perspective of divine design and eternal salvation.

> When I consider the tiny span of my life, which is swallowed up in the eternity which precedes and follows it, when I consider the tiny space that I occupy and can even see, lost as I am in the infinite immensity of Space which I know nothing about and which knows nothing about me, I am terrified and marvel to find myself here rather than there, for there is no reason at all why here rather than there, or why now rather than then. Who put me here? By whose command and under whose direction were this time and this place destined for me? [Pascal, *Thoughts*]

As Ionesco writes in his essay on Kafka,

> Absurd is that which is devoid of purpose.... Cut off from his religious, metaphysical, and transcendental roots, man is lost; all his actions become senseless, absurd, useless. [Ionesco, "Dans les Armes de la Ville"]

Another writer whose view of the absurd springs from this religious, absolutist point of view is Arthur Adamov. To Adamov the world must have some hidden, transcendent purpose which guarantees the significance of the world as a whole and everything in it. When we lose sight of this transcendent meaning and purpose, we are completely lost, our lives thoroughly wasted and futile. It is no longer a question of simply putting the pieces of our lives back together; only a transcendent source, such as God, can guarantee meaning in this sense.

> From whatever point he starts, whatever path he follows, modern man comes to the same conclusion: behind its visible appearances, life hides a meaning that is eternally inaccessible to penetration by the spirit that seeks for its discovery, caught in the dilemma of being aware that it is impossible to find it, and yet also impossible to renounce the hopeless quest. [Adamov, "The Endless Humiliation"]

And, of course, this presupposes that, like Sartre's paper-knife, the world has a meaning, that behind the world of experience there is something, however elusive, which gives it meaning. Adamov's play *L'Invasion* (1950) is a brilliant parable exposing the hopeless quest for the transcendent meaning or purpose which will make sense of and unify a mass of otherwise unintelligible, unrelated phenomena. In the play Agnes is left with a mass of posthumous papers which she tries to decipher and put into some intelligible order. But she can't find the code, and the action of the play expresses that frenetic activity which really accomplishes nothing. Here meaning stands for harmony, the purposive fitting together of parts within a whole. But for Adamov this is only possible by means of a key or code, that is, meaning in the sense of a transcendent purpose or design for the system as a whole. Nothing short of this will show us how the pieces of the puzzle fit together.

SAMUEL BECKETT. Meaninglessness from the absolutist standpoint turns on a very special view of time which is probably best expressed in the work of the Irish playwright Samuel Beckett. For Beckett the span of time (as seen from the standpoint of eternity) collapses, leveling and shortening everything in its path. We "stretch" out our lives with the accomplishment of our purposes; without purpose, time "snaps back" to something long in boredom and short in significance. In *Waiting for Godot* (1952), Estragon and Vladimir are seen aimlessly waiting, passing time, and idling away the hours, under a fragile illusion of purposeful anticipation and meaningful expectation. But since in Beckett's view nothing important or significant ever really happens or is accomplished, meaningful change is an illusion. Without the possibility of meaningful, purposeful action time contracts, and there is no more significance to the space of 80 years than to 80 seconds. Hence the sense of a man stretching out his life with activity and accomplishment is an illusion; he is dead (or as good as dead) as soon as he is born. As one of Beckett's characters, Pozzo, says,

> Have you not done tormenting me with your accursed time? . . . One day, is that not enough for you, one day like any other day he went dumb, one day I went blind, one day we'll die, the same day, same second. . . . They gave birth astride of a grave, the light gleams an instant, then it's night once more. [Beckett, *Waiting for Godot*]

And yet, ironically, the absence of purposeful accomplishment which makes life so short, also makes it boringly long! When we are bored, time drags by endlessly, yet when asked what we have been doing all day, we reply, "Nothing," which is certainly all we will remember of it later. On the other hand, when we are deeply engrossed in something, the hours fly by and we remember it as a full day with scarcely enough hours to pack in all the activities, and this stretches a day which in another sense was so short.

Ultimately it is death which, on this view, flattens and shortens life, swallowing up any would-be purposeful "end" of life and action in the final temporal "end" of each man's life. Death, like the infinity or eternity of time, not only annihilates man, but retrospectively annihilates the point of any human action, robbing it of reason and purpose. If I look at my own projects or national or international projects from the point of view of their eventual and inevitable end, I can no longer attach any point or purpose, and hence reason, to these activities. To act meaningfully is to act purposefully, doing one thing for the sake of another. This presupposes the possibility of accomplishing certain ends. This is the point of Camus' reference to Sisyphus, who was condemned by the Greek gods to roll a stone to the top of a hill. But the sentence is an exercise in futility because each time Sisyphus gets the stone to the top of the hill it rolls back down and must be pushed up again and again through all eternity. However, death, when viewed from the absolutist standpoint, seems to rob any possible action of its accomplishment. In the short run things may appear to be worthwhile, but not in the long run from the standpoint of eternity. If I plan a career, or the education of my children, or work toward a system of international security, then, however successful I am in the short run, all of this will be negated in the long run by the death of myself and my children and the eventual cosmic death of our planet.

THINGS WITHOUT SENSE. The existentialists also interpret "meanings" as human values which we attach to things that in themselves are meaningless. When the human meanings are stripped from things, we are brought face to face with the brute, alien, inhuman aspect of these things. Because these things are without significance, they are in a sense *nothing* and consequently ethereal, fleeting, and unreal. Existentialist writers often present two alternating views of the world: one in which a character is oppressed by all the objects and things in the world, the other in which he feels a vast sense of emptiness because there is nothing in the world. In their plays and novels, existentialists often present a surrealistic picture of the world in which tension exists between the all-too-real and the dreamlike quality of things. The playwright Ionesco writing about his plays explained the two interpretations of the meaning of things in this way:

> Two fundamental states of consciousness are at the root of all my plays . . . those of evanescence on the one hand, and heaviness on the other; of emptiness and of an overabundance of presence; of the real transparency of the world, and of its opaqueness; of light, and of heavy shadows. [Ionesco, "Point of Departure"]

Sartre calls this experience "nausea"—the sense of things as totally alien to us, encroaching on us and threatening us simply because they are not like us. Reality is stripped of man's projected meanings, and things exist without meaning. Because inanimate objects are alien, they are vaguely repulsive. In his famous novel *Nausea* (1938), Sartre explores this in depth.

> Objects should not *touch* because they are not alive. You use them, put them back in place, you live among them; they are useful, nothing more. But they touch me; it is unbearable. [Sartre, *Nausea*]

To say that things are inhuman is not just to say that they are not human beings, but that humanly projected meanings will no longer attach to them. They transcend the uses which we assign them, umbrellas to shed rain, dark clouds to warn of rain, and soon our concept of an object and the object itself are no longer lodged together. Sartre further dramatizes this experience in *Nausea*:

> I murmur: "It's a seat," a little like an exorcism. But the words stay on my lips: it refuses to go and put itself on the thing. It stays what it is. . . . Things are divorced from their names. They are there, grotesque, headstrong, gigantic and it seems ridiculous to call them seats or say anything at all about them; I am in the midst of things, nameless things. Alone without words, defenseless, they surround me.

In Sartre's description the brute, bullying otherness of things alien to us weighs in upon us with the suffocating heaviness described by Ionesco. But the next moment we experience the alternative lightness and emptiness of things. Without a human meaning attached to them, things exist, are just there, heavily and oppressively; but shorn of meaning they are also nothing. In Chapter 2 we discussed Aristotle's reasons for supposing that the being of an object is both individual existence and general essence. In this sense mere things have existential being but no essential being. *What* are these things (what do we call them, what meaning do we attach to them)? Nothing. Hence, they are in this sense nothing; they have existence in the technical sense of reality without meaning, but they have no being-as or essence. The objects and things are there, but they don't exist *for us*. Hence their overt heaviness dissolves into an empty, hollow unreality.

> Today they fixed nothing at all: it seemed that their very existence was subject to doubt, that they had the greatest difficulty in passing from one instant to the next. I held the book I was reading tightly in my hand; but the most violent sensations went dead. Nothing seemed true; I felt surrounded by cardboard scenery. [*Nausea*]

Since meaning cannot be attached to these things, we can no longer explain, identify, or define them. Like Camus, Sartre's view of reality without meaning is the image of an absurd, irreducible, and recalcitrant element.

> Absurd, irreducible; nothing . . . could explain it. . . . The world of explanation and reasons is not the world of ex-

> istence. A circle is not absurd, it is clearly explained.... But neither does a circle exist. This root [of a tree], on the other hand, existed in such a way that I could not explain it. Knotty, inert, nameless.... In vain to repeat; "this is a root" —it didn't work any more. I saw clearly that you could not pass from its function as a root, as a breathing pump, *to that*, to this hard and compact skin of a sea lion, to this oily, callous, headstrong look. [*Nausea*]

The circle is thoroughly explainable because it is nothing but the creation of man's intellect. But the root exists over and above our talk and thoughts about it. Consequently, there is always a gap between the root and what we say about it (see Chapter 3). We can never completely, exhaustively describe or explain or understand it; it transcends all our humanly oriented, purposive (functional) accounts of it—it is *just there*. Sartre stated that "The essential thing is contingency. I mean that one cannot define existence as necessary, to exist is simply to *be there*." No matter how good our explanations are, they are always and necessarily partial; they never exhaust the object.

For Sartre the emotional response to the world of objects devoid of meaning is twofold: a repugnance at this proliferation of alien things choking and crowding us, and a sense of being unwanted and not at home in such a world.

> I sank down on the bench, stupefied, stunned by this profusion of beings without origin: everywhere blossoming, hatching out.... It was repugnant.

> We were a heap of living creatures, irritated, embarrassed at ourselves, we hadn't the slightest reason to be there, none of us, each one, confused, vaguely alarmed, felt in the way in relation to the others. *In the way*. [*Nausea*]

The main factor in Sartre's account of this alien reality is the separation of being from meaning; existence in this sense is pure being without essence or purpose. And in Sartre's view reality is made up of pure being or existence—there is no meaning.

> I was not surprised, I knew it was the World, the naked World, suddenly revealing itself, and I choked wth rage at this gross, absurd being. [*Nausea*]

This is perhaps the most philosophically interesting concept of meaninglessness, especially as it has been developed by contemporary English-speaking philosophers, like John Wild and H. J. Blackman. As Blackman puts it,

> The intelligible world constructed by personal existence, in which man feels safe and at home, the world of meanings, is nihilated and he is plunged back into the sheer "is-ness" of what is.... This is an experience of brute existence denuded of meanings.... It uncovers the marvellousness of pure "is-ness," contingency, which reason covers up, and is therefore a revelation of Being. [Blackman, *Six Existentialist Thinkers*]

Wild also sees meaninglessness as the clash between being and meaning, the awareness of being as lacking meaning. Part of Wild's justification for this view is that it accords with our experience of absurdity, that "clashing dissonance between being and meaning that has been widely experienced in our time."

> Being is not necessarily joined with meaning as the major stream of Western thought, and also Heidegger, have supposed. Contrary to these teachings they may fall apart, and they may have fallen apart in the world of our time. [Wild, "Being, Meaning and the World"]

The crux of the problem of meaninglessness is that meaning is a human projection which has finally become dislodged from things. But why exactly is this tragic? Eastern philosophers (see chapter 5) have acknowledged for centuries the humanly projective nature of ordinary meaning, but they regard this discovery as a joyous awakening. Why is this reflection received so pessimistically in the West?

THE TRAGIC SENSE OF MEANINGLESSNESS

To answer this question let us return to our earlier analysis and examine how the three basic types of meaninglessness are related to one another. Just as meaning-1 presupposes meaning-2 which in turn presupposes meaning-3, and so on, so the reverse with meaninglessness. Meaninglessness as the loss of purpose and intention (4) leads to meaninglessness as the loss of any systematic interrelatedness (3), leading to meaninglessness as the loss of being-as (2), which in turn leads to meaninglessness as the loss of linguistic meaning (1). If we ask, in a mood of religious reflection, what is the ultimate purpose of life or the world as a whole and can find no answer, we may be overcome by the dizzying experience that the world is falling apart. We are then no longer able to relate one thing to another, nor ourselves to anything in a system or pattern of meanings. As a result things lose their familiar, recognizable shape and take on a disturbing strangeness. When this happens words cease to convey meaning or to disclose a meaningful world and become themselves disconnected, meaningless "things" which separate us from the world. Just as the midnight discovery we discussed earlier seems pale in the light of day, so the total removal of "subjective" involvement turns words into mere sounds, talk into noise.

So, the dialectical root of meaning is purpose. But the basic character of meaning would seem to be the human ability to project purpose on to the world. Meaning is transcendentally traceable to purpose, but the important point about purpose is not the psychological fact that men can entertain thoughts about what they want, but that they can see the world *in terms of* their purposes. Purpose is important, in other words, primarily as an explanation of *being-as*. Although the source of meaning is purpose, the key to understanding it is interpretation and projection. We want to think of "meaning" primarily as a projective understanding or interpretation of reality.

Projection

Existential meaninglessness, put simply, is the realization that the meaning we find in the world is a human projection or accomplishment, and not something possessed by the world itself. In Kierkegaard's terms, meaning is subjective, not objective. In order to understand this sense of meaninglessness, we must have a clear sense of the kind of meaning it denies, namely, objective essential meaning which we attach to things. Thus, existentialism is a rejection of Realism, the belief in the reality of essences. However, we are all Realists in our everyday projection of meaning because projection is primarily a blind interpretation, an automatic, unselfconscious understanding of things.

This definition of projection turns on two basic elements, the fact that it is an interpretation or way of seeing the world from a human point of view, and the fact that we are unaware that it is an interpretation. Projection is not just seeing that some part of reality could be interestingly explored from a certain point of view, it is the attachment of this point of view to the world and a failure to see that it is a human point of view. This naive view of meaning then gets translated into philosophical Realism, the belief in real essences or natural kinds (see Chapter 2), but it springs from our ordinary, unsophisticated view of the world. Normally, when I say "It's a seat," in direct contrast to the experience of "nausea," the word sticks to the object; I don't realize that it's mine at all. The word "projection" is used to describe another's view of the world and not one's own. I judge that *he* is reading into events his own biases, preferences, and interests, whereas I see myself as simply reading off objective characteristics of a situation. Psychologists and anthropologists often use the term "projection" when referring to other people's (generally false) conceptualizations and rationalizations of the world. Usually when we recognize ourselves making a projection we see this as a mistake which we try to avoid in the future. Or if we see ourselves as being under a constant illusion which we can neither correct nor abandon, then we may become depressed and feel trapped in this illusion.

Throughout Western philosophy projection ("subjectivity") has been looked upon as a sin to be avoided at all costs. Genuine knowledge (see Chapter 3) can only occur when my concept of a thing corresponds exactly with its essential nature. If it does not, then that concept is sheer fantasy and worthless for understanding the world.

Martin Heidegger contends that it is projection which enables us to get interested and absorbed in the world. We identify our meanings with the world and are thereby drawn into it, losing ourselves in it like Narcissus lost in his own reflection. In Wild's discussion, projection is presented as the ordinary, naive sense of the unity of being and meaning; it is the act of seeing meaning as a necessary and inseparable part of being, or rather, since it is never quite so explicit as this in everyday life, the failure to distinguish meaning from being (essence from existence). Thus projection must be naively blind; as soon as we see what we are doing, that the meaning is really ours, the illusion is shattered and meaning begins to separate itself from being, and this divorce of being and meaning is what we call an experience of meaninglessness. The *awareness of projection* is therefore the experience of meaninglessness. But this is ironic! Since meaning is a form of projection, meaninglessness is simply an awareness of the nature of meaning! Perhaps, as we will see, this indicates a flaw in the existentialist's thinking.

Two questions remain in regard to projection: (1) to what extent is our view of the world a projection and (2) how do we become aware of it as projection? Although projection is universal, it is capable of degrees of transparency which represent the various stages of our awareness of it. At first we see projection in others, especially the more obvious forms of projection as in primitive superstitions and childish explanations. From this point we may go on to discover more and more examples of projection of a more fundamental kind, getting closer and closer to us until we are led at last to the conclusion that everything we experience is a humanly projected interpretation.

In the search for pure objective knowledge, Western philosophy has always been against subjectivity and projection and has sought to root it out wherever possible. Ideal knowledge must be purified of all subjective biases, so whenever we discover some bias we naturally try to eliminate it. But ironically, since meaning *is* projection, the removal of projection only succeeds in removing meaning from the world. When we have removed all bias, nothing is left. It's like peeling the layers of an onion to get to the good part inside—pretty soon there is nothing left of it. When we trace our intellectual history from the Greeks through the medieval period into the modern era, we find a gradual but steady erosion of meaning in the name of pure objective knowledge. Searching for real essence has ironically led to meaninglessness.

Typical of this attitude is the well-known, early twentieth-century French philosopher Henri Bergson. In *Introduction to Metaphysics* (1913), Bergson characterizes all conceptual, analytic thinking as an imposition of human concerns on reality, which simplifies, rearranges, and thereby distorts reality. Analytic, intellectual thought "depends on the point of view at which we are placed and on the symbols by which we express ourselves." In this sense, he argues, analytic thinking simply "moves around" the object, like the "objective knowledge" discussed earlier in the chapter, focusing on certain aspects which this object shares with others, but leaving us always "outside" the object. "Symbols and points of view ... place me outside it; they give only what it has in common with others, and not what belongs to it alone." But this is at best "a translation, a development into symbols, a representation."

Projection is not an entirely worthless pursuit, however. In a practical sense it is not only useful but absolutely necessary for classifying objects into general, abstract kinds (see Chapter 2), without which we could surely neither think nor speak. The mistake lies in identifying the concept with the thing or, as the Zen Buddhists say, mistaking the pointing finger for the moon to which it points.

> Concepts ... —especially if they are simple—have the disadvantage of being in reality symbols substituted for the object they symbolize.... Examined closely, each of them ... retains only that part of the object which is common to it and to others, and expresses ... a *comparison* between the object and others which resemble it. But as the comparison has made manifest a resemblance, as the resemblance is a property of the object, and as a property has every appearance of being a *part* of the object which possesses it, we easily persuade ourselves that by setting concept beside concept we are reconstructing the whole of the object with its parts, thus obtaining, so to speak, its intellectual equivalent.... There precisely is the illusion. [Bergson, *Introduction to Metaphysics*]

The translation of an object falls short in two respects; it is partial and it is abstract and general. To say a golf ball is round, white, and hard is to describe it truthfully, but this description includes only a few of many possible aspects under which it could be viewed and which could be applied to it—a golf ball is also dimpled, expensive, and so on. The description also breaks it up and analyzes it into a series of generalized features which it shares with many other things—white fences, round melons, and hard biscuits. We can never offer more than a list of partial, abstract features; yet no finite list of such features, however long, can ever exhaust the thing or be identical with it. The golf ball is not just a round, white, hard ball, although this is an accurate and true description of it. As we saw in our discussion of the essence-existence distinction, a list of abstract, general qualities never seems to fix the simple, unique object. It is a mistaken view of language and the nature of human thought to suppose that an object should be fixed, captured, or exhausted by words and human concepts.

According to Bergson, conceptualization is useful and necessary even though it renders an incomplete account of things. The whole point of conceptualization is to fasten on to relatively stable aspects of things which we can symbolically represent to ourselves as objects and properties and in terms of which we can classify other objects. We must do this if we are to understand the world and be able to communicate with others. How many colors are there in the color spectrum? Obviously, as many as we like. We can slice it up any way we choose, but for purposes of communication, we had best break it up into a fairly tidy and manageable list of some eight or ten main colors. And so with all our conceptualizations. To think and communicate with others we must act as though the world were broken up into static objects and their fixed properties. But by this very token we are constantly falsifying the continuous, fluctuating, transient character of things.

> Our mind, which seeks for solid points of support, has for its main function in the ordinary course of life that of representing *states* and *things*. It takes, at long intervals, almost instantaneous views of the undivided mobility of the real. It thus obtains *sensations* and *ideas*. In this way it substitutes for the continuous the discontinuous, for motion stability, for tendency in the process of change, fixed points marking a direction of change and tendency. This substitution is necessary ... to positive science. [Bergson, *Introduction to Metaphysics*]

Despite this persistent and necessary deception, the *ideal* of knowledge is to form a conception of a thing which exactly corresponds with the objective essence of the real thing itself and which is identical with it. How is this possible? How can an idea of X be X? Does it make any sense to suppose that a view of the world, however superior, could ever be anything other than a view of the world? Are not the ideas of "essence" and "thing" which metaphysicians and other philosophers form merely human projections—perhaps the ultimate projections? If this is so, then the whole philosophical tradition concerning meaning rests on a colossal mistake. There is no perfectly objective view of the world;

we can only project a view from a given point of view. Therefore, projection is not the villain it has been made out to be. In fact, quite the opposite, projection is precisely what makes meaning possible. The world is meaningful only in so far as we interpret the world and project meaning; meaning is a feature not of things in themselves, but of being-as. But what is tragic about that?

THE PROBLEM OF NEGATION. There must be something else involved in the feelings of nausea, dread, and anguish experienced and popularized by twentieth-century existentialists than the mere fact that meaning is projection, that being is being-as. If we examine our negative attitude toward meaninglessness closely, we will see that the missing ingredient is to be found not so much in what meaninglessness is as in what it is not. The tragic modern sense of meaninglessness presupposes and makes no sense without the assumption that a meaningful world *ought* to be one in which meaning is simply a part of or identical with reality. The modern experience of meaninglessness is a response to the loss, divorce, and obscurity of meaning in the traditional objectivist sense.

In *Existentialism and Humanism* (1946), Sartre contrasts the purpose of the paper-knife with the lack or loss of a comparable purpose for mankind. In Wild's discussion meaninglessness is described as a "clashing dissonance between being and meaning." Expressed abstractly, the modern experience of meaninglessness is the perception of the clash between meaning as naively identified with reality and meaning as projected. The awareness of projection or being-as is tragic because it fails to match up to our a priori concept of reality—our concept of the real nature of a thing free of human interpretation, absolute reality purified of any subjective interference.

Projection and being-as bear tragic consequences not of themselves, but because the awareness that meaning is human projection leads to a sense of the loss of objective meaning. Like crying over spilt milk, the rich man who has lost all his money views his poverty more tragically than the man who has never had anything. The modern fictional literature of absurdity approaches the clash of meaning and reality in two ways, as we saw: as the loss of a transcendent source and guarantee of meaning and as the confrontation with a brute matter stripped of meaning—man cut off from God and man cut off from nature.

The Tragic Sense of Meaninglessness

In Camus the tragic sense of the absurd springs from a comparison of projection with the ideal of a world of objective meanings. Without this absolutist ideal the fact that we project meaning would not lead to the problem of suicide we find in Camus.

> The mind's deepest desire ... is an insistence upon familiarity, an appetite for clarity. Understanding the world for a man is reducing it to the human, stamping it with his seal. ... The mind that arises to understand reality can consider itself satisfied only be reducing it to terms of thought. [Camus, *The Myth of Sisyphus*]

But this projection must be blind. To satisfy this deepest desire the humanly oriented familiarity and clarity must seem an objective, inseparable feature of reality, and not something stamped on it by its human admirers.

Projection is what makes a meaningful world possible, and, ironically, this follows from the thesis that meaning is projection. If meaning is projection, then there is as much meaning as there is projection. Since we do project, we have a meaningful world. If meaning *is* projection, projection can take away from meaning only if projection is understood as displacing the *non*-projective ideal of meaning; only where "meaning is projection" is understood to mean "meaning is *not* a real part of the thing itself." Like the old double-question, "Have you stopped beating your wife?" the affirmation that the world is meaningful and the denial that it is not presuppose the same questionable premise—that it makes sense to suppose that the world *ought* to be meaningful. Camus is himself keenly aware of this.

> I said before that the world is absurd, but I was too hasty. This world in itself is not reasonable, that is all that can be said. But what is absurd is the confrontation of this irrational and the wild longing for clarity whose call echoes in the human heart. ... Absurdity consists in the *disproportion* between intention and reality. ... The magnitude of the absurdity will be in direct ratio to the distance between the two terms of my comparison. ... The absurd is essentially a divorce. It lies in neither of the elements compared; it is born of their confrontation. ... The world is neither rational nor irrational. It is unreasonable and only that. [*The Myth of Sisyphus*]

REJECTING AND ESCAPING PROJECTION. Upon examination, it might be said that Camus' view is an equally absurd position and itself a form of projection. We cannot say that the world is ugly because there are no objective values. Nor can we condemn the world as wicked on the grounds that goodness is a human convention. Likewise, it does not follow that the world is insane just because it lacks human reason. In ordinary English we distinguish something's being immoral and something's being amoral. Something is immoral if it is wicked, but it is amoral if, like a carrot, it is neither moral nor immoral. To say that something is immoral presupposes that it *could* and *should* be moral, an assumption not implied in the claim that it is merely amoral. Similarly, we need to distinguish what is simply not reasonable from what is irrational. The *tragic* sense of meaninglessness springs from the idea that the world is irrational, meaning that it ought to be something which it is not. But as Camus argues, the world is not irrational, it is just not reasonable. A stone is not reasonable, neither is a cabbage, but there is nothing tragic about this since no one thought they should be reasonable in the first place. As one leading commentator, Alain Robbe-Grillet, said recently, "The world is neither meaningful nor absurd. It simply is."

Like Camus and Sartre, Ionesco's denunciation of the absurdity of life also seems to presuppose an alternative, the possibility of rising above it in some way.

> If I denounce the absurd, I transcend the absurd by the very fact of my denunciation. For by what right should I declare a thing to be absurd, unless I had before me the image . . . of something that was *not* absurd? [Ionesco, "Dialogue avec Ionesco" with Lerminier]

If we are irretrievably stuck in the midst of absurdity, as all these writers maintain, how do we transcend it? How is it possible to defy death in the manner of Camus' heroes or to aspire to the Heideggerian "authentic" life? If this is possible at all, it is only possible from the absolutist point of view discussed earlier. When we are engaged in the mundane events of everyday life, we are not aware of, and so cannot condemn, meaninglessness. But in rare moments such as a death in the family or an important turning point in one's life, or simply during a walk along the beach at night, when we stand back and look down on things from an olympian height, the same mundane problems may appear pointless and absurd. It is from this "higher" perspective that existentialist writers describe man's absurd existence, but it seems they are projecting and interpreting the world themselves. Is the absolutist perspective from which the absurdity of the world is condemned any truer or more basic or more genuine than the mundane attitude of everyday existence? Is "the lucid perception of meaninglessness . . . itself a meaningful—the only meaningful—act," as Ionesco's biographer, Richard Coe, suggests, or is this, as Ionesco seems to affirm at times, itself an absurd act?

> We cannot soar above it all, we cannot be superior to the Divinity. . . . That's a piece of folly. . . . We cannot reject the world. . . . To say that the world is absurd is equally ridiculous; . . . it is absurd to say that the world is absurd. [Ionesco, *Fragments of a Journal*]

The tragic sense of meaninglessness therefore lies in the failure of the world to live up to our ideal, arising from a sense of what ought to be there but is not. But is this ideal justified? Why should the world live up to our idea of it? Perhaps the onus for meaninglessness falls on this ideal rather than on the world for failing to live up to it.

TRANSCENDENCE. The tragic contrast between man and an alien world of mere things is ascribed by Heidegger to man's "transcendence." The being of man ("existence" or *Dasein*) is understood by contrasting it with the being of something like a stone. A stone just is, it doesn't know that it exists, nor does it foresee what it might become. It cannot understand itself in terms of an idea, hope, or desire realizable by planning and thoughtful action. In this sense it is stuck in what it is; it cannot rise above this. But man is different; he understands and judges his existence and that of other things. He can experience dissatisfaction with the status quo and imagine preferable alternatives, some of which he can bring into being through his own efforts. Even where he can't bring about change, he knows how things stand and he can imagine what they might be like. In this sense, man transcends his existence, he rises above mere being.

But this is not a triumphal transcendence. Man still finds

himself plunked down in an alien world on which he is dependent. He has not chosen to be, nor to be in this particular world of objects which do not know and judge their own being and which are recalcitrant to his ends and projects. Ultimately he knows he is part of this world and that he will finally be dragged down by and into this world through death. He transcends the world of things in understanding, but he does not rise above the world like a god standing apart. He is stuck in between complete godlike transcendence and utter stonelike immanence. This position is what is tragic. If he were a stone, he would not be unhappy or dissatisfied. If he were a god, surveying all, complete master of his own destiny, he would not be unhappy. But he is neither; he is stuck in the world and he becomes anxious and dissatisfied.

In this sense man's being is flawed, cracked, and incomplete. He is not a completed whole as are stones and gods. The stone is complete in itself, finished and thus static; the being of man is constantly reaching out beyond itself and is thus dynamic and necessarily incomplete. It is through this "crack" that nothingness enters human awareness, and if we can make sense of this difficult phenomenological theory of negation we will have succeeded in clarifying the tragic response to meaninglessness, for the sense of nothingness is possible only by this human ability to perceive negation.

PHENOMENOLOGICAL ANALYSIS OF NEGATION. In the 1930s English-speaking philosophers had a good laugh over Heidegger's assertion that "negation negates nothing" as the prime example of philosophical nonsense. Out of context Heidegger's phrase is perhaps not as clear a piece of philosophical writing as one would like. But the critics may have been too hasty. The view which Heidegger proposed and Sartre later tried to develop was that negation was not a fact about the external world, but a peculiarly human way of perceiving things. If you listed all the objects in the world, negation would not be one of them. Negation is a human perception of something missing, something absent—something which ought to be there or which we expect to be there, but is not. Remember those picture puzzles for children in which you are asked to find what is missing in the picture? You are not asked simply to say what is not in the picture; that would be too easy. If the picture shows the interior of a house, you can truly say that there are no mountains, elephants,

The Tragic Sense of Meaninglessness 281

or locomotives in the picture. But this is not what you are asked to find; you are asked to discover what is mssing and this means what ought to be there but is not. You notice that a table has only three legs and the fourth is missing; you notice that the door lacks a handle, and so on. The point is that there is no such thing as something's being missing apart from the human conception of what ought to be there or what we expect to find there. Negation is not a thing in itself, a force in its own right; it is a human way of seeing rooted in man's projecting nature. Man understands the world in terms of his projects, purposes, possibilities; he can foresee what might exist that does not now exist. He sees what does exist in terms of what it needs, lacks, or requires. He looks at the table and says, "We need dessert spoons," or he looks in a cafe and sees that Bill is not there. This only makes sense on the supposition that Bill usually frequents this cafe or that he promised to be there on this particular night. It would make no sense, except as a bad joke, to say, "That's odd, Chairman Mao's not here tonight!"

The phenomenological theory seeks to answer the transcendental question, What makes negation possible? What conditions must be present before words like "not" and "nothing" can make any sense? The answer lies in man's ability to perceive things in terms of what they might become, to look ahead, and in throwing himself, as Heidegger puts it, ahead of himself. The point is, there is no real absence or gap in being; in themselves there is no negation or nothingness; there is only a falling away from human concepts and desires. There is a table with things on it, there is a cafe with people, tables, chairs, and so on in it. There is no "nothing." The question of "nothing" or "not" doesn't arise until someone—some person—asks, "Where are the dessert spoons?" "Where's Bill?" Only then do we get a "not."

Similarly when we say someone no longer exists, we mean he has died, and this only makes sense given the concept of a living person. As we saw in Chapter 2, things are constantly changing in various ways; some of these changes do not affect a thing's existence while other changes do. Bill survives the loss of his hair, but not the loss of his heartbeat. In another example, if a piece of wood is sawed in half the wood is still there, but if it is ground into pulp and made into paper then the wood has ceased to exist. Ironically, what determines the point at which a thing ceases to exist is our concept of that thing. "Things" only exist or cease to exist *as* this or that. Only projected being-as can "exist," or cease to exist, or be a particular thing. Without being-as, without human concepts, no "thing" would either exist or cease to exist. This is not an endorsement for idealism. It does not mean that in the absence of human beings there would be nothing in the world at all. What it means is that it is only by virtue of concepts that we can *say* or *think* that this or that exists or ceases to exist; only with human concepts and projection do we get the comprehensible distinction between existence and nonexistence. Without human concepts we could point to the world and say that there is "all that"; but we could not say *what* there is, we could not say there is this rather than that, we could not say that such and such used to exist but has now ceased to exist.

Thus to be able to say or recognize that something is not present it is necessary to have some prior human ideal or concept. The uniquely human condition of being dissatisfied with the status quo and the foundation for the tragic sense of nothingness rests on the fact that we can conceive of how things might or should be in contrast with how they actually are. However, no matter how objective we attempt to be, our concept of "how things should be" is itself projected, and the tragic sense of meaninglessness depends entirely on an ideal we have ourselves erected.

Toward a Solution

A kind of solution to the problem of meaninglessness, and the only way it can be solved, may be in dissolving the traditional objectivist ideal of meaning. Must the awareness of projection be tragic? In his definitive study of the theater of the Absurd, Martin Esslin points out that the tragedy results from "the awareness that there may be a meaning but that it will never be found." As Ionesco says, "By what right should I declare a thing absurd unless I had before me the image . . . of something that was *not* absurd?" Without this objectivist ideal the world would be seen as an interpreted world, but it would not be felt as absurd, senseless, or stupid. Without the nonprojective identification of meaning with reality, the awareness that meaning is projection would be an awareness of the nature of meaning, not its loss. As Esslin puts it, "Any conviction that the world is wholly absurd would lack this tragic element."

The question, therefore, is whether it is possible to renounce the objectivist ideal of meaning and embrace completely the projective nature of man and the interpreted character of the world. Can we "negate . . . this desire for unity, this longing to solve, this need for clarity and cohesion," which Camus rhetorically suggests we cannot? Is it "impossible," as Adamov believes, "to renounce the hopeless quest"? The vital question is whether we can, by renouncing the nonprojective ideal of meaning, find a positive, constructive side to the sheer meaninglessness of things in themselves.

First of all, it must be remembered that there is no alternative to projection, nothing we can do but project meaning and nothing we can even conceive as contrasting with projection. The awareness that meaning is projection is not the tragic denial that the world falls short of some real but unattainable goal; it is simply the realization of the conditions necessary for a meaningful world of human experience.

In itself there is nothing abhorent about projection; it is valuable in that it makes possible a meaningful world. What is bad is the false ideal of objective meaning. This ideal is not only impossible; it is itself a form of projection, a simplified reduction of ordinary experience into fixed categories of things and their natures. The awareness of projection is the realization that this is only a convenient way of speaking which does not strictly or literally correspond with reality. It is the realization that the "nature" of an object is an interpretation revealed by projection, and that the thing in itself has no meaning apart from some interpretation. The solution, put in another way, is not for Beckett's character Godot to come, but for Estragon and Vladimir to stop waiting.

Secondly, the absolutist point of view from which existentialist writers view the tragic sense of meaninglessness is no better or truer than the mundane point of view which reveals the interrelated meaning of things in everyday life. From the absolutist point of view, things are meaningless; from the mundane point of view they are meaningful. Both points are valid; both statements are true from the appropriate standpoint. The irony is that things *are* meaningful to me because I am engaged in them here and now, while viewed from a broader perspective they might not be meaningful. By concentrating on the latter point of view—"What will it matter 5000 years from now?"—the existentialists have made it seem as though absurdity is the last word. But this is only half the story. If we stand back from the normal course of events, we relinquish that sense of connectedness with things, and objects lose what meaning they previously had for us. When we reenter the ordinary realm, things once more become meaningful. When I first begin my new job I am appalled by the silly absurdity of petty office gossip; six months later when I have been drawn into the office life, this same gossip seems terribly important. In *Nausea* Sartre describes how Antoine observes lovers in a cafe from his lonely and detached point of view:

> They find the world pleasant as it is, just as it is, and each one of them, temporarily, draws life from the life of the other. Soon the two of them will make a single life, a slow, tepid life which will have no sense at all—but they won't notice it.

To the lovers their affair is of the utmost significance and importance, highly charged with meaning. But Antoine, who is detached from them, and from love and life in general, sees it as just one more human coupling since time began. This does not mean that the lovers are blind or that Antoine is a fool; it is just that in ordinary circumstances we can and do see the world in both ways. The world will yield up either aspect.

Some existentialists incorrectly suppose that the awareness of absurdity or the revolt against it transcends absurdity. The heroic posture of Camus' heroes defying the absurdity of ordinary existence is not the one meaningful act with which we contrast the senseless routine of everyday life. The awareness of absurdity is just as absurd as the plain man's naive acceptance of the meaningfulness of things—and just as meaningful. As intelligible aspects of the world exhibited from particular human points of view, both the acceptance and the rejection of absurdity are equally meaningful; as interpretations of the world both are equally projections, and in this (misleading) sense, "meaningless." The revolt against absurdity, as Coe points out, is "again absurdity, raised to the nth degree." To see that all is ultimately meaningless is a true reflection from the absolutist point of view, but it does not reveal the thing as it really is, shorn of all human interpretations, for it is itself a human achievement with a distinct cultural (late Romantic) background. The experience of absurdity is not the perception of the "naked World" itself, but the realization that the world as we experience it comes clothed in human projection. But to see that a man is clothed is obviously not to seem naked! We rise above the meaninglessness of life by becoming aware of it, not by escaping it. As Coe says of Ionesco, "Between the total and the sham reality there is, in the final analysis, no effective contrast. Both are gratuitous, both are void, both are meaningless." Because Ionesco never completely renounced the ideal of nonprojective meaning, he failed to see that both are equally meaningful as well.

The world as we know it is a recognizable world of meaningful items bound together into a more or less familiar system. In themselves things have no meaning, but the world we know and experience is a world which we interpret and understand in terms of human concepts and forms of thought. The world in itself is not something we could experience; the world we can experience is by that very token a world we experience in terms of human categories. Thus to say that the world in itself is meaningless is really a tautology. It is saying that the world minus human reason and interpretation is a world without reason and interpretation. On the other hand, to say that the world we know and experience is reasonable and meaningful is also a tautology—it is saying that the world which we interpret and explain to ourselves is an interpreted and explainable world. And since this is the world we are really concerned about, the one we actually live and move about in, the problem of meaninglessness properly understood does not have the enormous tragic proportions it is generally reputed to have.

Thus we reject meaninglessness in the only sense in which it hurts, the loss of a coherent world, and we accept meaninglessness only in the sense that there is no meaning without projection. We reject the meaninglessness of things as we experience them, and accept only the meaninglessness of the hypothetical thing-in-itself. Putting it the other way around, we accept the meaningfulness of the world we live in and reject only the contradictory idea of the meaningfulness of things in themselves. Looked at it in this way, the awareness of meaninglessness ceases to be a demoralizing, debilitating, tragic reflection and becomes instead simply the awareness of the nature of meaning. "Meaning is projection" has two handles, we say; things in themselves are meaningless and things in the world as we conceive it are meaningful. The existentialists have grabbed hold of the first, ignoring the second. We must now offset this imbalance by embracing both, as two sides of the same coin. To say that meaning is projection is to say that meaning is a matter of interpretation, a

286 Existentialism—The Philosophy of the Absurd

human achievement; without interpretation, without some limited human perspective, things in themselves are meaningless. And this puts meaninglessness in a more manageable and less tragic perspective.

In a sense, there is a "return to square one." At first we naively suppose that things are meaningful because meaning seems objectively to attach itself to objects. Later when we discover that this is not the case, that meaning is projection, we tend to scepticism, idealism, and meaninglessness. But this is logically inconsistent, as we have seen. When we complete the argument we reaffirm that things are meaningful precisely because we project meaning. So, we're back where we started, but with this important difference in our attitude toward projection. In the first case we project blindly; in the second case, reluctantly, despairingly; in the third case, we accept projection knowingly and with responsibility. Only in this sense is the awareness of projection "authentic." There is no alternative to projection; only differing interpretations of it—the tragic and misleading interpretation that it is a source of meaninglessness and the interpretation we are urging that *it is a source of meaning*. This view has been beautifully expressed by the Chinese Buddhist philosopher, Ch'ing-yuan.

> Before I had studied Zen for thirty years, I saw mountains as mountains, and waters as waters. When I arrived at a more intimate knowledge, I came to the point where I saw that mountains are not mountains, and waters are not waters. But now that I have got its very substance I am at rest. For its just that I see mountains once again as mountains, and waters once again as waters. [Ch'ing-yuan, *Ching-te Ch'uan-teng Lun, Record of the Transmission of the Lamp*]

We begin by supposing that objects are identical with our way of describing them; we naively accept a meaningful world of projected meanings. Later we see that these meanings are projected and this leads to the idealist denial that there are any mountains or waters in reality. However, it does not follow from this that we do not live in a meaningful world of being-as. And so we are led to a final assessment which neither denies nor affirms, but simply takes note of the projective nature of meaning and the being-as character of the world. Naively, mountains are mountains, but this naive view is wrong; mountains are not simply mountains, that is, reality is not exhausted by, but overflows our concept of "mountain," and in this sense mountains are not mountains. But once we get beyond this naive view of meaning, we are free to say once again that in the sense that "mountain" does illuminate a perceptible aspect of the world from a certain point of view, mountains *are* mountains. In the end we live in a meaningful world of projected meanings knowing they are projections and valuing them as such.

CONCLUSION

Thought and language can never do more than point to reality; they cannot capture or fix it in the traditional objectivist sense. Once we thoroughly grasp this point we are free to accept and describe a meaningful world of humanly disclosed, projected meanings. Thus, we can reject the tragic sense of meaninglessness by affirming the essentially projecting nature of thought and language.

Existentialism has always been more an attitude of mind than a well-defined philosophical position. As such it can no more be disproved than attitudes of individualism or utopianism which continually reappear throughout our history. We may disagree with particular intellectual formulations of it, as we have in this chapter, but the underlying concerns remain like an illness we cannot be talked out of. In its emphasis on the individual and the precarious nature of human existence, its most significant achievement in literature, art, psychology, and social theory has been to counteract the continuing threat to individualism. So long as the total technological and bureaucratic "system" threatens to swallow up the individual, we will continue to turn to the existentialists to reassert the dignity and importance of the individual person.

TOPICS FOR DISCUSSION

1. Are we really as free as Sartre says? What about social and psychological conditioning?
2. Chairs neatly arranged in the middle of a super-highway look ridiculous because they are out of place. How do Surrealist painters, like De Chirico, Dali, Ernst, and Tanguy, achieve a similar feeling of absurdity and alienation?

3. What is a forest in reality? Compare the different perceptions of a forest by
   a) the original Indians,
   b) the first white settlers,
   c) people today living in a commune,
   d) vacationers,
   e) the Sierra Club,
   f) a botanist,
   g) a timber company.
4. Sartre is both an existentialist writer of fiction (for example, *Nausea*, *No Exit*) and a phenomenologist concerned with existentialist themes (for example, *Being and Nothingness*). How are these two aspects of his writing related?

SELECTED BIBLIOGRAPHY

Primary Source

Adamov, Arthur. "The Endless Humiliation." 1938. Translated by Richard Howard. *Evergreen Review*, 1959.

Beckett, Samuel. *Waiting for Godot*. 1952. London: Faber and Faber, 1959.

Bergson, Henri. *An Introduction to Metaphysics*. 1913. Translated by T. E. Hulme. New York: The Liberal Arts Press, 1949.

Camus, Albert. *The Myth of Sisyphus*. 1955. Translated by Justin O'Brien. New York: Vintage Books, 1960.

Heidegger, Martin. *Being and Time*. 1927. Translated by McQuarrie and E. Robinson. London: S. C. M. Press, 1962.

Ionesco, Eugene. "Point of Departure." Translated by L. C. Pronko. *Theatre Arts*, 1958.

——. *Fragments of a Journal*. Translated by Jean Stewart. New York: Grove Press, 1968.

Jaspers, Karl. *The Way to Wisdom*. 1950. Translated by Ralph Manheim. Yale: Yale University Press, 1951.

Kierkegaard, Søren. *The Concept of Dread*. 1844. Translated by Walter Lowrie. Princeton: Princeton University Press, 1946.

——. *Fear and Trembling*. 1843. Translated by Walter Lowrie. Princeton: Princeton University Press, 1946.

——. *Repetition*. 1843. Translated by Walter Lowrie. Princeton: Princeton University Press, 1946.

Nietzsche, Friedrich. *The Portable Nietzsche.* Translated and edited by Walter Kaufmann. New York: Viking Press, 1954.
Sartre, Jean-Paul. *Being and Nothingness.* 1943. Translated by Hazel Barnes. New York: Philosophical Library, 1956.
——. "Existentialism and Humanism." 1946. In *The Age of Reason,* edited by Morton White. New York: Mentor Books, 1955.
——. *Nausea.* 1938. Translated by Lloyd Alexander. Norfolk, Connecticut: New Directions Books, 1959.
Wild, John. "Being, Meaning and the World." *Review of Metaphysics,* 1964.
Wittgenstein, Ludwig. *Philosophical Investigations.* Translated by G. E. M. Anscombe. New York: Macmillan, 1953.

Secondary Source

Barrett, William. *Irrational Man.* 1938. New York: Doubleday, 1962.
Blackman, H. J. *Six Existentialist Thinkers.* New York: Harper and Row, 1952.
Coe, Richard. *Ionesco.* London: Oliver and Boyd, 1961.
Collins, James. *The Existentialists.* Chicago: Regnery, 1952.
Esslin, Martin. *The Theatre of the Absurd.* 1961. Hammondsworth, England: Penguin Books, 1968.
Evans-Pritchard, Edward. *Social Anthropology.* London: Cohen and West, 1951.
Gould, James and Willis Truitt, eds. *Existentialist Philosophy.* Encino, California: Dickenson, 1973.
Kaufmann, Walter, ed. *Existentialism: From Dostoevsky to Sartre.* Cleveland, Ohio: World Publishing, 1956.
Levi-Strauss, Claude. *Structural Anthropology.* Translated by Jacobson and Schoepf. New York: Basic Books, 1963.
Marcel, Gabriel. *Man Against Mass Society.* 1951. Chicago: Regnery, 1962.
Stewart, David and Algis Mickunas. *Exploring Phenomenology.* Chicago: American Library Association, 1974.

CHAPTER 9

Aesthetics

The Philosophy of Art

WHAT IS AESTHETICS?

Aesthetics is probably as hard to define as philosophy itself, with aestheticians disagreeing among themselves as to whether it is an independent science, a branch of psychology, or simply a loose assortment of philosophical issues related to art. The term "aesthetics," which comes from the Greek word for human sensibility, was introduced by the German philosopher Alexander Baumgarten in the eighteenth century to broadly cover the investigation of the sensual dimension of human experience. But the concern with the human delight in art and beauty goes back to the beginnings of philosophy, especially the work of Plato and Aristotle, and continues today in a somewhat different form. Because of the complex nature of art, "aesthetics" (sometimes anglicized "esthetics") is used in different ways by different people, depending on their relationship to the arts. Some books on aesthetics concentrate on the appreciation of art, others emphasize art criticism, and still others approach aesthetics as a general theory or explanation of art. In our discussion we will regard aesthetics primarily as a branch of philosophy—the philosophy of art.

Aesthetics is concerned with the way the critic, the art educator, the art teacher, and the ordinary lover of art think and talk about art. It considers conceptual problems surrounding the meaning of terms such as "imitation," "realism," "representation," "expression," "form and content," "intuition," "intention," and "work of art," and attempts to understand and clarify artistic concepts and terms. This, of course, is only one of many valuable ways of approaching the arts. We can produce art, as when we compose a song (creating); we can simply enjoy it, as in listening to a symphony (appreciation); we may praise or condemn a work of art or try to say what it means (criticism); or we may even try to find out why artists produce works of art (the psychology of art). Over and above these activities, we may also get interested in the way we go about describing the creating, appreciating, and criticizing of works of art, and this is aesthetics.

This is not to say that these different activities are altogether unrelated. Just as the interpretation of a work of art elucidates a prior feeling or response, so analysis of the conceptual framework in which the interpretation is made brings to light assumptions and presuppositions contained within it. There are different levels of involvement in the arts, and even though the talk about a work of art presupposes some experience of it, many people enjoy art without feeling the need to talk about it. But when we do talk about art, problems can arise which attract the interest of the aesthetician.

Consider, for example, the well-known problem of expression which first appeared toward the end of the nineteenth century as an outgrowth of Romanticism. We all find it perfectly natural to say that a work of art expresses the artist's emotion, but when we reflect on this a little, it begins to sound rather strange. Emotion is a psychological process going on in someone's head; a work of art, on the other hand, is a physical object. The emotion is private and internal; the work of art, public and external. How can the one express the other, or, as the twentieth-century British aesthetician Bernard Bosanquet put it, "How can the feeling be got into the object?" Some philosophers, who understood aesthetics to be part of psychology, argued that the relationship between the two is *causal*—the feeling explodes into a work of art (creativity) and the work of art then causes those same feelings in us as members of the audience (appreciation), an idea suggested in Romantic metaphors of art as the "outpouring" or "overflowing" of human emotion. This psychological theory of art, however, does not solve all the conceptual problems. On the creativity side, what is the difference between a work of art and the violent curse you utter each time you hammer your thumb instead of the nail? On the appreciation side, what differentiates a work of art from the injection of a drug which will produce exactly the same feeling in you? The *causal* relations would seem to be identical. The difference seems to be that in a work of art the feeling is in the *object* and not in the person producing or enjoying it, but how can that be? This sounds like animism!

Autonomy

The problem of expression is really part of a much larger concern which has dominated the history of aesthetics from its origins in Greek thought, that of autonomy. Much of the work of aesthetics over the centuries has been to discover whether there is a domain peculiar to art and the experience of beauty, some special experience or value which we find in art and nowhere else, and if so, what this autonomous feature is. Theories which stress the internal character and value of a work of art we will refer to as "autonomous"; those which stress external factors will be called "heteronomous." Since the publication of Immanuel Kant's *Critique of Judgment* at the end of the eighteenth century, the concern with autonomy has pretty well defined the scope of aesthetics. The problem is that most of the things we want to say about art, like expression, seem to imply that art is not autonomous, and yet intuitively we feel that it is, that there is something special about art which cannot be reduced to anything else.

Art as Imitation

The first theory of art was the Greek view that art imitates reality, and we still talk about art in this way today. This theory suggests that a work of art is to be judged according to how well it mirrors a reality outside the work of art, and many critics have supported this view. Thus, if a human being is more valuable than a grasshopper, then a picture of a man is more valuable than a picture of a grasshopper, a view held by a number of critics from the Renaissance to the late eighteenth century. If a grasshopper has six legs in reality, then a picture of a grasshopper must have six legs. The belief that art must correctly reflect the real world has been made continuously from Plato's objection to inaccuracies in the artistic portrayal of things like beds and saddles to the objection heard today that the brutality portrayed in *Straw Dogs* is totally out of keeping with the quiet demeanor of contemporary rural England. This criticism would reduce art either to morals or to science, in either case judging works of art heteronomously by standards *outside* of art and running contrary to our best instincts about artistic autonomy. Intuitively we recognize that the value of a work of art lies in the special and unique way that a subject matter is presented in a particular poem or painting, not the subject matter itself. Children, who love stories about events they would be terrified to witness in real life, seem to draw a distinction between the internal value of a story and the value of events outside the story. There is a recognizable distinction between art and life and the peculiar value of each. The problem is how to square this with the view that art imitates reality and must therefore faithfully represent it.

When Plato criticized the artist in *The Republic* for not being realistic, Aristotle tried to modify his position to allow the *aesthetic* value of portraying things which *in reality* were false and ugly. When artists in the seventeenth century began to worry about the discrepancy between poetic and scientific accounts of the world, critics like John Dryden tried to defend the artist by shifting the critical criterion from the heteronomous standard of objective *truth* to the autonomous principle of internal *plausibility*. A contemporary offshoot of this problem is the ongoing controversy over state censorship. Censorship feeds on the heteronomous view that what is bad in real life cannot be good in art, and the best defense against censorship is to insist on artistic autonomy and to maintain that what is harmful in real life can be of value when portrayed in art.

The problem of expression in art also involves a debate over autonomy which centers not on the *external* reality *represented* in the work of art but on the *subjective* emotional state of the artist and his audience which is *expressed* in a work of art. If we view a work of art in terms of (1) the reality represented in it, (2) the art object itself, and (3) the feelings of the artist expressed in the work of art, then we can characterize both the Imitationist and the Expressionist positions as heteronomous in emphasizing factors outside the work of art proper. Imitationism stresses the external reality and Expressionism emphasizes the internal state of mind. Autonomy is represented by the twentieth-century position known as Formalism which holds that a work of art must be judged by its own standards and in terms of its own inner structure or "form." But this position seems to deny that the real world, including the emotions of the artist and audience, has any artistic relevance. As the English Formalist Roger Fry said about painting,

> Now I venture to say that no one who has a real understanding of the art of painting attaches any importance to what we call the subject of a painting—what is represented. [Fry, *Vision and Design*]

But this is just as debatable as the Imitationist heteronomy it seeks to replace. As we will see, much of contemporary art is directed against Formalist autonomy in favor of artistic "relevance."

The Autonomy-Relevance Problem

As with many philosophical difficulties, the problem is how to have one's cake and eat it too—how can we say that the concern of art is to represent the real world and express human emotion without denying its autonomous role? How can we combine autonomy with relevance? This has been the central question in Western aesthetics, with special significance today.

The source of the problem lies in the nature of the words we use when speaking about art—words such as "imitate" and "express." There is no language, vocabulary, or concept especially designed for aesthetic discussion. In talking about art we borrow terms from some area outside of art. The solution therefore lies in a careful analysis of the meaning of ordinary words used in an aesthetic context. As we have seen repeatedly, words from ordinary speech have a logical life of their own and commit us to all sorts of unwelcome implications which we cannot easily foresee at first. It may turn out that the idea of art "expressing emotion" or "imitating reality" may not be as good a way to talk about art as we had first supposed.

The central problem of aesthetics has nothing to do with the way works of art are produced and appreciated. It arises directly out of the ways in which we think of works of art and the terminology used to express ourselves. As Bishop Berkeley once put it, our vision is obscured by a "learned dust" which we have raised ourselves! Aesthetic terms are like metaphors, and we must always be aware of the dangers of taking any such metaphorical expression too literally. Do works of art "express emotion," have "formal structures," "imitate" or "represent" reality, are they "true" or "meaningful"? We must be prepared to approach all such questions in the relatively more sophisticated way we approach metaphors, with a yes and no—in a sense (which we must go on to specify) yes; in another sense (which must also be specified) no.

Because of this persistent source of misunderstanding, philosophers today are wary of grandiose theories of the nature of art in general, and prefer instead to tackle particular conceptual problems as they arise in the ongoing critical discussions of art and works of art. The best way to learn aesthetics is therefore to take a closer look at a few of these aesthetically interesting problems. The first is a question of great contemporary interest: What is a work of art? Moreover, are works of art the sorts of thing which can be said to be true, or at least meaningful?

THE CONCEPT OF A WORK OF ART

Normally we are not greatly concerned about what is and is not a work of art. In most cases our ordinary criteria serve us quite well. But when an artist offers such works as a room filled with dirt, a closed gallery, or 4 minutes and 33 seconds of silence, we begin to wonder just what *is* a work of art? This question seems to call for a definition. To arrive at such a definition it might seem profitable to begin by asking what all works of art have in common. If art is autonomous, as most aestheticians have argued since the end of the eighteenth century, it seems natural to suppose that there is something common to all works of art. Many philosophers today think this would be a grave error, a mistake which Ludwig Wittgenstein, the founder of the contemporary "analytic" school, has called "essentialism." Wittgenstein argued that when we try to define "games," to use his favorite example, we are apt to begin looking for some feature common to all games, something one could find in football, boxing, bingo, roulette, solitaire, hide-and-seek, and so on. The problem is that there just doesn't seem to be any such common denominator in all these very different games—some are played for fun, but not all; some, but not all, are competitive, and so on.

The same would seem to apply in the case of "work of art." What common feature can be found in the *Swan Lake* ballet, the statue of the Dying Gaul, *The Wasteland*, *Aida*, *Sons and Lovers*, a Franz Hals portrait, the Parthenon, the first Bruch Violin Concerto, and a Picasso ceramic owl—not to mention the room filled with dirt? There will be some similarities—there is something common to *Sons and Lovers* and *The Wasteland*, to *Aida* and the violin concerto, and to *Sons and Lovers* and *Aida*—but is there anything which is common to all of them?

Wittgenstein suggests that the impulse to search for the common denominator or essential feature is encouraged by a false view of language and the assumption that there must be something common to all these things, without which we wouldn't be able to correctly identify them as works of art. Essentialism goes back to the long-standing tradition derived from Aristotle that the being of an object and what we can know of it lies in its essential nature which it shares with others of that kind. Traditionally, being, knowledge, and meaning are tied to essence. Wittgenstein maintains that this tendency leads either to oversimplified accounts of what we mean by "a work of art" or to definitions which are too vague to be very helpful. Assuming there must be something common to all works of art, philosophers have been led to say that works of art are objects of sense constructed solely for the sake of sensual delight. This is a fair definition, but it oversimplifies the notion of a work of art. How could we fit *War and Peace* or *Hamlet* or Picasso's *Guernica* into such a definition? On the other hand, if we try to find some defining notion which is broad enough to cover any possible example, it is apt to be hopelessly vague. If we say that the defining feature of a work of art is "form," meaning the structure which a thing has, then it is true that all works of art have form. But so does everything else. If we mean anything more specific by "form," all works of art will not fit into such a category. If the definition is clear, it is too narrow; if it is broad, it tends to be vague. This is another reason aestheticians today shy away from all-embracing theories.

Although there does not seem to be a single feature common to all works of art, this does not mean that the expression "work of art" is meaningless or that it means something different every time it is applied to a specific work of art. Philosophy is concerned with concepts because the world is concept-laden, but concepts do not always isolate what all objects in a given group have in common. Objects are identified and placed into different groups according to humanly significant similarities and differences. Commonality lies in *our use of a word* rather than in the objects designated. We use the word "game" in roughly similar ways even though there doesn't appear to be anything common to all games. There may be a common use of the term even though there is no common feature in the objects defined. If we interpret the question "What is a work of art?" to mean, not what do all works of art have in common, but how do we employ the expression "work of art," we may be able to answer it.

Human Intention

The term "work of art" is used in one sense to indicate an object which is the result of human intention. You would probably not call a piece of driftwood lying unnoticed on the beach a work of art, however visually attractive it was. However, if someone stood it up on end and placed stones around it to form a circle, we might be more inclined to call it a work of art. There would be some tendency to call it art, even though after deliberating we might decide not to. If someone were to take the driftwood home and mount it on the wall and illuminate it with spotlights, most people would be inclined to call this a work of art in a limited sense. Finally, if a person were to sand the whole thing down, char large sections of it, paint other parts, and then raise it from the floor by steel supports, although this may not be your cup of tea, it would be a work of art. The point of this series of examples is to discover what it is about the context in which the driftwood is placed which would incline us to call it a work of art. The feature which seems to characterize the object as art is the presence or absence of noticeable intention. It is important that the intention be noticeable, for it might be that an artist had sculpted what we took to be driftwood from a large block of wood and secretly left it lying on the beach as a joke. We would call it a piece of driftwood because it appears to be a natural object in which the hand of man has played no part which we can see. (Of course, if we discover the joke, we will tend to call it a work of art precisely because we now know that it was made by someone.)

In order to be called a work of art an object must be fashioned, or at least used, by someone in a deliberate way. The way in which it has been constructed must be and seem to be intended by some person or persons. The object itself is the same, in some sense at least, in all of the above examples except the last, which is precisely why it is hard to define art by common features, as Wittgenstein said. In what sense is the difference between the driftwood lying on the beach and the driftwood stood up on end and surrounded by stones a difference in human intention? The man who set it up selected this object from many others and chose a particular angle and position for the driftwood over other possible stances. He intends that it be looked at in this way and in no other way. Perhaps he thinks it looks graceful or that it will evoke the feeling of some fantastic bird. There is in this situation just enough of an idea of intention to incline us to say that this is a work of art, though a limited or borderline case.

Aesthetic Value

Not everything deliberately made by man is a work of art. An ordinary chair, for instance, is not a work of art. How are works of art differentiated from other man-made articles? Often we use the expression "work of art" to indicate the use, or rather the *lack* of use, to which objects are put. An adjustable lamp could conceivably be as beautiful or aesthetically interesting as a piece of metal sculpture, but we would tend to regard only the latter as a work of art. A lamp is made to do a job of illuminating objects, whereas a piece of sculpture cannot be used, or at least is not intended to be used, for anything except looking at and enjoying (if you choose to call these latter activities "uses"). This was not always so; during the ancient and medieval periods "art" included any human activity involving skill which could not be reduced to mechanical rules, a meaning we still retain in such expressions as "arts and sciences," or "the culinary arts." Since the eighteenth century, aestheticians have stressed the nonutilitarian aspect of works of art and emphasized detachment and disinterestedness as the correct aesthetic attitude toward works of art. Beauty could be perceived, it was held, whether in works of art or in natural objects like a rose, only when we detached ourselves from any practical, theoretical, or moral interest in such objects. In the eighteenth century, beginning with the work of British aestheticians such as Alison, Burke, Shaftesbury, Kames, Hume and culminating in Kant's *Critique of Judgment,* the first attempts to formulate aesthetic autonomy, at least negatively, in terms of *dis*interestedness and *de*tachment were made. According to these theorists, "aesthetic" referred to the peculiar value of art and the unique mode of our perception of it. Most philosophers during this period agreed that the defining character of aesthetic experience was its disinterestedness and detachment. If a man's sole interest in a painting of a nude is a sexual interest in the model or a desire to own the painting, then his attitude is "interested" and not aesthetic. Or, if someone were to rush onto the stage and wrestle the villain to the ground, his attitude would not display the proper aesthetic detachment. This view of aesthetic experience was widely held until recent times, although its meaning was never very carefully explained.

Unfortunately, its negative formulation led to the view that works of art do not play an important role in our lives. However, people have since realized that areas of natural beauty are not just a luxury for those who can afford it, but a necessary condition for the well-being of the whole community. The more positive view now emerging is that art plays a vital, useful, and even necessary part in our lives, individually and socially. Nonetheless, one important use of the expression "work of art" is to draw attention to the autonomous *aesthetic* uses of an art object (whatever these are) as opposed to purely functional uses.

There are interesting exceptions and borderline cases, however, especially in contemporary art, where aesthetic autonomy has come under vigorous attack. Is a urinal in a men's room a work of art? Most of us would say no, but what about Marcel Duchamp's famous urinal which shocked the art world in the 1910s? This work is looked upon as a work of art. Why? What's the difference? The difference seems to be that Duchamp's urinal is meant to be viewed aesthetically; Duchamp intends us to behold and reflect on this object in a special and unusual light. He calls attention to this object and uses it to make an artistic "point" or "statement," ironically rejecting the eighteenth-century view that a useful or practical object could not be "fine art." In a curious way Duchamp's intention to eradicate the distinction between art and manufactured articles is self-defeating since it is precisely that intention which distinguishes Duchamp's urinal from all the other Parisian urinals. We know Duchamp's intentions not from the urinal alone, but from the aesthetic context or setting in which he placed it. The object is displayed in an art gallery and reproduced in art books, and we know it has been displayed by the same artist who painted *Nude Descending a Staircase*. Also, Duchamp inverted the urinal from its customary functional use and inscribed on it the words "R. Mutt, 1917." All this makes it clear that it is being displayed *as* a work of art.

Often we cannot tell whether contemporary pieces are works of art without contextual clues. Suppose you are sent into the attic of an old mansion with the task of bringing down all the works of art. Let's say you find a framed canvas painting of a seascape and immediately recognize it as a work of art; you spot a marble bust and add it to your collection. Suppose you also see a urinal, or a bicycle wheel, or a soup can, or a red plank of wood. If you don't know anything about contemporary art, you will assume they are not works of art. But if you have heard of Warhol, Oldenberg, and Duchamp you may be genuinely puzzled. In the case of older, more traditional art we know it by the look of it; with more recent pieces we may not know until we have more contextual information.

Social Acceptability

With some contemporary pieces it is not always enough to know that it was made or even owned by an artist. Marcel Duchamp also displayed a bicycle tire in the early 1900s as a work of art. What is the difference between an old auto tire lying in Duchamp's garage and his famous bicycle tire? While the auto tire belongs to an artist, it is not being put forward by him as a work of art. If I were to advertise my old auto tire as a work of art, I probably wouldn't get away with it and certainly would be unable to sell it for half the value of Duchamp's bicycle wheel. If I did pull it off, it would be because someone thought I was an artist and because he had heard of things like Duchamp's bicycle wheel. Our knowledge of what is and is not a work of contemporary art depends on a certain give and take between knowing whether someone is an artist or not and recognizing whether the object in question is or is not the kind of thing currently accepted as a work of art. We can know either given the other.

To become an artist one has to produce or display objects of the kind people currently consider works of art (including things like red planks, soup cans, urinals, erased drawings, and so on). Once a person becomes a recognized artist he can try something new. Let's say I cut out beer ads from old magazines and offer these for sale in art galleries as works of art. I might get away with it and people might begin to call this sort of thing art. And so it goes, stage by stage, step by step: we accept as art what is produced by artists, then we accept as artists those who produce what is accepted as art, and so on.

There is a similar problem with religious carvings which have, or were originally meant to have, a nonaesthetic, ceremonial use. Perhaps functional and aesthetic interests are not as incompatible as they have often been made to appear. To fulfill its religious function, the music of the Mass must sound solemn and profound, and appreciating it religiously presupposes appreciating it aesthetically. It is then possible to separate the two aspects, more or less, enabling the atheist to enjoy Bach's B Minor Mass.

In the same way it is possible for Europeans to appreciate the terror and dignity of African tribal masks without a deep knowledge of their ceremonial use. A medieval crucifix is a work of art because we put it into an aesthetic setting and consider it as such, but this is by no means an arbitrary decision on our part. The crucifix is a better candidate for a work of art than a piece of a saint's thigh bone because the religious function of the former, but not the latter, demands that it look a certain way, and this look can then be appreciated more or less for its own sake. What determines whether something is a work of art is rather different in this case than in the case of contemporary avant-garde art. With Duchamp, it is the artist's intention which is decisive; in the case of primitive and religious art it is the viewers who decide whether such objects are works of art. In either case, the decision depends on social acceptability and the tastes of the time.

Originality

The expression "work of art" indicates uniqueness and individuality. It would be very unusual to call something which is mass produced a work of art. This is one reason why handcrafted articles such as pottery, weaving, and wood-working are being reexamined as works of art despite their utilitarian function. However similar, no two cups made by a potter are exactly alike.

The criterion of individuality is closely related to the idea of originality. When an art museum discovers that one of its sixteenth-century Raphaels is a fake, the painting is removed and sold as a curiosity at a fraction of the original painting's value, even if it's just as good. This is because part of our concept of a work of art is that it be original and not a copy. Suppose someone turns up today who can write poetry in the style of and as well as John Donne, or music in the style of Haydn. We would tend to treat such works as curiosities, not because they are fakes (since there is no deception involved), but because such works deserve none of the credit of the original artist who developed this mode of expression. In this sense, originality forms part of our concept of a work of art. It is not easy to write music like Haydn, but it is a lot easier today than it was in Haydn's time. On the other hand, if a leading Pop artist were to display a print of the Mona Lisa in a New York or London gallery, we would probably call it a work of art on the basis of the contemporary artist's *use* of the

Mona Lisa to make some "statement" of his own ridiculing bourgeois culture.

Artistic Boundaries

We often use the expression "work of art" to express a value judgment. Clothing and pieces of furniture are generally not considered works of art, except in special cases in which the objects fulfill other criteria for a work of art—that it is meant to be viewed aesthetically, that it is an original creation, and so on. The manufacture of clothing, furniture, and other skilled crafts is somehow more humble and pedestrian than the production of works of art—another legacy of the eighteenth-century isolation of fine art from utilitarian enterprises. Conversely, if someone says that a gourmet delicacy is a work of art, this is obviously meant as a compliment. It is because we do not usually prize food so highly that this can be used as a compliment.

The distinctions between works of art and articles made by skilled craftsmen are by no means sharp. Some might consider a well-designed tapestry or a hand-loomed carpet to be works of art, while others might view them as highly artistic examples of workmanship. There is nothing about the ordinary concept "work of art" which enables us to answer this question decisively, which is precisely why this is an interesting field of controversy. Nor do we have to decide such questions philosophically. The main task of the philosopher of art is to point out the ordinary criteria involved in making such decisions.

Borderline cases provide the most fruitful controversy, not because we have to fix the boundaries more precisely, but because it is here that our ideas have room to change and evolve. This evolution takes place either by including more (or less) in the original concept than before, or, more frequently, by altering the boundaries of the original concept; that is, we either alter the examples to fit the concept, or the concept to fit the examples. The debate over whether something is a work of art sometimes involves a judgment whether to include this item in the concept as it stands, but more often the debate centers on the conceptual boundaries themselves. In the intense debates about art going on today, artists seek to tear down or to expand the concept of art which has separated art from the rest of the world since the eighteenth century.

The distinction between arts and crafts was not sharply drawn in the Middle Ages. The eighteenth-century interest in the autonomy of art drove a wedge between the two, creating a division which the current movement toward relevance attempts to heal. Part of the reason for the recent interest in the art-craft distinction is the attempt to upgrade certain crafts to the level of art. The point of this movement is to persuade us to regard handmade articles with the same veneration we regard paintings and pieces of sculpture.

Most contemporary debates about works of art are not just over whether to include a particular object in the category of art, but what that category should be. Professor Gallie, a respected contemporary aesthetician, recently suggested that concepts like work of art are "*essentially* contested," meaning that by their very nature they are constantly open to revision. A hundred years ago African masks and bicycle wheels fell very definitely outside the concept of art and realistic illustrations fell definitely within that concept. Today the position seems to be somewhat reversed! Continuity is provided, fortunately, by a host of examples of unquestionable works of art—the music of Beethoven, the paintings of Raphael, the plays of Shakespeare.

The situation today is further complicated by the fact that some artists pointedly challenge traditional artistic boundaries. Today a boundary is seen as a barrier—and a fair target to be shot down. When an artist displays as a work of art his own grandmother in a rocking chair or his erasure of another artist's drawing, he is challenging the concept of art and the concept of a work of art. He is denying that art is autonomous, that it must be removed in any essential way from life, that it be eternal, elevating, or sacrosanct, as the traditional concept requires.

The Contemporary Challenge

The nineteenth-century German Idealist G. W. F. Hegel once said that art eventually destroys itself by turning into philosophy. Today many artists appear to be fulfilling Hegel's prophecy. A great deal of contemporary art can only be understood intellectually, as a comment *about* art, a comment on the art world, the traditional conception of art, and so on. A few years ago one of the best known American artists, Oldenberg, sent out invitations to the art world in and around New York City announcing an important retrospective showing of his recent work on certain dates which the announcement specified. At the bottom of the invitation appeared the postscript that the gallery in which the show was to be held would be closed during those dates! Here art is virtually swallowed up in the concern *about* art. Oldenberg's invitation is a joke on the art world, a derisive comment on the chic New York art establishment and its elitist attitudes about art.

Much of the current debate is therefore rhetorical; it is not designed to show that our existing criteria either do or do not include this or that item, but it is an appeal either to expand or to retain the existing boundaries. Conservatives argue for the retention of the old values and revolutionaries try to open the boundaries up, or in some cases, to do away with them altogether. Where a concept is contested and in a period of transition, it tends to be used somewhat differently by different subgroups within the same society. Today many people identify art with cheap Woolworth's landscapes and would never dream of calling an ordinary plank of wood painted red a work of art. At the opposite extreme are art students and other people who believe that everything is a work of art (except, possibly, the Woolworth canvases). Most of us find ourselves somewhere in between, happy to call Beethoven's Seventh Symphony a work of art, content to extend the term to Schönberg, and frankly puzzled what to say about John Cage's *Silence—4 Minutes 33 Seconds*, in which a pianist sits at a piano for 4 minutes and 33 seconds in complete silence.

Artists have probably never been so alienated from the general public as they are today. Much of the contemporary art protest has been an attempt to replace aesthetic autonomy with relevance, though ironically this has been widely misunderstood by the general public. Many contempory works, as we have seen, are a revolt against the detachment of art from life. But the attempt to bring art out of its ivory tower back to the man on the street is precisely what appears so foreign to the man on the street! He has come to accept the eighteenth-century view that art is autonomous, and he therefore finds the attempt to make it thoroughly relevant puzzling. When he goes to see a play, for example, he expects to observe the performance from his detached point of view as a member of the audience; he is flabbergasted when he is asked to come up on stage and take the part of one of the actors! The problem of how to reconcile autonomy with relevance is therefore very far from being solved.

Aesthetic Meaning

The expression "work of art" is also used to indicate the presence or absence of "meaning." We do not usually consider an ash tray or an automobile or a dress as a work of art; while such an object may be visually pleasing or satisfying, it does not hold our attention, nor is it meant to hold our attention as though to convey something to us. As we will see, whatever meaning is conveyed by a work of art must be somehow autonomously contained within the work itself, which is what critics refer to when they say that artistic meaning must be "concretely presented." However, as Immanuel Kant pointed out, "meaning" is used in a rather special way in referring to art since we can never say exactly what the meaning is (see Chapter 8). The point is that we respond to a work of art and approach it *as* a thing of meaning for us. We patiently savor it, mull over its manifold relationships, as though it had something to say to us.

Practically anything can be seen aesthetically, provided we adopt the appropriate attitude toward the object. However, a work of art need not be perceived aesthetically, especially if we approach it in a lazy or inappropriate way. While a work of art can leave us quite cold, an oil smear on a river can appear beautiful in the moonlight. Thus, "aesthetic" cannot be defined exclusively in terms of "work of art" nor "work of art" in terms of "aesthetic"—neither is necessary to the other. Yet works of art do seem to have some more intimate connection with aesthetic experience. Somehow one is more likely to have such an experience with a work of art than by looking at an oil spill on a river.

Works of art are different from other things which can be perceived aesthetically in that the artistic materials have been arranged or constructed in an intentional, or at least quasi-intentional, way, which makes it more likely that they will be viewed aesthetically. As opposed to a cloud or a stone which can be viewed in many ways, aesthetic and otherwise, a work of art tends to limit itself to one or more aesthetic possibilities. In a work of art the audience is led or guided by the perceptible features of the work to the intended aesthetic aspect. The aesthetic aspect is therefore permanently, uniquely, and objectively present in a way not to be found in other public objects, whether natural or man-made, however appealing and charming in other respects. The beautiful rainbow effect is only one of many ways of seeing an oil smear (as opposed, for example, to its repulsive pollution aspect), but this aspect is permanently locked into a painting which captures this effect indelibly on canvas. Despite the functional use of an African mask, it seems designed to draw our attention to a particular point of view, clearly and forcefully conveyed. Whatever its psychological intention, its noticeable intention is aesthetic.

If it is held that aesthetic value is self-contained within the perceptible features of the work, then what about the red plank or the Brillo box which have been set forth as art in contemporary circles? These count as works of art because they are used by an artist to make an artistic "point" or "gesture" concerning our popular culture and our traditional view of fine art. But after the point has been made, are such pieces still aesthetically enjoyable? It remains to be seen; it may turn out that this sort of thing has a very short-lived appeal. Perhaps this is all the artist intends it to have. However, it may turn out that the best pieces are those which are also aesthetically pleasing, as Duchamp's urinal and Warhol's *Campbell's Soup Can* surely are.

One of the great powers of art is its ability to lead us to view things from unaccustomed points of view—often from points of view we otherwise reject as repugnant or falsifying. Willy Loman, the central character in Arthur Miller's play *The Death of a Salesman*, would be an intolerable bore and a repugnant, pathetic, and uninteresting person in real life; but in the play we are drawn into the world as seen and lived by Loman and his family and are able to sympathize with and become involved in him. It is, at least in part, this power of art to draw us into unusual perspectives which can engage our interests in ordinary motifs, such as a chair or a few bottles, which in a mundane context are utterly without significance or interest.

The majority of events occurring in everyday life have little impact on us; it is difficult to relate to them in any single, concerted, or totally engaged way. Our attention is too confusedly scattered to have much intensity or direction. The "clarity" of a work of art lies in its isolating the essential meaning of a situation as seen from a limited human perspective. Because of its unity and clarity, a work of art can engage us more directly and powerfully than most situations in real life. Real people we may never get to know thoroughly; they never have the sharp and clear character delineation of even the most complex characters of fiction. By "detaching" us from a mindless absorption in everyday affairs, a work of art can provide us with a new and wider perspective.

This suggests that works of art present us with a view of the world, that they *mean* something and are therefore true or false. But doesn't this reduce art to science? Can art be meaningfully and truthfully relevant to the world we actually live in and remain autonomous?

MEANING IN ART

There is a strong tendency on the part of people who read and enjoy poetry to ascribe meaning either to the parts or to the whole of a poem. Robert Frost's famous poem "Stopping by Woods on a Snowy Evening,"[1] has been often interpreted as a reflection on death. We suspect that the last part of Dylan Thomas's "A Winter's Tale"[2] has something to do with resurrection, an idea also reflected in the lines of Yeats's poem "Death," "Many times he died,/Many times rose again."[3] Poetry in par-

1. The woods are lovely, dark and deep.
   But I have promises to keep,
   And miles to go before I sleep,
   And miles to go before I sleep.
2.   For the bird lay bedded
   In a choir of wings, as though she slept or died,
   And the wings glided wide and he was hymned and wedded,
   And through the thighs of the engulfing bride,
   The woman breasted and the heaven headed
                     Bird, he was brought low,
   Burning in the bride bed of love, in the whirl-
   Pool at the wonting centre, in the folds
   Of paradise, in the spun bud of the world,
   And she rose with him flowering in her melting snow.
3. Nor dread nor hope attend
   A dying animal;
   A man awaits his end
   Dreading and hoping all;
   Many times he died,
   Many times rose again.
   A great man in his pride
   Confronting murderous men
   Casts derision upon
   Supersession of breath;
   He knows death to the bone—
   Man has created death.

ticular and art in general, therefore, seem to be relevant to the world we actually live in.

On the other hand, there is an equally strong reaction on the part of certain critics against any such suggestion, and a very cautious attitude on the part of the poets themselves. It was customary to ask Frost on his lecture tours whether the last lines of "Stopping by Woods on a Snowy Evening" were a reflection on death. Did he mean that the desirability of death was offset by the more onerous duties in the here and now? To which Frost always replied, "no"; the lines, he said, described a man stopping his carriage to view a field newly filled with snow before going on to the next town. Picasso is similarly reported to have denied that his painting of a red bull's head depicted the dangerous emergence of Fascism. What the painting showed, he went on, was the head of a red bull. Faulkner, who was always suspicious of academics and especially and understandably so of aggressive doctoral candidates, is said to have replied to the suggestion that the spotted horse in *As I Lay Dying* referred to the blemished moral nature of man, "Well, I wouldn't know, I never had much education."

Autonomy and Meaning

Certainly few critics then or now would fault Faulkner's response, which seems a straightforward, if naive, support of the critic's defense of poetic autonomy, the essential unity of poetic form and content. As the Formalists have said for years, what a poem means cannot be isolated from how the meaning has been expressed in the particular poem. This was first clearly formulated by the early twentieth-century Italian philosopher Benedetto Croce as the identity of "intuition" and "expression"; the original idea cannot be distinguished from the way it is expressed in that particular work of art. Hence, as T. S. Eliot said, a poem is "untranslatable." To offer a translation of a poem is to propose two different expressions identical in meaning—that is, two forms of speech having the same content or meaning. In the case of poetry, the contention is that this simply cannot be done. The meaning of a poem is unique and internal to it and cannot lie in anything outside the poem, such as Christian imagery, sexuality, death, or responsibility. More recently, Susan Sontag has criticized meaning as a threat to autonomy, a concern aptly summed up in Marshall McLuhan's famous epigram "The medium is the massage."

And this we all must surely applaud. How awful for the ghost of Tolstoy if someone were to put aside *War and Peace* with the remark "Right, war is bad; now what else has he got to say?" Or to abandon Picasso's painting with a brusque "Oh yes, the Fascists; terrible time that was." Or worse, in the case of Frost and Yeats, "How true, how true." Whatever meaning is contained within a work of art must be considered and contemplated in its own unique context.

But it is one thing to applaud a slogan and quite another to defend its truth as a sober proposition. Archibald Macleish states that "A poem should not mean/But be," but is this strictly true? He further contends that "Form is inseparable from content," and "a work of art is unique and all its values internal to it." Most people tend to agree with the spirit of these slogans, but is it really true that aesthetic values are "unique" and "internal"? Does this kind of autonomy imply the rejection of all meaning?

With what, for example, is this internal-uniqueness criterion of poetry meant to be contrasted? With prose statements presumably. But what is said linguistically always depends on the way it is said. If I change "slammed the door" to "shut the door" the meaning is different. Similarly, there are important shades of difference in the meanings of expressions like "come if you possibly can," "come if you can," "come if you like," "come if you want," "come if you really want," "come if you must," and so on. So, if the meaning of poetry is internal and inseparable from its form, then the same seems to be true more or less outside of poetry.

Conversely, turning the argument around, we can ask if the meaning of poetic language ever is or can be strictly internal. As R. K. Elliot has recently pointed out, the poet's comparison of old men to spaniels who mumble the game,

> So well-bred spaniels civilly delight
> In mumbling of the game they dare not bite,

will mean little to one who doesn't already know, outside the poem, that spaniels are game dogs noted for the care they take in retrieving birds without mangling the flesh. Similarly, assuming the lines "Many times he died,/Many times rose again" have some implied reference to the crucifixion and resurrection of Christ, this will mean little to the ordinary Burmese Buddhist. And a person totally unfamiliar with snow will scarcely understand certain poems by Frost. Nor are these examples exceptional. The poet, like any writer, must rely on a wealth of common experience and understanding which is completely general and external to the poem.

The dichotomy between autonomy and meaning, like the dichotomy mentioned earlier between aesthetic autonomy and function, seems to be a false dichotomy. Because aesthetic relevance seemed to exclude autonomy, Formalists rejected all relevance. But art *is* relevant to our lives, so contemporary artists and critics, in the belief that autonomy excludes relevance, want to throw out autonomy and make everything a work of art. And so, the pendulum swings back and forth, from one extreme to the other, while the problem of reconciliation remains unresolved. Can we have our cake and eat it too? Let's at least try.

Reconciling Autonomy and Relevance

While we must accept the autonomy principle that the meaning of a poem cannot be given entirely in some other, say, prose statement, we must reject the antirelevance suggestion supposedly implied by this—that it is always wrong to discuss the meaning of a poem (or to try to say what a poem means). Rejecting in a strict or literal sense the distinction between meaning which is "internal" and unique to a work of art and that which is external and generalizable outside that work of art, we might begin by trying to define and defend this distinction in a looser, relative sense. Let us say that if understanding a line of poetry or the poem as a whole requires no more common experience or understanding outside the poem than what we could reasonably expect any educated adult of that society to possess (the boundaries of which are admittedly much open to question), and if the meaning of these lines is not exhausted by the external meaning presupposed for any qualified reader, then we will say that the meaning is "internal and unique" in our newly formulated sense. If understanding the meaning of a line of Pound's *Cantos* depends on an extensive knowledge of ancient Indian or Chinese philosophic thought, then we can safely assume that this meaning lies "outside" the poem. And if there is no or little more to be got from a poem than some commonplace moral or religious sentiment with which we are all too familiar outside the poem, then we are surely justified in withholding our approval since the poem deserves none of the credit for meanings which it derives exclusively from outside the poem. But if the common meaning already understood outside the poem is only necessary but not sufficient to an understanding of the poem (for example, a general knowledge about spaniels), then we can say that the meaning is internal and unique to that poem in our new, more cautiously defined sense. In this sense a poem's meaning can be both relevant *and* autonomous.

This is true, for example, of that special sense of resurrection internal to the last stanza of Thomas's poem "A Winter's Tale," referred to earlier. The particular, unique meaning of this work is strictly dependent on every part of the poem and the particular way in which these parts hang together. Aside from the presupposed background of common experience, this meaning does not depend on anything else. The precise meaning of practically every word and phrase is determined by its relation to every other word and phrase in the poem, and it's not until we imaginatively reconstruct the totality of these relationships that we get the particular sense of the poem.

For example, the "bird" of the first line is a bird in the ordinary sense, but in conjunction with the "choir of beings" in the second and the notion of "hymned" in the third, the bird also takes on the meaning of the heavenly angels and the Holy Spirit as represented in Christian symbolism by a dove. This amplified meaning is reinforced and further modified by the expressions "bedded," "slept," "thighs," "bride," "breasted," "bride bed of love," and others, which in their obvious suggestions of love, sex, and marriage connote further the quasi-sexual relation of the dove of the Holy Spirit and Mary, the mother of Jesus. The meaning of *this* bird is amplified further by the expressions "burning" and "melting snow" which suggest the image of the phoenix rising from its own ashes. This forms the transition to another set of relationships. The notion of "bud" and "flowering" taken in conjunction with the phoenix image and the expression "rose" in the last line suggests the idea of resurrection, though a very special sense of resurrection which we have never encountered before. The unique meaning internal to the poem is determined contextually by the organic form of the work.

But granting one can make out the distinction between "inner" and "outer" meanings along these lines, can one *say* what the "internal" meaning of a poem is? And if not, does it make any sense to speak of the meaning of a poem? Isn't it like asking for examples of "inexpressible thoughts"? Either we cannot say what it means and thereby demonstrate our acceptance of an apparently vacuous philosophical position, or else we can say what the meaning is and tacitly contradict our previous assertion that the meaning is truly internal and unique. Which brings us back to the dilemma of how artistic meaning can enjoy an internal autonomy and still be relevant outside that particular work of art.

How to get around this dilemma? Can we say what a poem means? Obviously we cannot in the narrow linguistic sense of an exact translation, but this is not the only kind of meaning (see Chapter 8). Sometimes "meaning" signifies purpose and intention, as in "I mean to help him if I can" or "It was meant to be a footstool." Sometimes "meaning" refers to interrelationships between things, as "Passage of this bill will mean the end of second-class citizenship" or "Dark clouds mean rain." In either of these senses a work of art, like life or one's job, can be said to have, or to lack, meaning. "What does this mean?" (of a work of art) is usually understood purposively to mean "Why is it there?" or "How is it related to this or that?" In these senses there is no disgrace in being unable to *say* what the meaning is (except in an English exam). If you say your job is meaningless or that your relationship with your sweetheart is meaningful, it is inappropriate to ask *what* it means or doesn't mean. A work of art, like life or a job or a relationship with someone, has meaning (or the lack of it), but not *a* meaning.

But even if we understand poetic meaning in an exclusively linguistic sense, it is not clear that one cannot say in some sense or other what a poem means, just as we agreed in the previous chapter that one could explain in a roundabout way what a chair means in our society. It all depends on what we mean by "saying what something means." If saying means providing an alternative form of words identical in meaning, then we cannot say what a poem means. But neither can we "say" in this sense what anything means. But if we mean by "saying" something like suggesting, indicating, illuminating, or as the Zen Buddhists say, pointing, then we surely can say what a poem means. We can at least place the meaning within certain limits on which most of us can agree. Frost's poem has something to do with death or nihilism or something of the sort. "Resurrection" brings out the meaning of the last stanza of "A Winter's Tale" in a way "assassination" does not. Opinions will vary as to the precise meaning of Yeats's poem, but most of us can agree that its meaning falls within a closely knit group of related attitudes towards death. While we may disagree among ourselves as to which of the possible interpretations within this limit is the best, we can agree more or less on what the range of meanings should be.

In this sense, then, there seems no reason to deny that one can say what a poem means. The anxiety of the poet and the hostility of the critic stem from the other sense of "saying," that is, providing a complete and exact translation identical in meaning. But can one ever say what anything means in that sense? After a generation of "language analysts" most philosophers today are inclined to say no. They tend now to disparage the view that language, even ideally, just "states facts" or "mirrors the world." Meanings, we are now prepared to say, are ways of understanding things, not labels permanently affixed to the world, while words are viewed as tools we use to illuminate, suggest, or point out aspects of things which interest us in one way or another—and this is as true of science and everyday speech as of poetry and criticism.

Meaning is not, then, opposed to poetic integrity, and in this instance at least, relevance is not irreconcilable with aesthetic autonomy. The fact that a poem is untranslatable in one sense does not mean that we cannot say what it means in some other sense, just as we *can* put into words, roughly and with a clear sense of inadequacy, thoughts which are in another sense inexpressible. To say that X is inexpressible, then, is not to be understood as disallowing any talk about X, but as a warning about the sort of meaning which cannot be given. Like much of the Zen literature (see Chapter 5), it serves to mark a recognized inadequacy of language and to caution our confusing what we can and cannot do with words.

Similarly, the assertion that a poem is untranslatable should not be understood to mean either the impossibility of translating a poem into a prose statement nor the inadvisability of ever trying to do so. The assertion that a poem is untranslatable should be taken as a warning not to mistake a suggestion of the meaning of a poem, which we *can* give, for an exact equivalent of its meaning, which we *cannot*. In the Zen epigram mentioned earlier, don't mistake the finger for the moon. The worry over saying what a poem means, then, is primarily a statement of the limitations of critical discourse, an attempt to define the boundaries between what critical discouse can and cannot do. But acknowledging the limitations of critical language should not force us to abandon the attempt to discuss poetry in terms of meaning. Rather, having accepted these limitations, we are able to go right on using that language though now *aware* of its dangers and limitations. In the same way, I do not stop driving my car when I become aware of the dangers involved; I simply drive more carefully. Once we understand the legitimate use of critical talk about meaning, we are free to continue to use it in that way.

TRUTH IN ART

Assuming works of art can mean something in some sense, do they mean or assert something which can be said to be true or false? Do literary works of art, to take the simplest case, tell or show us the truth? They often seem to, and we frequently talk as though they did. But how can they since even figurative, representational works of art deal with fictional entities and illusory objects? In a broader perspective, the problem is how the autonomous, internal structure of a story can have any heteronomous relevance to the world outside the story. If truth is the correspondence of an assertion to the real facts of the world, how can fictional statements be true? Perhaps they are true in some other sense, but if so, in what sense? How, in short, can a description of fictions and illusions tell us something about the real world? Indeed, can statements about fictional entities be true even of fictional entities? There has been a lively philosophical discussion of this problem in the twentieth century which, though it lies outside the realm of aesthetics proper, provides a good beginning for our inquiry.

Fictional Referring

Philosophers have pondered whether the statement "Tom Sawyer ran away from home" is true or false. The answer to this apparently simple question has been complicated by an extensive philosophical debate surrounding it. Around the turn of the century, the German philosopher Alexius Meinong said in effect that the statement was true, which is certainly the answer a freshman English teacher expects. But, reminiscent of Plato (see Chapters 2 and 3), Meinong preserved its truth only by introducing an ontological category of nonexistent beings! The statement is true, Meinong said, of a nonexistent, fictional entity, Tom Sawyer. Bertrand Russell, who thought this was patent nonsense, argued that since the statement in effect claims that there was a Tom Sawyer who ran away from home and there was no Tom Sawyer, the statement is false. More recently, the English philosopher P. F. Strawson, trying to settle the dispute amicably, said that the statement is neither true nor false, since it fails to meet one of the necessary conditions for something's being a statement in the first place. In order for something to be true or false, Strawson argued, it must refer to something existing in the world about which the statement makes some assertion. Unlike Russell, Strawson denied that the proposition states that Tom Sawyer exists; it merely presupposes this as a necessary condition for the successful act of making a statement, and so the question of the truth or falsity of the statement simply doesn't arise. In Strawson's view, truth is irrelevant to literary art.

But Strawson's account won't do, either. For one thing it won't get us through freshman English, where "none of the above" is counted an incorrect answer, and for another, it doesn't do justice to the speaker and his intentions. The speaker is not trying to refer to a real person, nor is he pretending to refer to a real person. The speaker is openly and knowingly using an accepted convention of referring to people and places in fictional stories. The problem with understanding fictional referring is that we don't have a clear enough picture of what ordinary referring is, and the root of this problem is that referring is perceived in terms of a paradigmatic relation between a description and an *existing thing*. But that relation, as we will see, is preceded by the more fundamental referential relation of thought to an object of thought, whether real or imaginary. In Heideggerian language (see Chapter 2), the question of being (what is it?) precedes the question of reality (does it really exist?). "Are there any dragons?" makes no sense until we know what a dragon is. This is what Pooh, a bear of admittedly small brain, failed to understand in his search for Woozles.

Strawson correctly notes that expressions can refer to something without denoting an actually existing object, but his insistence that the reality of the object is presupposed obscures the more fundamental question of how descriptive sentences become descriptions of an object in the first place, whether real or imaginary. The fundamental question is how a sentence like "He slowly reached over and turned off the alarm" is immediately understood in terms of a complete context of objects and events, not all of which are actually mentioned in the sentence—a full-bodied, flesh and blood man with two arms, legs, and so on, asleep in a bed in a room in a house, early one morning, being awakened by the ringing of the alarm clock, reaching over in half-sleep and annoyance to turn it off. Descriptive expressions work, not by asserting or implying real existence, but because we accept and understand that they are partial and generalized accounts of complete, concrete situations. Individual objects or events must be understood in an interrelated context of objects and events; every isolated remark, if it is to be meaningful, brings with it a context in which it makes sense, a context which we perceive as a "world" or "environment." In that sense every description is a description of a whole world. As a fact about our descriptive use of language, you can't describe less than a whole world. Our understanding of this world may be very sketchy, or even "blank" in places, but it is given all at once, in one shot, from the first sentence.

A clearer understanding of the ordinary descriptive use of language makes its use in fiction less puzzling. Basically, the problem is the same in both cases: somehow a world is given independently of ontological questions of real existence. To demonstrate the basic parity of ordinary and fictional usage, let's consider a series of cases deviating progressively from the supposed paradigm in which the referring expression is said to pick out a real object in the real world and describe it. (1) Consider the sentence "My uncle is a wealthy merchant from Burma" said in the presence of my uncle as part of an introduction. Here the sentence, with the aid of head and eye movements, picks out an object at hand and identifies him. But (2) what if my uncle is asleep upstairs or away at his home in Burma? The sentence obviously can't pick out an object in this case in the same way it did in the previous case. In this case you must get a sense of what I am talking about without pinning the descriptive tag on an independently identifiable object. Of course, you assume he exists, though you can't see him. But (3) what if I am lying? Obviously it makes no difference to your understanding of my statement whether he exists or not. Otherwise, lying would be impossible. In either case you take the statement to describe a complete male human being, living in a full-blown environment down to the last details. even though you don't know very many of these details. He lives somewhere, though you don't know exactly where; he eats something, but you don't know what; he wears clothing, but you don't know what kind.

Of course, it's true that you supposed this full-blown setting to be part of the real world, and this part of your understanding will be shattered when you discover that I am lying. But (4) what if I introduce my remark by saying "Wouldn't it be nice if I had a rich uncle in Burma," or invite you to imagine this or suppose it to be true. This makes perfectly good sense. Actually, we do this sort of thing frequently when we want to talk about the past or the future or to make plans or to speculate about what "might have been" or what "could be." Again, as in all the above cases, the description is immediately understood to describe full-bodied objects in a total setting—with this crucial difference, that this object and setting are understood to have no place in the real world of everyday experience. From this ordinary referential use of language it is only a gentle, gradual transition to (5) its use in fiction. I begin a story to a small child, "Imagine you and I are hunters in the far north..." The child knows we are not really there, but he understands the words referentially, that is, as a partial, generalized illumination of a whole world, a world of animals, mountains, rivers, trees, and so on. He understands the story to be about objects in a contextual setting even though he also knows that these objects do not exist.

Without such an understanding we would be utterly unable to follow the simplest sort of story, whether real or imaginary. As soon as we are out of sight of the object described, it is essential both in fiction and nonfiction to take the descriptive phrase as a partial, generalized account of a whole object in a complete setting and to relate other descriptive phrases to the same object. Suppose that in the midst of relating the story of Goldilocks and the Three Bears we say, "and then they returned to the cabin," and the child asks, "Who? What cabin?" Why, the three bears, of course, and their cabin. We thought the child had understood that. Or the child asks, "How did they get back? You didn't say whether they walked, ran, skipped, or hitch-hiked. And how did they get in? You didn't mention opening the door," etc., etc. The child has failed to understand (fully) the elementary referential use of language. And this has nothing to do with the reality of the object in question. Such a child would also fail in exactly the same way to understand a true account of my father's first hunting trip with his uncle, which began, "My father and his uncle left their cabin early the next morning to look for deer. Finding none, they returned to the cabin." As we saw in the previous chapter, a description of an object can never contain more than a partial list of abstract features which it shares with other objects. In order to understand any such description, whether factual or fictional, we must therefore place the description in a complete context or setting. This is the crux of referring: understanding partial, generalized descriptions to be descriptions of complete, concrete objects and organizing different descriptions around the same objects, gradually clarifying, filling in details about objects which are nonetheless given in their totality from the outset.

It is the intuitive recognition of some of these aspects of referring which leads to the supposition that in fiction we create an imaginary world of imaginary people. But this is not so much an explanation of fictional characters and fictional worlds as a figurative, and often misleading, way of calling attention to the fact that we can and do refer meaningfully to people and situations which do not exist. We do not, or at least we need not, produce a mental picture of a man on a bed hearing the sound of the alarm and then turning it off to understand the narrative sentence given earlier. It is just that the case in which the object doesn't exist is precisely like the case in which the object does exist in being understood in the same way to be about an object with all the properties an object of that kind is supposed to have in a setting with all the features which a setting is supposed to have—even though we don't *know* what any of these properties are except the one or two mentioned in the referring expression. Since we also understand, in fiction, that neither the object nor the setting are contiguous with the real world, it is tempting to fall back on the idea that although they are not real people in a real world, they are nonetheless imaginary people in an imaginary world. But this doesn't explain anything except by way of either the suspect Meinongian ontology of existing and nonexisting beings or the false psychological view that we always form mental pictures in reading novels and the like. The fact is that we may form such mental pictures in reading historical accounts of real events, but we needn't do it in order to understand a story.

Credibility: Coherence Truth in Fiction

Our account of referring should help explain what people mean when they talk about imaginary entities in imaginary worlds. Moreover, our account of partial referring could illuminate various related literary phenomena, such as the sense in which we speak of the "world of the novel," or our treatment of fictional characters as quasi-people, passing judgment on them, worrying about them, sympathizing with them, and so on, and the sense in which we feel that a fictional account is internally "realistic" or "believable" and can at the same time shed light on the outside world. Let's consider for a moment our treatment of fictional characters as quasi-people. From the very first sentence a whole world is given, but it has large blank spots which can be progressively filled in. But this is very much like our knowledge of real people. We begin almost immediately forming judgments or hypotheses about new acquaintances or people we have only heard about which new information will either confirm or throw into doubt. If I tell you that my rich uncle from Burma is asleep upstairs, you know that he is a man, since this follows analytically from the statement that he is my uncle. But there are other things you only suspect but do not know for sure. You will probably assume that he is middle-aged or older because this is what uncles of adults usually turn out to be. Equally reasonable assumptions are that he is asleep on a bed since this is where people usually sleep, and that he is an American since most known relatives of Americans are themselves Americans. But you will probably leave open such questions as color of eyes, hair, weight, build, and so on, since there are no probabilistic rules of thumb to follow here. You will assume that he *has* eyes and that these eyes have color because this is typical of people, but you probably won't infer more specifically as to what color. When I tell you that he is medium-build, with brown eyes and greying hair, you will not be surprised, but "fill in" these details, on the basis of which you will go on to make further assumptions (he is probably not very handsome, is probably a hard-nosed business man, and so on) and to ask further questions (such as, is he married?). Certain new information will be consistent with your expectations and provide additional knowledge which "fill in" the details, while other information will only confirm what you expected. But some new information may correct your anticipations, though it is fully consistent with previous information. You will be surprised to learn, for example, that he is a seventeen-year-old Frenchman sleeping on his head, and you will have to correct your view of things accordingly.

The point is that there is no difference in the filling-in of details between my telling you about my real uncle and my telling you a bedtime story about an imaginary uncle. Indeed, in reading these pages, you don't know for sure whether my uncle is real or imaginary; nor does it matter for your understanding of what has been said about him. We make the same assumptions, which can be confirmed or disconfirmed as the story unfolds, or which lead to new, more specific information. In both cases our assumptions are guided by what we take to be ordinary probabilities from everyday life. The credibility of a story, whether true, fictional, or an outright lie, depends equally on the sorts of things likely to happen in the real world. If I am late for work because I found a tiger sitting in the front seat of my car, I will be sorely tempted to excuse myself untruthfully by saying that I had a flat tire. As Aristotle said, "a likely impossibility is always preferred to an unconvincing possibility." The same is equally true in a story. What is believable in a story, whether real or imaginary, does not depend on what actually happens in concrete cases but rather, as Aristotle said, on general probabilities. Even in Tolkien's *The Hobbit*, which is pure fantasy, the fact that the dwarves forgot Thorin, their leader, in their escape from the spider people is completely believable in the story because outside the story it is generally expected that anyone's presence of mind will sag a little in the midst of extreme danger.

But of course, what is probable in one context is not probable in another context, and so, in constructing a story we can make almost any given incident believable by selecting the appropriate context of probabilities. In this sense every story-probability, whether real or imaginary, depends indirectly on real probabilities, but directly on the particular context of selected probabilities. Thus, while it is highly improbable, other things being equal, that a tiger should be sitting in my front seat, it is not so unlikely if the story takes place in India where I have raised as a pet a tiger cub who is occasionally allowed to ride in my car. Given all this, and what we know independently about the habits of pets, it is highly probable that he would want to come and sit in the front seat of my car. So the most improbable events can be made believable by placing them in the proper contexts, although these contexts are themselves constructed out of ordinary probabilities.

Here we can begin to see a resolution of the false dichotomy between autonomy and external reference in art. As the correspondence to an independent, objective reality there is, of course, no "truth" to a fictional story. But in the sense in which we speak of truth as the coherent relation of events into a plausible, consistent unity, there certainly is fictional truth. To be plausible, even a lie must reflect what people believe to be true and be constructed according to our ordinary sense of everyday probability.

Our understanding of fictional characters, then, is very much like our understanding of real people. We know there are no such persons, but we understand the narrative as the revelation of a whole complex person, indicating, for example, general character traits which nonetheless leave room for speculation as to what he is like in other respects. Through our referential use of language, the character in a work of fiction is treated as a partially disclosed entity about whom more can be learned, who therefore contains more than our description of him, and in that sense, transcends the actual descriptive sentences about him. In short, because of our referring use of language, we treat him as a whole person over and above the sum of properties actually attributed to him in the novel. This is what lies behind (and a better way of putting) the confusing idea that a fictional character is a nonexistent *object*.

The source of judgments of character, based indirectly on our sense of ordinary probabilities, are certain relatively "hard data," points stated explicitly in the story; as descriptions of the referential object, these descriptions are either true or false. "Tom Sawyer is irresponsible" is a debatable judgment. But "Tom Sawyer ran away from home" is not; it is a true description of the Tom Sawyer referred to in Twain's novel. "Tom Sawyer" does not refer to an object which exists in the ordinary phenomenal world of space and time, but it does refer to a character in a novel who did run away from home. Meinong gave the right answer, then, but for the wrong reason. There is no ontological entity of which the story is true, but only a grammatical or logical "object" which carries no metaphysical overtones.

Realism: Interpretive Truth in Fiction

The sentences of the novel, we have said, are understood to describe a person; this fictional person's credibility is based, indirectly, on our ordinary understanding of ordinary probabilities about ordinary people. This brings us to the third and most important question, the realism of events in the story and the ability of the novel to describe "real life" outside the story. The credibility of the story derives indirectly from our understanding of real life, but it follows directly from the author's selection of the appropriate context of real life probabilities, and it is here that the author can create a bias or slant which reflects back on real life. In constructing the right context, he can draw us into a sympathetic understanding of his point of view, his way of looking at things, and since the context is derived from real life probabilities, this way of looking at things spills over necessarily and deliberately into the way we look at things in real life. The world of our experience, we have been saying, is a humanly interpreted world, and art is one of the ways we achieve this interpretive focus. In addition to fictional coherence truth, then, there is also an interpretive truth in literary art, in which the story establishes a point of view from which the outside world is perceived and judged.

But again, this is exactly what we do in constructing true stories about real people. I want you to like my rich uncle, but I'm afraid your Maoist leanings will prejudice you against him. So, I construct the story of his life, consistent with the facts, though not, of course, the "whole truth," in a way which puts my uncle in a favorable light. I tell you about his impoverished, deprived childhood, of his vow to overcome his humiliating situation, of his lonely struggle and deserved successes, tempered always by his immense generosity to those less fortunate. Even though he is a real person completely independent of your opinion of him, your *idea* of him may now be more favorable. And if you find my story sufficiently credible to begin to like my uncle, I will have succeeded in some small way in subverting your general Maoist inclinations. A few more such believable stories and you may find your political position dangerously compromised. So, by borrowing from ordinary probabilities which you already accept, I have created a favorable impression of my uncle, which in turn creates a slightly better impression of others of his type in the real world.

Of course, other people may tell you a very different story about my uncle, and here the similarity with fiction ends. A real person can be analyzed indefinitely, and there are consequently many possible views of this person from many possible points of view. There are many story-tellers about real people, but only one story-teller of a fictional character. In this sense the novelist is irrefutable, if not omniscient. It makes no sense to propose an alternate version of some fictional character, unless you want to write another and better story, and even here there are no independent criteria for judging which is the most accurate. In short, there is no correspondence truth in art.

All the novelist has to do, then, is construct *one* plausible account, and we are generally prepared to accept it. We generally allow ourselves to be drawn into the perspective of the author, even though we might not normally share that point of view outside the novel. Of course, the author can fail to make the story convincing, just as I might fail to convince you of my uncle's magnanimous character. (Perhaps you suspect that people who vow to overcome deprived childhoods usually turn out to be ruthlessly aggressive.) But if the novelist is successful in creating a plausible account out of real life possibilities, he will draw us into sharing a point of view which we may not normally share. Thus, if the story of my rich uncle is a work of fiction, and you find it convincing, you will, for the moment, share my point of view and find this type of man attractive. And since this *type* of man exists in the real world as well as in my story, you will, at least for the moment, share my view of the real world as the stage for the great individual, overcoming the herd instinct of the masses, and so on, even though you would normally regard this as so much nonsense.

Sometimes the spell of the novel lasts only so long as we are reading it. Occasionally, however, it continues to project its point of view on the real world long after we have put the book down. Like Don Quixote's, many of our attitudes about love and adventure are formed more by novels, plays, and films than by real life. In this sense, nature imitates art, as the English playwright Oscar Wilde playfully noted, and this is the sense in which people live within a cultural framework which allows certain well-defined aspects of reality to be perceived more readily than others. Certainly, as we saw earlier, fictional characters are more clearly and sharply drawn than their counterparts in real life. Because the author is only required to create one plausible view, his vision is far more coherent and compelling than the ordinary vagueness of indefinitely analyzable real-life people—who have no commitment to conform to our opinion of them!

Thus, works of fiction describe the world in general terms with which we may agree or disagree, and in this sense they can be said to be true or false. As with all interpretive truth, this involves a comparison with an independent, objective reality which nonetheless falls short of direct correspondence. Like metaphysical statements (see Chapter 2), independent facts will tend to confirm or disconfirm such interpretations, but they cannot absolutely verify or falsify them, because the facts themselves are being judged by the interpretation in question. Imagine how difficult it would be to convince a pessimist he was wrong. Everything you could point to he would interpret differently. Facts are relevant, but they are not conclusive—as they would be, say, in verifying the correspondence of the statement that the door is red to the red door. But we must be careful to distinguish the ordinary interpretive truthfulness in a novel from its special literary truth. We generally agree or disagree with the novel in the sense that we are prepared to see the world in that light, *not* in the sense that we compare the "statement" of the novel (for example, that life is hard) with our assessment of life independently of the novel. The novel shows the world in a certain light, and we either fall prey to its spell or we don't. Its truth is purely presentational, and in that sense, autonomous. We can also dispute the realism of the author's point of view, as people have Thomas Hardy's perspective, but in comparing the novelist's "message" with independent evidence, the novelist is in no more privileged position than anyone else who may care to voice an opinion. The special power of the novelist and the playwright is his ability to show us the world in that light. If it's convincing there is little to be said by way of refuting it, though we may feel that his point of view is limited, narrow, bizarre, or whatever. The special sense of literary truth, then, lies in presenting a glimpse of the real world from a certain standpoint. Since this may shake us out of a stereotyped vision of the world, it is often of greater value than the truth of statements supported by independent factual evidence. The latter confirms whether this way of seeing the world is consistent with the facts; the former shows us how to see the world like that in the first place. Both are necessary to what we call the truth.

Do works of art tell the truth? The answer, like the answer to most philosophical questions, is yes and no. In the sense of a strict correspondence truth, no; in the sense of coherence, interpretive, and especially presentational truth, yes. And this suggests a kind of truthful relevance in art consistent with aesthetic autonomy. The only kind of truth which denies autonomy is correspondence truth, which literary art does not possess. Interpretive and presentational truth, on the other hand, depends entirely on the peculiar construction of events within that particular story and is thus internal and autonomous, despite the inevitable reflection of its unique point of view, which we at least momentarily adopt, back on the real world.

TOPICS FOR DISCUSSION

1. Duchamp's original urinal was actually stolen and replaced. Suppose that now the original were found. Would it be worth replacing? Why or why not?
2. If it is just as good, why is a fake Raphael less valuable than a genuine one?
3. There have been thousands of performances, interpretations, individual responses, and copies of Beethoven's Seventh Symphony. Which of these is the *real* Seventh Symphony? (See Margolis.)
4. Is a poem untranslatable, as Eliot said? If so, should critics keep quiet, as John Cage has recently requested?
5. Does art imitate nature, as Aristotle thought, or does nature imitate art, as Oscar Wilde said? (See Arnheim and Gombrich.)
6. What is the "problem of expression"? (See Tolstoy, Santayana, Tomas, Bouwsma, Croce, or Collingwood.)

SELECTED BIBLIOGRAPHY

Primary Source

Aristotle. *The Poetics*. Translated by Ingram Bywater. In *The Basic Works of Aristotle*, edited by Richard McKeon. New York: Random House, 1941.
Arnheim, Rudolf. *Art and Visual Perception*. Berkeley: University of California, 1957.
Bosanquet, Bernard. *Three Lectures on Aesthetics*. 1934. New York: Macmillan, 1954.
Bouwsma, O. K. "The Expression Theory of Art." In *Aesthetics and Language*, edited by William Elton. Oxford: Blackwell, 1954.
Collingwood, R. G. *The Principles of Art*. 1938. New York: Oxford University Press, 1958.
Croce, Benedetto. *Aesthetica*. Translated by Douglas Ainslie. London: Macmillan, 1909.

Dewey, John. *Art as Experience*. 1934. New York: Putnam, 1958.
Fry, Roger. *Vision and Design*. 1920. Cleveland: Meridian Books, 1963.
Gombrich, E. H. *Art and Illusion*. London: Phaidon Press, 1960.
Hegel, G. W. F. *The Philosophy of Fine Art*. 1832. Translated by F. P. B. Osmaston. London: G. Bell, 1920.
Isenberg, Arnold. "Critical Communication." 1958. In *Introductory Readings in Aesthetics*, edited by Hospers. New York: Free Press, 1969.
Kant, Immanuel. *Critique of Judgment*. 1790. Translated by J. H. Bernard. New York: Hafner, 1951.
Langer, Susanne. *Feeling and Form*. 1953. New York: Scribner's, 1956.
Margolis, Joseph. "The Identity of a Work of Art." *Mind*, 1967.
Plato. *The Republic*. Translated by Benjamin Jowett. New York: Random House, 1957.
Russell, Bertrand. "On Denoting." 1905. In *Readings in Philosophical Analysis*, edited by Feigl and Sellars. New York: Appleton-Century-Crofts, 1949.
Santayana, George. *The Sense of Beauty*. 1896. New York: Dover, 1955.
Strawson, P. F. "On Referring." 1950. In *The Theory of Meaning*, edited by Parkinson. London: Oxford University Press, 1968.
Tolstoy, Leo. *What is Art?* Translated by Louise and Aylmer Maude. London: Oxford University Press, 1896.
Tomas, Vincent. "The Concept of Expression in Art." 1952. In *Philosophy Looks at the Arts*, edited by Joseph Margolis. New York: Scribner's, 1962.
Wittgenstein, Ludwig. *Philosophical Investigations*. Translated by G. E. M. Anscombe. New York: Macmillan, 1953.
Wolfflin, Heinrich. *Principles of Art History*. 1932. Translated by M. D. Hottinger. New York: Dover, 1950.

Secondary Source

Aldrich, Virgil. *Philosophy of Art*. Englewood Cliffs, N. J.: Prentice-Hall, 1963.
Beardsley, Monroe. *Aesthetics*. New York: Harcourt, 1958.
Elliot, R. K. "Poetry and Truth." *Analysis*, 1967.
Osborne, Harold. *Aesthetics and Art Theory*. New York: Dutton, 1970.

Index

A

Abortion, 222–224
Absurd, 248, 253, 258, 261–263, 268, 270, 278, 282, 284
Absurdist literature, 245, 261
Action, 122, 123, 126, 127
Actuality/potentiality, 14, 58, 60, 62
Adamov, Arthur, 261, 264, 265, 283, 288
Aesthetic, 298, 299, 305
Aesthetics, 290, 291, 294
Agni, 167
Alienation, 162, 164, 165, 249, 252, 253, 258, 262, 263, 280
Analysis, 11–13, 15–17, 40, 44, 55, 57, 63, 66, 68, 71, 75, 82, 101, 161, 229, 233, 291
Analytic, 3, 40, 41, 63, 64, 99, 102, 105, 114, 115, 273
Analytic philosophy, 77, 185, 253, 313
Anatman, 176
Anaximander, 34, 56
Anaximenes, 34, 56
Anselm, Saint, 15

Anxiety, 249, 252, 253
A posteriori, 45, 63, 65, 114
Appearance, 45, 46, 171
A priori, 39, 45, 63, 64, 114, 217
Aquinas, Saint Thomas, 38, 60
Argument, 6, 7, 16–18, 20, 24, 27–29
Argument from analogy, 29, 138
Argumentum ad Absurdum, 21
Aristotle, 18, 36, 38–40, 48, 49, 52–54, 56, 57, 60–63, 69, 71–75, 80, 81, 83, 102, 103, 108, 120, 127, 129, 132, 144, 157, 162, 227, 251, 259, 268, 293, 296, 320, 325
Arjuna, 168
Art, 290, 291, 300–304
Assertion, 101
Atman, 167, 168, 170, 171, 175, 176, 184
Atomists, 35, 36, 38, 39
Atoms, 44, 47, 57
Austin, 41
Authentic, 252, 278
Autonomy, 235, 292–294, 304, 308–311, 313–314, 321
Ayer, A. J., 45, 63–68, 70, 72, 75, 82, 83, 99, 152

B

Baier, Kurt, 145–148, 227
Baumgarten, Alexander, 290
Beauty, 290
Beckett, Samuel, 245, 261, 265, 266, 283, 288
Becoming, 60
Behavior, 127, 138, 139, 152, 153, 155, 156
Behaviorism, 133, 138, 149, 152, 156
Being, 48, 53, 54, 75, 76, 80–82, 273
Being-as (seeing-as), 258, 259, 268, 276, 281
Belief, 85, 86, 105–107, 109, 110, 116–120, 128, 319, 320, 322, 323
Bergson, Henri, 273–275, 288
Berkeley, George, 29, 46, 60, 83, 96, 294
Bhakti theism, 168
Bodhisattva, 178
Bradley, F. H., 45
Brahma, 168
Brahman, 167, 168, 170, 171, 173–175
Brain process, 139–148, 153
Buddhism, 11, 159, 164, 165, 170, 173, 174, 176–179, 182–184, 186, 188–191, 194, 198

C

Camus, Albert, 245, 261–263, 266, 277, 278, 283, 284, 288
Categorical Imperative, 216–218
Causality, 9, 23, 57, 62, 69, 72, 74, 75, 79, 80, 104, 138, 175, 180, 291
Certainty, 39, 85, 92, 107, 109–111, 114, 115, 118, 121, 128, 145–148, 155

Change and permanence, 10, 46, 47, 50, 52, 54, 56, 58, 71, 106, 107, 172, 175, 176
Chih-k'ai, 184
Ching-yuan, 196, 286
Chi-tsang, 194, 196
Choice, 121, 122
Civil disobedience, 238–240
Class, 18, 51, 52, 55, 58, 61, 71, 251, 259, 272, 274
Coherence, 319, 321
Coleridge, Samuel, 30
Common sense, 48, 49, 52, 53, 55–58, 63, 74–76, 109, 122
Communication, 32, 33
Concept, 3–7, 10, 11, 13, 15, 16, 38, 40, 42, 51, 54, 55, 58, 61, 63, 74, 82, 83, 103, 133, 149, 150, 160, 161, 165, 166, 184, 186–188, 191, 229, 232, 233, 258, 274, 275, 282, 287, 295, 302–304
Conclusion, 16, 19, 20, 24, 25, 27, 28
Confirmation, 26, 28, 73, 324
Confucianism, 160, 165, 178, 179, 181, 182, 198
Consciousness, 125, 137, 139, 140, 141, 143, 144, 146, 147
Consequence, 28, 213, 215, 219, 220
Consistent, 17, 47
Contextual meaning, 255–259, 312, 317, 320
Contingent, 108, 115
Contradiction, 6, 7, 9, 14, 17, 37, 45–47, 55, 64, 76, 104, 107, 172
Copleston, 68
Correspondence, 111, 272, 314, 321, 323, 324
Crafts, 302, 303
Criteria, 5, 6, 42, 123, 124, 126, 152, 154–156, 203–205, 208, 213, 214, 217, 218, 220

D

Death, 11, 252, 253, 266
Decision, 121
Deductive, 16, 17, 90, 105
Definition, 12, 15, 21, 221, 296
Democritus, 35
Denying the consequent, 21, 27
Deontological, 213, 214, 218, 226
Descartes, René, 39, 65, 79, 83, 96, 108–110, 112, 118, 120, 129, 132–138, 142, 148, 149, 157, 172
Descriptive versus revisionist metaphysics, 71, 73
Determinism, 180
Dewey, John, 124, 127, 128, 130, 180
Dialectical, 20, 22, 25
Dialogue, 21, 22
Disposition, 127, 149, 151
Double effect, 222, 223
Dualism, 132–135, 137, 138, 142, 143, 147, 149, 151, 152, 155, 156, 171, 188, 195
Duchamp, Marcel, 299–301
Duns Scotus, John, 38

E

Eastern philosophy, 159, 161, 270
Education, 120, 123, 128
Ego (self), 11, 137, 165, 166
Egoism, 205–207, 214, 215, 225, 226
Einstein, Albert, 25
Eleatics, 35, 37
Empirical, 24, 26, 63, 65, 92, 96, 99, 107, 112, 114, 214, 217, 231
Empiricism, 39, 45, 46, 63, 86–90, 94–97, 99, 101, 110, 175, 177
Emptiness, 176, 183, 184, 186–188, 191, 193–195

Epiphenomenalism, 134
Epistemology, 85, 86, 96–100, 128
Essence, 52, 55, 58, 60, 62, 71, 251, 259, 271, 272, 275, 283, 295, 296
Essence-existence problem, 58, 60, 75, 243, 249, 268, 269, 272, 274
Ethics, 160, 201, 228
Euclid, 22
Evidence, 16, 28, 99, 128
Existence, 10, 15, 48–52, 58, 63, 71, 110, 137, 142, 148, 149, 153, 251, 252, 279, 282, 315, 316
Existentialism, 30, 58, 60, 163, 242–245, 248, 251–253, 261, 267, 271, 284, 287
Expediency, 225–226
Experience, 13, 45, 69, 70–73, 86–90, 93–95, 97, 98, 102, 104, 128
Expression, 153, 156, 290, 291, 293, 294
Extrasensory reality, 44, 66, 74, 174, 175, 181, 197

F

Facts, 24, 26, 42, 64, 73
Fallacy, 28
Falsification, 26, 27, 65, 73, 111, 115
Fiction, 315, 316, 318, 321–323
Formal argument, 18
Formal Cause, 58
Formalism, 293, 294, 310
Forms (Ideas), 37, 38, 46, 47, 52, 55–58, 60, 62, 88, 94, 102, 107, 112, 186
Fourfold truth, 173, 175
Freedom, 8, 179, 180, 206–208, 229–232, 236, 237, 249, 250, 253

330   Index

Frost, Robert, 307, 310
Fry, Roger, 293, 294, 326

G

God, 7, 14, 15, 29, 38, 53, 60, 71, 75, 83, 110, 162, 167 168, 174, 175, 178, 181, 197, 257
Good, 23, 201, 204, 205, 207, 209, 211, 213, 215, 217–221
Grammar, 48, 54, 67, 102

H

Habit, 124, 126
Haiku, 197
Happiness, 208–211, 221
Hedonism, 205, 209, 210, 212, 213
Hegel, G. W. F., 31, 303, 326
Heidegger, Martin, 41, 77, 80–82, 242, 248, 249, 252, 257, 261, 272, 278–280, 288
Hinayana, 175–178, 181, 194
Hinduism, 159, 164, 165, 167, 168, 170, 171, 184, 186, 189, 198
Hobbes, Thomas, 39, 205, 206
Huang-po, 187, 188, 190–193, 196, 199
Hui-neng, 189, 190, 193
Humanism, 251
Human nature, 163, 164, 243, 248, 250, 257
Hume, David, 15, 29, 32, 39, 42, 60, 63, 64, 66, 67, 72, 73, 83, 96, 114, 115, 130
Husserl, Edmund, 41, 189, 194, 199, 248, 249
Huxley, Aldous, 164, 199
Hypothesis, 22, 25–28, 72, 73, 98, 321, 323
Hypothetical, 20–22, 24–26, 97, 216, 220
Hypothetical syllogism, 20

I

Idea, 46, 86, 87, 94, 96, 100
Idealism, 35, 38, 46, 60, 62, 186, 189, 195, 197, 282
Identity, 136, 144, 147, 164, 166, 259
Identity Theory, 136, 139, 140, 141, 143, 147, 148
Imitation, 290, 292, 294
Implication, 20, 25, 63
Inconsistency, 21
Independence, 49, 50, 56, 58, 60, 63
Individual, 229–233, 243–244, 247–250, 287, 301, 311
Indra, 167
Induction, 24, 28
Informal argument, 18, 27
Innate, 88–90, 93–95, 98, 99, 101–104
Intelligent, 122, 123, 126–128, 151, 152
Intention, 211, 214–216, 223, 224, 254, 255, 297, 301, 305
Interactionism, 134, 138
Interested/disinterested, 206–208, 230, 231, 298
Intuition, 32, 58
Invalid, 19, 24, 27, 42
Ionesco, Eugene, 245, 261, 267, 278, 282, 285, 288

J

Jen, 182
Justice, 12, 21, 212
Justification, 99–101, 116, 236, 237, 240

K

Kant, Immanuel, 15, 22, 23, 40, 69, 71, 72, 74, 83, 102–104,

130, 213–218, 226, 227, 243, 292, 298, 305, 326
Karma, 165, 166, 169, 170
Kierkegaard, Søren, 242–249, 252, 271, 288
Knowledge, 39, 44, 85, 86, 88–90, 96, 105–107, 109, 110, 112, 116–121, 128
Krishna, 168

L

Language, 43, 54, 67, 154, 155, 165, 166, 177, 183–186, 191–193, 195, 196, 253, 256–259, 275, 287, 294, 312, 313
Lao-tzu, 179, 199
Leibniz, Baron Gottfried Wilhelm, 39, 60, 73
Leucippus, 35
Locke, John, 39, 60, 87, 89, 93–96, 98–102, 109, 110, 114, 130
Logic, 16–18, 40, 91, 104, 107, 114
Logical Positivism, 44, 45, 63, 73

M

Madyamika, 175, 177, 183, 184
Mahayana, 175–178, 181
Malunkyaputta, 173, 174, 176–178
Mao Tse-tung, 182
Material Cause, 58
Materialism, 36, 39, 46, 53, 55–57, 133, 138, 139, 141–143, 147–149, 156
Mathematics, 40, 64, 90–92, 107, 112, 114
Matter, 44, 46, 47, 55–58, 60, 75
Matter and form, 40, 55, 56, 58
Maya, 171, 186
Meaning, 3, 13, 14, 16, 17, 40, 55, 63–68, 70–72, 75, 99, 101, 144, 154, 155, 196, 253–255, 258, 259, 261, 265, 267, 269, 273, 276, 277, 285–287, 296, 305, 307–313
Meaninglessness, 62, 253, 254, 258, 260, 265, 266, 270, 271, 273, 276, 279, 283, 285, 286
Meinong, Alexius, 314–315
Metaethics, 201, 202, 218, 219
Metaphor, 160, 294
Metaphysics, 44–46, 48, 52–54, 56, 60, 63, 64, 66–69, 71, 73–75, 82, 83, 143, 161, 171–176, 181, 183–186, 188, 189, 193, 194, 198, 324
Milesians, 34, 35, 168
Mill, John Stuart, 205, 207, 208, 217, 219, 220, 226, 227, 229, 230–232, 241
Mind, 44, 46, 78–82, 122, 132, 133, 150, 151, 153
Mind-body problem, 75, 76–79, 82, 123, 133–135, 137–139, 148–150, 152–156
Moksa, 166, 170
Monism, 132–134, 137, 153, 155, 156
Moore, G. E., 213, 227
Moral, 161, 169, 201, 202, 204–208, 211, 212, 216, 217, 220, 224–226

N

Nagarjuna, 159, 161, 183, 184, 193
Naive Realism, 189, 196, 197
Nama-rupa, 185, 186
Nan-ch'uan, 187
Nature, 12, 13
Naturalistic Fallacy (ought-is), 220–222
Nausea, 267–269, 276, 284
Necessary, 15, 28, 106, 108, 109, 115, 118, 214
Negation, 266, 267, 276, 280, 281
Negative Way, 192

Newton, Sir Isaac, 25
Nietzsche, Friedrich, 242, 244–246, 248, 249, 289
Nominalism, 38, 40, 61
Nomological danglers, 142, 143, 145, 148
Noncontradiction, 35
Nonduality, 193
Normative, 201–203, 218, 219, 231

O

Object, 48, 50, 52–54, 60, 69, 70, 74–76, 80, 83, 105, 116, 185–187, 196, 251, 261, 267, 268, 274, 275, 282, 287, 315, 318, 321
Objectification, 35–37, 60, 192
Objective, 118, 242, 244–247, 271, 273, 275, 282, 283, 287
Obligation, 201, 205, 207, 211, 213, 217, 218
Occam, William of, 38
Oldenberg, 303, 304
One and Many, 34, 37, 172, 173
Ontological Argument, 15
Originality, 301
Other minds, 29, 133, 135, 138, 139, 148, 152, 153, 154, 156

P

Pacificism, 222, 224, 225
Parallelism, 134
Parmenides, 31, 35, 45
Pascal, Blaise, 244, 264
Perennial Philosophy, 164, 179, 181
Personal identity, 9, 10, 42
Phenomenalism, 39–41
Phenomenology, 75, 77, 189, 244, 248, 249, 261, 280, 281
Philosophy, 1–8, 11, 13, 15, 16, 52, 159, 160, 161, 183–185, 242, 243, 303
Plato, 12, 20–23, 25, 36–39, 40, 42, 45–47, 52, 53, 55, 57, 58, 60, 62, 63, 83, 88–91, 93–95, 98–103, 105–108, 111, 112, 116, 118–120, 127, 130, 132, 157, 165, 171, 185–186, 227, 242, 243, 293, 326
Pleasure, 209, 210, 212, 213, 221
Practical, 121–123, 127, 128, 161, 202
Prediction, 26, 28, 98
Premise, 16, 19, 20, 24, 25, 27, 28
Probability, 92, 113, 320–322
Problem of Evil, 7, 14
Projection, 192, 196, 197, 267, 270–278, 281–283, 285
Proof, 26–28, 72, 209–211, 217
Property, 48, 50, 54, 60, 67, 69, 70, 74, 75, 80, 81, 83, 162, 196
Psychology, 13, 96, 100, 132, 133
Purpose, 254–257, 258, 259, 261–264, 266, 269, 312
Pythagoras, 35–37

R

Rationalism, 35, 39, 45, 86, 88, 92, 95, 99, 111, 242–245, 248, 251
Realism, 38, 57, 62, 271, 272, 292, 293, 319, 322, 324
Reality, 35, 37, 38, 44–49, 52, 54–57, 60, 80, 81, 89, 103–107, 164, 171, 175, 176, 179, 192, 195–197, 287
Reason, 16, 20, 24–26, 28, 30–33, 39, 86, 103, 116, 119–121, 172, 213–215, 216, 217, 242–244, 258, 261, 262, 278, 285
Recollection, 89, 90
Reference, 67, 314, 315, 317, 318, 321
Reincarnation, 165
Relation, 54, 80, 81

Relativism, 105, 117, 202–204, 207, 214, 215, 225, 226
Relevance, 294, 304, 308–310, 314
Religious, 159–162, 164, 166, 167, 171, 172, 181, 183, 197, 300, 301
Represent, 293
Responsibility, 248–253
Revolt against reason, 30, 242, 261
Revolution, 236, 237
Right, 201–206, 208, 209, 211, 213, 214, 217–220, 225, 231
Romanticism, 30, 163, 244, 291
Russell, Bertrand, 315, 326
Ryle, Gilbert, 41, 77, 80, 121–124, 126–128, 130, 149, 151–153, 158, 180, 213

S

Samsara, 166, 170
Sankara, 161, 170, 171
Santayana, George, 57
Sartre, Jean-Paul, 41, 61, 242, 249, 252, 257, 261, 265, 267–269, 276, 284, 289
Saving the Appearances, 46, 47
Scepticism, 60, 110
Science, 24, 38, 39, 44, 45, 56, 72, 82, 83, 97, 104, 108, 109, 112, 141–143, 250
Seng-chao, 161, 188
Sensation, 39, 45, 64, 65, 111, 141, 142, 145–147, 154, 212, 213
Sentential Calculus, 20
Shiva, 168
Siddhartha Gautama, 170, 172, 185
Skill, 124, 126, 151
Smart, J. J. C., 136, 139, 140, 142, 143, 145, 147, 153, 158
Socrates, 7, 21, 22, 36, 37, 89, 90, 238, 239, 244
Socratic Method, 21, 246
Solipsism, 133, 155

Sophists, 22
Space, 6, 36, 44
Spinoza, Benedict, 39, 53, 64, 65, 171, 172
Strawson, P. F., 41, 48, 69, 71, 73–75, 82, 84, 315, 326
Subjective, 118, 244, 246, 247, 273
Substance, 34, 48, 52, 53, 55–58, 60–64, 67, 69–71, 75, 76, 79–83, 134, 135, 150, 162, 168, 171, 184, 259
Syllogism, 18
Synonymity, 139–149
Synthetic, 63–65, 114, 115

T

Taoism, 164, 165, 178–182
Teleological ethics, 169, 170, 204, 205, 208, 213, 216, 226
Testing, 26, 28
Thales, 1, 34, 56
Theology, 38, 162
Theoretical, 121–123, 128, 161, 162
Theorize, 121–123, 128, 151
Thomas, Dylan, 307, 311
Tien-tai (Lotus School), 183, 184
Time, 106, 108, 265, 266
Transcendent, 23, 176, 264, 279, 280, 284
Transcendental, 22, 23, 25, 69–71, 74, 90, 281
True/false, 16, 19, 20, 26, 27, 65, 101, 108, 116–118, 122, 245–247, 314, 321, 323, 324

U

Universality, 203, 204, 207, 214, 215, 217, 218, 224, 225, 242, 244, 247–249
Utilitarianism, 205, 208, 212, 213, 215, 219, 220, 226
Utility, 300, 301

V

Validity, 16–20, 27, 42
Value, 93, 201, 202, 210, 211, 213, 218, 246
Varuna, 167
Vedanta, 170–172, 175, 176, 178, 186
Verifiability Criterion, 65, 68
Verification, 65, 70, 71, 73, 99
Vidya, 166, 170
Violence, 33, 224, 225, 229, 233, 235, 236
Virtue, 22
Vishnu, 168

W

Whitehead, A. N., 57
Wittgenstein, Ludwig, 41, 153, 154, 158, 166, 185, 196, 200, 257, 289, 295, 296, 326
Work of art, 13, 197, 290, 291, 293, 295–298, 301–303, 305
World, 12, 13, 69, 82, 251, 258, 261, 276, 277, 283, 285, 287, 316–318, 322, 323

Y

Yeats, William Butler, 307
Yi, 182
Yogacara, 175, 177, 178

Z

Zen, 30, 165, 182–184, 186–188, 189, 191, 195–197, 274, 312, 313
Zeno, 6, 11, 35